Beginning Microsoft Word 2010

Ty Anderson
Guy Hart-Davis

Apress®

Beginning Microsoft Word 2010

ISBN 978-1-4302-2952-0

ISBN 978-1-4302-2953-7 (eBook)

9 8 7 6 5 4 3 2 1

President and Publisher: Paul Manning
Lead Editor: Ben Renow-Clarke
Technical Reviewer: Paul Milbourne
Editorial Board: Clay Andres, Steve Anglin, Mark Beckner, Ewan Buckingham, Gary Cornell,
    Jonathan Gennick, Jonathan Hassell, Michelle Lowman, Matthew Moodie, Duncan Parkes,
    Jeffrey Pepper, Frank Pohlmann, Douglas Pundick, Ben Renow-Clarke, Dominic Shakeshaft,
    Matt Wade, Tom Welsh
Coordinating Editor: Anita Castro
Copy Editor: Mary Ann Fugate
Compositor: MacPS, LLC
Indexer: BIM Indexing & Proofreading Services
Artist: April Milne
Cover Designer: Anna Ishchenko

Distributed to the book trade worldwide by Springer Science+Business Media, LLC., 233 Spring Street, 6th Floor, New York, NY 10013. Phone 1-800-SPRINGER, fax (201) 348-4505, e-mail orders-ny@springer-sbm.com, or visit www.springeronline.com.

For information on translations, please e-mail rights@apress.com, or visit www.apress.com.

Apress and friends of ED books may be purchased in bulk for academic, corporate, or promotional use. eBook versions and licenses are also available for most titles. For more information, reference our Special Bulk Sales–eBook Licensing web page at www.apress.com/info/bulksales.

Contents at a Glance

Contents

About the Authors

 **Ty Anderson** is partner at Cogent Company in Dallas, Texas. He spends his time consulting and building software using Microsoft technologies. In addition to consulting, Ty speaks and writes frequently about Microsoft technologies, especially Microsoft Office and SharePoint. His work has been published on MSDN, Microsoft TechNet, Devx.com, Devsource.com, Simple-Talk.com and CIO.com. He also maintains a blog at http://officedeveloper.net. Sometimes he blogs…sometimes he doesn't.

 **Guy Hart-Davis** is the author of more than 60 computer books on subjects that range from Microsoft Office to programming Visual Basic for Applications and networking both PCs and Macs.

About the Technical Reviewer

 **Paul Milbourne** has been an enterprise level interface developer in the greater Washington DC area for the better part of a decade. He is currently a Software Engineer and Senior Flash Developer for Zynga (the makers of FarmVille). Paul has written and edited several books focusing on user interaction and client-side software development.

Acknowledgments

Ty Anderson would like to thank:

- Guy Hart-Davis for agreeing to help write the book.
- Steve Anglin for believing in the book and convincing me to help write it.
- Anita Castro for keeping us organized and everything moving.
- The rest of the Apress team including, but not limited to, Ben Renow-Clarke, Mary Ann Fugate, and Gary Cornell.
- Cogent Company
- My wife Amy

Guy Hart-Davis would like to thank the following people:

- Ty Anderson for creating the outline and asking me to help write the book.
- Steve Anglin for handling the administration.
- Ben Renow-Clarke for developing the manuscript.
- Paul Milbourne for reviewing the manuscript for technical accuracy and contributing helpful suggestions.
- Mary Ann Fugate for editing the manuscript with care and a light touch.
- Anita Castro for coordinating the book project and keeping things running.

Introduction

Do you need to get your work done with Microsoft Word—smoothly, easily, and quickly? If so, you've picked up the right book.

Who Is This Book For?

This book is designed to help beginning and intermediate users get up to speed quickly with Word 2010 and immediately become productive with it.

If you need to learn to use Word to accomplish everyday tasks, at work or at home, you'll benefit from this book's focused approach and detailed advice. You can either start from the beginning of the book and work through it, or use the Table of Contents or the Index to find the topic you need immediately, and then jump right in there.

What Does This Book Cover?

Here's what this book covers:

- **Chapter 1**, "The Word 2010 Primer," shows you how to work with Word's Fluent User Interface, using the Ribbon, the Quick Access Toolbar, and the new Backstage view to control Word. You'll also learn how to create and save documents, plus how to view a document's structure.

- **Chapter 2**, "Creating and Editing Documents," explains how to write text, how to edit text, and how to correct errors in it. You'll also learn how to use Word's powerful Outline view, how to paste content in the format you need by using the Paste Options feature, and how to find and replace text.

- **Chapter 3**, "Adding Style to Documents," covers the use of Word's most important types of formatting. You'll learn to format documents swiftly and efficiently by using styles, and how to add headers and footers to identify pages and make their content clear.

- **Chapter 4**, "Reusing Content," shows you how to make the most of Word's many features for reusing content you've already created. You'll get the hang of building documents from Quick Parts, create AutoCorrect entries to save you time and effort, and tame the helpful but volatile AutoFormat As You Type feature.

- **Chapter 5**, "Making Your Documents Display Information Effectively," teaches you how to present information clearly by using bulleted, numbered, and multilevel lists; how to create tables to lay out information precisely; and how to apply co-ordinated formatting easily by using Word's themes and their components.

- **Chapter 6,** "Completing a Document," first walks you through the process of adding a cover page and a table of contents to a document. You then learn how to customize a document's page layout and margins, how to finalize and secure a document, and how to print either a whole document or only those parts of it you need.

- **Chapter 7,** "Editing Pictures Within Word," shows you the easy way of making your pictures look good in your documents—by using Word's features for editing pictures. You'll gain the skills of inserting pictures, resizing them, and cropping them as needed; you'll also learn to correct the color balance in a picture or even remove its background.

- **Chapter 8,** "Using Media with Word," explains how to ginger up your documents by adding graphical objects to them. You can use Word's extensive collection of clip art, insert your own pictures, or create exactly the shapes and SmartArt illustrations you need. If your documents require them, you can also insert computer screenshots, audio files, or video files.

- **Chapter 9,** "Working with Others," teaches you to use Word's powerful features for working with other people on documents. You'll learn to mark revisions with the Track Changes feature, add comments to a document, and merge either marked or unmarked changes from two versions of a document. You'll also find out how to restrict edit rights on a document and how to take linked notes using OneNote.

- **Chapter 10,** "Taking Your Use of Word to the Next Level," shows you how to customize Word so that you can work faster and more easily in it. You'll use the Word Options dialog window to set essential options the way you prefer; customize the Ribbon, the Quick Access Toolbar, and the status bar; and even record time-saving macros to automate repetitive tasks. You'll also learn to save time by editing a document simultaneously with your colleagues and by creating documents with the Mail Merge feature.

Conventions Used in This Book

This book uses several conventions to make its meaning clear without wasting words:

- **Ribbon commands.** The > sign shows the sequence for choosing an item from the Ribbon. For example, "choose Insert ➤ Illustrations ➤ Clip Art" means that you click the Insert tab of the Ribbon (displaying the tab's contents), go to the Illustrations group, and then click the Clip Art button.

- **Special paragraphs.** Special paragraphs present information that you may want to pay extra attention to. Note paragraphs contain information you may want to know; Tip paragraphs present techniques you may benefit from using; and Caution paragraphs warn you of potential problems.

- **Check boxes.** Word many check boxes—the square boxes that can either have a check mark in them (indicate that the option is turned on) or not (indicating that the option is turned off). This book tells you to "select" a check box when you need to put a check mark in the check box, and to "clear" a check box when you need to remove the check mark from it. If the check box is already selected or cleared, you don't need to change it.

- **Keyboard shortcuts.** In Word, you can often save time and effort by using a keyboard shortcut rather than a Ribbon command. This book uses + signs to represent keyboard shortcuts. For example, "press Ctrl+S" means that you hold down the Ctrl key, press the S key, and then release the Ctrl key. "Press Ctrl+Alt+T" means that you hold down the Ctrl key and the Alt key, press the T key, and then release the Ctrl key and the Alt key.

Visit the *Beginning Microsoft Office 2010* Blog!

Word is a powerful program with many capabilities, and a book this size can cover only some of them.

For further information on Word 2010 and the other Office 2010 programs, please visit the *Beginning Microsoft Office 2010 Blog* at http://www.ghdbooks.com. Here you'll find tips, resources, and a form for asking questions you'd like to see covered on the site.

CHAPTER 1

The Word 2010 Primer

It's time to open Word 2010 and gain some understanding of how the good people at Microsoft built it. Believe it or not, they didn't build in to torture you as you try to write you term paper, thesis, management report, or novel. Microsoft invests millions of dollars researching and speaking with people to make Word a better product. These investments have produced some startling innovations in the last two releases of Microsoft Word.

Microsoft dramatically revamped the Word's user interface in Word 2007 by adding the Office Fluent User Interface (a.k.a. the ribbon) to replace the outdated Office toolbars. Microsoft made a big bet that the Ribbon would make life incredibly easier for users to create documents using Word (and other Microsoft Office applications that utilize the ribbon). My experience as a consultant as well the experience of many of my peers and clients prove that the ribbon is a success.

In Word 2010, Microsoft has released another dramatic user interface innovation known as the Backstage. This user interface (UI) element is now the location of all activities that are not part of actual document authoring or creation. Tasks like opening, saving, closing, sharing, and printing documents are now backstage and not found on the Ribbon.

Dramatic changes like the Ribbon and Backstage require some adjustment on your part, particularly if you have lots of experience with previous version of Word. If you are new to Word, you are starting with a clean slate and will not have to learn new methods of accomplishing tasks.

The goal of this chapter is to give you a solid overview of the Word's basic mechanics. We start by covering the basics of working with documents and end with a discussion of the UI elements within Word.

At the end of this chapter, you will know the basics of navigating Word 2010, including the following:

- Navigate the Ribbon and know the purpose of its different tabs
- Use the Backstage view
- Open, close, and save documents

Before we take a look at the UI elements, I believe it is best to start by performing a few basic tasks in Word to get your feet wet. These tasks will give you a bit of a primer to working with Word and will possibly generate some questions about Word's user interface that I will explain in the latter half of the chapter.

Learning the Word 2010 User Interface

Learning any new application can be a frustrating experience, especially if time is tight and you need to be productive now. The learning process isn't unlike learning a new sport, for example swimming, which I recently decided to learn how to do for exercise. With sports, understanding technique and investing time to master it can make all the difference. To be a good swimmer, I had to spend some time going slow while focusing on my stroke and breathing. Doing so eventually meant I could go faster, much faster than if I hadn't focused on technique.

The same principle applies to learning software. The technique in this case is learning how the software works and how you should interact with it. You need to invest some time in understanding how the product team designed the program, and you need to learn what the manufacturer has to say about the best practices for using the software. To do otherwise can result in a serious amount of frustration and leave you flailing in a pool of expletives.

The first step in learning proper Word technique is understanding Word's user interface so that you know where to go to execute the actions you want. The purpose of this section is for you to become familiar with Word's main user interface elements like the Ribbon and the Backstage view. As a bonus, you will learn how to perform some basic customizations so that you can have easier access to the commands you use most.

Understanding Word's Fluent User Interface

Microsoft introduced the Fluent User Interface (Fluent UI) in the Office 2007 suite of applications, of which Word is a part. The goal of the Fluent UI was to simplify Word's complex menu and toolbar structure and build a system that presented, or made available, the relevant Word commands when you need them.

The result is a major improvement over previous versions. That isn't to say that everyone loves the Ribbon, because not everyone does. People who have been Word users since the '80s especially don't like it. But since this book is for beginners, you most likely aren't carrying any baggage and just need to understand how the different command elements are laid out within the user interface.

Figure 1–1 illustrates some the major components of the Fluent UI.

The Ribbon (item 1 in Figure 1–1) is the component of the Fluent UI that receives most of the press, good and bad. But it is only one part of the entire UI system. The system includes other elements like task panes, galleries, the File button, and more. In the following sections, I provide you with a description of each element to satisfy your curiosity for now, and you'll learn more as we move through this chapter's exercises:

Figure 1-1. Word displaying some elements of the Fluent User Interface

The Ribbon

The Ribbon is the user interface element that replaced the traditional Word menus and toolbars. It is a collection of tabs organized by task type. The Home tab contains the most common types of commands for activities like the following:

- Cutting, copying, and pasting
- Formatting text (e.g., changing fonts, applying bold formatting, and changing text colors)
- Changing text alignment
- Working with styles

Other tabs in the Ribbon are more specialized just as their name implies. For example, the Insert tab contains commands for inserting objects like cover pages and images into your document. The Page Layout tab is where the options for fine-tuning how each page in your document will display and print. The References tab has the commands for—you guessed it—annotating your document. We'll work more with each tab in subsequent chapters.

The File Button and Backstage View

The name for the File button user interface element is confusing and is the result of its implementation in Word 2007. The File button has been updated for Word 2010 to be a tab within the Ribbon. In Word 2007, it was a circular button displaying the Office logo and was slightly elevated above the Ribbon. In Word 2010, the File button is the blue tab labeled File. It might make more sense to simply call it the File tab but that isn't the case; according to Microsoft, its proper name is the File button. To keep things simple and because it looks like a tab, I will refer to it as the File tab. Now that you know that somewhat needless bit of trivia, let me tell you what it does.

The File tab displays the Backstage view (see Figure 1–2), which is itself a new feature to Word 2010. The Backstage view is intended to provide a central location for all commands that work *with* the document instead of *on* the document.

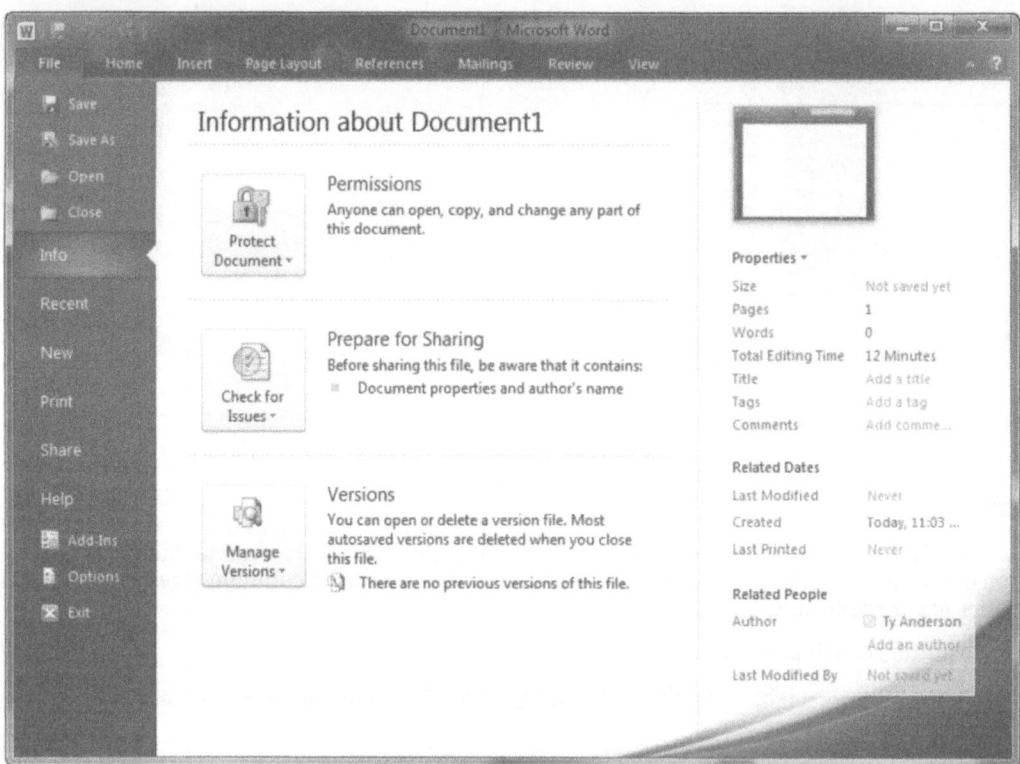

Figure 1–2. The File button activated to display the Backstage view

For example, activities like printing, sharing, opening, saving, and editing Word's option settings are not part of the actual writing of a document and thus are found in the Backstage view. In contrast, activities like formatting, editing the page layout, and inserting images are part of document creation and are found on the ribbon.

Task Panes

Task panes are vertical windows that dock on either side of the Word window. Task panes exist to help you complete a specific task by providing quick access to relevant commands within the pane and are only visible when requested. They don't automatically appear when you first open Word. An example is the Styles task pane that displays all the styles available for formatting the current document. Other panes available in Word 2010 include the Navigation pane, the Research pane, and the Reviewing pane.

Galleries

Galleries provide a set of results for you to choose from when working with your document. Figure 1–1 shows the Styles gallery residing on the Ribbon's Home tab. Each gallery control displays a result that you can choose to apply to text in your document.

These are the obvious components of the Fluent UI, but there are many more, including the Quick Access Toolbar, the Mini toolbar, and contextual tabs. I leave them out here only because I think they are easier to understand by completing a few exercises.

Learning to Use and Navigate the Ribbon

The Word 2010 ribbon contains eight tabs by default: File, Home, Insert, Page Layout, References, Mailings, Review, and View (see Figure 1–3). Each tab contains related commands that correspond to the name of the tab where they reside. Microsoft isn't trying to confuse anyone with the Ribbon; the idea is to make it simple for you to find the command you want when you want it.

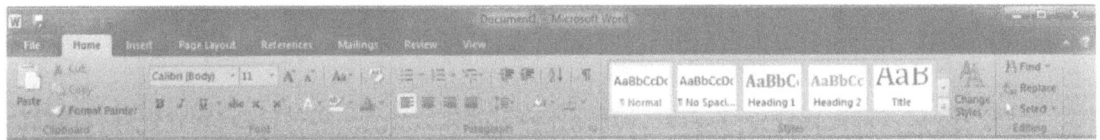

Figure 1-3. The Word 2010 Ribbon displaying the Home tab

For this first exercise, I'll ask you to open Word, and click around the different tabs just to become familiar with what's there. In some places, I'll suggest that you click one of the available commands to see the different types of controls on the Ribbon and how they work. The focus in this section is less on what these commands do to the current document than on learning to work with the Ribbon.

Now then, go ahead and open Word 2010 if you haven't opened it already, and let's get started with the first exercise.

1. Click the Home tab to activate it as the current tab.

2. Scan each of the groups available on the tab. You should see groups labeled Clipboard, Font, Paragraph, Styles, and Editing. Commands are not only located on Ribbon with related commands but they are also further grouped within each tab. This grouping really helps you find a desired command and understand what a set of commands does. Want to copy some text to the clipboard? It's a good bet you'll find what you are looking for in the Clipboard group.

3. Still in the Home tab, find the Styles groups, and click the More button—the down-pointing arrow located just to the right of the available styles (see Figure 1–4). This control is a good example of a gallery control. In this case, the control lists styles available for formatting your document's text.

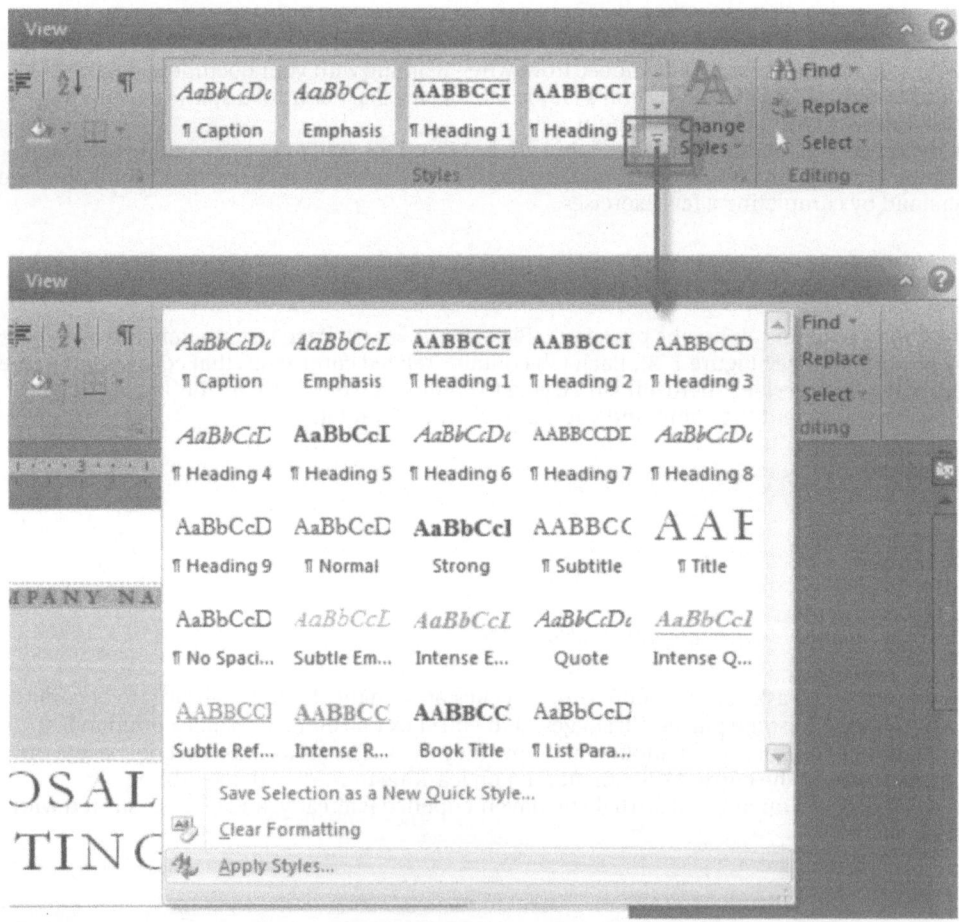

Figure 1–4. The Styles gallery available in the Ribbon's Home tab

4. Each control in the gallery provides a preview of how text will display when given that style. If you have text in your document, Word will provide you a feature called Live Preview to show you how the style looks when applied to your text. As you hover over different styles, the text changes too. Only when you click a style does Word actually apply it to the text in your document. Without clicking any of the styles, click the arrow again to hide the gallery.

5. Look in the Font group, and notice the several controls that display a downward-facing arrow next to their pictures (see Figure 1–5). When a control has an arrow like this, it typically offers additional options that you may choose. For example, in the Font control, clicking the arrow displays a full listing of fonts available on your system.

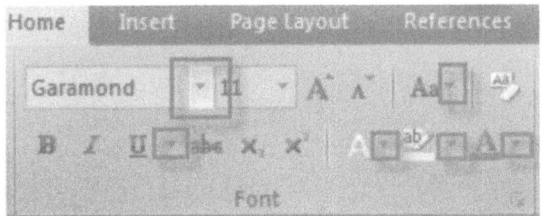

Figure 1–5. The Font group contains several control arrows that offer different options

6. Take a moment to click each of the arrows in the Font group to see what they offer. When you're finished, look for other controls with related downward-facing arrows. Click them to see what they allow you to do.

■ **Tip** The Ribbon groups are not all-inclusive, and some commands are indeed hidden. Something that isn't obvious is that several groups within the various tabs have a hidden Options dialog window. These highly detailed dialog windows provide all the options related to that group in a single location. Keep in mind that the Ribbon's purpose is to place the most common commands at your fingertips. An arrow in the bottom right-hand corner of a group signifies the existence of an Options dialog window for that group. Click the arrow to display the Options window and discover even more commands.

The Ribbon actually contains more than eight tabs. These additional tabs are known as contextual tabs and they become available only in certain circumstances.

Using Contextual Tabs

Contextual tabs are just like Word's eight main ribbon tabs except they display only when you perform certain tasks, like working with images or tables. When you edit an object type that has an associated contextual tab, the tab becomes available and provides options that only apply to that object type. A good example of this is the Picture Tools Format tab. Anytime you have an image as the active object in your document, this tab becomes visible (see Figure 1–6) and provides tools specifically for formatting the selected image.

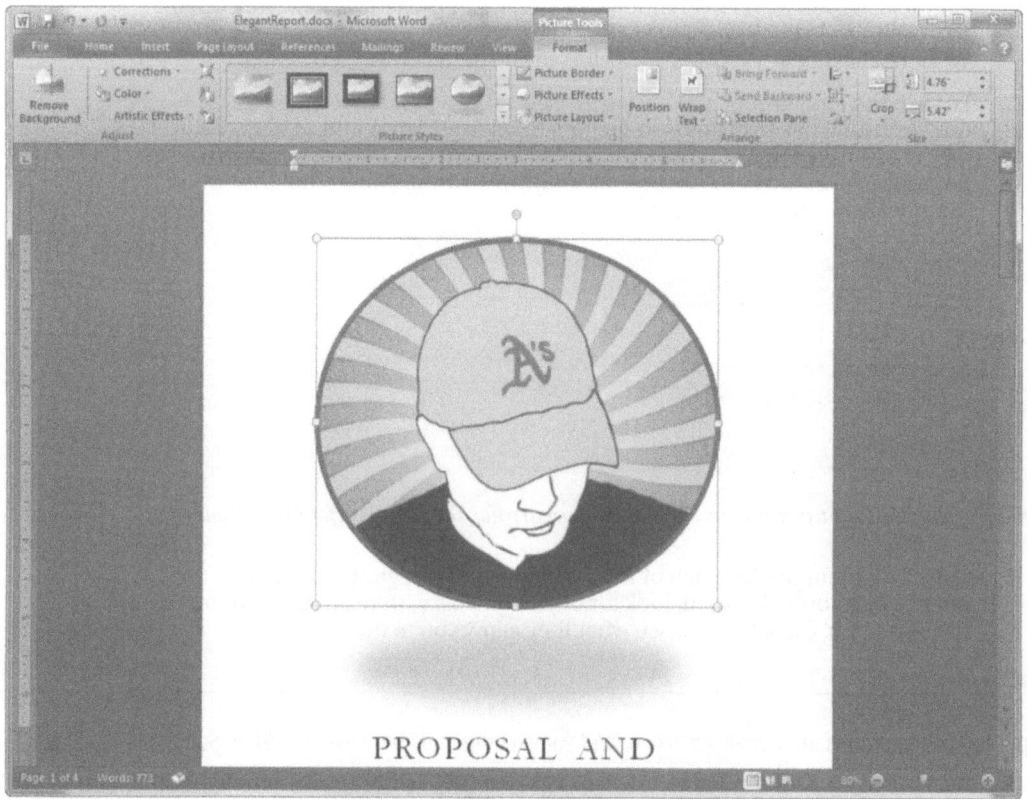

Figure 1–6. Word displaying the Picture Tools Format contextual tab

---

■ **Tip** Microsoft isn't afraid to try new ways to help people learn its products, like building a game to help you become familiar with the ribbon. For Office 2010, Microsoft released *Office Ribbon Hero*, a game that will help you increase your skills quickly by playing a game that is both cheesy and fun. You can download the game from the Microsoft Office Labs web site at http://www.officelabs.com/Lists/Posts/Post.aspx?ID=88.

In the following steps, I will show two different contextual tabs and point out some of the commands available within them:

1. With Word open, click the Insert tab available on the Ribbon.

2. Click the Picture button to display the Insert Picture Dialog window. This window allows you to locate an image on your hard drive, select it, and insert that image into the current document by clicking the Insert button. Go ahead and locate a picture, and insert it into your document.

3. After Word inserts your selected image, Word selects the images and keeps it as the active object within the document. Since the image is the active object, the Picture Tools Format tab is now visible.

4. In the Picture Tools Format tab, find the Adjust group, and click the Artistic Effects button. You should see a list of effects you can apply to the image. Hover over each result with your mouse to view a live preview of the effect on you image without actually applying it. Apply one by clicking it.

5. Locate the Picture Styles group, and click the down-facing arrow attached the Picture Styles gallery. Hover over each style with your mouse, and view how each applies to your image. Apply your desired style by clicking it.

There are more features for editing images but this is enough for now. Next, let's look at another contextual tab that allows you to format tables.

1. Delete the image in your document by clicking it with your mouse and pressing the Delete key on your keyboard.

2. Click the Insert tab available on the Ribbon.

3. Find the Tables group in the Insert tab, and click the Table button to display the Insert Tables gallery (see Figure 1–7).

4. The top section of the Tables gallery is a series of squares, ten columns wide and eight rows deep. The idea behind this section is for you to quickly define a table with your mouse and then insert the new table into your document with a single mouse click. Give this a try by hovering your mouse to define a table four columns wide and six rows deep. Once you are satisfied with the dimensions, left-click to insert the new table.

5. After Word inserts the new table, you have two new table tools contextual tabs named Design and Layout.

6. Click the Table Tools Design tab, and locate the Table Styles groups. Click the down-facing arrow of this group to display the Table Styles gallery. Choose a style that suits your fancy, and click it to apply the style to your table.

7. Click the Table Tools layout tab, and locate the Rows & Columns group.

8. Click the Insert Above button to insert a new row above the currently active row in your table (the row that contains the cursor is the active row).

9. Click the Insert Right button to insert a new column to the right of the currently active column.

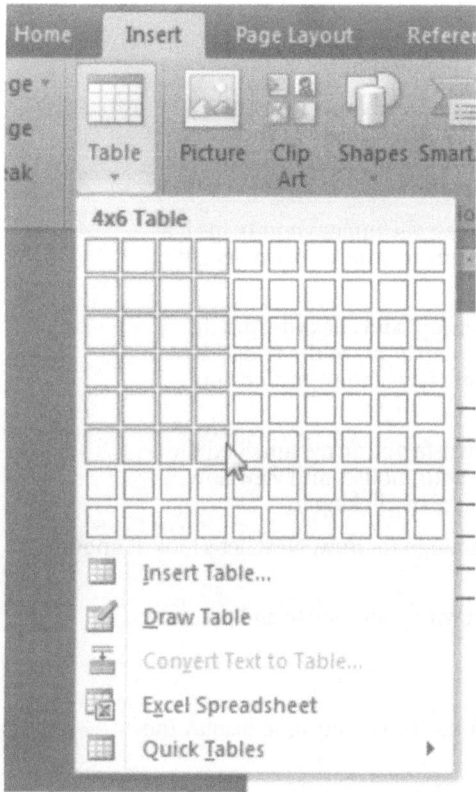

Figure 1–7. Inserting a table in Word using the Tables gallery

Each these contextual tabs contains many more features that I will leave to you to play around with to discover what they do. The idea here is to expose you to the Ribbon and provide an overview of how it is organized and how you work with its controls to affect your document. As you move through the remaining chapters, you will learn more about the available ribbon commands of each tab.

Using the Quick Access Toolbar

The Quick Access Toolbar (see Figure 1–8) resides in the upper left-hand corner of the Word window. It exists to provide you with quick access to the commands you use most and is always on display, no matter which Ribbon tab is active. This makes the Quick Access Toolbar the ideal location to place the commands you love and use most often. It is intended for you to customize it by adding your favorite commands available within the different Ribbon tabs.

Figure 1–8. The Quick Access Toolbar as it looks without any customizations

Adding a Button to the Quick Access Toolbar

You can add a command to the Quick Access Toolbar (QAT) with just a few clicks. In fact, it is so simple you will be tempted to add a plethora of commands right off the bat just in case you can't find them later. Go for it, because I will show you how to remove commands as well. Here is how to add a command:

1. Navigate to the Home tab, and find the Copy button. If you need a hint, the Copy button resides in the Clipboard groups.

2. Right-click the Copy button with your mouse to display a context menu that provides additional commands related to the button.

3. Click "Add to Quick Access Toolbar" as shown in Figure 1–9.

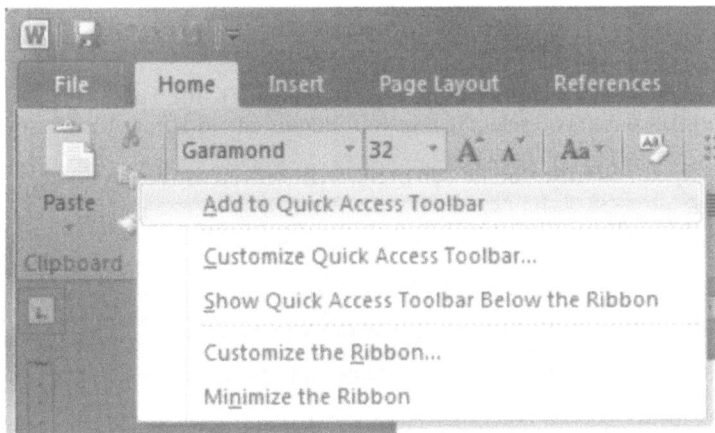

Figure 1–9. Selecting Add to the Quick Access Toolbar

4. Review the QAT to see the newly added Copy button.

5. Add some text to your document, and select it. Then, click the Copy button residing on the QAT to test that it works.

6. To verify the new Copy button does indeed work, now click the Paste button residing on the Home ribbon tab. You should see the copied text pasted into your document.

The process of adding QAT buttons is quick and easy and allows you to place a command you are using frequently, either temporarily or everyday, in a convenient location. Now, what if you placed a button on the QAT but now want to remove it? That's next.

Removing a Button from the Quick Access Toolbar

Removing a button is just as easy as adding one; it follows a similar sequence. Let's remove the Copy button added in the previous exercise by completing these steps:

1. Right-click the Copy button in the QAT to display its context menu.

2. Click "Remove from Quick Access Toolbar" to remove the button.

3. Review the QAT, and verify the removal of the Copy button.

The ease with which you can customize the QAT means that you can add and remove frequently used buttons as you wish. If buttons drop out of favor and you find you don't use them enough to make them QAT-worthy, you can quickly remove them.

The Mini Toolbar

The Home Ribbon tab contains the majority of styling and formatting commands. It is well organized and makes it easy to find these types of commands for use in your document. But what do you do when you have a different tab, for example the Insert tab, as the active tab but want access to formatting and styling commands? You could customize the QAT by adding slew of additional buttons but that will quickly congest the QAT.

Fortunately, there is an additional toolbar called the Mini toolbar (see Figure 1–10). This toolbar is a type of context menu that becomes visible when you select text in your document and move the cursor away from the selection.

Causing the Mini toolbar to display can be tricky, but it's all in the wrist, as you can see by performing the following actions:

1. Open Word (if it isn't open already), and add some text to a document.

2. Use your mouse to highlight the text, making it the selected text.

3. Slowly move your mouse above the selected text to display the Mini toolbar.

4. When the Mini toolbar displays, click the Bold and the Italics buttons to edit the selected text's format.

5. Move your mouse away from the Mini toolbar to hide it again.

The Mini toolbar is a nice time-saver, because it allows you to format your text without moving your mouse to the top of the Word application window. It does require a bit of practice however, as it sometimes likes to pop up when you are not expecting it.

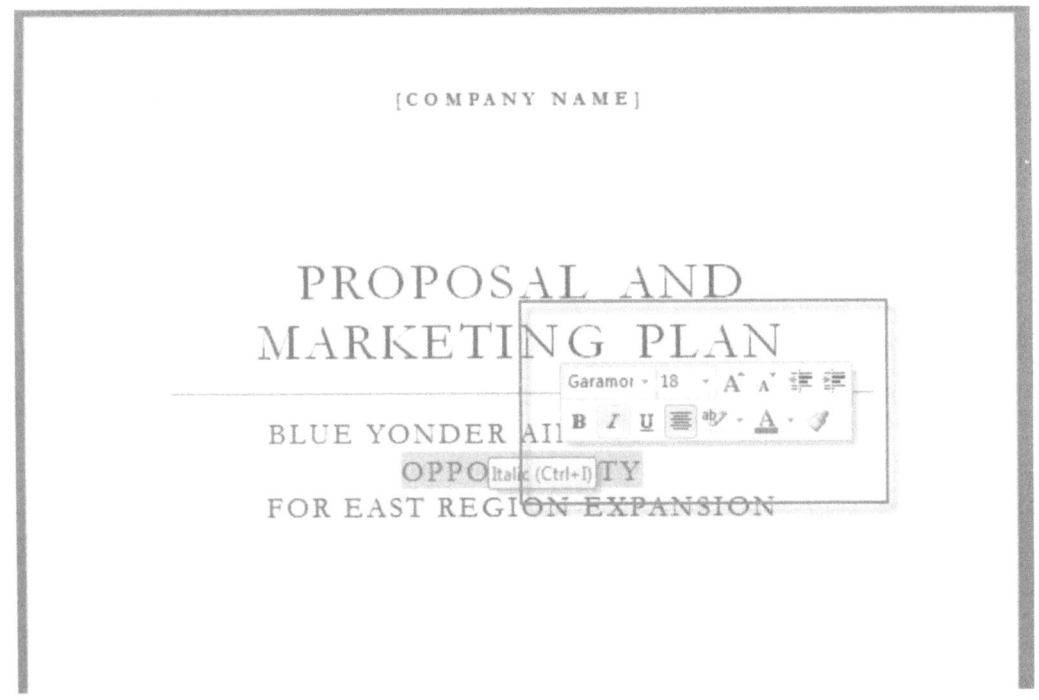

Figure 1–10. The Mini toolbar provides inline access to common formatting commands

Using the Microsoft File Button and Backstage View

As I explained in "Learning the Word 2010 User Interface," the File button activates the new user interface element known as the Backstage view (see Figure 1–2). The Backstage view is the location for all commands that work around the document, like all the activity that occurs back stage in a theater production.

Like the Ribbon, the Backstage view organizes commands according to category. In effect, the Backstage is a vertical subribbon, with panels located along its left-hand side (does that mean they are located stage right?) instead of tabs. The top left-hand section contains commands for saving, opening, and closing documents. This location makes sense, because these are the actions most associated with File commands.

The Backstage view panels follow:

- **Info:** This panel provides information about your document. Here, you can see common document metadata like the file path, size, page count, last modified date, and author information. In addition to the metadata, this panel contains commands for working with document permissions and cleaning document properties in preparation for document sharing, as well as managing document versions.

- **Recent**: This panel lists the most recently opened documents. The list displays each file name along with its file path and an icon that represents the file type (e.g., Word document, Word template, or Rich Text file). In addition, each file listed has a pin icon next to it. You can click this icon to pin a document to the top of the Recent Documents listing. The Recent panel places all pinned documents at the top of the list in alphabetical order.

- **New:** The New panel contains a listing of available document templates that you can utilize as the basis for a new document. At the top of the panel reside the most common document templates: Blank Document and Blog Post. This area also includes links to Recent Templates, Sample Templates, and My Templates. The bottom section of the New panel lists templates available at Office.com. These templates are categorized into folders. To view the templates for a category you double-click the folder. The right-hand section of this panel displays a preview of each template as you select them with your mouse, providing you with a glimpse of the document format and structure without requiring that you create a document from the template first. You can find more information about templates in Chapter 4.

- **Print**: As you would expect, this panel is all about tools and commands for printing your documents. It allows you to select a printer and specify the number of copies to print. A print preview resides to the right of the panel allowing you to page through your document as well as zoom in and out to see how your document will print. Additional print settings are available here as well, including settings that allow you to specify which pages to print, one-sided or two-sided printing, collation, and number of pages per sheet. Chapter 6 covers printing and printing options that will help you ensure your documents look good!

- **Share**: If you write a document, chances are you will want to share it with someone. The Share panel contains the commands for sharing a document via e-mail, SkyDrive, SharePoint, or a blog post. In addition, this panel provides tools for changing the file type to formats like Adobe PDF and Microsoft XPS, formats that don't require Microsoft Word to display and will preserve the formatting of the document.

- **Help:** This panel contains links to local Microsoft Office help file. It also includes links to the "Getting Started with Word 2010" online resource, where you can find in-depth articles with content straight from the Microsoft Word product team that help you, uh, get started with Word.

- **Options**: This button really displays the Word Options dialog window, which allows you to fine-tune Word's environment. Here, you can change Word's editing, proofing, and character display behavior; change the file location for templates; customize the Word Ribbon; and even more stuff that will lead to trouble at this point. I don't recommend using this tool when beginning to learn Word.

■ **Caution** To close the Backstage view, click the File tab again. Don't click Exit, or you will close your document and exit Word. Even though I have warned you of this, you will do it anyway! But after a couple of times, you will remember not to click Exit.

Working with Basic Documents

It's time to get your hands dirty by performing a few basic tasks related to working with documents. In this section, you will learn the skills needed create and save documents on your computer's file system.

Creating a New Blank Document

In this exercise, you will create a new document. Go ahead and open Word 2010, and wait for it to load. When Word displays inside Windows, you should see a blue tab in the upper left-hand corner labeled File. Click it to display the Backstage view (see Figure 1–11).

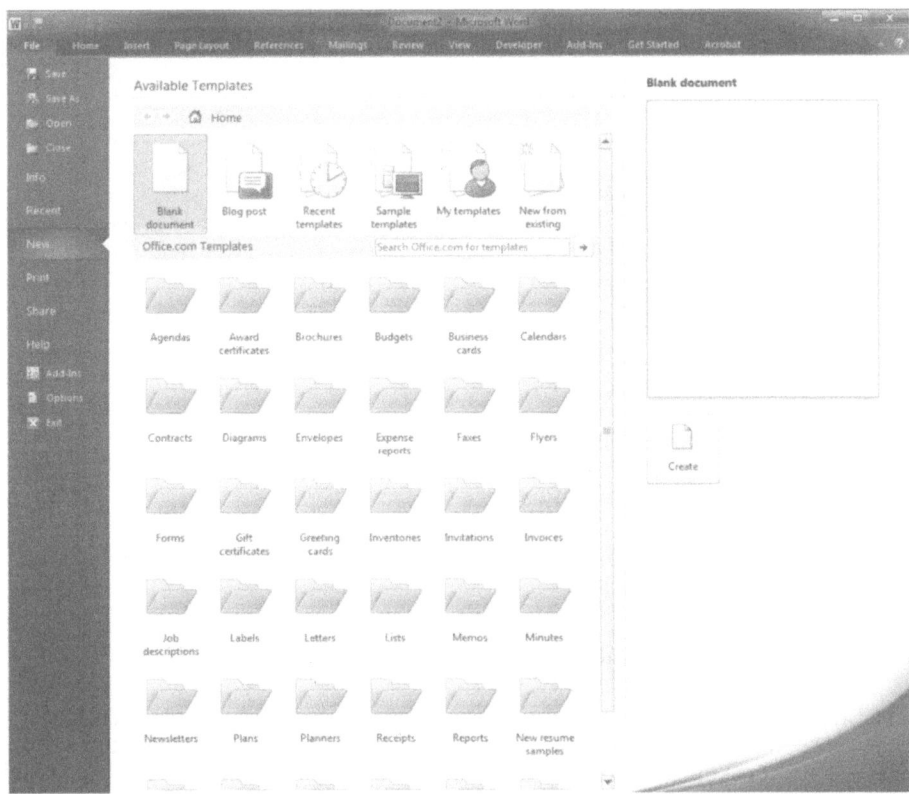

***Figure 1–11.** The Backstage view displaying the New Document section*

Figure 1–12 displays the various templates available to you as the basis for your new document. You have the option to choose from the available templates, saving you time in document construction and formatting, or you can choose to start from scratch. In this task, we will start from scratch by performing the following steps:

1. If you haven't done so already, click File ➤ New from the Ribbon to display all available templates.

2. Select the Blank document template by clicking it.

3. Click the Create button, available on the right-hand side of the screen (see Figure 1–12)

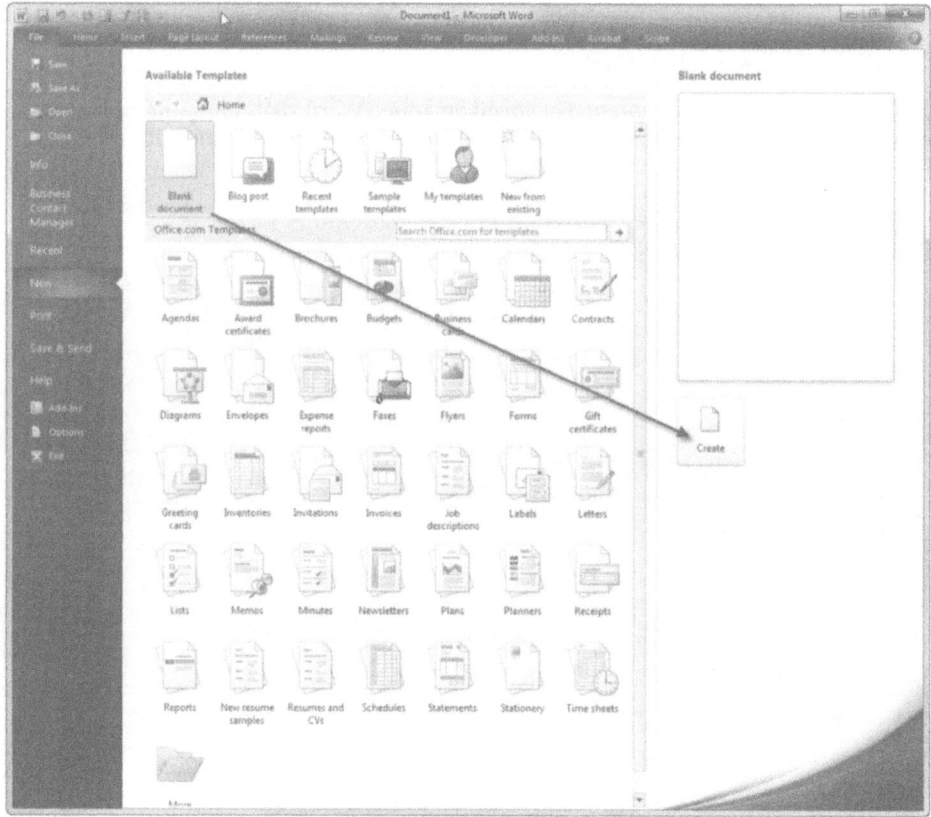

Figure 1–12. *The Create Button visible in the Backstage view's New section*

After clicking the Create button, Word will display a new document that is really a blank canvas awaiting your brilliant prose—or boring status report. Either way, you have a clean document to work with and structure as you please. Don't give in to the temptation to start typing something. We'll end this task here, as we will delve into document construction in Chapter 2. The same goes for the other tasks in this section. The idea is to get your feet wet working with documents at a high level.

Next, you will create a document using preconstructed template built by Microsoft.

Creating a New Document from a Template

Microsoft provides a plethora of templates for you to use as the basis of your documents. There is no pride of authorship here, so it makes sense to use templates to your benefit. Templates save you time by providing a prestructured and preformatted document, leaving you with only the task of adding your content.

There many templates available to you, with thousands more available at Office.com. In this exercise, you will create a new document using one of the available report templates by completing the following steps:

1. Click the Ribbon's File tab to display the Backstage view.

2. Select the New section to display the list of available templates (see Figure 1–13).

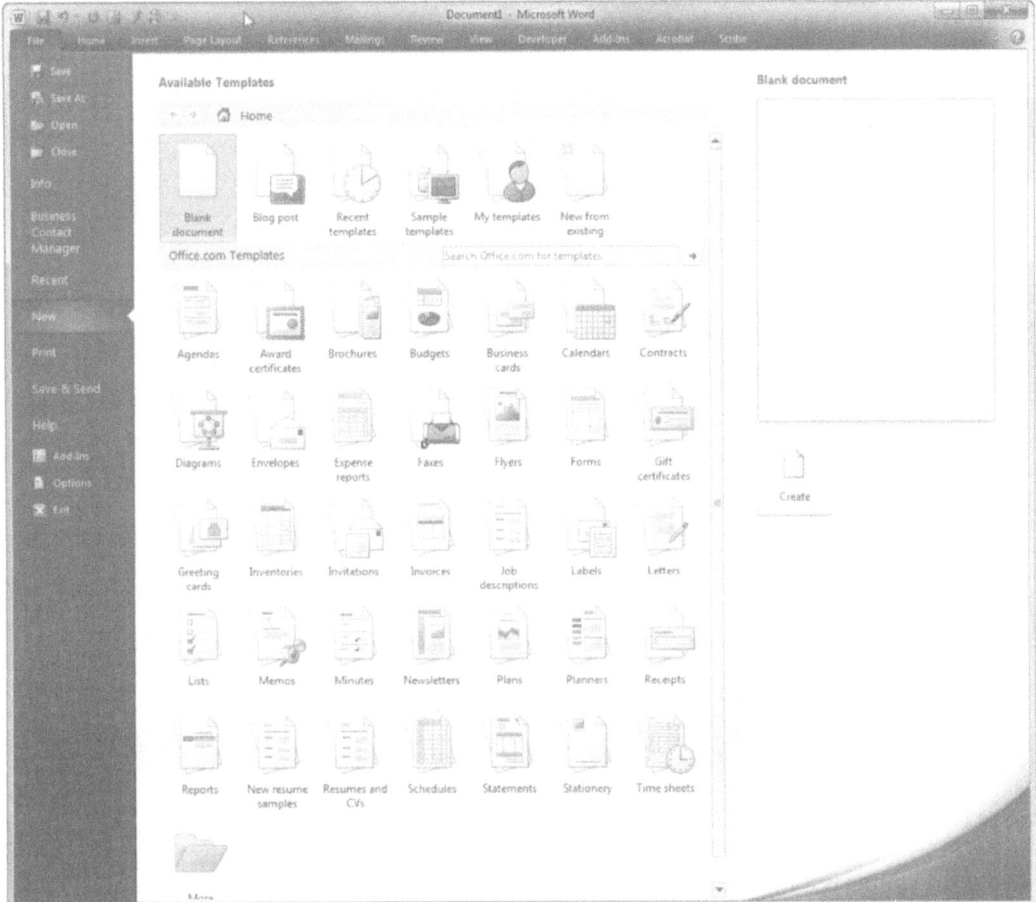

Figure 1–13. The list of templates by type

3. Click the Reports folder to open the list of report templates (see Figure 1–14).

4. Select the Business report (Elegant design) template.

5. Click Download to download the template from Office.com to your local system and display it in Word.

The result of these steps is a nice-looking document loaded into Word that includes both structure and formatting (see Figure 1–14).

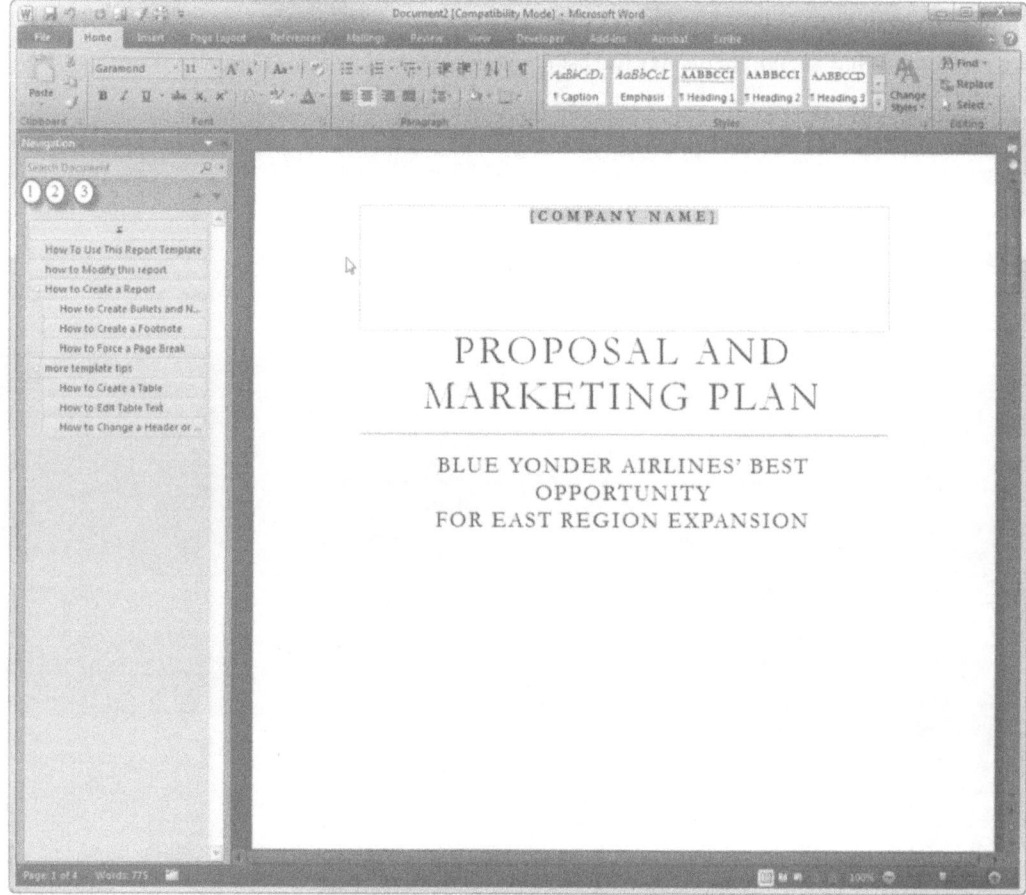

Figure 1–14. The elegant report template viewed within Word

The formatting is easy to see given the various fonts and design elements (like lines and tables) employed. After Word creates the new report document from the template, it also displays a special task pane called the Navigation pane. This pane displays all the sections with the document and allows you to quickly move between the major sections defined in your document. The next step will show you how to easily view and navigate a document's structure. Keep this document open, because it will help with the next task.

Viewing a Document's Structure

As you format a document by defining headings, subheadings, and the like, you are defining the document's structure or hierarchy. If you are familiar with Windows Explorer and the tree-like structure it uses to organize folders and files, you might be comforted to know that Word provides a user interface that resembles the tree-view structure (see Figure 1–15).

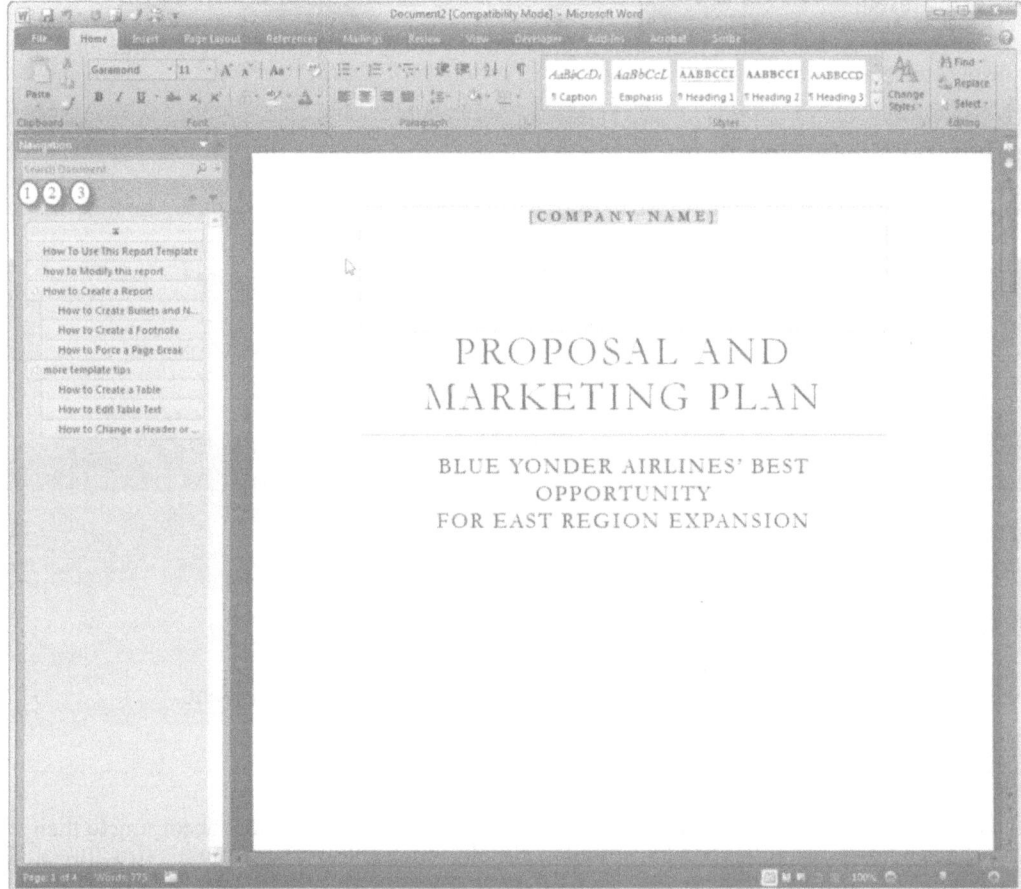

Figure 1–15. The Navigation pane

The Navigation pane hosts features for moving within your document. There are three tabs in the pane, numbered 1, 2, and 3 in Figure 1–16. Each tab has specific purpose as follows:

1. **Headings browser tab**: This tab lists all content in the document that is formatted using any of the defined heading formats like Heading 1, Heading 2, or Heading 3. This tab makes it easy to quickly move to major sections of your document.

2. **Pages browser tab:** This tab lists all the pages included in your document. You can click the page you want to make the active page, and Word will take you right to it. The tab lists each page as a thumbnail image, hopefully making it easier for you to identify a desired page simply from the thumbnail image.

3. **Search results tab:** This tab lists results from a search query using the text you input in the Navigation pane's search box. If the search finds any matches, the tab lists each result along with surrounding text to help you identify the context of the result.

Let's give each of the Navigation pane tabs a quick trial by completing a task for each one. First, you need to display the Navigation pane.

Displaying the Navigation Pane

Displaying the Navigation pane is really just an exercise in knowing where to look within the Ribbon. To display it, perform the following steps:

1. Click the View tab in the Ribbon to display Word's view settings (see Figure 1–16).

2. Look for the grouping labeled Show, and find the Navigation Pane check box.

3. Click the Navigation Pane check box so that it is selected (i.e., enabled).

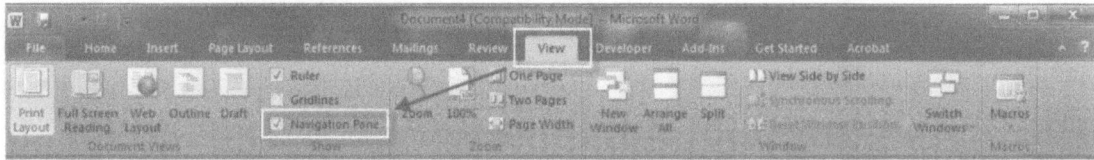

Figure 1–16. The View tab of the Ribbon showing the Navigation Pane setting enabled

When visible, the Navigation Pane displays the hierarchy of the opened document.

Using the Headings Browser Tab

As I stated previously, the headings browser tab lists all headings in your document according to their hierarchy. The headings are a series of tabs, nested to visually represent your document's structure and hierarchy. For example, Heading 2 items are listed under their related Heading 1 item. Try out the headings browser tab by doing the following actions on your current elegant report:

1. Click the "How to Create a Report" hierarchy tab. You should now be taken to page 3 of the elegant report.

2. Click the "How to Create a Table" hierarchy tab to navigate to page 4.

3. The hierarchy tabs can be expanded and collapsed, enabling you to display or hide heading levels as you please. Double-click the "How to Create a Report" hierarchy tab to hide that heading's child headings. You can also click the arrow displayed within the tab to achieve the same effect.

4. Double-click the "How to Create a Report" hierarchy again to display its child headings.

The headings browser does a great job of simplifying navigation within in a document. It is one of my favorite features and something I immediately display when working on any meaningful document that spans more than a couple of pages.

Using the Pages Browser Tab

Once you have a handle on using the headings browser, the pages browser is a cinch. This tab provides a visual listing of all the pages in your document. Each document is represented by a thumbnail image that more or less resembles the full-size page when rendered in Word.

There is more to the thumbnails browser than meets the eye. To demonstrate, please do the following items:

1. With the Navigation pane open, click the pages browser.

2. Practice navigating within the document by clicking pages, 2, 3, and 4 of the elegant report you created earlier.

3. Be super impressed, because navigating within Word can be super easy.

I have a tip about the pages browser, but I will save for the next topic, the search results tab, because it ties directly to search results.

Using the Search Results Tab

The search results tab provides a listing of results that match the search query you enter in the search text box. You can click on any of the listed results to move to that section of your document. Give it a try by following these steps:

1. Still using the elegant report created in "Creating a New Document from a Template," type **quotation** into the Search text box located at the top of the Navigation pane, and press the Enter key. You can also click the magnifying

   glass icon 🔍 to initiate the search.

2. Word should list five results that match the search text. Select any of the listed results to change the current location of your document. Now comes something I believe is a great enhancement to Word in version 2010—the search results appear not only in the search results tab but on the pages listed on the pages browser tab. This enhancement greatly simplifies navigation within search results.

3. With the search results for "quotation" still active, click the pages browser tab to display the documents that include this text within the page (see Figure 1–17).

Simple yet oh-so-very powerful, this is search works as it should have in all previous versions of Word.

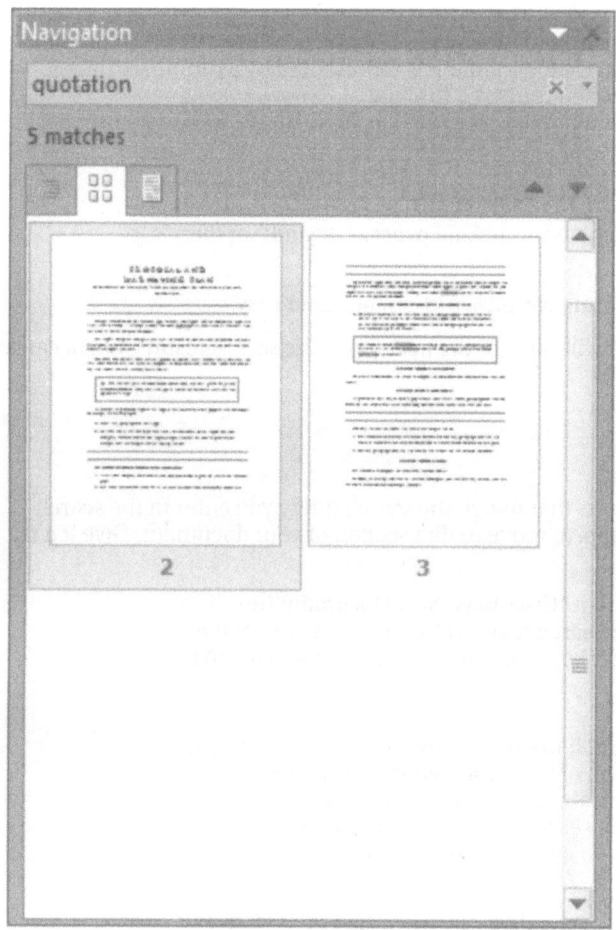

Figure 1–17. *The Pages Browser tab displaying filtered results*

Saving and Closing Documents

There are a couple of scenarios when you want to save your document. The first scenario is after writing a significant block of text. Maybe after finishing a page, a paragraph, or a sentence—your goals may vary. Either way, you want to commit your changes to your hard drive to decrease the chance of Word bugging out on you before your save and thus causing you to lose your work. In this scenario, you click the Save button to commit your changes to your hard drive and continue working on your document. You keep the document open and keep writing after saving.

The second scenario occurs when you have completed working on your document and wish to close and save it your work. Here, you can choose to perform a save action followed by a close command, but I like to be efficient and do both within a single action.

Saving a Document While Leaving It Open

You've done some typing and made enough progress on your document that you think you should go ahead and commit your progress to the hard drive by performing a save action. However, you don't want to close the document; you want to keep it open so you can keep typing. To save your progress while keeping your document open for further editing, follow these steps:

1. If you don't already have a document open, open one, and make some changes to it by typing—really, any change will do. You can format something bold, change the font size, and so on.

2. From the Ribbon, click File to display Backstage.

3. Click Save (see Figure 1–18). If you have previously saved this document, nothing further is required. If it is the first time you have saved the document, you need to perform step 4.

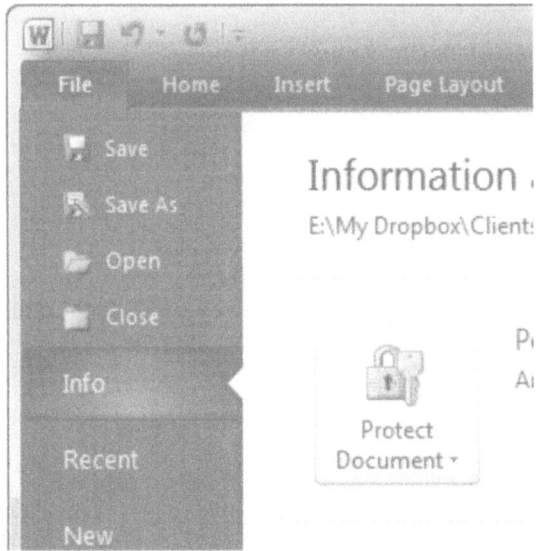

Figure 1–18. Saving a document using the Ribbon's File ➤ Save command

4. If this is the first time you have saved your document, Word will prompt you to specify a file name and folder location for your document. Save the document by browsing to your desired folder, naming the file, and clicking Save (see Figure 1–19).

■ **Tip** I perform the Save command all the time, after almost every sentence I write. Whenever I complete a thought by typing it out in Word, I save using one of the shortcut key combinations built into Word (and just about any other Microsoft Windows compatible program). The shortcut key combination is CTRL + S. I use it so frequently that I often press these keys multiple times while thinking about what to type next. The result of this habit is that what's represented in Word is almost always the same version saved to disk, greatly reducing the chances of losing my work. That said, Word has an auto-save feature that automatically performs a save at a given interval. You can find the settings for auto-save in Word options (File ➤ Options ➤ Save). Just enable the "Save AutoRecover information every minutes" option. Keep in mind that automatically saving is not a substitute for manually saving your document, but it can be a lifesaver if Word crashes.

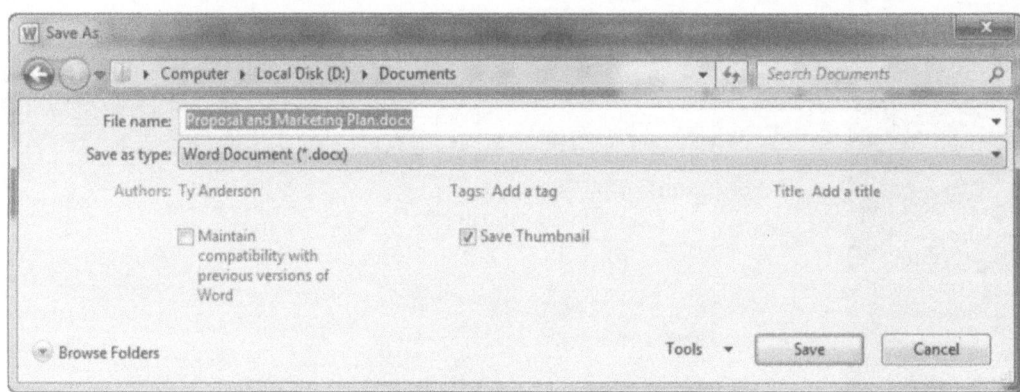

Figure 1–19. Defining a folder location and file name during Save

Closing and Saving a Document

If you are finished with your document either because you have completed it or you are taking a much-needed break from your PC, there is a quick way to close Word and save your document in one action:

1. From the Ribbon, click File ➤ Close. If you have any unsaved changes, Word will kindly ask you if you would like to save them (see Figure 1–20). All you need to do is click Save, and Word will save the document and close.

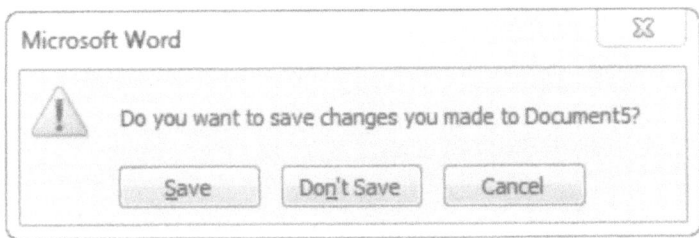

Figure 1–20. Word asking if you would like to save your changes

    2. Alternatively, click the red "X" in the upper right-hand corner of the Word window (see Figure 1–21). This action has the same affect as the previous step: Word will prompt you to save any unsaved changes and then close.

Figure 1–21. The red "X" just waiting to be clicked

Whichever method you employ, each of these is much more efficient than saving and closing the document separately and achieves the same end.

Summary

Understanding how an application organizes its commands and other user interface elements (windows, panes, toolbars, ribbons, dialogs, etc.) is half the battle. It might be even more than half because it seems that most complaints I hear are the result of simply not knowing where on earth a command resides in the UI.

This chapter provided you with an overview the Office Fluent User Interface and explained how to use it to perform common Word tasks. In addition, this chapter explained the nuts and bolts of working with Word documents. We will build on these skills in the next chapter, where we cover document creation and editing in further detail.

CHAPTER 2

■ ■ ■

Writing and Editing Text Basics

"Writers write," or so the saying goes. It's a well known phrase, but there is a related, lesser-known, saying that is familiar to anyone who has ever attempted to put creative thoughts into a cogent, coherent document using Word: "Writers don't write, they beg and plead to get Word to work with them." In my experience, it's best to play nice with software by learning how it is intended to work and let go of how you think it should work.

This chapter teaches you the basic skills required for creating documents with Word 2010. Because you will spend the majority of your time manipulating text, it is essential that you at least be a proficient at such tasks as typing text where you intend, as well as moving text around by cutting and pasting.

At the end of this chapter, you will know how to

- Manipulate text by typing it, selecting it, cutting and pasting it, and more

- Quickly navigate to section a within your document

- Correct grammatical and spelling errors

I'll move fast, but after reading this chapter and performing the tasks I have included, you will be well on your way to not only befriending Word but becoming a proficient user. Instead of becoming frustrated with Word, you will be able to instead focus on the struggle of putting the ruminations of your mind onto paper (so to speak).

Note For each task in this chapter, I assume you already have a document open. The reason for this assumption is that I didn't want to ask you to make sure you have a document open as step 1 of each task. I respect you too much for that, so I am notifying you now. Open a document before completing any of the tasks in this chapter. If you don't have a document, create a new one using any of the included Word templates.

Working with Text

Text is the essence of a document. Yes, you can include other elements like charts and images, but they only serve to highlight the narrative that is your text. Ever see a document that included only pictures that wasn't something intended for a two-year-old? No, you haven't. Do people prefer documents that include pictures and other types of illustrations that serve to make a document more enjoyable to read? Yes. But without text, your message loses its punch. Therefore, knowing how to write and edit text in your documents is an essential Word skill.

It is a document's nature to go through several iterations of changes. Rarely will you write perfect prose in your first attempt. Communicating your point requires constant revision up to the point you decide it is ready for your audience. Knowing how to be quick about your edits will help you focus your mind and crank out quality documents that impress everyone. This section explains what you need to know to go about your writing and editing business.

Letting the Cursor Point the Way

In Word 2010, the cursor (see Figure 2–1) marks what is known as the *insertion point*. The insertion point is a blinking vertical line that signifies the current focal point of the document. When you start typing, the blinking line lets you know where Word will insert the text you type.

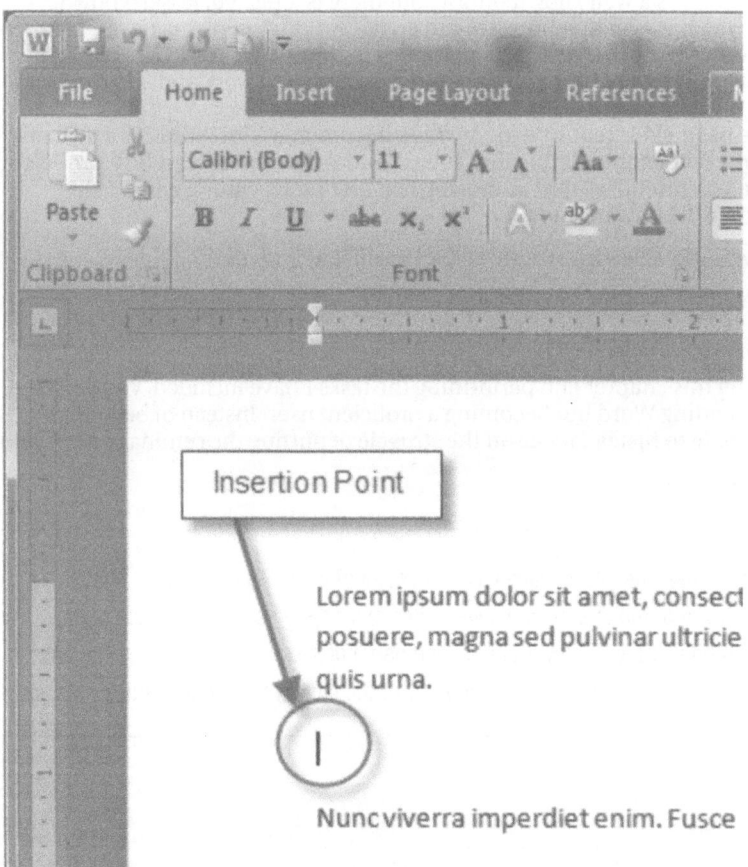

Figure 2–1. The insertion point displayed in a Word document

You can change the insertion point in your document using a couple of methods. The first is to use your mouse to find a different location in your document and then click where you want to insert text.

The second is to use your keyboard. Let's complete a couple of exercises that show how to utilize each method.

■ **Note** If you are working with a blank document, a single click is not enough to change the insertion point. Instead, you need to double-click the location where you want to move the insertion point.

Method 1: Using the Mouse to Change the Insertion Point

Using the mouse is maybe the most common and simplest way to change the insertion point. Most likely, you are already familiar with this method, as it is a rather routine skill employed in every Windows application. However, if you are not familiar with this technique, you can follow these steps to make it happen:

1. I know I said I wouldn't do this, but since this is the first task of the chapter, I'll ask you to open a Word document! OK, I won't mention it again.

2. If you don't have any text in your document, type a few lines of random text or take advantage of the tip below and type **=lorem(10)**.

■ **Tip** Word has a great undocumented feature that allows you to automatically insert text. It's great for testing Word features without actually having to type a bunch of text. All you need to do is type **=lorem(*n*)**, where *n* equals the number of paragraphs you would like to insert, and press the Enter key. Word will then insert the specified number of paragraphs using pseudo-Greek text. Give it a try; it's quite useful.

3. Grab your mouse, and click anywhere in the document you'd like to specify a new insertion point (or double-click if it is a blank document)

4. Type some new text—whatever you like!

Most likely using your mouse is how you will change the insertion point 99 percent of the time. However, using your keyboard can prove very convenient, as it does not require you to move your hand and grab your mouse. Instead, you can employ various key combinations to quickly navigate within your document's text.

Method 2: Using the Keyboard to Change the Insertion Point

The mouse definitely rules, but the keyboard is oftentimes the quickest and best method for changing the insertion point. You can use the arrow keys alone or combine them with the CTRL key to hop around the document and change the insertion point. To change the insertion point using keyboard commands, complete the following steps:

1. Press the down arrow key on your keyboard to move the insertion point down a line (assuming your document contains more than a single line).

2. Next, press the left, right, and up arrow keys to move the insertion point in the corresponding direction.

These keys move the insertion point within the document one character at a time. But what if you want to make larger jumps within your document? This is where knowing some keyboard combinations come in handy. The following steps explain how to use some common keyboard combinations:

3. Press and hold the CTRL key and then click the down arrow. This keystroke combination moves the insertion point to the next paragraph.

4. Now, reverse it by pressing CTRL and the up arrow to move up a paragraph. These two key combinations allow you to move between paragraphs like a gazelle moves between rocks.

5. Next, press CTRL and the right arrow key. This combination moves the insertion point to next word to the immediate right of the current focus. As you might expect, CTRL + left arrow, moves the insertion point to word left of the insertion point.

■ **Tip** There are many other keyboard shortcuts, and it would behoove you to look them up in Word help and learn the ones most relevant to you. A few of other really useful combinations are: CTRL+Page Up and CTRL+Page Down to jump up and down from the current page and CTRL+Home and CTRL+End to jump to the document's beginning and end.

You can a full listing of keyboard shortcuts here: `http://office.microsoft.com/en-us/word/HP101476261033.aspx`.

The mouse is best when you want to quickly move large distances within a document. For example, you can use the mouse wheel to scroll several pages up or down and then click the desired page and start typing. The keyboard is best when you need to move only a few lines or paragraphs from the current insertion point.

Selecting Text and Deleting Text

Part of any editing process involves rewriting or massaging your text. The key skill with editing is the ability to select text, delete it, and type whatever changes you think would enhance your document.

To select text, you can you use your mouse or keyboard to select one or more word, sentence, or paragraphs. The following steps explain both methods for selecting text:

1. Type some text in your document.

2. Use your mouse to navigate between two words, and click (i.e., click the left mouse button) to position the cursor between them.

3. Click again and hold down the mouse button, and drag the cursor to the right to select several words. Once you have the selection you like, release the left mouse button. See Figure 2–2.

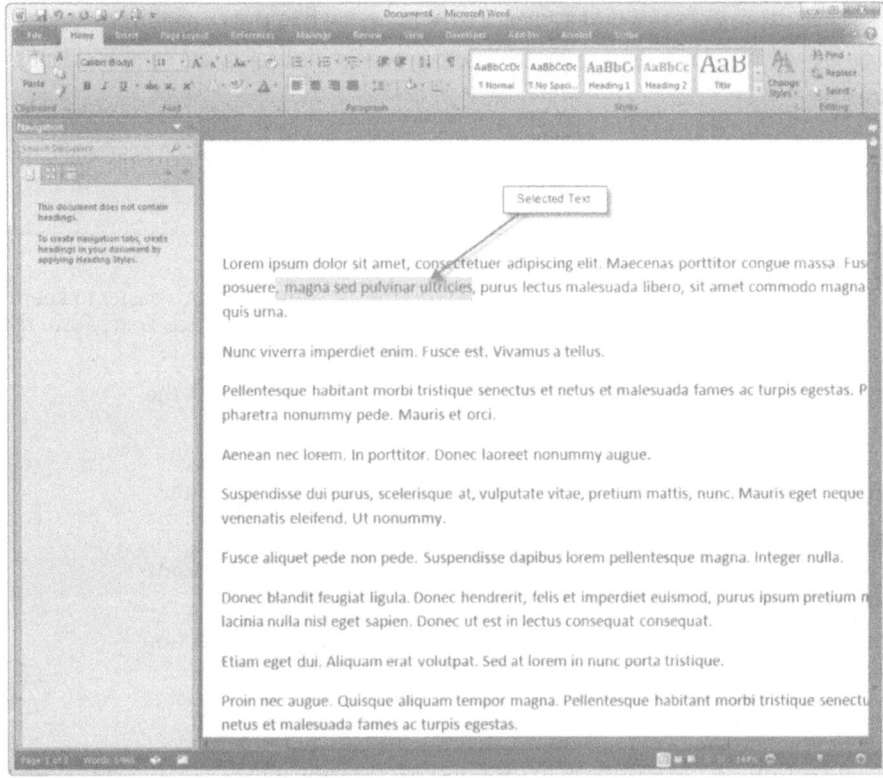

***Figure 2–2.** The highlighted text is known as the selection in Word .*

▪ **Tip** You can also select a word by double-clicking it with your mouse. If you want to select an entire paragraph, hold the CTRL key and double-click.

Now, you have a couple of options depending on what you want to do. If you want to type over the selected text and replace it, simply start typing. Word will delete the selected text and then insert what you type in its place. If you only want to delete the selected text, press the Delete key on your keyboard.

▪ **Tip** The Delete and Backspace keys are similar but different. They are similar in that they both removed content from your document but they differ in how they do it.

The Backspace key deletes the character behind the insertion point, pushing the cursor back one position and deleting the character you backed into. Any text preceding the insertion point shifts back by the number of times you press the Backspace key.

The Delete key deletes the character ahead of the insertion point. Any text preceding the insertion point shifts back by the number of times you press the Delete key.

The mouse is a great tool, but when you are banging out your thesis, sometimes, it's easier to keep your hands on the keyboard and use it to navigate within your document and select text. To perform the same actions listed but with a keyboard, give the following steps a try:

1. Use the keyboard combination Ctrl + right arrow to jump to the word just to the right of the current cursor location.

2. Now that you can move the cursor quickly with a nice keyboard combination, you need to know how to select text. This is done by adding the Shift key to the CTRL+arrow key combination. To select text, press Shift+CTRL+right arrow. You should see the word to right of the cursor selected. This method selects entire words or paragraphs depending on which arrow you employ. If you want finer control, read-on.

3. By dropping the CTRL key out of the combination, you can change the selection process to increment by letter instead of word when selecting horizontally. When selecting vertically, the selection increments by a single line versus a paragraph. Give this a try by pressing Shift+right arrow. You should see the selection include a new character each time you press the key combination. Now, try it with the up and down arrows to see how it works with lines.

Word has tons of keyboard combinations that are worth knowing and integrating into you authoring workflow, as they save time and make life a bit easier. Anytime you can keep your hands on the keyboard and leave the mouse alone, you are working more efficiently. To learn more keyboard combinations, open Word help by pressing F1. When the help window displays, type **keyboard shortcuts** in the search box to see everything Word has to say about the subject (see Figure 2–3).

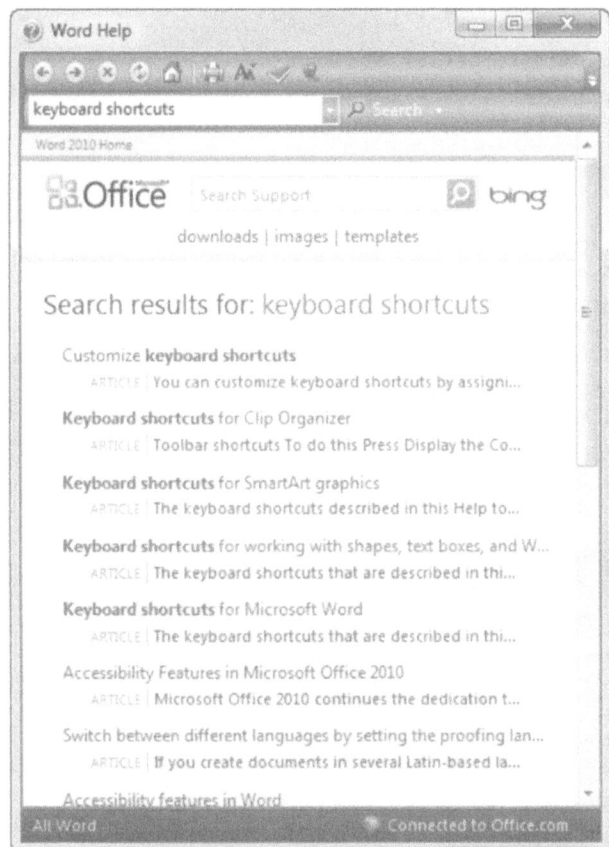

Figure 2–3. Word help displaying links for keyboard shortcuts

■ **Caution** Word has two typing modes: Insert mode and Overwrite mode. Insert mode is the default mode and causes text in the document to shift automatically as you type. This is the behavior you most likely expect Overwrite mode, instead of shifting text, replaces any text at the insertion point with what you type next. Overwrite mode looks as if it is eating your existing text and has the tendency to strike fear into users of all levels.

Luckily, Word 2010 does not enable Overwrite mode by default. If you should, for some reason, decide you want to enable it, open the Word options dialog box (click the File ➤ Options from the ribbon), and navigate to the Advanced panel (see Figure 2–4). Click the "Use Insert Key to control overtype mode" check box as well as the "Use overtype mode" check box to enable overwrite mode and the usage of the Insert key to toggle between modes.

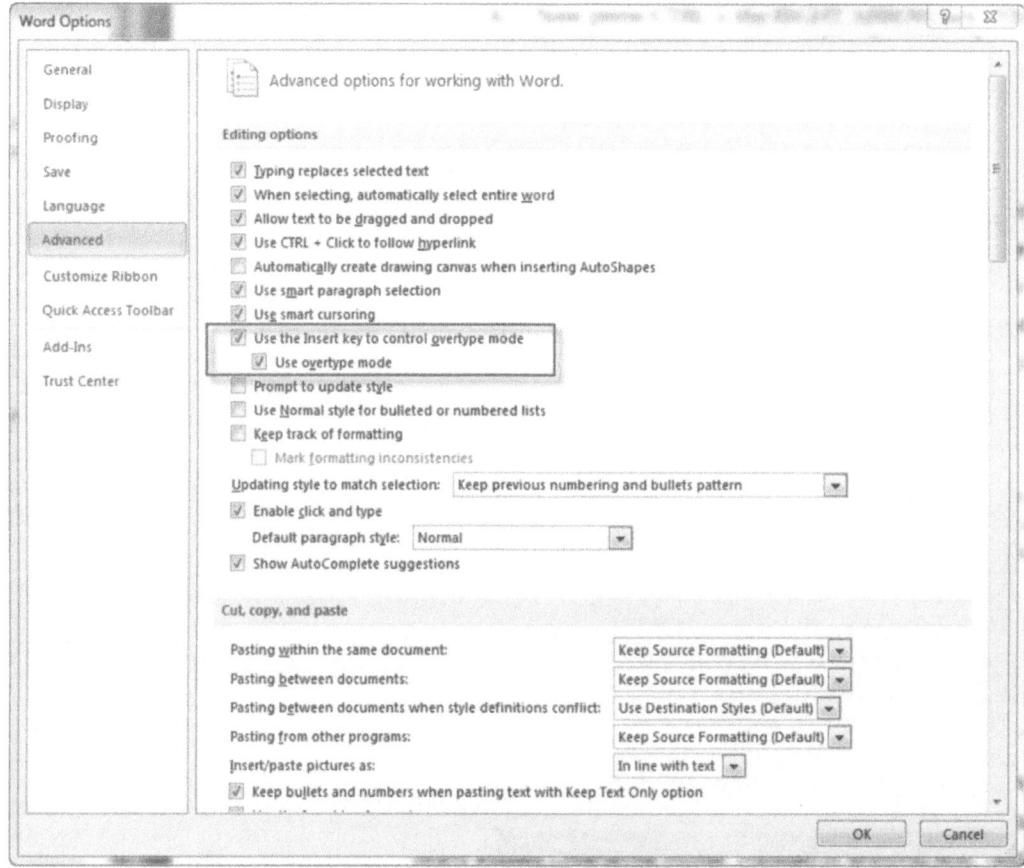

Figure 2–4. Enabling Overwrite mode in the Word Options dialog box.

With overwrite mode enabled, you can then toggle between the two modes by press the Insert key on your keyboard.

Cutting, Copying, and Pasting

Perhaps no set of skills is more important to your computing experience than the ability to cut, copy, and paste. These three commands truly distinguish word processing applications from typewriters. With these commands at you fingertips, you can make drastic decisions like turning your conclusion into your document's introduction without making a mess. All you do is select the text that serves as your document's conclusion, cut it, and then paste it at the beginning where introductions are typically found.

Cut and copy are very similar. The only difference is that cutting and pasting effective moves your selected text from one location to another within your document. Copying and pasting results in duplication of the selected text.

Using the Ribbon

Figure 2–5 shows the location of the Cut, Copy, and Paste buttons on the Ribbon's Home tab. If you are really sharp, you might have noticed that both the Cut and Copy icons are disabled. The reason for their disabled state is that when I took this screenshot, I did not have any text selected in my document. As a result of this "no text selected" situation, there is nothing to cut or copy, so the buttons are not enabled.

Figure 2–5. The Cut, Copy, and Paste icons displayed in the Ribbon's Home tab

To invoke these actions, you first need to select some text or any other type of content (charts, tables, images, etc.). Once you make selection, the Cut and Copy icons will be enabled (see Figure 2–6). To actually cut, copy, and paste using the Ribbon, simply do the following:

- *Cut*: Select some content in your document, and click the Cut icon on the Home ribbon tab (Home ➤ Clipboard group ➤ Cut).

- *Copy*: Select some content in your document, and click the Copy icon on the Home ribbon tab (Home ➤ Clipboard group ➤ Copy).

- *Paste*: Use your mouse or your keyboard to move the cursor to the location where you want to paste content (recall that the cursor location is called the insertion point). Paste the content clicking the Paste icon (Home ➤ Clipboard group ➤ Paste).

Figure 2–6. Cut and Copy icons are enable when you select Word conent, like text.

Using the Mouse

You can perform the same actions using your mouse. Say you are at the bottom of the Word application window, and you just do not feel like moving your mouse all the way up to the Ribbon. You are in some serious luck, as you can right-click to display a special menu known as the context menu (see Figure 2–7).

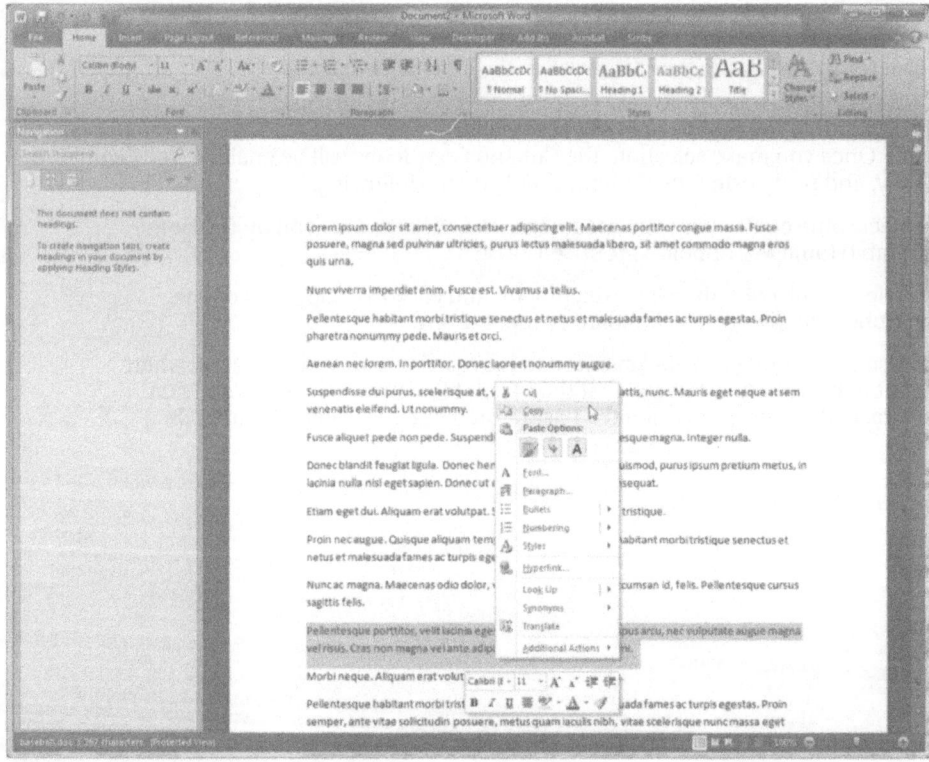

Figure 2–7. The Word context menu displaying the icons for Cut, Copy, & Paste.

Once you invoke the context menu, you can then choose Cut or Copy to place the selected content on the clipboard. To perform a paste, move the insertion point to your desired location, invoke the context menu again (right-click), and select the Paste icon.

Keyboard Shortcuts

My recommended method for cut, copy, and paste is to learn the keyboard shortcuts, as it is the fastest way to perform these actions—especially if you are right-handed and use the mouse with your right-hand. The keyboard shortcuts are:

- *Cut*: Ctrl+X
- *Copy*: Ctrl+C
- *Paste*: Ctrl+V

Also, it's worth knowing the keyboard shortcut for the undo function as well (Ctrl+Z). These four commands are in a convenient line for your left hand. It's worth taking the time to train your left hand to be proficient with these shortcuts. It will save you lots of time.

Using Paste Preview and Paste Options

Many people perform a copy and paste and then decide they don't like what they see. They either undo this action or delete the text. Well, Microsoft has introduced a feature that allows you to preview what a paste action will look like before actually pasting the text into your document (see Figure 2–8). When I first heard about this feature, I didn't think it was anything to write home about. I was wrong. After taking the time to test it, I quickly realized it is quite useful indeed, because it allows me to visualize the change to my document without actually committing it.

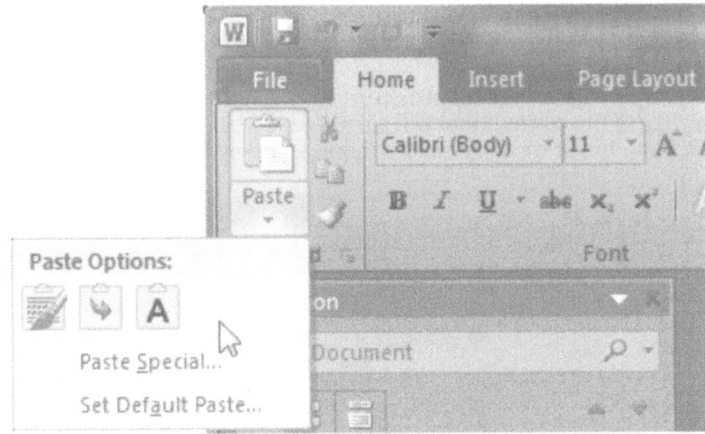

Figure 2–8. The Paste Options displaying underneath the Paste icon

The location of Paste Preview is not obvious at first glance. But if you look closely at the Paste icon in Figure 2–8, you will see an arrow underneath it. If you click this arrow, you will see three Paste options as follows:

- *Keep Source Formatting*: This paste option will insert the source text using the same formatting it had when you placed it on the clipboard via a cut or copy action. Figure 2–9 shows an example of this option.

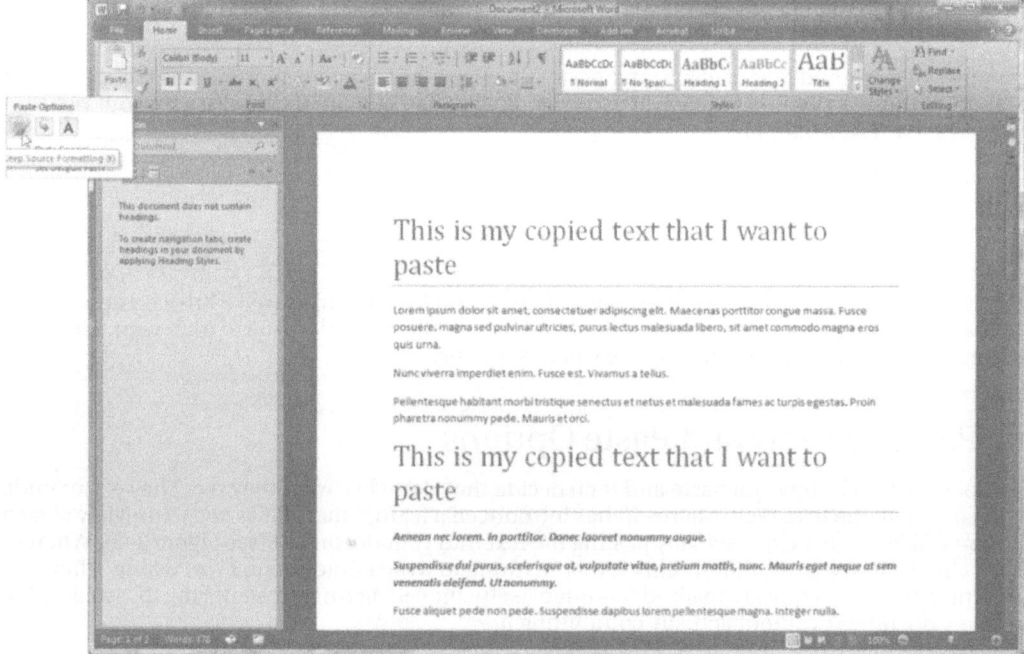

Figure 2–9. Paste Preview for the Keep Source Formatting option

- *Merge Formatting*: Merge attempts to preserve the structure of you copied content while merging it with the styling of the content that will surround it. The end result isn't always what you might want, but in most cases, Word makes a pretty good guess. See Figure 2–10.

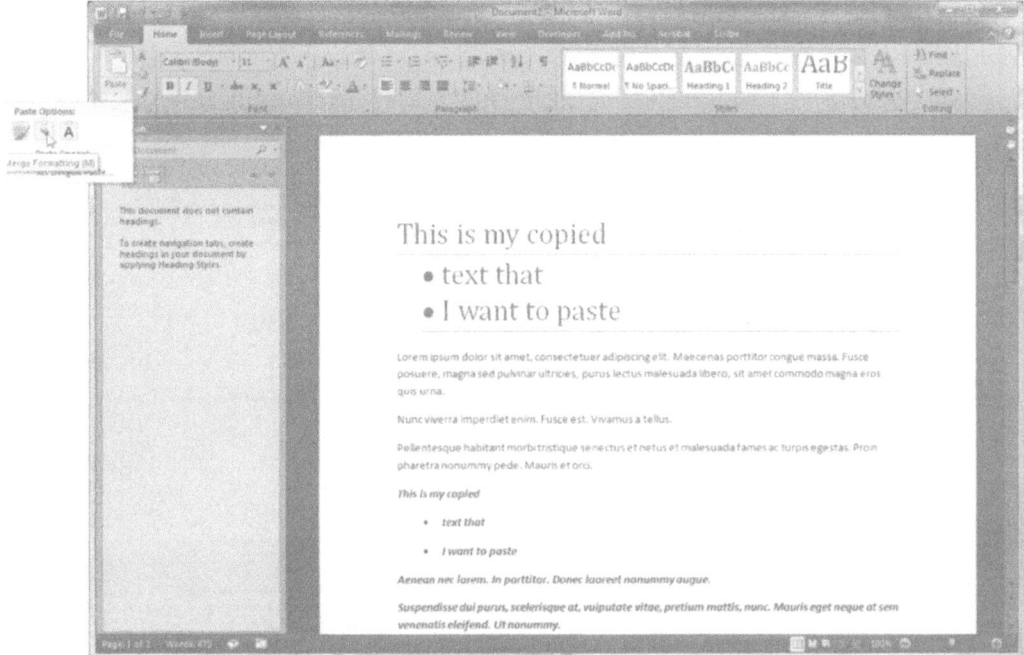

Figure 2–10. Paste Preview for the Merge Formatting option

- *Keep Text Only*: This option has no frills and no extra features. Use this option to insert the copied text as text without any formatting. The structure of the text will be preserved but no formatting will be applied.

Finding and Replacing Text

I write lots of documents and even reuse existing documents as templates for new ones. When I attempt to reuse an existing document, it is typically a contract where most of the content is the same, but I need to change the client name and the project name. Both are scattered throughout the document, which means if I try to scan the document with my eyes, I will invariably miss a reference to the previous client and embarrass myself.

Luckily, Word has a powerful search feature that allows me to quickly find text and replace it. Of course, I don't have to replace the text I find. You can perform searches for text without being required to replace it with different text. Just know the two are related and found in the same location.

Finding Text

As you create documents and write text, invariably you need to search for specific words or phrases. There are several reasons as to why you might want to execute a search in your document including (but not limited to): discovering where and how often the word is used, navigating to the location of the word, and replacing the text (covered next). Word's search features reside in something called the Navigation pane (see Figure 2–11)

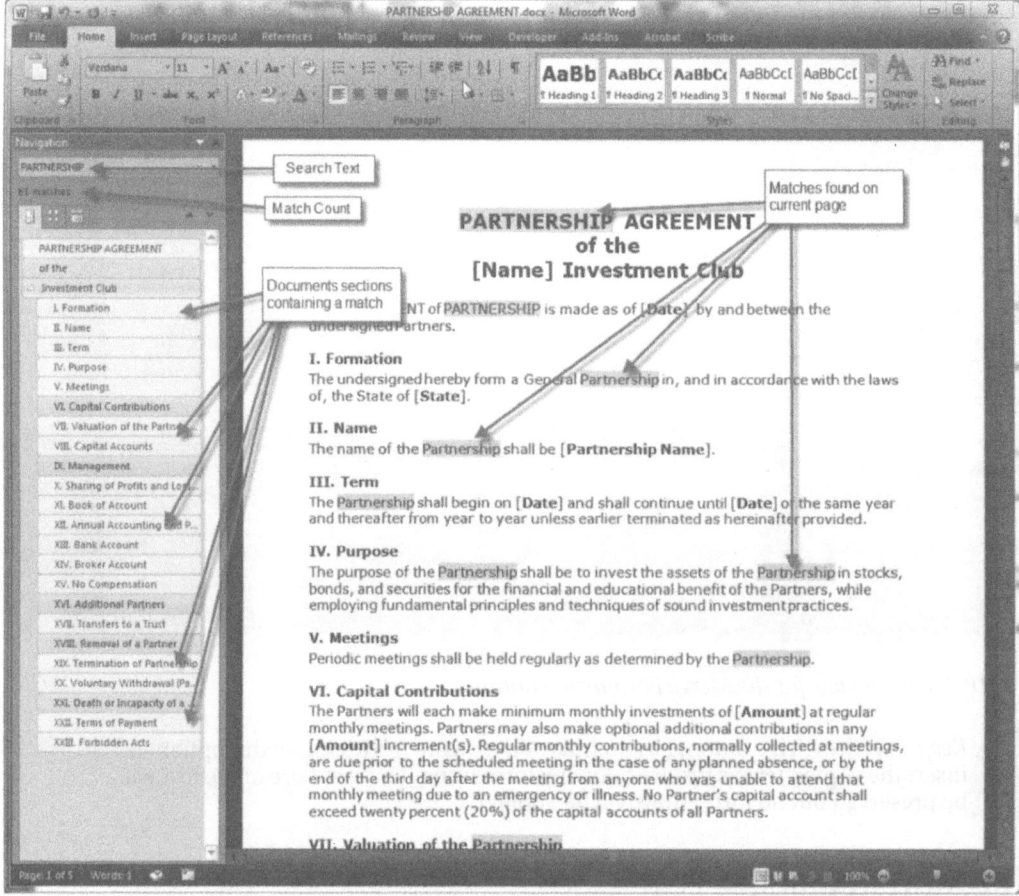

Figure 2–11. *The Navigation pane displaying search results*

To perform a search, click the Find icon on the ribbon (Home ➤ Editing group ➤ Find) or use the Ctrl+F keyboard combination. This action will display the Navigation pane, which contains an input field where you type your search query.

The Navigation pane contains three tabs that allow you to browse search results in three different ways:

- *Browse by Headings*: After executing a search, the tab lists in yellow all section headings that contain the searched text. The yellow formatting makes the sections appear lit-up and helps make it obvious where matches were found. You can click any heading, and Word will take you to the section containing the match.

> ▓ **Tip** The Navigation pane is available to you at anytime and isn't only for searching or finding text in your document. When I write long documents, I keep the Navigation pane open, so I can quickly move within the document sections I have created for my document. The key to this strategy is that I format my sections using the Heading 1, Heading 2, Heading 3, Heading *N* styles available in the Styles section of the Home ribbon tab. As you format sections using the heading styles, the Navigation pane displays the section hierarchy defined in your document.

- *Browse by Page*: This tab provides a thumbnail view of each page in your document (see Figure 2–12). Each search match displays with a yellow highlight so you can easily see pages containing a search match. Just click a page to navigate to it. The insertion point will always be at the top of the page each time to you move to a new page in this manner.

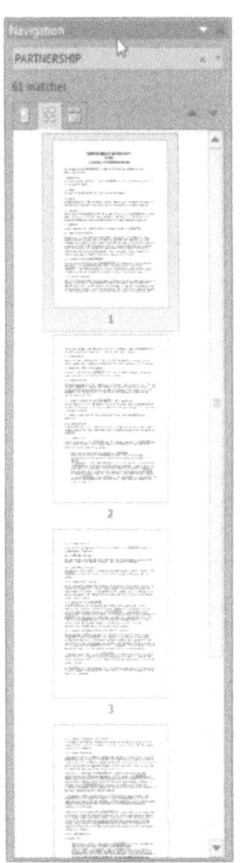

Figure 2–12. The Browse by Page tab shows page thumbnails in the Navigation pane

- *Browse by Text*: This tab lists each search result along with some surrounding text that helps show the context of the match (see Figure 2–13). Each result is encapsulated within a grey rectangle that serves to separate each result. You can jump straight to a search result by clicking it. When Word moves you to the location of the match, it selects the matching word or phrases, causing the match to become your current selection.

Figure 2–13. The Browse Results tab diplays search results in the Navigation pane

Searching for text is one very useful feature but what makes it truly useful is the ability to quickly find text and replace it with different text. This is exactly what we will do next.

Replacing Text

The replace text option resides in the Find and Replace dialog box shown in Figure 2–14 (the keyboard shortcut is CTRL+H). Using this dialog box you can enter the text you want to find and then enter the text you want to replace it with. The way Find and Replace works is that Word first searches the document for text that matches what you enter in the "Find what" field.

Figure 2–14. The Find and Replace dialog box

When Word finds a match, it stops to show you the matching text. You can then replace the text by clicking the Replace button. Once you click the Replace button, Word deletes the old text and inserts the text you entered in the "Replace with" field and moves to the next match. This methods works if you only want to replace certain instances of the matching text.

If you know you want to replace every match found, you can click the Replace All button. Clicking this button will cause Word to search through your document and replace every match found with the new text.

Refining Search by using Options

Finding text is nice and straightforward as long as you only want to find a given string of text and you don't particularly care how it is formatted. But what do you do if you want to find every instance of a word like "coffee" but only when it is capitalized? You make use of search options. Here's how:

1. Open the Find and Replace dialog box (Home tab ➤ Editing group ➤ Find)

2. In the lower left-hand corner, click the More button to display to the Search Options (see Figure 2–15).

3. Given the example mentioned previously, you would type **Coffee** into the "Find what" field.

4. In the Search Options section, click the "Match case" check box so that it is enabled (there should be a check in the box).

5. Click Find Next, and Word will move the selection to the next instance of the search text ("Coffee") within the document, but ignore any instances of "coffee" that it finds.

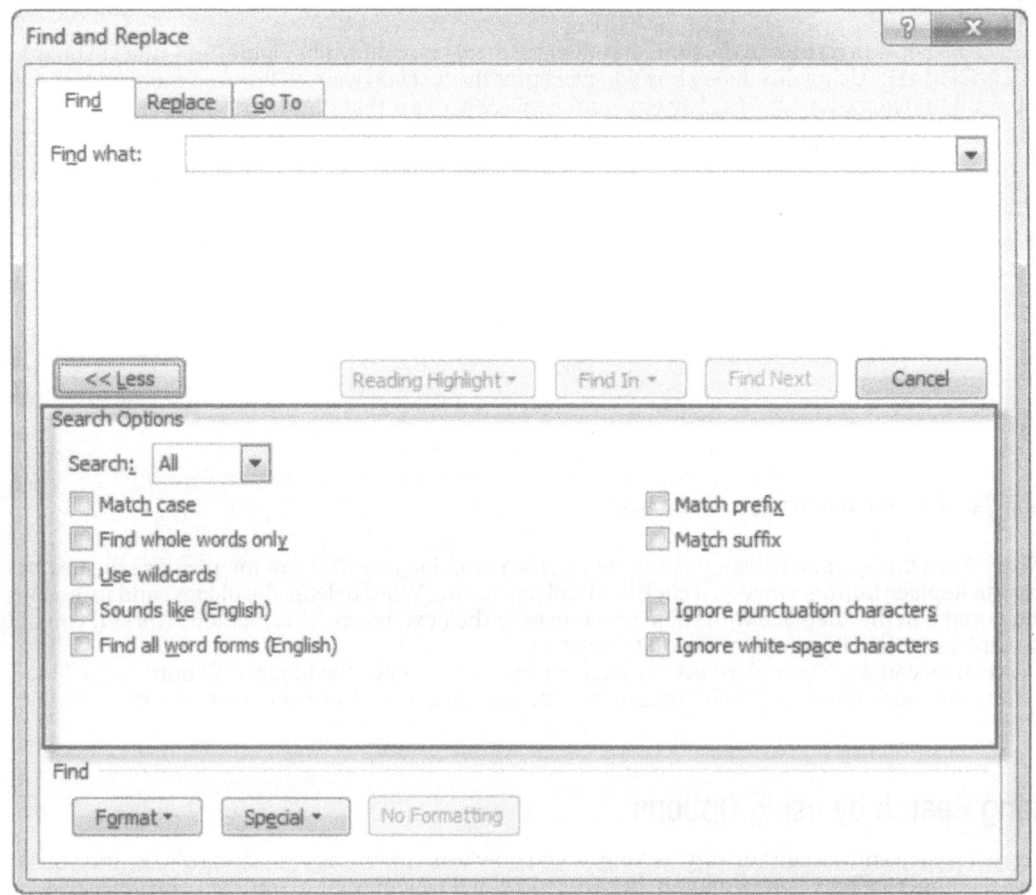

Figure 2–15. The Search Options group displayed in the Find and Replace dialog box.

Search options provide you with options akin to fine motor skills. Instead of retrieving every single instance of text regardless of it case, you can perform sophisticated searches. One option I find handy is "Find whole words only". This option will return only matching pieces of text that are each a separate word with in the document. If the search text is only contained within a word, it would not be returned in the results as it would not be a whole word. For example, searching for "in" as a whole word would not return "pin" or "inch."

Other options prove useful as well. Using the drop-down next to the Search label, you direct the flow of your search to move down the document from the current insertion point or to move up. If you select All, as shown in Figure 2–15, the search will move downward and the return to the beginning of the document after reaching the end, in essence starting over at the top.

Searching Within a Specific Format

Let's cover one last example before we end this chapter. Imagine you have a document that utilizes a sophisticated design template that contains a variety of different formats (we'll cover styles in Chapter 3, so this is a bit of a warm-up). Let's say you have used the Heading 1, Heading 2, and Heading 3 styles throughout your document. Now, what if you only want to search text that has the Heading 1 style applied to it? Well you'd be in considerable luck, as all you'd need to do is this:

1. Open the Find and Replace dialog box.

2. Enter your desired search text into the "Find what" field.

3. Click the More button.

4. Click the Format button to display the format search options (see Figure 2–16).

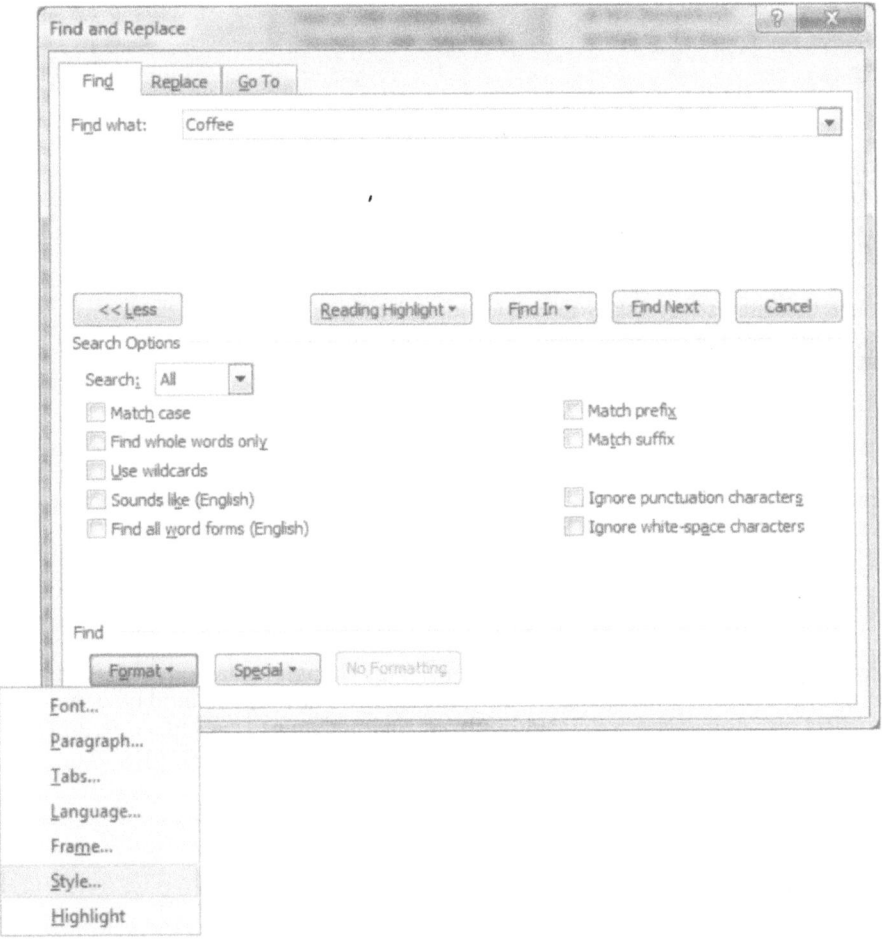

Figure 2–16. The Format buttons menu displaying the various format search option categories.

5. Click the Style option to display the Find Style dialog box (see Figure 2–17).

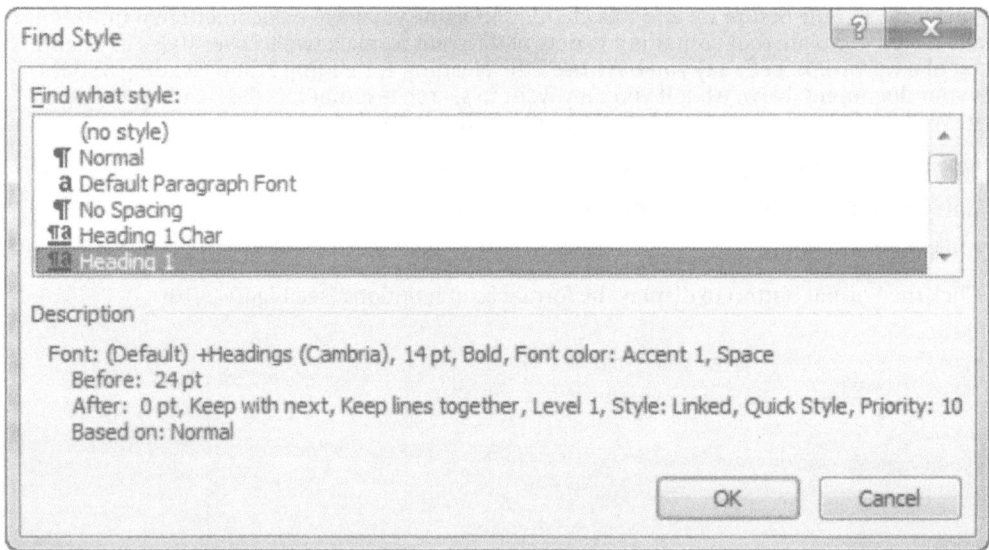

Figure 2–17. The Find Sytle dialog box.

6. Scroll through the listed styles until you find Heading 1. Select it, and click the OK button to close the dialog box. You will see the format appear under the "Find what" field.

7. In the Find and Replace dialog box, click the Find Next button.

The result of these steps is essentially a style filter that only searches text formatted as Heading 1. Learning to utilize the search options like style filters is a great way to fine-tune you text searching skills. It's worth the investment, because it will save you time, especially when working with long documents. To clear any formatting from a search field, click the No Formatting button.

Summary

Writing and editing text is the essence of authoring documents. This chapter explained the basics of working with text within Word 2010. If you read all the way through, you now understand how to position your cursor, select text, and delete text. In addition, you learned how to use cut, copy, and paste while experiencing the beauty that is Paste Preview. Last, you learned how to find text within a document and replace with it with different text.

CHAPTER 3

■■■

Adding Style to Documents

Having something to say and "putting pen to paper" (so to speak) are only part of the battle. Certainly, if you have something to say, you need to have text on a document and it needs to be somewhat coherent text at that. But there is another item you should consider when authoring a document...your audience. Your audience does not have the benefit of all the information bouncing around in your cabeza. They don't know how you arrived at your main points, so they are not able to infer your meaning. They need *your* help in order to understand *your* document.

This help manifests itself with document styling and formatting. With styling and formatting you can transform your document from page after page of text into an attractive piece of art that draws the eyes of your audience and makes your document a compelling read.

Good usage of styling and formatting increases the chances of your audience entering your mind and understanding your message. By implementing a well-designed style guide, you ease the pain of an already information-overloaded audience and guide them along a path of your choosing. This chapter shows you how to effectively format and style your documents for the sake of your readers as well as yourself.

Learning the Basics of Formatting

Good formatting provides both structure and emphasis to your documents. Applied effectively, formatting guides your readers through your document and draws their eye to key points or facts you want them to remember. The tools for formatting text reside in the Home tab of the Word 2010 ribbon (see Figure 3–1).

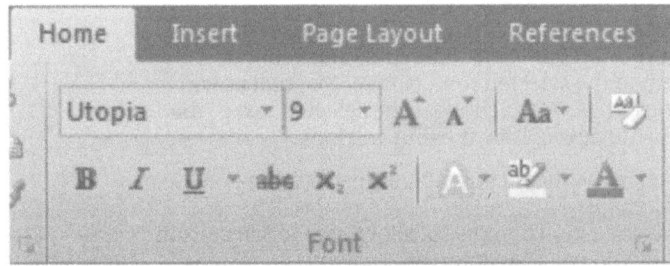

Figure 3–1. The Font group residing in the Home tab

In this tab you find a group of tools within the Font group. The tools found here provide the majority of the commands you need to format your text. The following series of steps takes you through each command in the font group and will help you become familiar with the text formatting options available to you.

1. Create a new, blank document in Word 2010.

2. Type "=lorem(1)", without the quotation marks (see Figure 3–2) into your document and press the Enter key. Word will insert one paragraph of Latin text into the document. This text serves as nice example text for the remaining steps.

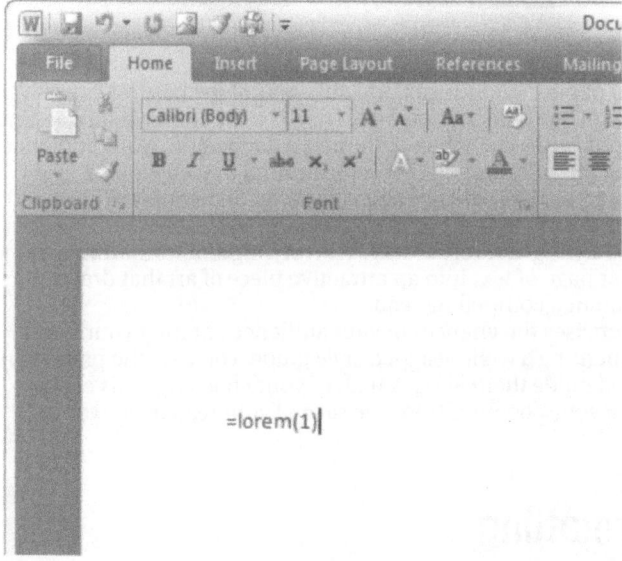

Figure 3–2. Creating the Latin paragraph to use as example text for formatting

3. Click anywhere in the word **Lorem** at the front of your new paragraph of text so that the insertion point is somewhere within that word. Click the down-arrow within the Font drop-down control ⌷Arial Black⌷. The Font drop-down will display a listing of fonts on your system. Select the Arial Black font to change the selected word **Lorem** to the selected font. Notice, too, that as you change the font in the Font drop-down, Word changes the selected text in the document to provide you with a preview of how the font will look.

4. While here, let's go ahead and change the font size of **Lorem**. Click the Font Size control ⌷24⌷ and select 24 as the size. This control allows you to select from the available list of font sizes, but you can also enter a size of your choosing.

5. To insert a font size value, click the Font Size control, replace the value 24 with a value of 36, and press the Enter key.

6. You can also change the font size by clicking the Grow Font and Shrink Font controls. Clicking Grow Font will increase the font size to the next larger value available in the Font Size control. Clicking the Shrink Font works the same way but in reverse. Click each button a couple of times to see how they affect your text.

7. Now click anywhere in the word **consectetuer.** This word needs to be formatted as bold, italics, and underline. There are three buttons that handle each of these tasks and they are appropriately named Bold, Italic, and Underline . Click each of these buttons to apply these formatting options to the word so that it looks like ***consectetuer***. Each button is a toggle button, meaning each click of the button toggles between applying and un-applying the format to the selected text. Another way to apply these three formats is to use their keyboard shortcuts. For bold, italics, and underline, the shortcut keys are CTRL+B, CTRL+I, and CTRL+U, respectively.

8. The Underline button contains a down-arrow that displays additional options for the underline format. Click this down-arrow and select the double underline option (see Figure 3–3).

Figure 3–3. The different format option available via the Underline button

9. Select the word **dolor.** Let's apply a strikethrough format to it by clicking the Strikethrough button . Strikethrough comes in handy when you want to show the reader that changes have been made to text.

10. Next let's use the Subscript ⬛ and Superscript ⬛ buttons to apply these formats to the words **adipiscing** and **elit**, respectively.

11. Next up is the Text Effects control ⬛. Select **Lorem** again and click the down-arrow in this control to see a list of available effects. Select the Red Fill option (see Figure 3–4) to apply this effect. Notice, too, that additional options are available that allow you to adjust the effects. Using these options you can adjust the outline, shadow, reflection, and glow. Take a moment to investigate these options and see how they change your selected effect.

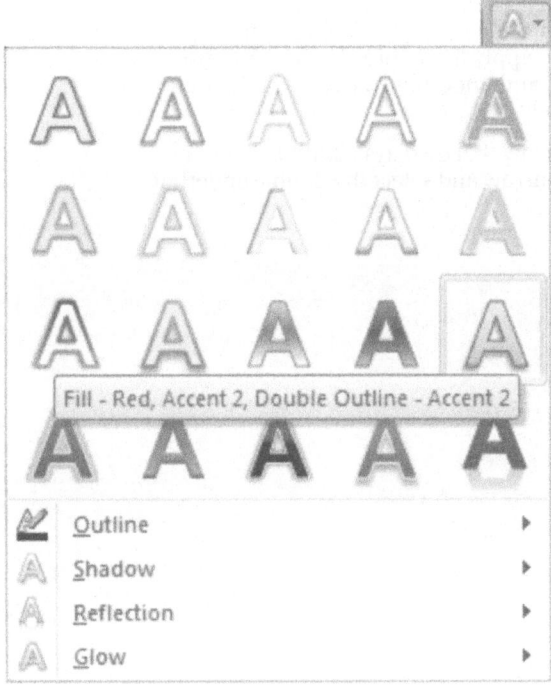

Figure 3–4. The Text Effects gallery of available effects and options

---

■ **Note** If the Text Effects control is not available, you might be in Word compatibility mode, meaning you are not working with the Office 2007–2010 file formats but with a Word 2003 or earlier file format (.doc file). If this is the case, you can convert the file to Word 2007–2010 format by choosing File ➤ Convert from the ribbon.

---

12. Select the words **Fusce posuere** and apply a yellow highlight to them by clicking the Text Highlight Color button [ab] . If you prefer, you can change the highlight color by clicking the button's down-arrow and selecting the color of your choosing. Like the bold, italics, and underline buttons, the highlight button is a toggle button, applying or removing the highlight format. You can change the highlight color by clicking the arrow and selecting from one of the displayed colors. Lastly, you are not required to select text before applying a highlight. If you do not have any text selected, when you click the highlight button, the cursor changes to a highlight cursor. You can then use the cursor like a physical highlighter—just select text in your document to apply a highlight.

■ **Tip** If you want to apply highlights to non-sequential text, you can double-click the Text Highlight Color button. A double-click will cause the tool to stay in highlighting mode until you decide you are finished highlighting. You can then move throughout your document, making as many highlights as you like without clicking the highlight button over and over again. When finished, either click the Text Highlight Color button again, or press the ESC key on your keyboard.

13. Select the word **pulvinar** and click the Font Color button [A] to change the font to red. The Font Color button also has a down-arrow that displays additional colors for your selection (see Figure 3–5). When you select a color, the Font Color button will update to display the active color. For example, if you select blue, the underline below the A of the Font Color button will change to display blue.

■ **Tip** The Font Color button lists the colors according to color sets or themes (see the following). These groupings simplify the task of choosing colors that play well together. In addition, if you want to use a color not included in the Theme Colors or Standard Colors sections, you can click the More Colors button to open a color mixer that allows you to "build your own." Also, there is a set of pre-set gradient colors available via the Gradient menu option. You can click the Gradient option to view the available gradient colors. And if the pre-sets are not quite to your liking, you can customize them via the More Gradients option.

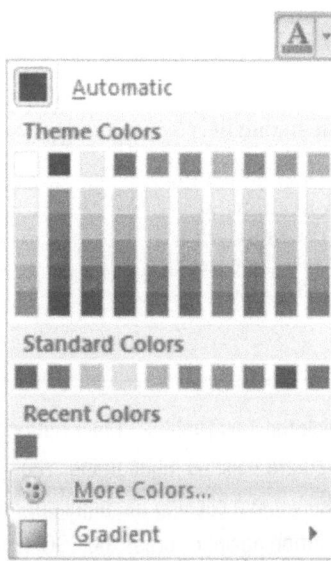

Figure 3–5. *The Font Color Picker control displaying color options*

14. Select all text in the document using your mouse or the key combination Ctrl+A. Change the case of the text by clicking the Change Case button and selecting **Capitalize Each Word.** This button enables you to quickly change the case of selected text to sentence case, lowercase, uppercase, or toggle case, as well as to capitalize each word. This button is quite handy when you aren't too good with the Shift key. You can type away and then quickly format your text to sentence case. Also, if you decide a certain sentence makes for a good heading, changing its case to title case makes it happen.

15. Lastly, click inside the word **Lorem** and then click the Clear Formatting button . This button removes all formatting applied to the selected text, making it easy to remove formatting and start anew if desired.

If you followed all of these steps your document will resemble something similar to Figure 3–6.

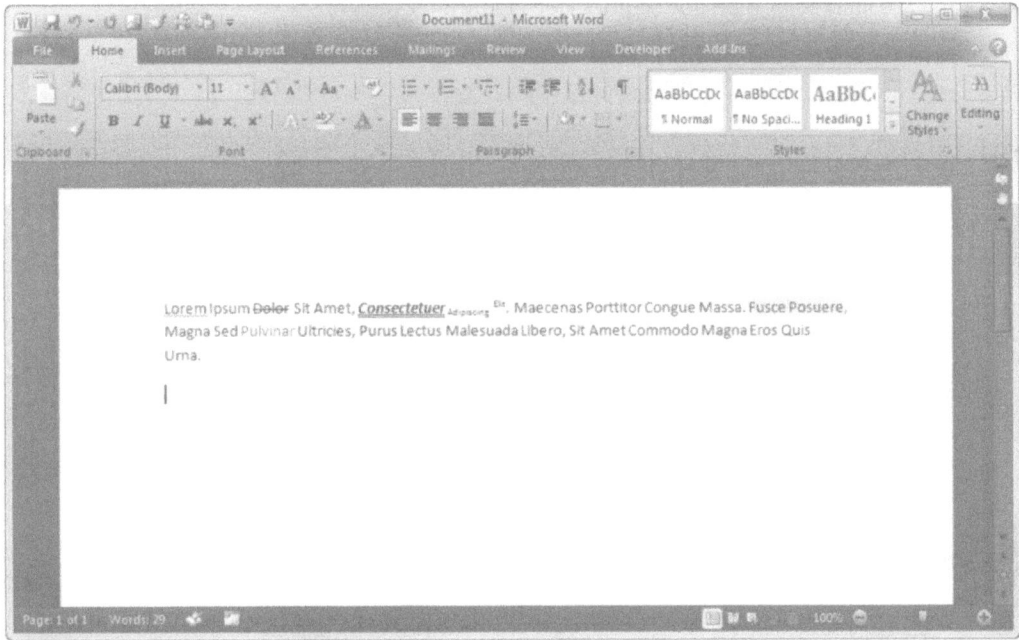

Figure 3–6. The document with all the formatting applied in Steps 1–15

With the tools included within the Font group, you have all the text formatting commands you need at your fingertips. Next we will take a look at how to add some style to documents via headers and footers.

Formatting Headers and Footers

Headers and footers are regions on each page of your document that allow you to display such things as page numbers, the document title, the document date, a special image, and more. The header displays at the top of each page while the footer resides at the bottom of each page. You can create headers and footers that are the same throughout a document, or you can create multiple headers and footers that change in each section of a document, for example.

The key point is that you should insert data elements in these regions that will help your readers know what it is they are reading (ie., document titles, section titles, etc.) as well as their current location in the document (ie., page numbers). This section shows you how to create basic headers and footers as well as a few other tricks along the way. We'll start by learning how to enter what I call "Header/Footer Edit Mode."

Entering Header/Footer Edit Mode

Every document you create with Word has headers and footers…even if they do not contain any text, images, or other types of content. In fact, Word doesn't allow you to edit headers and footers unless you enter "Header/Footer Edit Mode." This mode is a special view where the main document content displays in gray and is not editable. While in this mode, the header and footer sections of the document are editable and are marked by blue dotted lines (see Figure 3–7).

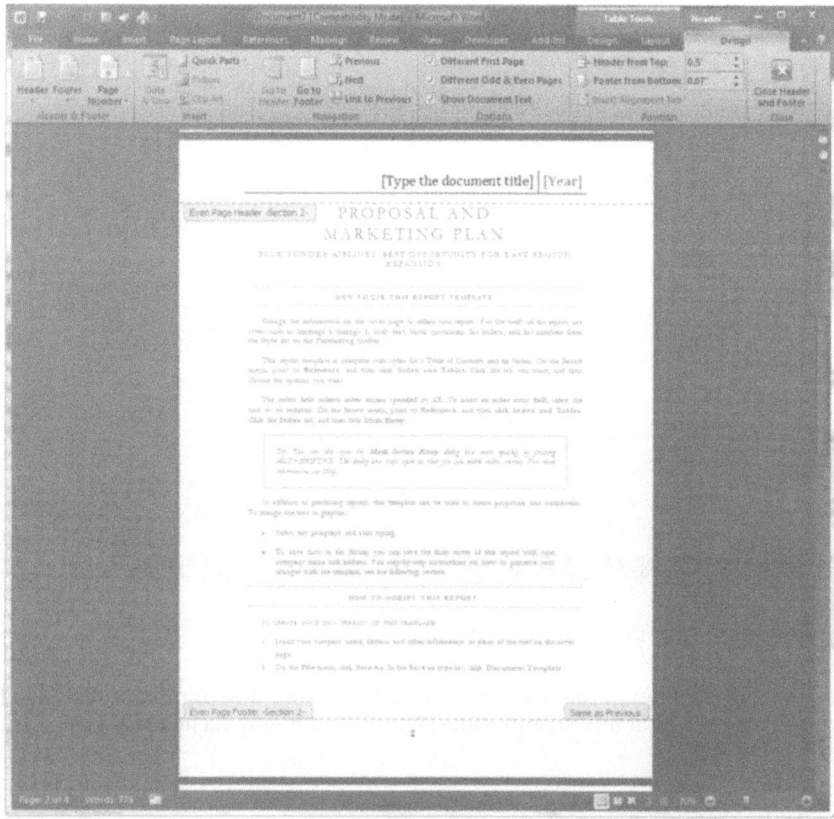

Figure 3–7. A Word document displayed in "Header/Footer Edit Mode"

Each section allows you to edit its contents as you would the main contents of a document. You can type whatever you like and have it appear on every page. You can also insert images, bullet lists, tables…whatever suits your fancy. The only limit is your style, creativity, and what is proper for your readers. The last point in that list will most likely overrule any desire to be too creative, forcing you to go with traditional elements like page numbers.

You can enter "Header/Footer Edit Mode" using a couple of methods.

1. **Double-click the header or footer region:** This is my preferred method as it allows me to enter edit mode without actually inserting any information into either region. All you need to do is double-left-click your mouse at the top or the bottom of a page in your document. This will cause Word to display your document so that it resembles Figure 3–6. Once enabled, you can edit the header and footer as you wish.

2. **Insert Method:** This method requires that you choose an element from the Header & Footer section of the Insert tab of the Word ribbon (see Figure 3–8).

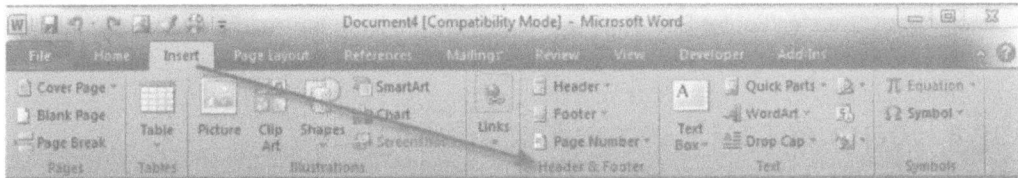

Figure 3–8. The Header & Footer group as found in the Insert tab

3. This tab contains content gallery controls for the header and footer as well as an additional control for page numbers. If you click either of these controls, Word displays content "chunks" (see Figure 3–8), each one representing a pre-defined template. You can automatically enter "Header/Footer Edit Mode" by selecting a content chunk for the Header, Footer, or Page Number content gallery controls. After Word inserts the content into either the header or footer, it leaves the document in "Header/Footer Edit Mode" to await any further edits you wish to add (see Figure 3–9).

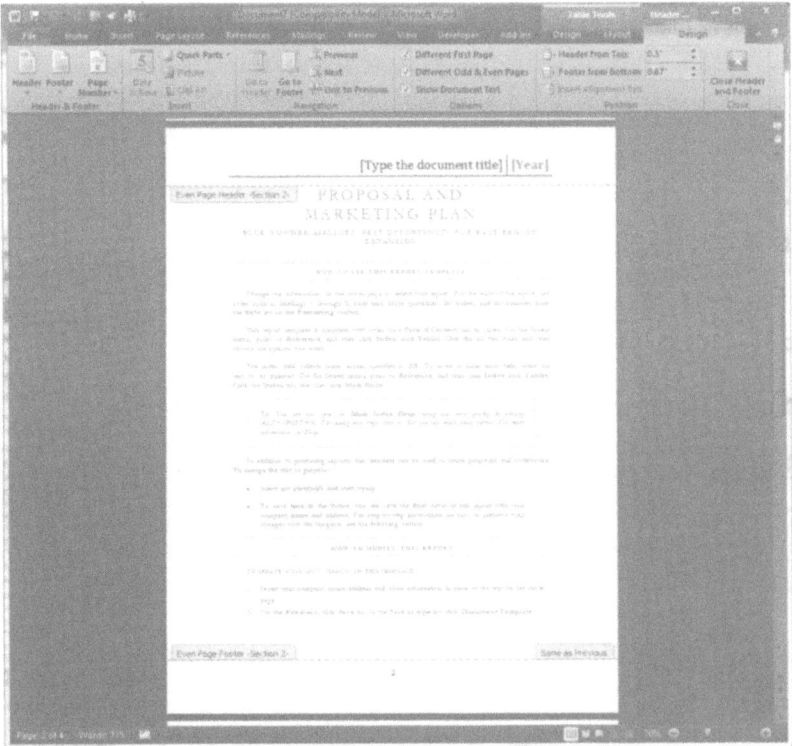

Figure 3–9. *The Header & Footer group as found in the Insert tab*

Knowing how to enter edit mode and making edits are two related but entirely different tasks. Now that you know about "Header/Footer Edit Mode," you are ready to learn how to create some simple yet useful footers and headers.

Adding a Document Title to the Header Region

One of the more common document headers employed by document authors is to place the document's title in the header. You can utilize the Header content gallery to quickly insert a pre-formatted header. The other method is to manually insert the document's title property and insert the value into the header.

To insert a pre-formatted header, follow these steps:

1. Click the Insert tab of the Word ribbon.

2. In the Header & Footer group, click the Header gallery control. The control will list all available pre-formatted headers (see Figure 3–10).

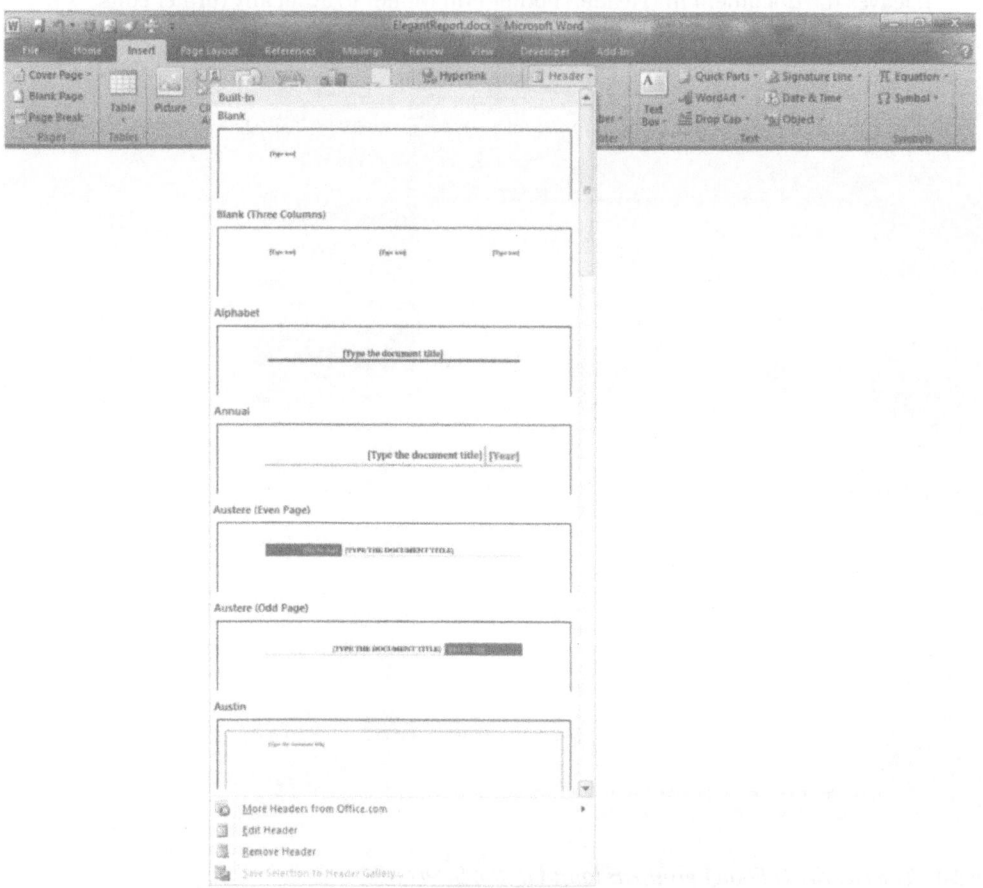

Figure 3–10. Pre-formatted headers displayed in the Header content gallery

3. Select the header named Annual to insert it into your document. Once Word inserts the header, your document's header should resemble the one shown in Figure 3–11. Notice the highlighted text, "Type the document title," is encased by a gray rectangle labeled Title. This is a content control that directly maps to the document's title property.

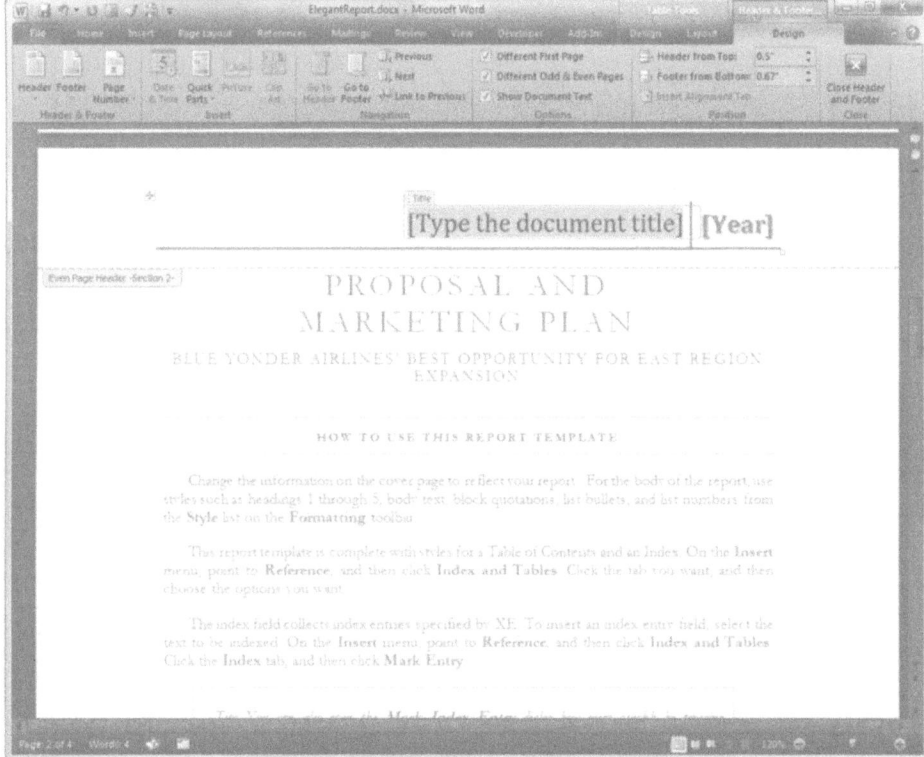

Figure 3–11. Pre-formatted headers displayed in the Header content gallery

4. Select the text inside the Title content control and delete it.

5. Type "Bravo Corp Proposal" or any text that you prefer. Once you replace the default text, "Type the document title," the text you enter becomes the value of the document's Title property. You can verify this is true by opening the Backstage and viewing the information about the document (see the following tip).

■ **Tip** Document properties reside in the new Backstage feature (see Figure 3–12). To view them or edit them, click the File button on the ribbon to display the Backstage. The document properties reside in the Info panel. If the Backstage does not default to the Info panel, click it to display the document's information. The document properties reside in the far-right column.

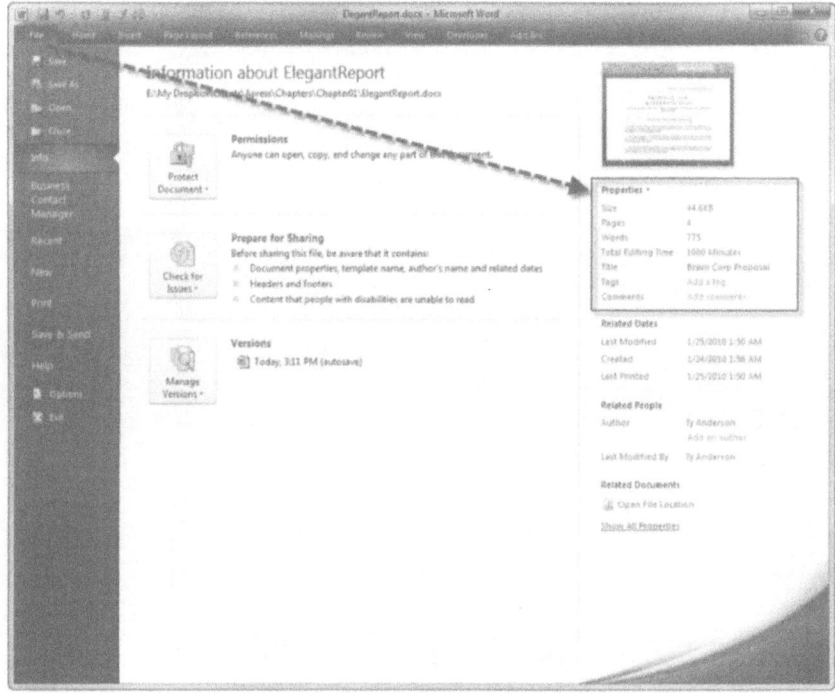

Figure 3–12. Documents properties shown in the Backstage view.

What if you don't want to use a pre-formatted header? What if you already have a document title and you want to simply insert the title document property into your header? All you need to do is follow these steps:

1.   Double-click the Header region of the current page in your document. This action will activate the "Header/Footer Edit Mode."

2.   The insertion point will be in the Header region and the ribbon will display a new tab named Design (see Figure 3–13).

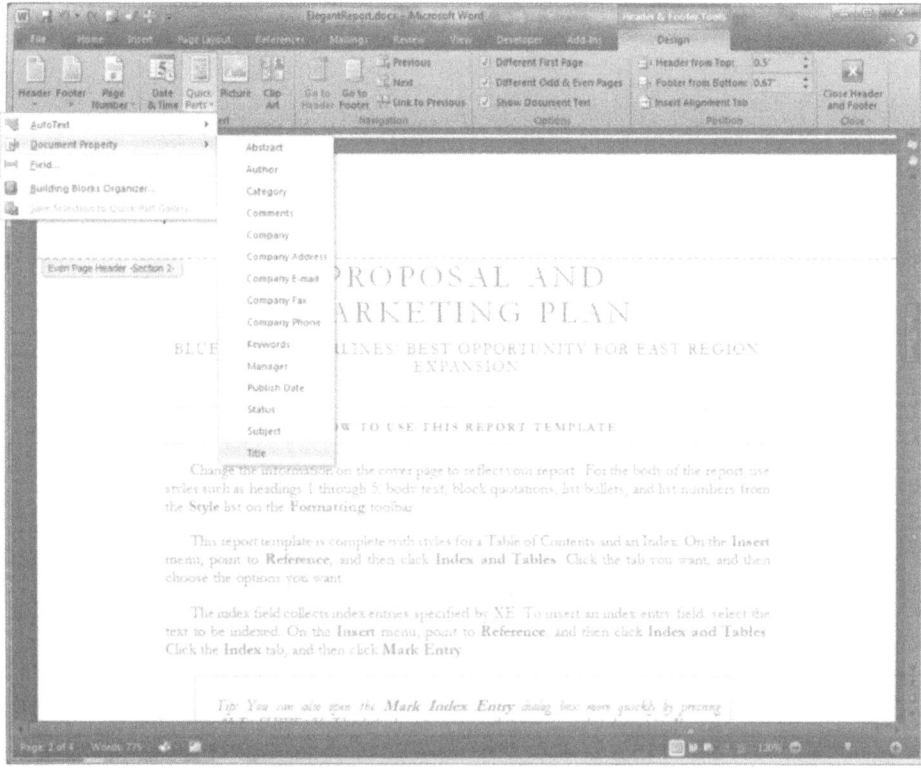

Figure 3–13. Document Properties listed as part of the Quick Parts content gallery

3. Find the Insert section of the Design tab. Click the Quick Parts content gallery to display fields available for insertion into the header.

4. Click the Document Property section of the displayed Quick Parts gallery to see a list of available document properties.

5. In the list of document properties, click Title to insert the title property into the header (see Figure 3–14).

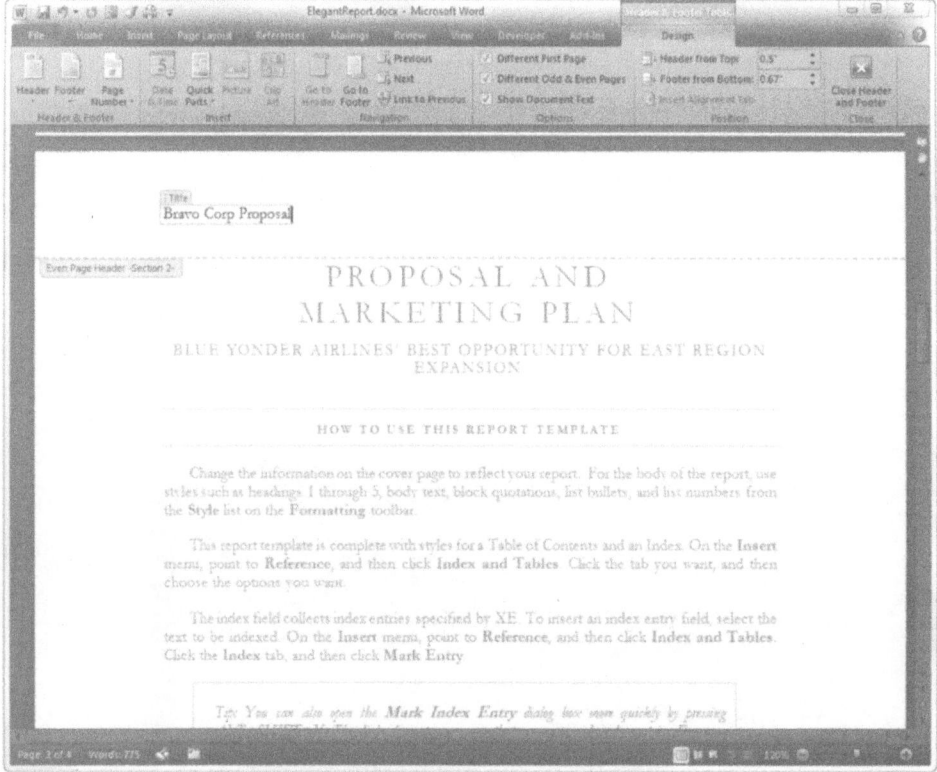

Figure 3–14. *The unformatted document Title property residing in the header region*

Once you add content to the header (or footer for that matter), you can use formatting and alignment tools to create a look that matches your document.

Adding a Page Number to the Footer Region

If the document title typically resides in the header, page numbers are typically found in a document's footer region. Now that you have some experience with headers, adding content to a footer will look very familiar. To add a page number to a document, follow these steps:

1. Click the Insert tab of the Word ribbon.

2. In the Header & Footer group, click the Page Number ➤ Bottom of Page to display pre-formatted page number options (see Figure 3–15).

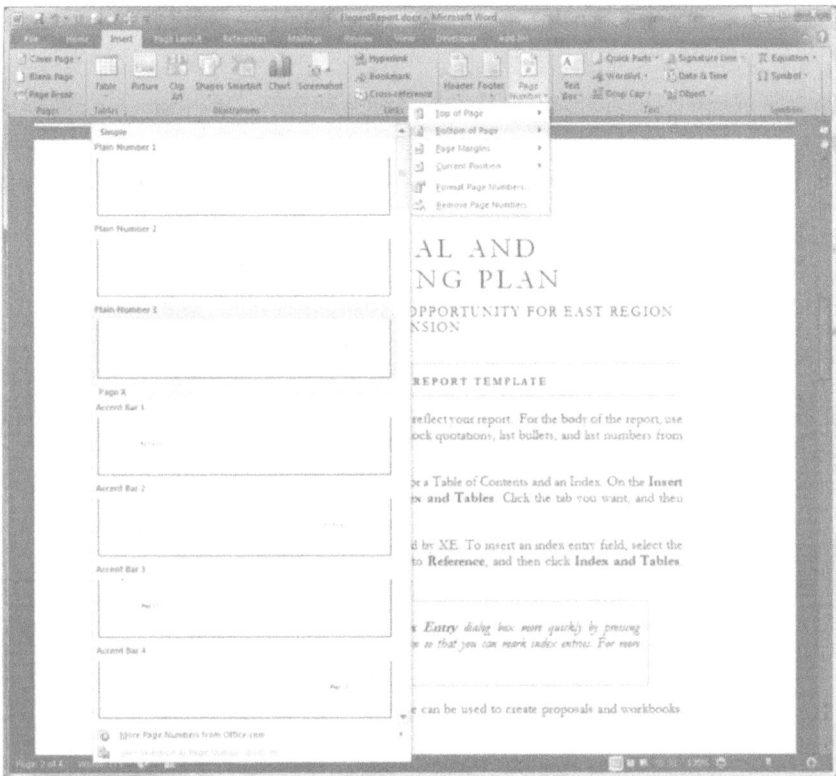

Figure 3–15. Pre-formatted page numbers available for insertion into a document

3. Click the **Plain Number 3** option to insert it into the document footer. The document will now display the page number in the lower-right corner of every page in your document (see Figure 3–16).

Now clearly, sometimes you might prefer to have the page numbers in the header. If so, just follow the same steps as you did for the footer but instead add them to the header. There really are not any hard and fast rules imposed by Word. Such rules are typically imposed by your business, organization, or professor.

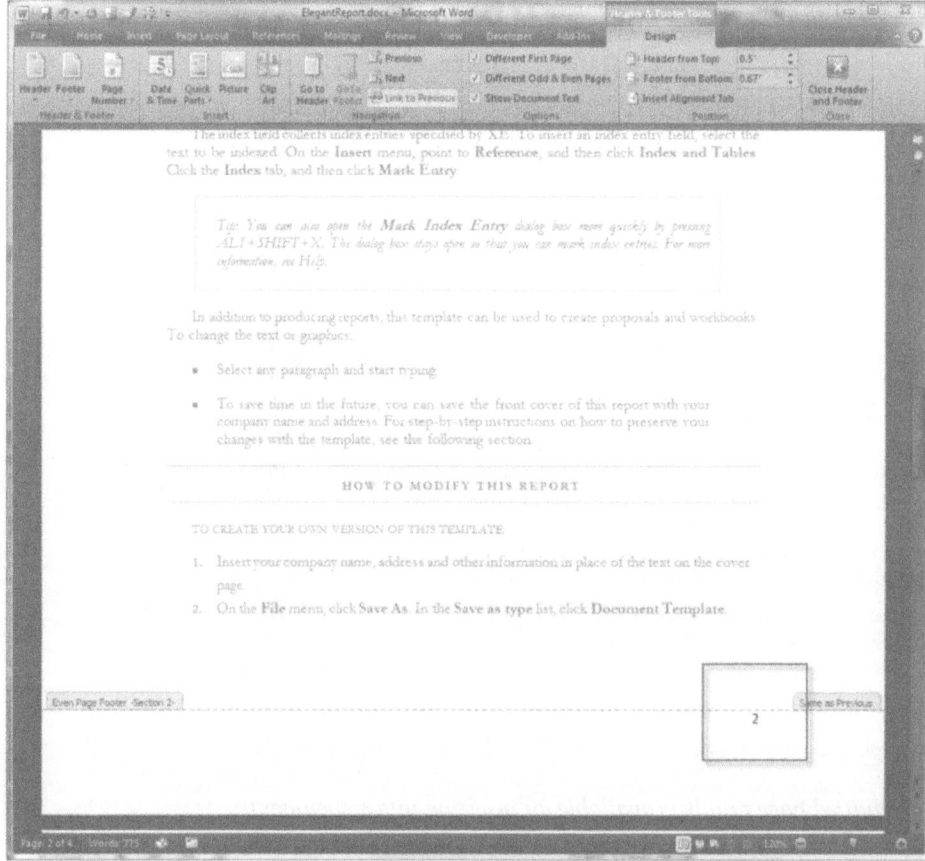

Figure 3–16. The page number visible in the document footer

Create a Unique Footer for One Page

So far, what I have shown you regarding headers and footers is fine as long your document is rather simple and does not contain such things as multiple sections that each require a different header and/or footer. In these cases, you will be glad to know Word 2010 allows you to quickly and easily define footers for each section.

The first step is to create additional sections in your document. Once done, you can create different headers and footers for each section. To accomplish this feat, make sure you are in the main section of the document (as opposed to the header or the footer section) and complete the following steps:

1. First, let's create a new section in your document. Click the Page Layout tab in the Word ribbon.

2. In the Page Layout tab, find the Page Setup group and click the Breaks button to display a content gallery of available break options (see Figure 3–17).

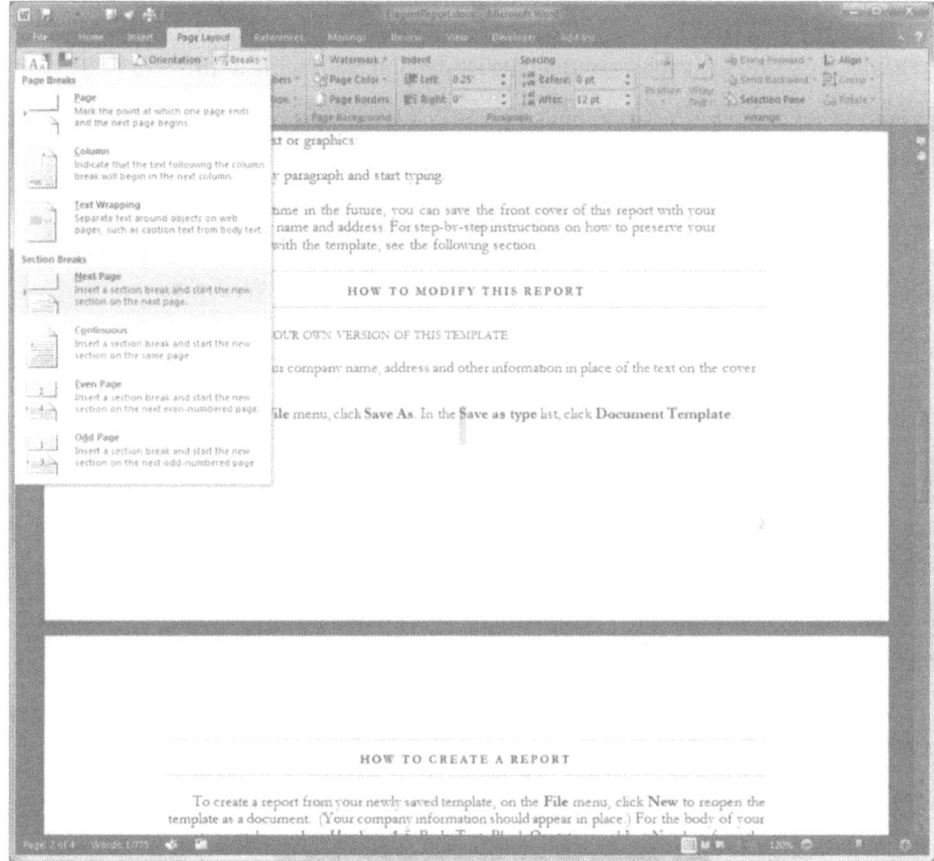

Figure 3–17. Inserting a section break

3. In the Breaks content gallery, find the Section Breaks section and click the Next Page option. This selection will cause Word to insert a new section that begins with the page after the current page. According to Figure 3–17, the new section would begin with Page 3.

■ **Note** Section breaks work a bit like page breaks. Whereas a page break defines the beginning and end of a page, a section break defines the beginning and end of a section. You want to use section breaks to divide major portions of your document.

4. Now that we have a new section, insert a pre-formatted header in the first section by clicking Insert ➤ Header ➤ Alphabet.

5.   Next, move to the page where the second section begins in your document.

6.   Currently, this section has the same header as the previous section. To change this behavior, find the Navigation group in the Design tab (see Figure 3–18).

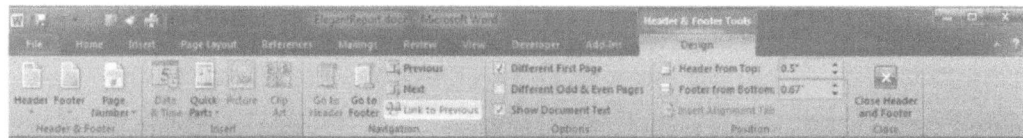

Figure 3–18. The Link to Previous toggle button visible in the Design tab of the Word ribbon

7.   Click the Link to Previous button to turn off the link to the previous section's header.

8.   Add a different header to this section by clicking Design ➤ Header ➤ Tiles.

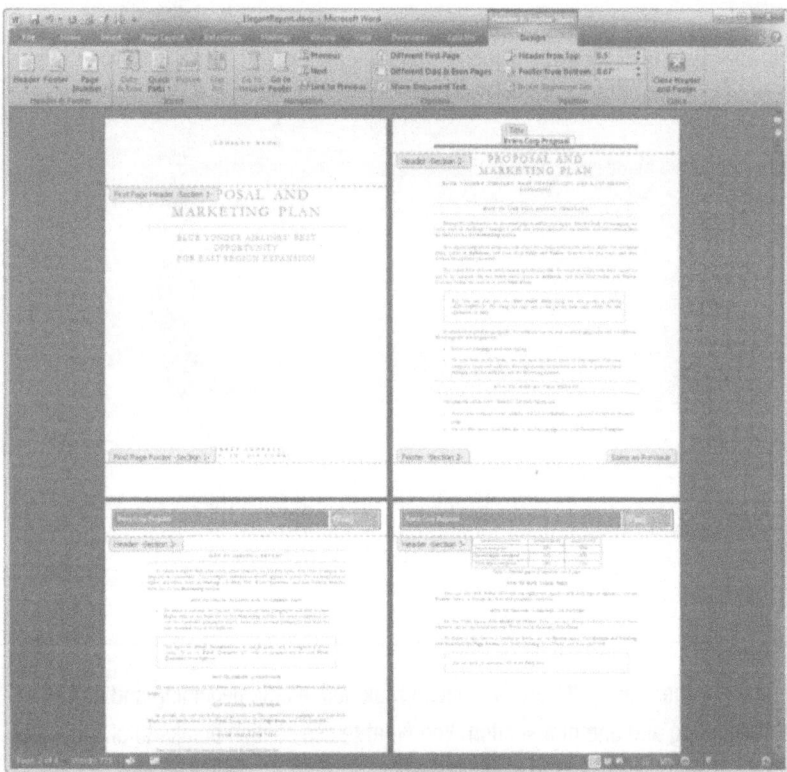

Figure 3–19. Multiple headers within a single document

The end result is a document that begins with one header in the first section and a different header in the remaining pages. The document in Figure 3–19 contains three sections. The title page has a header that displays a placeholder for a company name. The second section utilizes the Alphabet header inserted in Step 4, while the remaining pages have the Titles header inserted in Step 8.

Tip You have several options when designing separate headers and footers. First, you can use the same header and footer on every page in your document. This is the easiest way to go. Second, you can define one header and footer for the first page (i.e., a cover page) and then utilize a different header and footer set for the subsequent pages. Third, you can create a header and footer for even pages and a different set for odd pages. Fourth, you can mix and match these options as well as incorporate different headers and footers for each section. It's up to you as Word provides you with the flexibility you need.

Using Styles

Formatting text is one way to add some style to your documents. As I said previously, you can use text formatting to draw attention to important information in your document. By implementing styles in your document you can build some structure to your document via the effective use of headings. In addition, you can quickly change the overall design of your document by changing its style set. Style sets are design templates available in Word that include style definitions.

This section begins by showing how to use styles to build a document structure or content hierarchy. The remaining sections then use the document as a guinea pig, showing you how to apply different styles to your document and how to quickly change color sets and font styles—all without having to apply them manually.

Building Structure Using Styles

By applying styles to your document, in effect, you build a content hierarchy. Take a look at the available styles found in the Styles group of the Home tab (see Figure 3–20).

Notice the styles named Heading 1, Heading 2, Heading 3, and so on, until Heading 9. As you apply these heading styles to content in your document, you are defining how your content relates to other content in the document. For example, the top level is Heading 1 and should be used to format or stylize the main points or sections within your document. Within a main point, you apply Heading 2 to the points or sections that support the corresponding main point.

Headings make key points and sections within your document obvious to your readers while also building a content hierarchy. Let's see how to achieve this result by following these steps:

1. Open Word and create a new blank document (File ➤ New ➤ Blank Document).

2. On the first line, type "This is the Document Title". After typing the text, select all of it and apply the Title style by clicking the down arrow (see Figure 3–21) in the Styles gallery and selecting the Title style.

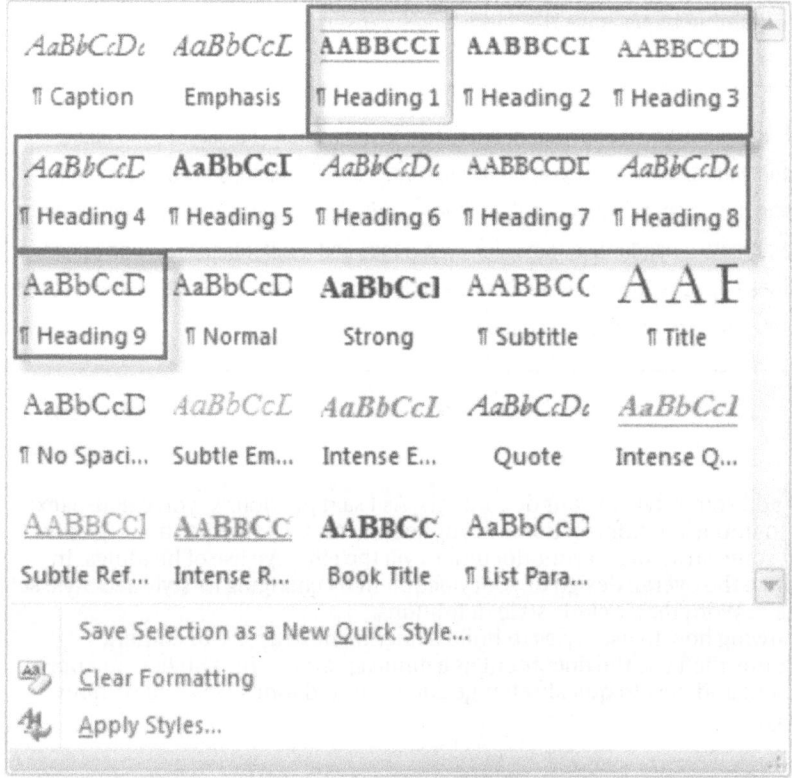

Figure 3–20. The Styles gallery displaying available styles

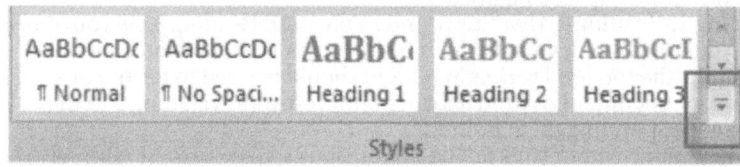

Figure 3–21. The Styles gallery down arrow

3. Press the Enter key to create a new line in the document. Type "Key Point 1" and format it as Heading 1.

4. Create a new line, type "Supporting Point 1", and format this line as Heading 2.

5. Create a new line and type "Additional info about Supporting Point 1". Format this line as Heading 3.

6. Create one last new line, type "Supporting Point 2", and apply the Heading 2 style to the text.

7. Click the View tab on the ribbon and click the Navigation Pane check box. The check box resides in the Show group of the View tab. Once you click this check box, it should display Word's Navigation Pane.

After following these steps, your document should resemble Figure 3–22, which includes a bit more text in order to further illustrate the document's hierarchy. Anything with a Heading 1 format resides to the far left of the navigation pane.

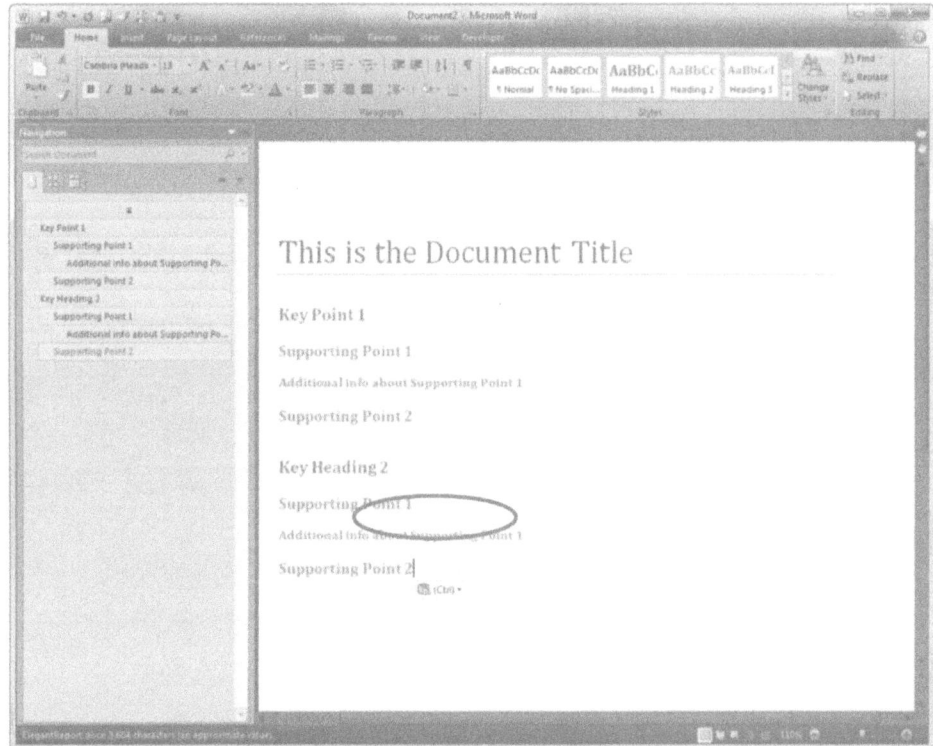

Figure 3–22. *A sample document containing a content hierarchy thanks to application of Heading styles*

Underneath the Heading 1 panels are its child headings—basically, the text beneath it that is formatted as Heading 2 through Heading 9. The child headings are indented to indicate they belong to a parent heading.

Keep this document open, since, in the next section, it will help demonstrate the power of using styles for quickly changing a document's design by applying Quick Styles.

Using Quick Styles

Quick Styles, or Style Sets, are document design templates included with Word that allow you to change the design of your document with three quick mouse clicks. Word includes 14 templates that might just fit your styling needs, especially if you are pressed for time and don't feel the need to create a custom design that properly represents your creative genius. But if you are the finicky type and want to build your very own quick style, you can, and Word's help file contains content explaining how to do it. For now, I want you to learn the basics of using quick styles by doing the following:

1. Using the document from the previous section, click the Home tab on the ribbon.

2. In the Styles group, click the Change Styles button (see Figure 3–23) to display its sub-menu. From the sub-menu select Style set to see a listing of quick styles. Just as with the font drop-down, as you hover your mouse cursor over a style, the document will preview the style's formats in your document.

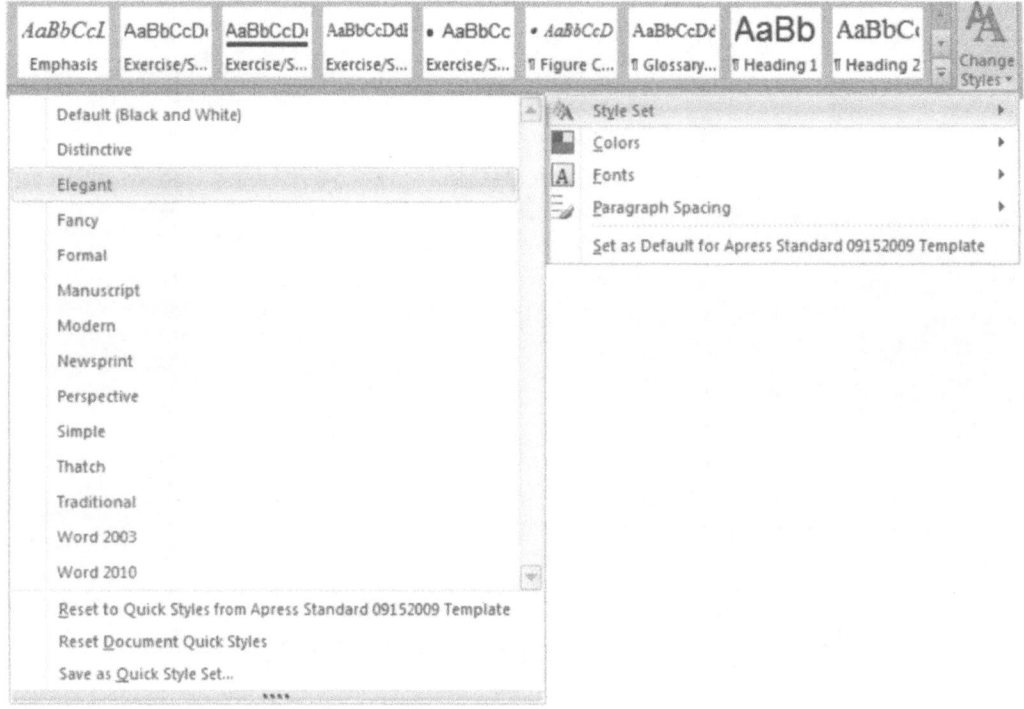

Figure 3–23. The listing of Quick Styles available in the Change Styles gallery

3. Select the Modern style. Your document should now resemble Figure 3–24.

4. Try out the other quick styles by applying them to the document.

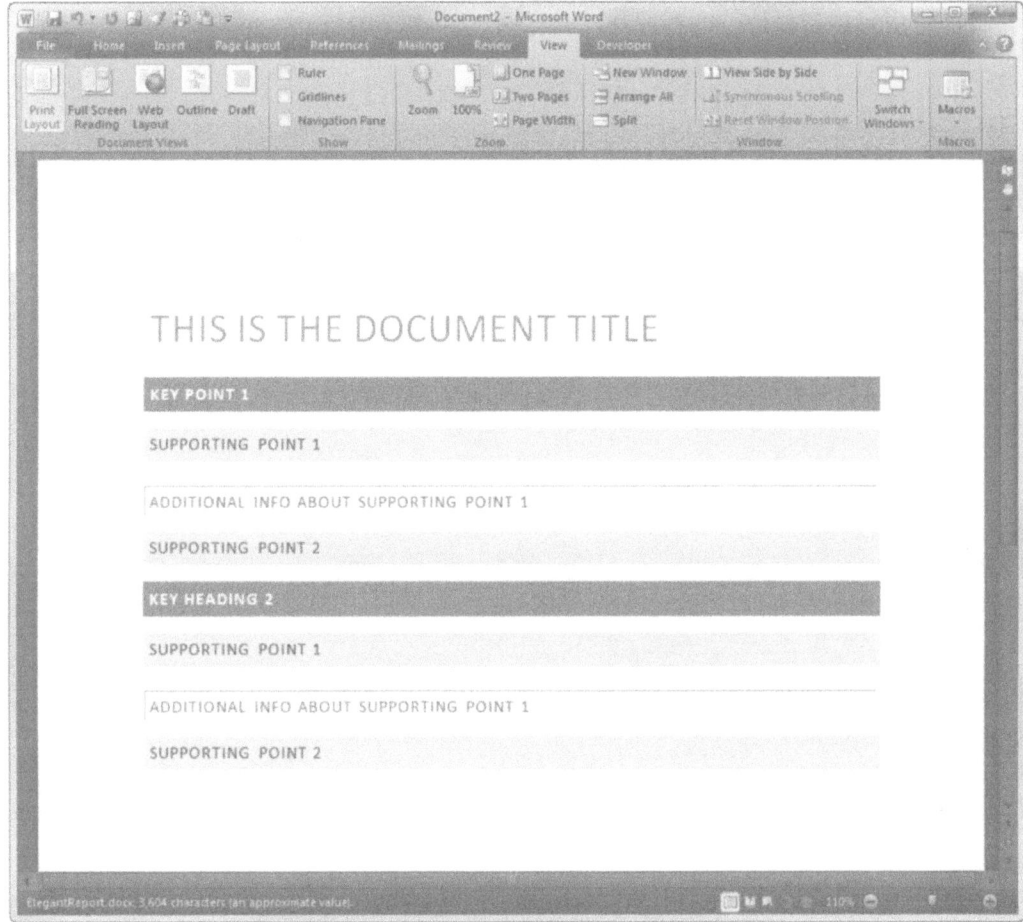

Figure 3–24. A document formatted using the Modern quick style style set

Over time you might find you prefer one of the quick styles and decide to adopt it as your own. If not, you can try your hand at building your own.

Like the Style But Not the Color? No Problem!

The quick styles do a great job of defining the look and feel of the text within your document. But what if you like a particular style but decide you don't like the color? First simply apply the quick style you prefer and then change the color as follows:

1.   From the Home tab, click Change Styles ➤ Colors to see a listing of color sets, or themes (see Figure 3–25).

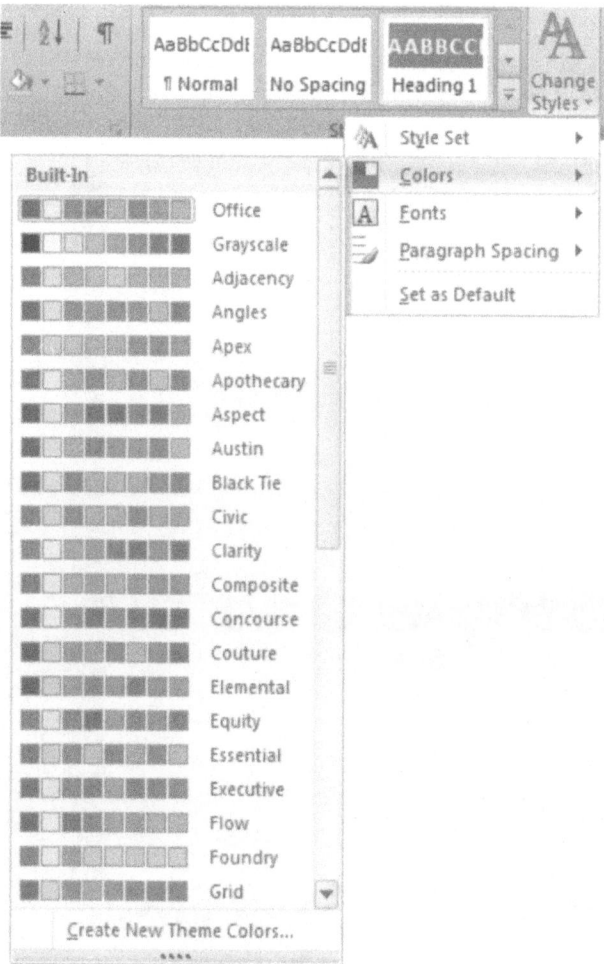

Figure 3–25. The listing of color sets available from the Change Styles button

2. From the listing, scroll down and choose the Slipstream theme.

Using color sets allows you to change the colors of your document text without the need to do so manually throughout your document. Features like color sets and quick styles reinforce the need to utilize styles in your documents because doing so separates the styling of your text from the text itself. This separation enables the easy style changes explained in this chapter. Just remember to use styles to define your document's content and then pick or build a style set that suits your document's needs.

■■■

CHAPTER 4

Reusing Content

Perhaps the greatest thing about computers is how easy they make it to reuse your content without having to retype it or create it again from scratch. In this chapter, I'll show you how to use Word's powerful features for reusing your content quickly and easily.

We'll start by reviewing Word's different tools for reusing content so that you have an overview of the weapons at your disposal. We'll then look at how to create documents quickly based on templates—and how you can create templates of your own.

After that, we'll move on to Quick Parts, a feature that enables you to quickly insert prefabricated sections in your documents. We'll look at how the AutoCorrect feature can save you time, effort, and frustration, talk about whether you should switch on Math AutoCorrect, and discuss how to choose sensible settings for the volatile AutoFormat As You Type feature.

Finally, I'll show you how to format a document in moments using the AutoFormat feature.

Understanding Your Different Options for Reusing Content

As you'll know from working with computers, there are two standard ways of reusing content:

- **Open a document and save it under a different name.** This move gives you a separate file containing the same content as the original document. You can then change the new file as needed—for example, deleting the parts you don't need and adding fresh content in their places. This approach works well when you need to use most of the document

- **Open a document and copy the parts you need to another document.** This move lets you cherry-pick content from the existing document and is good when you need only some of the content.

You can use either of these approaches in Word just as you can in any other program. But Word also includes carefully thought-out features that let you base one document on another, add standard parts to a document, and save yourself typing, time, and effort.

These are the Word options we'll investigate in this chapter:

- **Base a document on existing content.** To do this, you use a template, as discussed in the first section of the chapter.

- **Insert a document's content into another document.** You can copy content from one document to another, but Word also provides an easier way of inserting all of one document's content into another document. If you set up the source document with electronic markers called bookmarks, you can insert a bookmarked chunk of it instead of the entire contents.

- **Assemble a document from standard parts.** Word's Quick Parts feature enables you to quickly add standard parts to your documents. For example, you can add canned headers and footers (as discussed in Chapter 3), text boxes for pull quotes, sidebars, and other items.

- **Keep a library of ready-made content that you can insert in your documents.** You can create your own Quick Parts, containing exactly the content you need, and then insert them into your documents in moments.

- **Insert boilerplate text in your documents.** If your documents require standard text, you can insert it quickly by using either the AutoCorrect feature or the AutoText feature.

- **Insert automatic information and keep it updated.** If a document requires a standard piece of information, such as the current date or its own file name, you can insert it by using a field. Word can then automatically update the information for you.

In this chapter, we'll go through these options in that order. Roughly speaking, this works from largest to smallest—you'll save the most time and effort by using a template to create a new document with content, whereas inserting small items such as fields makes more modest savings but is still useful.

Creating Documents Quickly by Using Templates

The quickest way to create a complete document is by basing it on a template. Word comes with a healthy number of built-in templates, and you can download many other templates from the Office.com web site. But to save the most time, you'll most likely want to create custom templates of your own that contain exactly the content and the formatting you need.

Understanding What Templates Are and How You Use Them

In Word, a *template* is a document on which you can easily base another document. A template can have anything from no content at all to all the text, formatting, and other content (for example, graphics) needed to create a new document in an instant.

Note Technically, a Word template file has a couple of minor differences from a Word document file, such as using a different file extension (by default, templates use the .dotx file extension, whereas documents use the .docx file extension). In practice, the most important difference is that you store templates in one or two specially designated locations. In these locations, the templates show up in the New pane in the Backstage view, from where you can easily create new documents based on them.

UNDERSTANDING THE NORMAL TEMPLATE

Word includes a template called Normal (usually referred to as "the Normal template") that it loads each time you start the program. The Normal template contains Word's default settings, including any changes you make to them.

Word uses the Normal template as the basis for any "blank" document you create in Word. You can save various changes in the Normal template, including your default font, default page setup, and so on.

The Normal template also contains formatted AutoCorrect entries and can contain AutoText entries, building blocks, and VBA customizations. You'll learn about AutoCorrect, AutoText, and building blocks in this chapter, and about VBA in Chapter 10.

If you make any changes to the Normal template, or if you add any of these items to it, you need to save the changes in order to keep them. You can either have Word save the changes for you automatically or save them yourself manually.

Let's look at the automatic mechanism first. When you exit Word (for example, by choosing File ➤ Exit or by closing the last document window that's open), Word usually saves any changes you've made to the Normal template. If Word displays the Microsoft Word dialog window shown in Figure 4–1, prompting you to save changes to the Normal template, you'll normally want to click the Save button.

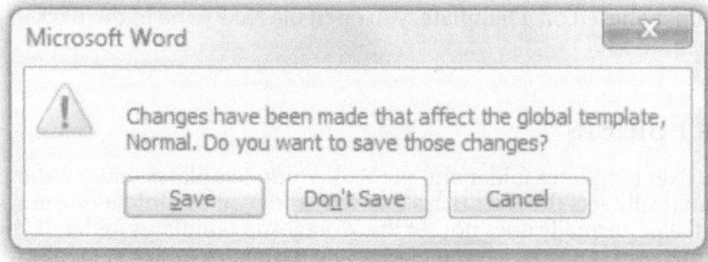

Figure 4–1. If Word prompts you to save changes to the Normal template, click the Save button.

If you want Word to save changes to the Normal template automatically rather than prompting you to save them, follow these steps to change the setting that controls the prompt:

1. Choose File ➤ Options to display the Word Options dialog window.

2. In the left pane, click the Advanced category to display the Advanced options.

3. Scroll down to the Save heading (most of the way down to the bottom).

4. Clear the "Prompt before saving Normal template" check box.

5. Click the OK button to close the Word Options dialog window.

If you make extensive changes to the Normal template, it's a good idea to save them manually in case Word crashes. To do so, you need to put the Save All button on the Quick Access Toolbar (or create a keyboard shortcut for it). Follow these steps:

1. Right-click any button on the Quick Access Toolbar, and then click Customize Quick Access Toolbar to display the Quick Access Toolbar category in the Word Options dialog window.

2. Open the Choose commands from the drop-down list, and then click Commands Not in the Ribbon. The list box below the drop-down list shows all the commands that don't appear in the ribbon.

3. Scroll down to the Save All command, and then click it.

4. Click the Add button to add the Save All command to the box on the right.

5. Click the OK button to close the Word Options dialog window. Word adds the Save All button to the Quick Access Toolbar.

Once you have done this, you can simply click the Save All button on the Quick Access Toolbar when you want to save all the changes. When Word prompts you to save the changes to the Normal template, click the Save button.

To save the most time with templates, you will probably want to build a separate template for each different kind of document you create frequently. For example, if you create marketing plans, marketing reports, and business letters, you'll normally need three separate templates. While it's possible to have a general-purpose template that you can use for a variety of document types, it usually means that you end up doing more work in each document because the template is less specific to the types of document you're creating.

When you need to create a document based on a template, you open the New pane in the Backstage view and choose the template you want to use.

Setting Your Templates Folders

Word uses two template folders, the User templates folder and the Workgroup templates folder. When you install Office, the installer automatically sets the User templates folder for you to a folder on your PC. For a normal installation, the installer normally does not set the Workgroup templates folder. If you share templates with others on your network, you can set the Workgroup templates folder manually to point to this folder by using the technique described in this section.

To set your templates folders, or to check which folders Word is using for them, follow these steps:

1. Make sure you have a document open. If not, press Ctrl+N to quickly create a new blank document.

2. Choose File ➤ Options to display the Word Options dialog window.

3. In the left column, click the Advanced category to display the Advanced pane.

4. Scroll down all the way to the bottom of the pane.

5. Click the File Locations button to display the File Locations dialog window (see Figure 4–2). This dialog window shows a list of the file types and the folders used for them, but the folder paths for most items are usually too long to appear fully in the dialog window.

Figure 4–2. Use the File Locations dialog window to check or change the folder in which Word stores your templates.

6. In the File types list box, click the type of file for which you want to see or change the path. For example, click the User templates item.

7. Click the Modify button to display the Modify Location dialog window. The address box shows the full address of the folder.

■ **Tip** If you need to open the folder in a Windows Explorer window so that you can move your templates to it, click the address box in the Modify Location dialog window. Word displays the folder path (for example, C:\Users\Jan\AppData\Roaming\Microsoft\Templates) and selects it. Press Ctrl+C or right-click and choose Copy to copy the address to the Clipboard. Click the Start button, right-click the Search box and choose Paste, and then press Enter to open a Windows Explorer window showing the folder.

---

8. To change the folder, navigate to the folder you want to use, click it, and then click the OK button. Word closes the Modify Location dialog window and displays the new path (or as much of it as will fit) in the File Locations dialog window.

9. Change any other file paths (for example, you may want to set the Workgroup templates path), and then click the OK button to close the File Locations dialog window.

10. Click the OK button to close the Word Options dialog window.

Creating Your Own Templates

To get the most out of templates, you'll most likely want to create your own templates that contain exactly the text, elements, and formatting you need to enable you to create finished documents quickly.

Starting a New Template

To start a template, click the File button to open the Backstage view, and then click New in the left column to display the New pane. You can then create a new template by using either a sample template or one of your templates.

To create a new template from a sample template, follow these steps:

1. Click the Sample templates item to display the list of sample templates (see Figure 4–3).

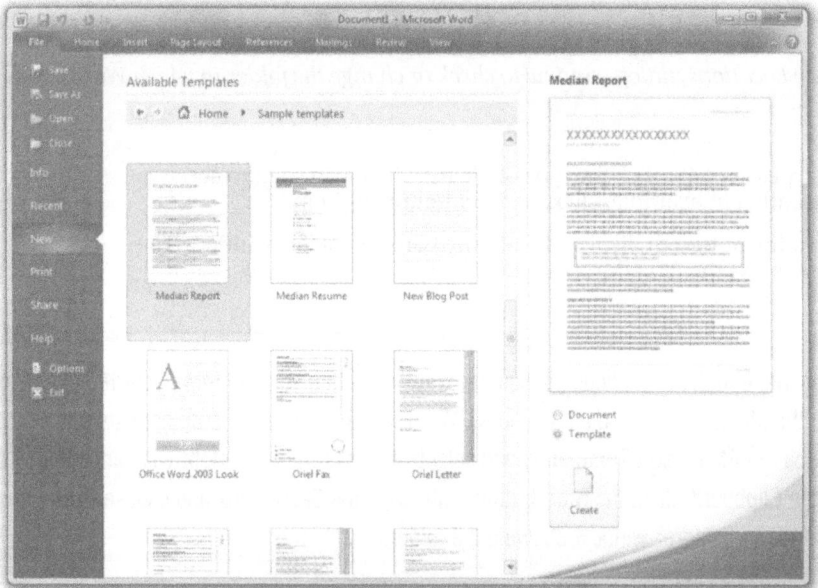

Figure 4–3. *To create a new template based on a sample template, select the Template option button on the right side of the New pane, and then click the Create button.*

2. Click the template you want to use.

3. On the right side of the New pane, under the preview of the template, select the Template option button instead of the Document option button.

4. Click the Create button. Word closes the Backstage view and displays the new template, which it gives the temporary name Template1 (or the next available number, such as Template2).

To create a sample template based on one of your own templates, follow these steps:

1. In the Available Templates box in the New pane in the Backstage view, click the My templates item to display the New dialog window (see Figure 4–4).

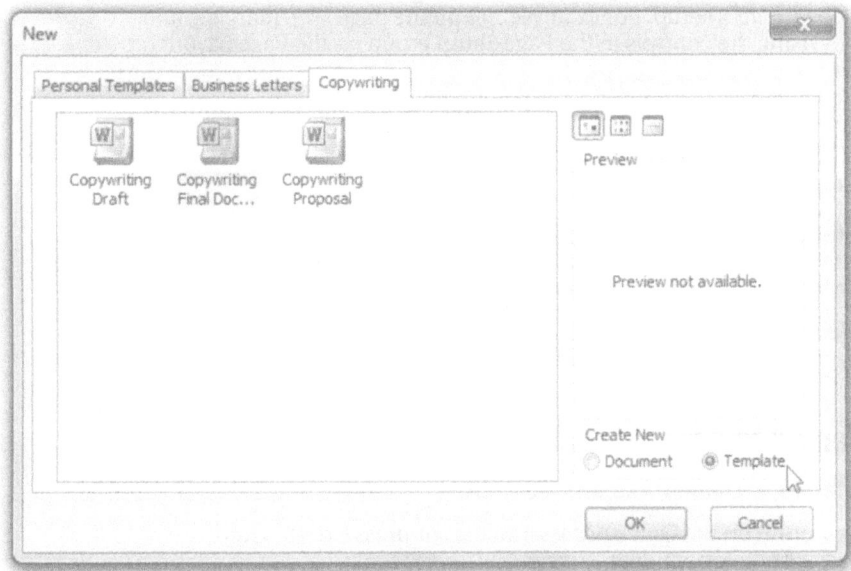

Figure 4–4. To create a new template based on one of your own templates, select the Template option button on the right side of the New dialog window, and then click the OK button. Until you add further templates, the New dialog window may contain only the Personal Templates tab.

2. Click the tab that contains the template you want to use.

■ **Note** At first, the New dialog window contains only the Personal Templates tab. When you create other templates folders, they appear in the New dialog window.

---

3. Click the template on which you want to base the new template.

4. In the Create New box above the OK button and Cancel button, select the Template option button instead of the Document option button.

5. Click the OK button. Word closes the New dialog window and the Backstage view and displays the new template. Word gives the template a temporary name such as Template1.

Adding Content to the Template

Now set up the template with the text, other content, and formatting it needs. What the template needs will vary widely depending on what you're trying to do with it, but you'll probably want to do some or all of the following:

- **Format the document's setup.** For example, set up the page size, margins, and orientation by using the controls in the Page Setup group on the Page Layout tab of the ribbon.

- **Add text.** Type (or paste, or insert) any text the template needs. For example, if you're creating the template for a standard customer-response letter, you can add most of the text, leaving only the customer's name, address, and complaint to fill in.

- **Format the text.** Apply formatting as discussed in Chapter 3. By formatting the content in the template, you can reduce the amount of formatting each document based on the template needs to a minimum.

- **Add other elements.** Add headers and footers as discussed in Chapter 3. Insert and position pictures or diagrams as discussed in Chapter 8.

Saving the New Template You've Created

To save the new template you've created, follow these steps:

1. Click the Save button on the Quick Access Toolbar, or press Ctrl+S. Word displays the Save As dialog window.

2. Make sure that the Address box at the top of the Save As dialog window shows your Templates folder. Word should display this folder automatically; if not, you may need to navigate to it.

■ **Note** In a standard installation of Office 2010 on Windows 7, the Templates folder is in the AppData\Roaming\Microsoft\Templates folder within your user folder. If you can't find the Templates folder, click the Cancel button to close the Save As dialog window. Choose File ➤ Options and click the Advanced category on the left. At the bottom, click the File Locations button to display the File Locations dialog window. Double-click the User templates item to open the Modify Location dialog window. Click the Address box, right-click, and then choose Copy to copy the location. Close each of the three dialog windows. Now press Ctrl+S to display the Save As dialog window, paste the path into the Address box, and then press Enter.

---

3. If necessary, switch to a subfolder of the Templates folder. You can create a new folder if necessary by clicking the New Folder button under the Address box.

4. In the File name box, type the name you want to give the template.

5. Make sure that Word Template is selected in the "Save as type" drop-down list.

6. Select the Save Thumbnail check box if you want to save a thumbnail picture of the template to make it easier to identify.

7. Click the Save button. Word closes the Save As dialog window and saves the template.

Close the template (for example, choose File ➤ Close). You can then start creating documents based on the template.

TURNING A DOCUMENT INTO A TEMPLATE

If you're like me, you may create your most useful templates almost by accident. You create a document for a special purpose, put a lot of effort into it—and then realize you could reuse it. Frequently.

When this happens, you can create a template from the document. Normally, the best way to do this is as follows:

1. If the document is open, close it. For example, choose File ➤ Close.

2. Click the File button to open the Backstage view.

3. Click the New item in the left column to display the New pane.

4. Click the New from existing icon to display the New from Existing Document dialog window.

5. Select the document, and then click the Create New button. Word creates a new document based on the document you chose.

6. Make any changes needed to the document. For example, you may need to knock out specific content areas that you will replace with fresh information in the documents you create.

7. Press Ctrl+S or click the Save button on the Quick Access Toolbar to display the Save As dialog window.

8. Use the Address box to navigate to your Templates folder. If necessary, open the File Locations dialog window and the Modify Location dialog window, copy the folder location, and then paste it into the Address box.

9. In the File name box, type the name you want to give the template.

10. Open the "Save as type" drop-down list and choose Word Template.

11. Select the Save Thumbnail check box if you want to save a thumbnail picture of the template.

12. Click the Save button. Word closes the Save As dialog window and saves the template.

Close the template (for example, choose File ➤ Close). You can then create a new document based on the template.

Creating a Document Based on a Template

After you've made a template, you can quickly create a document based on the template.

1. Click the File button to open the Backstage view.

2. Click New in the left column to display the New pane.

3. In the Available Templates box, click the "My templates" item to display the New dialog window.

4. Click the template you want to use.

5. Click the OK button to close the New dialog window. Word creates the new document.

■ **Tip** You can also create a new document based on an existing document. To do so, click the New from existing icon in the New pane in the Backstage view, choose the document in the New from Existing Document dialog window, and then click the Create New button. This command is effectively a dressed-up version of the File ➤ Save As command. Its advantage is that it eliminates the risk of you opening the existing document intending to save it under a different name, making the changes, and then saving it under its current name by accident.

Inserting One Document into Another Document

Another way to reuse content quickly is to insert one document into another document. Doing this is a simpler way of opening the document that has the contents, copying them, and then pasting them into the target document.

Inserting one document into another document enables you to keep a library of pre-built content sections in separate documents and then quickly assemble documents from these sections. You can also use this command to insert only a part of one document into another. To do this, you need to mark that part of the document with a bookmark, as described later in this section.

■ **Note** There's one problem with inserting the contents of a bookmark: you need to know the name of the bookmark you want to enter. Word's Insert File dialog window doesn't give you a way to see which bookmarks a document contains. Ideally, you'd see a drop-down list of bookmarks so that you could pick the one you want— but as it is, you must type the name from memory.

Inserting a Document or Part of a Document

To insert a whole document or a bookmarked part of a document in another document, follow these steps:

1. In the target document, position the insertion point where you want to insert the content.

2. Choose Insert ➤ Text ➤ Object ➤ Text from File to display the Insert File dialog window (see Figure 4–5).

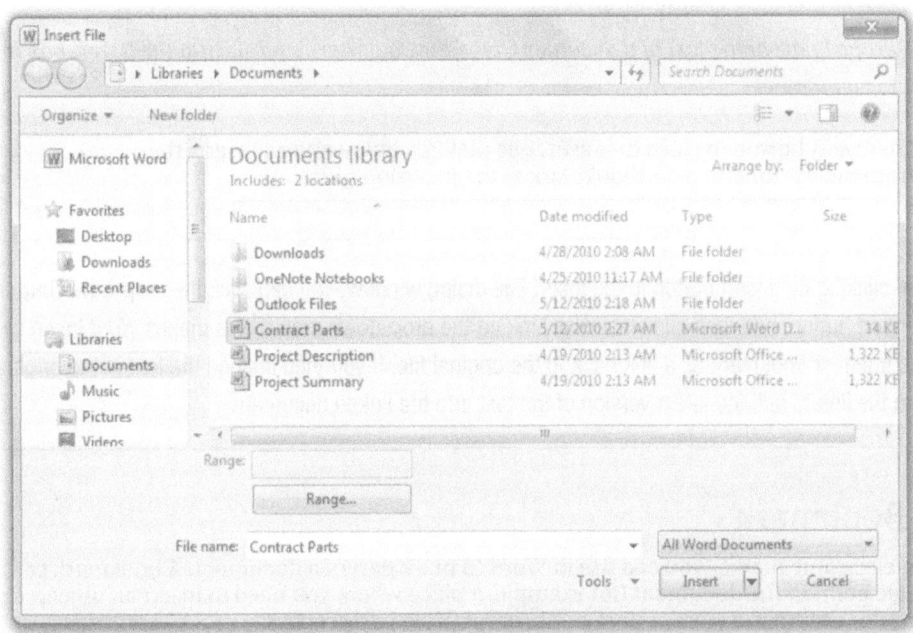

Figure 4–5. *In the Insert File dialog window, select the file whose text (or part of it) you want to insert in the active document.*

3. Navigate to the folder that contains the document, and then click it.

4. If you want to insert only the contents of a bookmark, click the Range button to display the Enter Text dialog window (see Figure 4–6). Type the bookmark's name in the Range box, and then click the OK button. Word enters the name in the Range box.

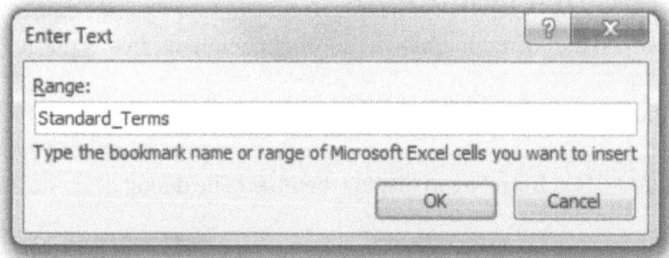

Figure 4–6. To insert just part of the text of a document, type the bookmark's name into the Range box in the Enter Text dialog window.

> 5. Click the Insert button to close the Insert File dialog window. Word inserts the text from the document or the bookmark at the insertion point.

■ **Note** Instead of clicking the Insert button in the Insert File dialog window, you can click the drop-down button to the right of the Insert button, and then click Insert as Link on the drop-down menu. This makes Word insert the contents of the document or bookmark as a link back to the original file. If you then change the text in the original file, you can update the link to pull the latest version of the text into the linked document.

Creating a Bookmark

A *bookmark* is an electronic marker you can use in Word to mark part of a document. A bookmark can mark either a single point in the document (for example, a place where you need to insert an object) or a section of content (for example, a word, a paragraph, or multiple paragraphs).

Bookmarks are useful for various purposes, including cross-references (as you'll see later in this chapter) and marking a part of a document that you want to insert in another document.

To create a bookmark, follow these steps:

> 1. Select the part of the document that you want the bookmark to mark. Here are some examples:
>
>   - To mark a paragraph, select the whole of that paragraph.
>   - To mark an object (such as a table), select that object.
>   - To mark a single point in text, place the insertion point there.
>
> 2. Choose Insert ➤ Links ➤ Bookmark to display the Bookmark dialog window (shown in Figure 4–7 with several bookmarks already created).

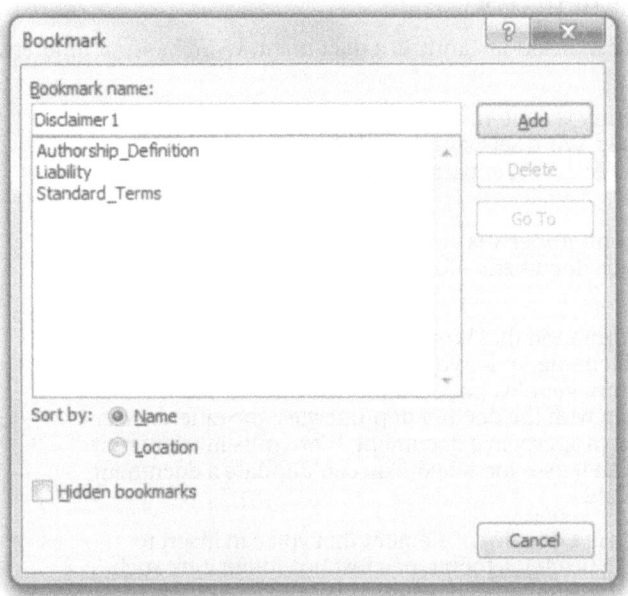

Figure 4–7. Use the Bookmark dialog window to create a new bookmark or to delete an existing bookmark.

3. In the Bookmark name box, type the name for the bookmark. You can create bookmark names freely provided you follow these rules:

- The name must begin with a letter.
- After that, you can use letters, numbers, and underscores in any combination.
- The name can be up to 40 characters long.
- The name cannot include spaces or symbols.

4. Click the Add button. Word closes the Bookmark dialog window and adds the bookmark to the document.

Reusing Content by Using Quick Parts

When you need to build part (or indeed all) of a document out of standard components, you can save time by using Word's Quick Parts feature. You can use either the Quick Parts that come built into Word or custom Quick Parts that you create. You'll probably want to do both.

Understanding What Quick Parts Are

A *Quick Part* is a pre-built element that you can insert instantly in a document. Word has four different types of Quick Parts:

- **AutoText entries:** An AutoText entry is an item containing text or other elements you want to be able to insert easily. Word sets you up with AutoText entries for your name and initials; any other AutoText entries you need, you must set up for yourself.

- **Document properties:** A document property is a piece of the information that Word automatically keeps for each document—for example, the document's subject, keywords, or author.

- **Field:** A field is a piece of the information that Word maintains automatically for the document (for example, its filename) or for your Word setup (for example, your name), or that it retrieves from your PC (for example, the time or date). Confusingly, Word's fields overlap with the document properties; the difference is that when you insert a document property in a document, Word puts in a different type of information container than it uses for a field. You can't update a document property, but you can update a field.

- **Building blocks:** A building block is a document element that you can insert to build a document—for example, a header, a footer, or a text box for an item such as a pull quote or a sidebar.

■ **Note** Building blocks include items such as headers and footers, which Chapter 3 shows you how to insert in your documents. Confusingly, Word also uses the term *building block* to include other types of Quick Parts, including AutoText entries.

Inserting an AutoText Entry in a Document

You can insert an AutoText entry either by quickly typing its name and pressing a shortcut key or by using the AutoText gallery.

Inserting an AutoText Entry Using the Keyboard

When you know the name of the AutoText entry you want to insert, type the name at the appropriate point in text, and then press F3 to make Word insert the AutoText Entry. You can also type just enough of the name to uniquely identify it.

Inserting an AutoText Entry Using the AutoText Gallery

When you're not sure of the name of the AutoText entry you want, insert the entry by choosing Insert ➤ Text ➤ Quick Parts ➤ AutoText, and clicking the item on the AutoText gallery (see Figure 4–8).

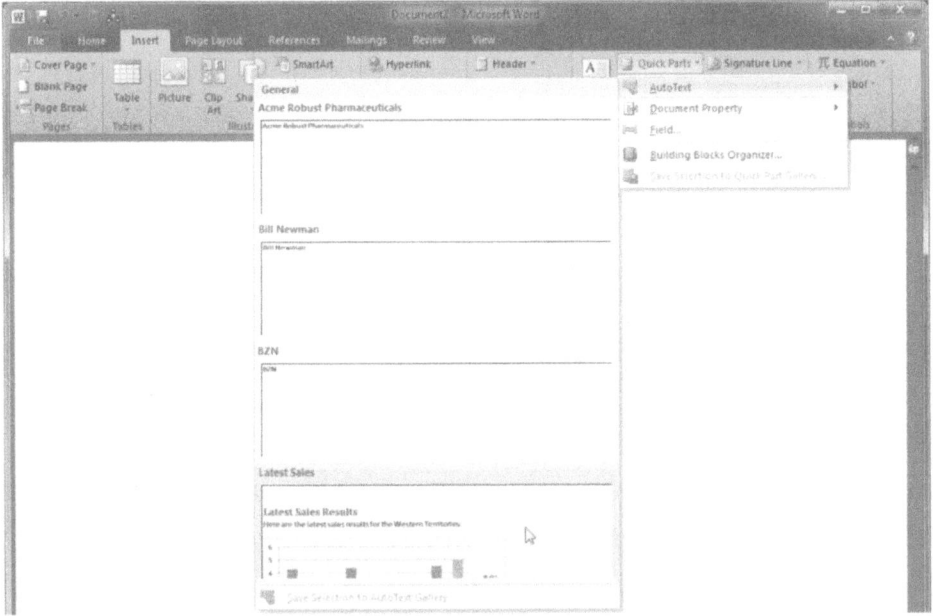

Figure 4–8. You can browse the AutoText gallery on the Quick Parts drop-down list to find the AutoText entry you want to insert.

Creating Your Own AutoText Entries and Building Blocks

Word's built-in Quick Parts are useful for many documents, but to save the most time, you'll almost certainly want to create your own Quick Parts. You can create either AutoText entries or building blocks. You use the same general technique to create both items; for simplicity, and because the dialog window you use is called Create New Building Block, the following discussion refers to building blocks rather than to AutoText entries.

To create a building block, follow these steps:

1. In a document, enter the text or other content you want the building block to contain. Apply any formatting and layout the building block will need.

2. Select the material for the building block.

3. Choose Insert ➤ Text ➤ Quick Parts ➤ Save Selection to Quick Part Gallery. Word displays the Create New Building Block dialog window (see Figure 4–9).

Figure 4–9. *Use the Create New Building Block dialog window to name a new building block, choose the gallery in which to save it, and select other options.*

4. In the Name box, type the name to give the building block. If your selection in the document contains text, Word suggests the first part of that text.

5. In the Gallery drop-down list, choose the type of building block you're creating:

   - The top part of the list contains the built-in galleries for AutoText, Bibliographies, Cover Pages, Equations, Footers, Headers, Page Numbers, Page Numbers (Bottom of Page), Page Numbers (Margins), Page Numbers (Top of Page), Quick Parts, Table of Contents, Tables, Text Boxes, or Watermarks. Choose one of these to put the new building block in a particular existing gallery.

   - The middle part of the list contains five custom galleries named Custom 1 through Custom 5. Choose one of these to put the new building block in so that you can access it quickly from that gallery. For example, you may want to put all the building blocks related to a particular project (or document type) in one of these Custom galleries.

   - The bottom part of the list contains a Custom gallery that corresponds to each of the built-in galleries: Custom AutoText, Custom Bibliographies, Custom Cover Pages, and so on. Choose one of these to put the new building block in a custom gallery, keeping it separate from the built-in building blocks of the same type.

Note The advantage of the Custom galleries is that you can put them on the Quick Access Toolbar and display them easily. For example, you can add your header building blocks to the Custom Headers gallery, put the Custom Headers gallery on the Quick Access Toolbar, and then be able to browse your custom headers without seeing the built-in headers.

---

6. In the Category drop-down list, choose the category in which you want to store the building block. Word starts you off with just the General category, but you can click the Create New Category item in the drop-down list and use the Create New Category dialog window to make a new category. For example, you could create a category for your business building blocks, or create separate categories for different types of projects.

7. In the Description box, type a brief description of the building block to help you (or your colleagues) identify it quickly in galleries or in the Building Blocks Organizer dialog window. The description appears in a ScreenTip in galleries and below the preview in the Building Blocks Organizer dialog window.

8. In the "Save in" drop-down list, choose where to save the building block. These are your options:

    • **Normal:** Choose Normal if you want to save the building block in the Normal template. This is good for text-only AutoText entries, but if you store large building blocks in Normal, it can quickly grow large and make Word run more slowly.

    • **Building Blocks:** Choose Building Blocks to store the building block in the Building Blocks template, along with all Word's built-in building blocks. This is the best place to store your building blocks apart from text-only AutoText entries.

    • **(Current Template):** If the active document is a template, you can choose to store the building block in that template. The building block is then available only when a document based on that template is open. Store a building block in the current template if you will need the building block only for documents based on that template.

9. In the Options drop-down list, choose how to insert the building block in documents:

    • **Insert content only:** This is the default choice, and the one you'll normally want to use. Makes Word insert the building block's text without creating an extra paragraph or an extra page.

    • **Insert content in its own paragraph:** Makes Word create a new paragraph when inserting the building block (in addition to any paragraphs the building block contains).

    • **Insert content in its own page:** Makes Word create a new page when inserting the building block. This is useful for items such as cover pages.

10. Click the OK button to close the Create New Building Block dialog window. Word creates the building block, and you can start using it in your documents.

Inserting a Building Block in a Document

You can insert a building block in a document quickly from the keyboard, by using the appropriate Building Block gallery, or by opening the Building Blocks Organizer dialog window and browsing to the building block you want.

Inserting a Building Block Using the Keyboard

When you know the name of the building block you want to insert, position the insertion point where you want the building block to appear. Type the name of the building block, or enough of the name to identify it uniquely, and then press F3 to make Word insert the building block.

Inserting a Building Block Using a Building Block Gallery

When you've decided which type of building block to insert, you can quickly insert it by opening the appropriate Building Block gallery, and then clicking the building block. For example, when you need to insert a text box, choose Insert ➤ Text ➤ Text Boxes, and then click the text box in the gallery. You can also right-click the gallery item (see Figure 4–10) to display a context menu with other commands. Of these, the most useful is the Organize and Delete command, which opens the Building Blocks Organizer dialog window and selects the building block you right-clicked.

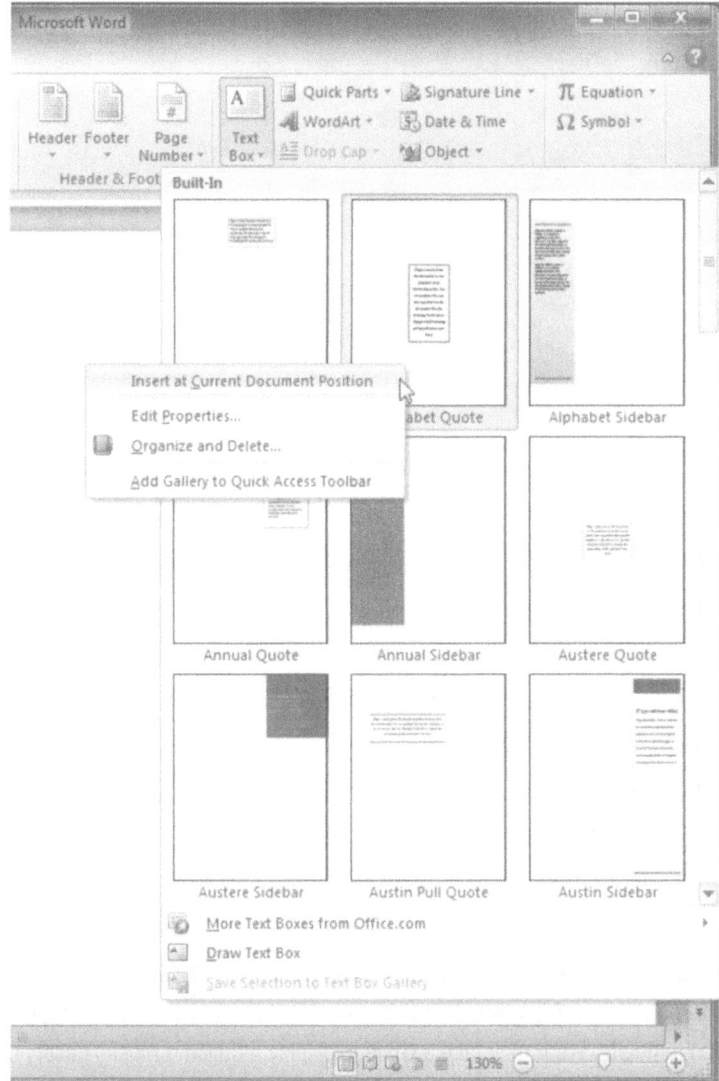

Figure 4–10. From a Building Blocks gallery such as the Text Box gallery, you can either insert a building block or open the Building Blocks Organizer dialog window.

Inserting a Building Block Using the Building Blocks Organizer Dialog Window

When you want to browse through all the available building blocks, choose Insert ➤ Text ➤ Quick Parts ➤ Building Blocks Organizer to display the Building Blocks Organizer dialog window (see Figure 4–11).

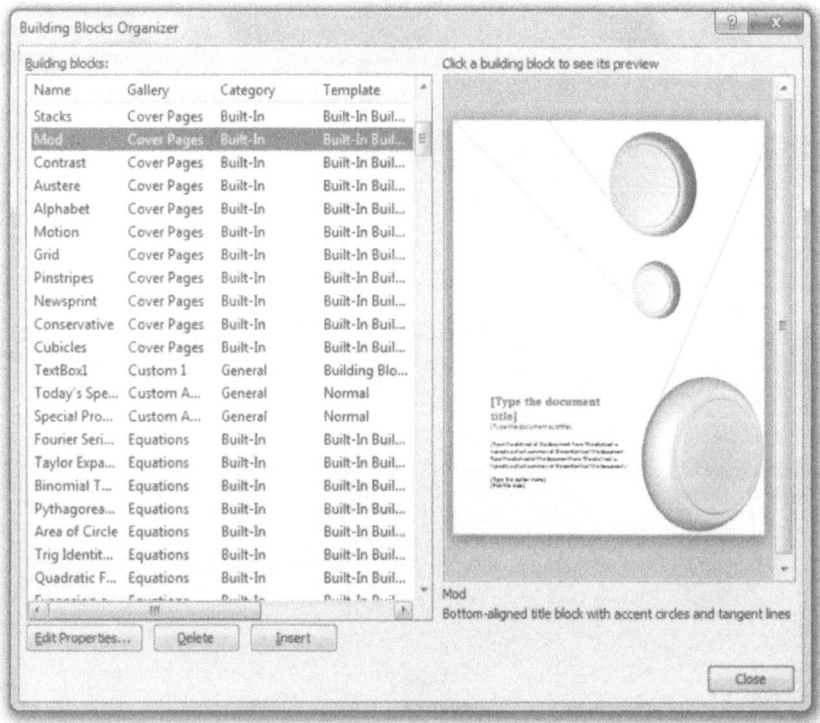

Figure 4–11. Use the Building Blocks Organizer dialog window to browse all the building blocks and insert those you need. From here, you can also edit and delete building blocks.

▪ **Note** Word stores most of its building blocks in a special template called Building Blocks. To keep down its usage of your PC's memory, Word loads this Building Blocks template only when you open a Building Blocks gallery or the Building Blocks Organizer dialog window. After that, Word keeps the Building Blocks template open until you exit Word. Because of loading the template, Word may take a while to display a Building Blocks gallery or the Building Blocks Organizer dialog window the first time you use them in a Word session. After that, they should display at full speed.

From the Building Blocks Organizer dialog window, you can take the following actions:

- **Browse the building blocks**: Scroll down the list of building blocks, and click the building block you want to preview.

- **Sort the building blocks**: Click one of the column headings—Name, Gallery, Category, or Template—to sort the building blocks list by that heading.

- **Jump to a letter**: Press a letter to jump to the first item in the Name list starting with that letter. For example, press T to select the first item whose name starts with *T*. This is most useful when you've sorted the building blocks by the Name column, but it still works when you've sorted them by another column.

- **Insert a building block**: Click the building block in the building blocks list, and then click the Insert button.

- **Delete a building block**: Click the building block in the building blocks list, click the Delete button, and then click the Yes button in the confirmation dialog window that Word displays.

■ **Note** If you delete a built-in building block, you can recover it by running the Office installation routine and choosing the option for repairing Office.

- **Edit the properties of a building block**: Click the building block in the building blocks list, and then click the Edit Properties button to display the Modify Building Block dialog window. Apart from its title, this dialog window works just like the Create New Building Block dialog window, which you'll meet in the next section.

When you have finished using the Building Blocks Organizer dialog window, click the Close button to close it.

Inserting a Document Property in a Document

To help you keep your documents organized, Word maintains a list of document properties that you can use to store key information about the document. You can quickly insert a document property in a document by using the Document Property gallery.

Table 4–1 explains the document properties for Word documents. The properties fall into two categories: a couple of properties that Word automatically assigns the appropriate information, and rather more properties to which you need to assign the information manually.

Table 4–1. Word's Document Properties

Document Property	Type	Explanation
Abstract	Manual	A short section of text explaining the document's contents
Author	Automatic	The creator of the document
Category	Manual	One or more categories you create to enable you to sort your documents
Comments	Manual	Comments you add to help you identify your documents
Company	Automatic	The company you entered in your Office user information
Company Address	Manual	Your company's address
Company E-mail	Manual	Your company's e-mail address
Company Fax	Manual	Your company's fax number
Company Phone	Manual	Your company's phone number
Keywords	Manual	Keywords or key phrases you add to help you find the documents you need
Manager	Manual	The manager's name you enter
Publish Date	Manual	The publication date you enter
Status	Manual	The document status you enter
Subject	Manual	The subject of the document
Title	Manual	The title of the document

To insert a document property in a document, follow these steps:

1. Position the insertion point where you want the property to appear.
2. Choose Insert ➤ Text ➤ Quick Parts ➤ Document Property to display the Document Property gallery.
3. Click the property you want to insert.

Inserting a Field in a Document

As well as document properties, you can insert fields in your documents. A *field* is a container for variable information that you may need to update during the document's life. For example, you can insert the SaveDate field to include the date and time when the document was last saved. When you update this field, it changes to show the latest value.

■ **Note** Many of Word's features that you'll learn about in other chapters use fields. For example, when you insert page numbers in your headers and footers, Word uses fields for the numbers so that it can update the information as the document changes. Similarly, cross-references, tables of content, and mail merge all use fields.

To insert a field in a document, follow these steps:

1. Place the insertion point where you want to insert the field.

2. Choose Insert ➤ Text ➤ Quick Parts ➤ Field to display the Field dialog window (shown in Figure 4–12 with the full list of fields displayed).

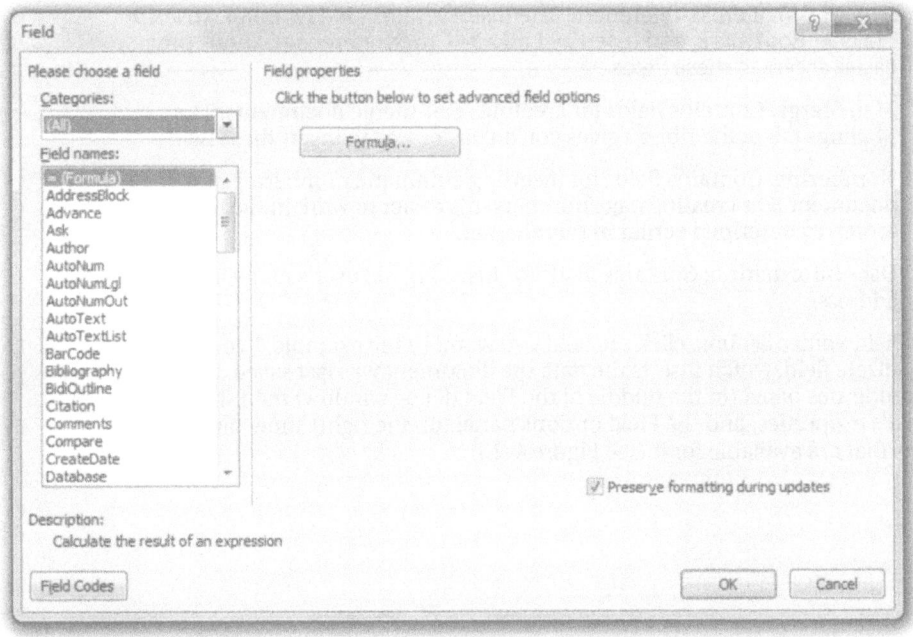

Figure 4–12. The Field dialog window includes a wide range of fields. Normally, you'll want to start by choosing the type of fields in the Categories drop-down list.

3. In the Categories drop-down list, choose the category of fields you want (see the following list). I'm using the Date & Time category as an easy example.

- **(All)**: Lists all the fields. This is useful when you know the field's name but not the category that contains it.

- **Date and Time**: Contains fields for entering dates and times, such as the current date or the time the document was last saved, in various formats. You can also insert a date, time, or both more easily by choosing Insert ➤ Text ➤ Date & Time and using the Date and Time dialog window.

- **Document Automation**: Contains fields for automating movement about the document, running macros, printing, and similar actions.

- **Document Information**: Contains fields for inserting information contained in the document's properties, such as the author name or file name.

- **Equations and Formulas**: Contains fields for inserting equations and formulas. Use these when the Insert ➤ Symbols ➤ Equation menu doesn't contain what you need.

- **Index and Tables**: Contains fields for creating indexes and content tables (such as tables of contents and tables of figures). The References tab of the ribbon contains controls for inserting these fields more easily.

- **Links and References**: Contains fields for inserting links (such as hyperlinks) or cross-references. The Insert ➤ Links ➤ Hyperlink, Insert ➤ Links ➤ Bookmark, and Insert ➤ Links ➤ Cross-reference options provide easier access to these fields.

- **Mail Merge**: Contains fields for creating mail-merge documents. The Mailings tab of the ribbon gives you an easier way to insert these fields.

- **Numbering**: Contains fields for inserting automatic numbering in a document. For creating page numbers, it's easier to work in the header or footer, as described earlier in this chapter.

- **User Information**: Contains fields for inserting the user's name, initials, or address.

4. In the Field names list box, click the field you want. In the example, I've clicked the SaveDate field, which inserts the date the document was last saved. The Field properties panel (in the middle of the Field dialog window) then shows the field's properties, and the Field options panel (on the right) shows any options that are available for it (see Figure 4–13).

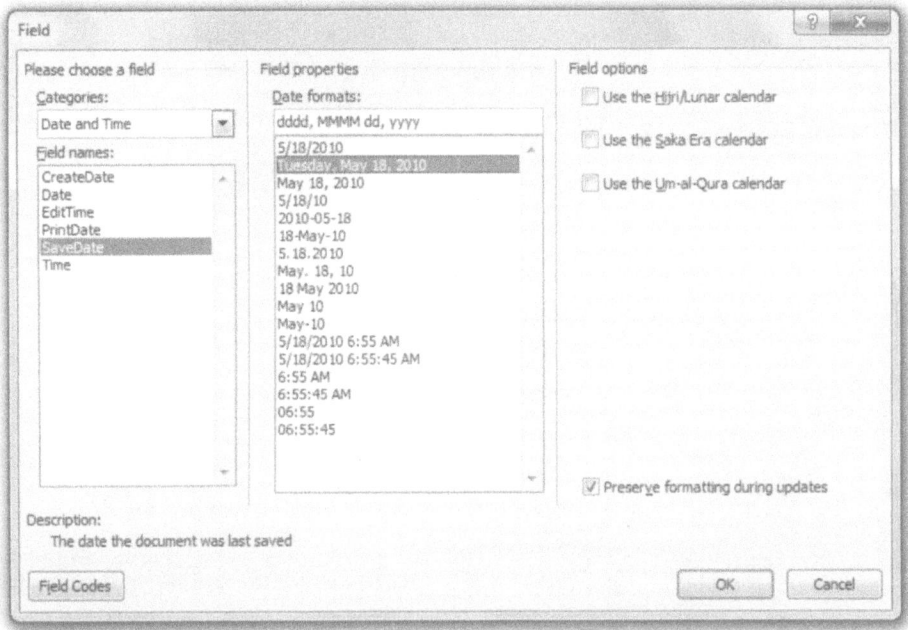

Figure 4–13. *Click the field in the Field names list box, and then set the field properties and field options you need.*

5. In the Field properties panel, choose the file properties you want. The available properties depend on the field you've chosen, but for date fields such as SaveDate, a Date formats list appears in which you click the format you want.

6. In the Field options panel, choose any options you want. Again, these depend on the field: some fields have no options, while the SaveDate field lets you select from various calendars.

7. Select the "Preserve formatting during updates" check box if you want to keep the field's formatting when you update it. This behavior is normally useful.

8. Click the OK button to close the Field dialog window and insert the field.

Examining and Updating a Field

Now that you've inserted a field, you can examine it. At first, the field displays the *field result*—the information that the field produces. For example, the SaveDate field displays a date in the format you choose.

Normally, the field result appears like normal text until you click in it or select it, at which point Word displays gray shading behind it to indicate that it's a field. To update the field, right-click anywhere in it, and then click Update Field on the context menu (see Figure 4–14).

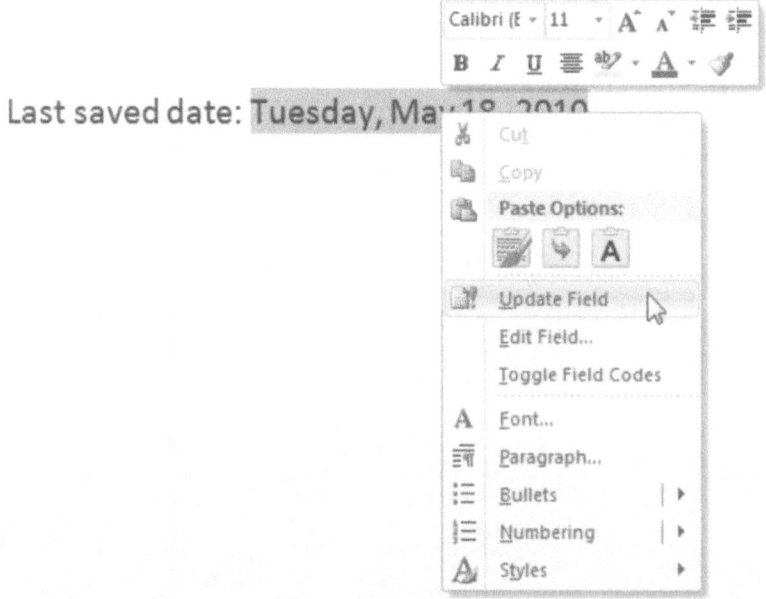

Figure 4–14. *To update a field, right-click it, and then click Update Field on the context menu.*

___

■ **Note** If you want to see field shading all the time, click the File tab, and then click the Options item to display the Word Options dialog window. Click the Advanced item in the left pane, open the Field shading drop-down list in the "Show document content" area, and click Always. You can also select the "Show field codes instead of their values" check box if you want to display field codes all the time. Click the OK button to close the Word Options dialog window.

___

If you want to see the field code that's producing the field result, right-click anywhere in the field and choose Toggle Field Codes. Repeat the command to return to the field result.

___

■ **Note** To change a field you've inserted in your document, right-click the field, and then click Edit Field on the context menu. Word displays the Field dialog window, and you can edit the field using the same techniques as when you inserted it.

Adding Custom Building Block Galleries to the Quick Access Toolbar

After you create your own building blocks and store them in the Custom galleries, you can add the Custom galleries to the Quick Access Toolbar to give yourself easier access to their building blocks.

To add a Custom gallery to the Quick Access Toolbar, follow these steps:

1. Right-click any button on the Quick Access Toolbar, and then click Customize Quick Access Toolbar to display the Quick Access Toolbar category in the Word Options dialog window.

2. Open the Choose commands from the drop-down list, and then click Commands Not in the Ribbon. The list box below the drop-down list shows all the commands that don't appear in the ribbon.

3. Scroll down to the list of Custom items—Custom AutoText, Custom Bibliography, Custom Bottom of Page, and so on.

4. Click the Custom item you want to add to the Quick Access Toolbar.

5. Click the Add button to add the item to the box on the right.

6. Repeat Steps 4 and 5 to add other items to the Quick Access Toolbar as needed.

7. Click the OK button to close the Word Options dialog window. Word adds buttons for the custom items you chose to the Quick Access Toolbar.

You can now click the button you added to the Quick Access Toolbar to open the custom gallery. This is great for quickly inserting the building blocks you've created and customized.

Saving Time and Effort by Using AutoCorrect

As you work in a document, the AutoCorrect feature watches the characters you type and springs into action if it detects a mistake it can fix or some formatting it can apply. AutoCorrect can save you a lot of time and effort, and can speed up your typing substantially, provided you spend some time setting it up to meet your needs and you define AutoCorrect entries to expand abbreviations and correct mistakes that you type.

Opening the AutoCorrect Dialog window

To set up AutoCorrect, open the AutoCorrect dialog window like this:

1. Click the File button to open the Backstage view, and then click Options to display the Word Options dialog window.

2. In the left pane, click the Proofing category to display the Proofing options.

3. Click the AutoCorrect Options button to display the AutoCorrect dialog window.

4. If the AutoCorrect tab (see Figure 4–15) isn't at the front, click it to display it.

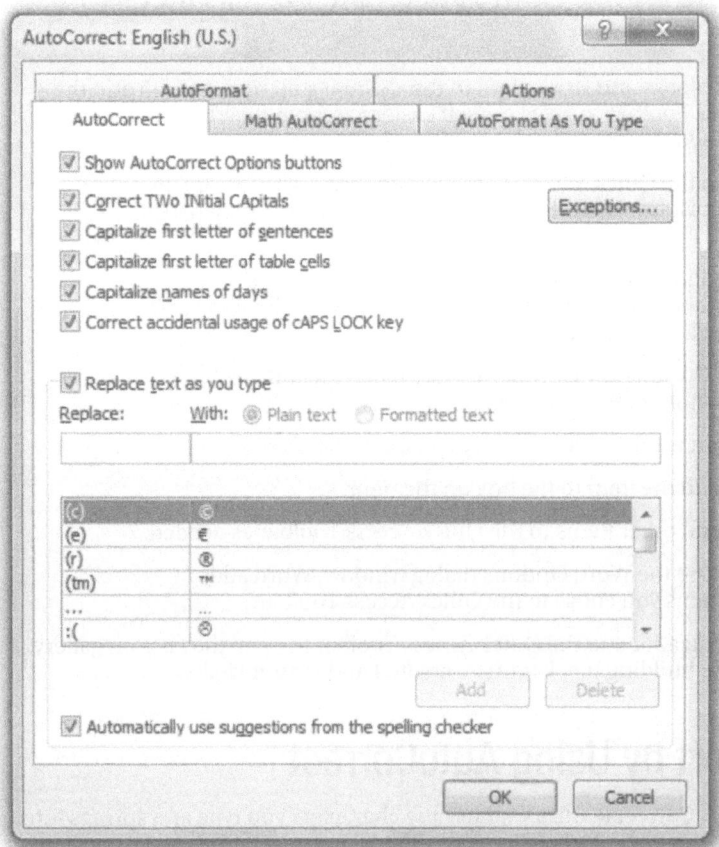

Figure 4–15. On the AutoCorrect tab of the AutoCorrect dialog window, choose which settings you want to use. This is also where you create AutoCorrect entries for the items you want AutoCorrect to replace automatically.

Choosing Options on the AutoCorrect Tab of the AutoCorrect Dialog Window

To control which AutoCorrect features Word uses, choose options on the AutoCorrect tab of the AutoCorrect dialog window. These are the settings:

- **Show AutoCorrect Options buttons**: Makes Word display a small button under each item AutoCorrect changes. You can hold the mouse pointer over this button to make the program display a menu of AutoCorrect-related choices, such as stopping this particular change. These buttons are usually helpful; but if Word displays a button in the way of what you're doing, press Esc to make it disappear.

- **Correct TWo INitial CApitals**: Makes Word apply lowercase to a second initial capital—for example, changing "THree" to "Three." This option is usually helpful.

- **Capitalize first letter of sentences**: Makes Word capitalize the first letter of the first word in a sentence or paragraph. Clear this check box if you prefer to write in fragments and then fix them afterward.

- **Capitalize first letter of table cells**: Makes Word capitalize the first letter of each entry in a table cell. Whether this option is helpful depends on how you work.

- **Capitalize names of days**: Makes Word capitalize the first letter of the day names (for example, Sunday). This option is usually helpful.

- **Correct accidental use of caps LOCK key**: Makes Word turn off Caps Lock if you start a sentence with a lowercase letter and continue in caps. This option is usually helpful.

- **Replace text as you type**: Turns on AutoCorrect's main feature, replacing misspellings and contractions with their designated replacement text. You will want to use this feature to make the most of AutoCorrect.

- **Automatically use suggestions from the spelling checker**: Lets the "Replace text as you type" feature use suggestions from the spelling checker as well as the entries in the list. This option is usually helpful too.

Creating AutoCorrect Entries

If you use the "Replace text as you type" feature on the AutoCorrect tab of the AutoCorrect dialog window, make the most of this powerful feature by creating a list of entries that will save you time and effort.

■ **Tip** You can create AutoCorrect entries up to 255 characters long—enough for several sentences. Longer AutoCorrect entries are great for quickly entering boilerplate text, such as addresses, company names, set phrases, or standard text for documents such as business letters or contracts.

Understanding Unformatted AutoCorrect Entries and Formatted AutoCorrect Entries

In Word, you can use two different types of AutoCorrect entries: regular, unformatted AutoCorrect entries, and formatted AutoCorrect entries.

An unformatted AutoCorrect entry consists only of text. You can create unformatted AutoCorrect entries in any of the major Office programs (for example, Excel, PowerPoint, and OneNote), and the entries are available in each program. For example, you can create an unformatted AutoCorrect entry in Excel, and then use it in Word.

A formatted AutoCorrect entry consists of text with formatting, and can contain other objects as well—for example, a graphic, a table, or an equation. You can create formatted AutoCorrect entries only in Word, and you can use them only in Word.

■ **Note** To create an AutoCorrect entry that includes a paragraph mark, you must create a formatted AutoCorrect entry rather than an unformatted AutoCorrect entry. This is because the paragraph mark contains formatting.

Creating Unformatted AutoCorrect Entries in the AutoCorrect Dialog Window

The standard way of creating an AutoCorrect entry is to use the controls on the AutoCorrect tab of the AutoCorrect dialog window. Follow these steps:

1. Display the AutoCorrect tab of the AutoCorrect dialog window, as discussed earlier in this chapter.

2. Type the error or the abbreviation in the Replace box. This is the text that, when you type it in a document, you want AutoCorrect to replace with the replacement text.

3. Type or paste the replacement text in the With box.

4. Click the Add button to add the AutoCorrect entry.

5. Repeat Steps 2 through 4 for each entry you want to create.

6. Click the OK button to close the AutoCorrect dialog window.

Creating Unformatted AutoCorrect Entries When Checking Spelling

When you're checking spelling in Word, you can quickly create an AutoCorrect entry that will fix a typo or spelling mistake in the future:

- **On-the-fly spell checking:** Instead of clicking the correct spelling on the contextual menu, open the AutoCorrect submenu, and then click the correct spelling (see Figure 4–16). Word corrects the error and creates an AutoCorrect entry that will take care of the error in the future.

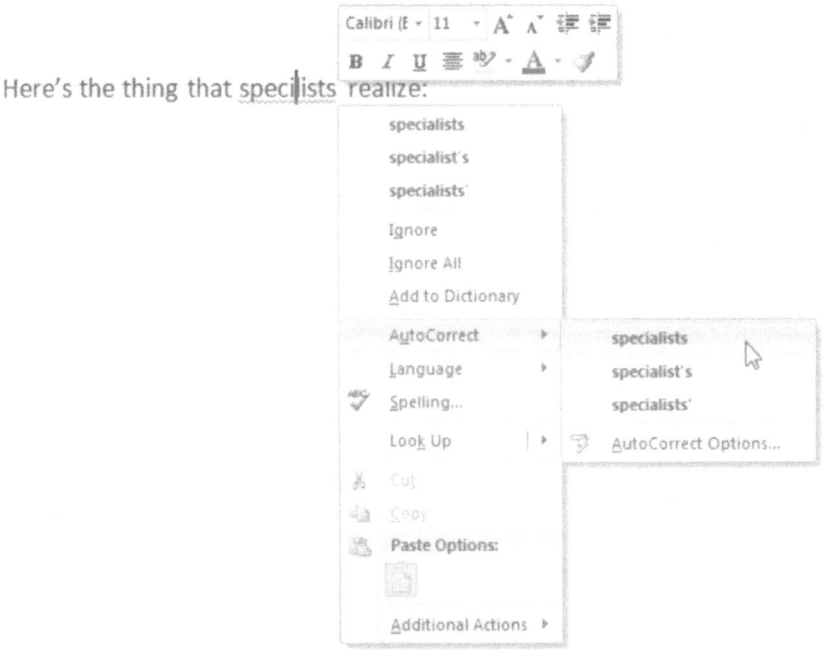

Here's the thing that speci|ists realize.

Figure 4–16. *When checking spelling with the contextual menu, use the AutoCorrect submenu to quickly correct any spelling mistake or typo you think you may repeat.*

- **Regular spelling check**: Click the correct spelling in the Suggestions box in the Spelling and Grammar dialog window, and then click the AutoCorrect button. Word fixes the spelling and creates an AutoCorrect entry for it.

Creating Formatted AutoCorrect Entries

Formatted AutoCorrect entries can be a great time-saver because they let you insert not only fully formatted text but also other objects, such as graphics or tables.

To create a formatted AutoCorrect entry, follow these steps:

1. In a document, create the entry as you want to be able to enter it. For example, type text and format it, add a graphic, or add a table.

2. Select everything you want to include in the AutoCorrect entry.

3. Open the AutoCorrect dialog window as described earlier. The first part of your selection appears in the With text box.

4. Make sure the Formatted text option button is selected. (If not, click it.)

5. In the Replace box, type the abbreviation you want to use for the entry.

6. Click the Add button to add the entry.

■ **Note** Word stores formatted AutoCorrect entries in the Normal template. Depending on the options you've chosen for Word, you may see a prompt to save Normal when exiting Word after creating a formatted AutoCorrect entry. If you receive this prompt, click the Yes button to save the changes to Normal.

Creating AutoCorrect Exceptions

As well as AutoCorrect entries, you can create AutoCorrect *exceptions*—specific terms when you don't want AutoCorrect to replace text when it normally would. To create AutoCorrect exceptions, follow these steps:

1. On the AutoCorrect tab of the AutoCorrect dialog window, click the Exceptions button. The AutoCorrect Exceptions dialog window opens (see Figure 4–17).

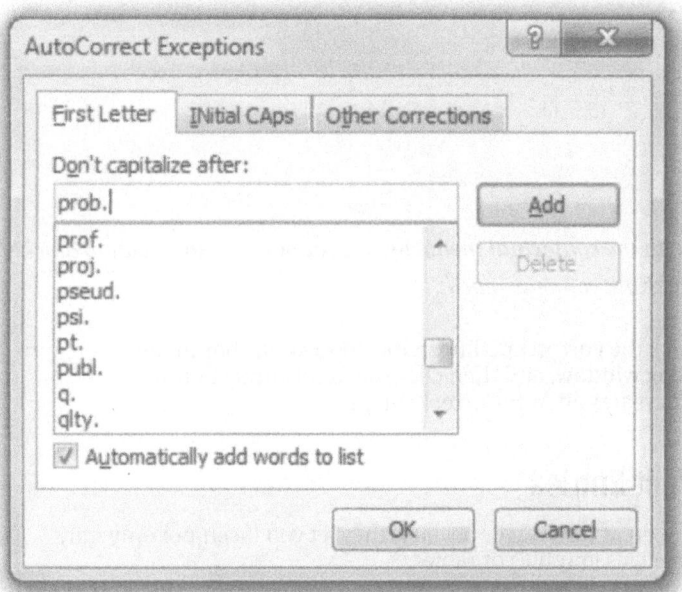

Figure 4–17. In the AutoCorrect Exceptions dialog window, you can create lists of terms that you want AutoCorrect to ignore.

2. Click the tab for the type of exception you want to work with:

   - **First Letter**: On this tab, list the terms that end with periods but after which you don't want the next word to start with a capital letter. Office starts you off with a list of built-in terms, such as vol. (for *volume*) and wk. (for *work*).

- **INitial CAps**: On this tab, list the terms that start with two initial capital letters that you don't want AutoCorrect to reduce to a single capital—for example, IPv6.

- **Other Corrections**: On this tab, list other terms that you don't want AutoCorrect to fix. These are typically terms that don't have first-letter or initial-caps issues, but that you don't want AutoCorrect to fix—for example, apparent misspellings that are, in fact, correct but that you haven't added to the dictionary.

3. Add and delete exceptions as needed:

   - **Add an exception**: Type it in the Don't Correct text box, and then click the Add button.

   - **Delete an exception**: Click it in the list box, and then click the Delete button.

4. Select the "Automatically add words to list" check box if you want the program to automatically add exceptions when you undo a correction it has made.

5. When you have finished working with exceptions, click the OK button to close the AutoCorrect Exceptions dialog window.

Inserting an AutoCorrect Entry

After you've created your AutoCorrect entries, you can insert an entry by typing the abbreviation for the entry (the Replace term) and pressing the spacebar or a punctuation key (such as the comma key or the period key). Word automatically replaces the abbreviation with the replacement text.

Choosing Whether to Use Math AutoCorrect

Math AutoCorrect makes it easy to enter characters and symbols used in math in your documents. For example, you can type \theta to enter a lowercase theta character (θ) without visiting the Symbol dialog window. Math AutoCorrect comes with a long list of entries for math characters and symbols.

If you use math in your Word documents, you'll do well to spend some time setting up the Math AutoCorrect options to meet your needs. Conversely, if your documents don't include math, you may want to turn Math AutoCorrect off.

To set up Math AutoCorrect, open the AutoCorrect dialog window, and then click the Math AutoCorrect tab (see Figure 4–18). You can then choose settings as needed:

- **Use Math AutoCorrect rules outside of math regions**: Allows Word to use Math AutoCorrect anywhere in your documents. To confine Math AutoCorrect to math areas, clear this check box.

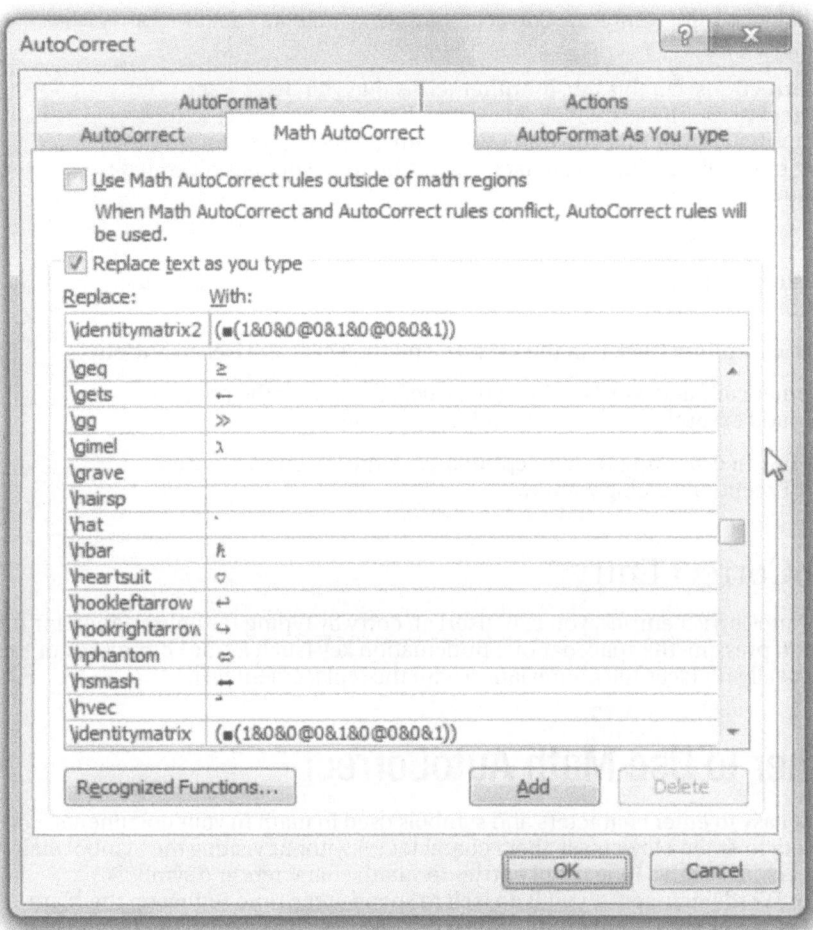

Figure 4–18. On the Math AutoCorrect tab of the AutoCorrect dialog window, choose whether to use Math AutoCorrect and whether to let it work throughout your documents or only in math regions, areas in which you've inserted equations.

- **Replace text as you type**: Enables Word to replace the text items listed in the main box with their math replacements.

- **AutoCorrect items**: To add an item, type the abbreviation or text version in the Replace box, type or paste the replacement text in the With box, and then click the Add button.

- **Recognized Functions**: To change the list of math expressions that Word recognizes and doesn't automatically italicize, click the Recognized Functions button, and then work in the Recognized Math Functions dialog window that opens.

Making the Most of the AutoFormat As You Type Feature

As you've seen earlier in this chapter, AutoCorrect's "Replace text as you type" feature automatically replaces your typos and predefined text shortcuts as you work. But AutoCorrect can also do much more than this—if you let it.

In this section, I'll show you how the AutoFormat As You Type feature works and suggest how to choose settings for it that will suit your needs. This feature can save you time and effort once you've learned its ins and outs and set it up the right way. If you just leave AutoFormat As You Type with its default settings, it will probably give you some surprises and will make changes that you need to undo.

Understanding How the AutoFormat As You Type Feature Works

Like the AutoCorrect feature, AutoFormat As You Type watches as you type and tries to analyze the patterns of characters. But unlike AutoCorrect, which replaces a predefined string of characters with replacement text (or formatted objects), AutoFormat As You Type tries to apply suitable formatting.

For example, Microsoft's developers know that many people create numbered lists manually—by typing the item number, followed by a period or a closing parenthesis, and then by a space or tab. Word's recommended method of creating numbered lists is to apply paragraph formatting that includes numbering, which means that Word can automatically renumber the paragraphs for you. So when you type a sequence that suggests you're trying to create a numbered list (for example, typing 1. and a tab at the beginning of a paragraph), the AutoFormat As You Type feature automatically applies numbered list formatting for you.

Once you know how AutoFormat As You Type works, you can use it to save time—or you can simply turn it off.

Choosing Settings for the AutoFormat As You Type Feature

To keep the AutoFormat As You Type feature under control, take a few minutes to choose suitable settings for it. Click the AutoFormat As You Type tab to bring it to the front of the AutoCorrect dialog window (see Figure 4–19).

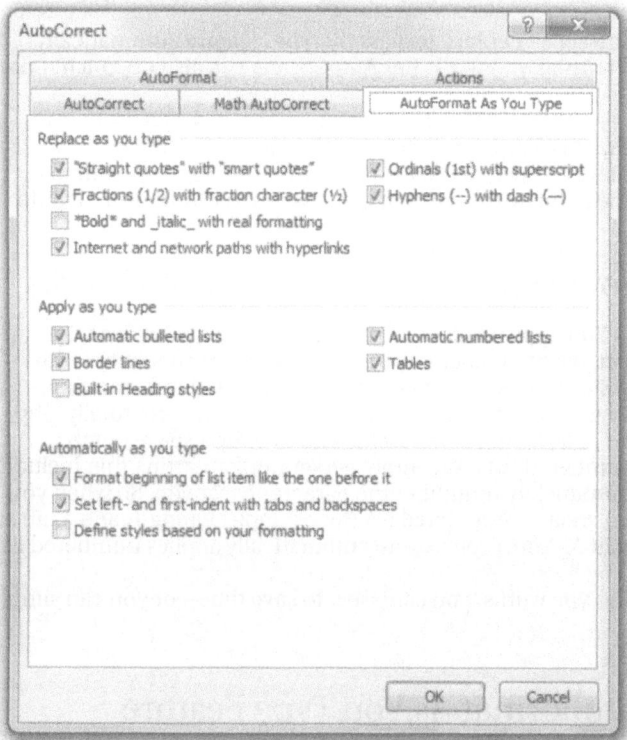

Figure 4–19. The AutoFormat As You Type tab of the AutoCorrect dialog window contains several genuinely helpful options, but other options try too hard to be helpful.

Choosing Replace As You Type Options

The "Replace as you type" area at the top of the AutoFormat As You Type tab contains most of the AutoFormat options that most people find useful. Here are the details:

- **"Straight quotes" with "smart quotes"**: Makes AutoCorrect replace straight-up-and-down quotes with smart or "curly" quotes. This is usually helpful.

- **Fractions (1/2) with fraction character (½)**: Makes AutoCorrect insert real fraction characters in place of fractions you type. This too is usually helpful.

- ***Bold* and _italic_ with real formatting**: Lets you apply boldface by typing an asterisk before and after a word, and apply italics by typing an underscore before and after a word. These are long-standing Internet conventions for indicating formatting in plain text, but usually it's easier to use keyboard shortcuts to apply the boldface (press Ctrl+B) or italics (press Ctrl+I).

- **Internet and network paths with hyperlinks**: Makes AutoCorrect insert a hyperlink when you type a URL (for example, www.apress.com) or a network path (for example, \\server1\public). If you want to create live hyperlinks in your documents automatically, select this check box; otherwise, clear this check box and use the Insert ➤ Links ➤ Hyperlink command when you need to insert a hyperlink.

- **Ordinals (1st) with superscript**: Makes AutoCorrect apply superscript to the letters of ordinals (for example, 1st, 2nd). This option is useful when you need fully formatted documents. If you don't need superscripted ordinals, clear this check box.

- **Hyphens (--) with dash (—)**: Makes AutoCorrect insert en dashes (–) in place of a hyphen preceded and followed by spaces, and em dashes (—) for two hyphens typed between words. This option is usually helpful.

Choosing Apply As You Type Options

The five options in the "Apply as you type" area in the middle of the AutoFormat As You Type tab cause many surprises to Word users. That means it's vital to understand how each option works so you can decide whether to use the option or turn it off.

Here's what you need to know:

- **Automatic bulleted lists**: Makes AutoCorrect automatically apply a bulleted list style when you start a paragraph with an asterisk, a hyphen, or a greater-than sign followed by a space or tab.

■ **Caution** If you're using styles to format your documents, turn off the Automatic bulleted lists feature and the Automatic numbered lists feature. This is because Word applies the bullets or numbering as direct formatting on top of the paragraph style the paragraph uses. When using styles, you're better off applying a bulleted-list style or a numbered-list style to the list paragraphs manually.

- **Automatic numbered lists**: Makes AutoCorrect automatically apply a numbered list style when you start a paragraph with a number or letter followed by a period or closing parenthesis, and then type a space or tab.

- **Border lines**: Select this check box to have AutoCorrect apply border lines when you type three or more characters at the beginning of a paragraph and then press the Enter key. These are characters and the lines they produce:

    - **Hyphens**: Thin line.

    - **Underscores**: Thick line.

    - **Equal signs**: Double line.

    - **Tildes**: Wavy line.

    - **Pound signs (hash marks)**: Three lines—thin on top, thick in the middle, and thin on the bottom.

- **Tables**: Enables you to create a table by typing a line of plus signs and hyphens. Each plus sign indicates a column border, so +--+--+--+ produces a three-column table. The number of hyphens indicates the relative width of the columns—in the previous example, the columns are of equal width. Usually it's easier to use the Insert ➤ Table ➤ Table command to insert a table.

- **Built-in Heading styles**: Select this check box if you want AutoCorrect to automatically apply Word's Heading styles when you create a short paragraph in the right way. Here are the details; in each case, AutoCorrect removes the tabs and the extra paragraphs after the heading, but it leaves the blank paragraphs before the heading.

  - **Heading 1**: Press the Enter key twice, type the heading, and then press the Enter key twice more.

  - **Heading 2**: Press the Enter key twice, press the Tab key, type the heading, and press the Enter key twice more.

  - **Heading 3**: Press the Enter key twice, press the Tab key twice, type the heading, and press the Enter key twice more.

  - **Heading 4**: Press the Enter key twice, press the Tab key three times, type the heading, and press the Enter key twice more.

Choosing Automatically As You Type Options

The bottom section of the AutoFormat As You Type tab of the AutoCorrect dialog window contains check boxes for controlling the three most confusing AutoFormat options. You may well want to turn all three options off:

- **Format beginning of list item like the one before it**. Makes AutoCorrect format the second and subsequent items in a list using the same formatting you've added to the beginning of the first item—for example, italic or boldface. This is sometimes useful, but if you feel Word is trying to wrest formatting control from you, clear this check box.

- **Set left and first-line indent with tabs and backspaces**. Makes AutoCorrect automatically move the left indent and first-line indent to the left when you press Backspace at the beginning of a blank paragraph, and move them to the right when you press Tab at the start of a paragraph. This feature tends to cause formatting surprises, especially if you're used to using Backspace to delete the beginning of a paragraph and return to the previous paragraph—so you may want to turn this option off.

- **Define styles based on your formatting**. Makes AutoCorrect automatically create styles when it thinks you need one. This feature is a recipe for confusion, so you'll probably want to clear this check box.

Formatting a Document Instantly with the AutoFormat Feature

When setting the AutoCorrect options, you'll probably have noticed that the AutoCorrect dialog window also contains an AutoFormat tab (see Figure 4–20). This tab contains settings for the AutoFormat feature, which you can use to apply automatic formatting to documents that lack formatting but are laid out with text-based formatting—for example, e-mail messages or text you've written on a mobile phone.

If you don't deal with such documents, you don't need to choose AutoFormat settings—Word doesn't apply them as you type, so they won't give you any surprises.

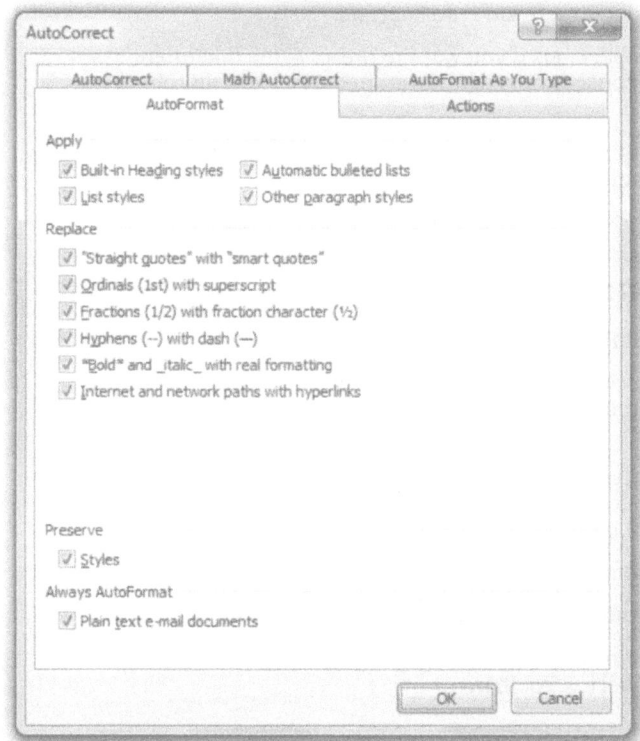

Figure 4–20. *If you need to apply automatic formatting to unformatted documents you receive, choose suitable settings on the AutoFormat tab of the AutoCorrect dialog window.*

AutoFormat is an orphan, because Microsoft has removed the command for running it from the ribbon. That means you'll need to customize the Quick Access Toolbar in order to access the AutoFormat feature.

Choosing Suitable Settings for AutoFormat

If you do need AutoFormat, choose the settings on the AutoFormat tab in the AutoCorrect dialog window. Most of the settings are almost identical to those on the AutoFormat As You Type tab:

- **Apply area**: To control which styles Word applies automatically, select the Built-in Heading styles check box, the List styles check box, the Automatic bulleted lists check box, and the Other paragraph styles check box.

- **Replace area**: To control which text-formatted items Word replaces automatically with proper formatting, select or clear the check boxes. For example, select the "Straight quotes" with "smart quotes" checkbox if you want Word to replace straight quotes with smart quotes. The only problematic option here is the "Internet and network paths with hyperlinks" check box; clear this check box if you don't want live links in the document you're formatting.

- **Preserve area**: Select the Styles check box if you want to preserve the document's existing styles. If the document consists only of unformatted text, clear this check box.

- **Always AutoFormat area**: Select the "Plain text e-mail documents" check box if you want AutoText to automatically format each plain text e-mail message you open.

Adding the AutoFormat Command to the Quick Access Toolbar

To use AutoFormat, you need to add the AutoFormat command to the Quick Access Toolbar like this:

1. Right-click any button on the Quick Access Toolbar, and then click Customize Quick Access Toolbar to display the Quick Access Toolbar category in the Word Options dialog window.

2. Open the Choose commands from drop-down list, and then click Commands Not in the Ribbon. The list box below the drop-down list shows all the commands that don't appear in the ribbon.

3. Scroll down to the AutoFormat command, and then click it.

4. Click the Add button to add the AutoFormat command to the box on the right.

5. Click the OK button to close the Word Options dialog window. Word adds the AutoFormat button to the Quick Access Toolbar.

Formatting a Document with AutoFormat

Now that you've added the AutoFormat button to the Quick Access Toolbar, click the button to display the AutoFormat dialog window (see Figure 4–21).

Figure 4–21. In the AutoFormat dialog window, choose whether to simply format the document automatically or to review each change that Word makes. You can also choose the document type.

In the upper part of the dialog window, you can choose between the "AutoFormat now" option button and the "AutoFormat and review each change" option button. What you'll probably want to do here is select the "AutoFormat now" option button and see what formatting you get. If the resulting document contains changes you don't want, click the Undo button on the Quick Access Toolbar, click the AutoFormat button again to display the AutoFormat dialog window once more, and this time select the "AutoFormat and review each change" option button.

In the "Please select a document type to help improve the formatting process" drop-down list, choose General document, Letter, or Email, as needed. This setting gives Word a heads-up on which types of elements to expect in the document. For example, a General document is likely to have headings; a Letter will have an address section, a salutation, and a sign-off line; an e-mail will have a sender, a subject line, a message body, and so on.

■ **Note** Clicking the Options button in the AutoFormat dialog window opens the AutoCorrect dialog window with the AutoFormat tab at the front. This lets you tweak the AutoFormat settings before Word uses them on this document.

Click the OK button to close the AutoFormat dialog window and run the AutoFormat operation.

If you selected the "AutoFormat now" option button, Word simply displays the formatted version of the document. If you selected the "AutoFormat and review each change" option button, Word displays the formatted version of the document with the AutoFormat dialog window shown in Figure 4–22 in front of it.

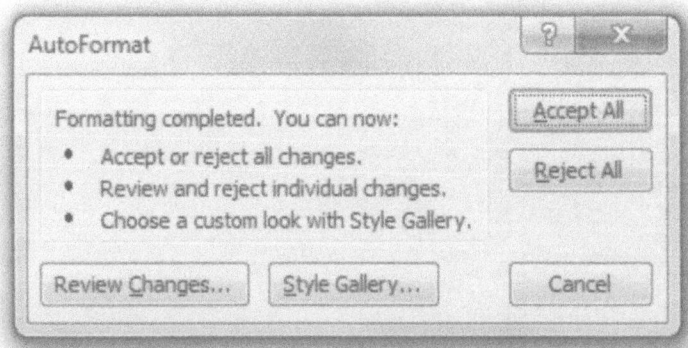

Figure 4–22. *From this AutoFormat dialog window, you can quickly accept or reject all the changes, review the changes, or use the Style Gallery to apply a different style.*

If the document looks okay, click the Accept All button to accept all the changes and close the dialog window. Conversely, if you want to get rid of the changes, click the Reject All button to reject the changes; again, Word closes the dialog window.

To review the changes that Word has made, click the Review Changes button. Word displays the Review AutoFormat Changes dialog window (see Figure 4–23). Click the → Find button to find the next change or the ← Find button to find the previous change. You can then click the Reject button if you want to reject the change; click the Undo button if you need to reverse a rejection.

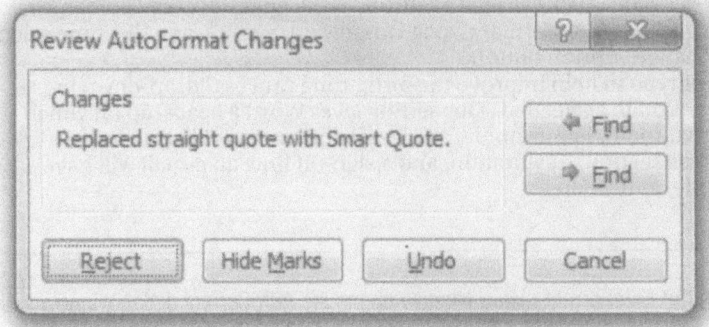

Figure 4–23. *Use the Review AutoFormat Changes dialog window to go through the changes Word has made, rejecting any you don't want.*

When you've finished reviewing the changes, click the Cancel button to close the Review AutoFormat Changes dialog window. You can then save the document, either under its current name, or under a new name by using the File ➤ Save As command.

Summary

In this chapter, you've learned how to reuse content both on a grand scale by using templates and on a smaller scale by using Word's other specialized reuse features, such as Quick Parts and AutoCorrect.

Along the way, you've learned how to create documents from templates, how to create templates of your own, and how to create your own building blocks for assembling documents quickly. You also know how to tone down the worst excesses of the AutoFormat As You Type feature and how to quickly format a text document by using the AutoFormat feature.

In the next chapter, I'll show you how to make your documents display information effectively. Turn the page when you're ready to start.

■ ■ ■

CHAPTER 5

Making Your Documents Display Information Effectively

In this chapter, I'll teach you how to make your documents display information effectively.

We'll start by creating bulleted lists, numbered list, and multilevel lists. As you'll see, you can create lists in several different ways—or you can even have Word create them for you automatically as you type.

After that, you'll learn how to create tables to lay out information clearly. Word's tables give you great flexibility and control, and you can even hide the table's borders so that the information appears not to be in a table. Better yet, Word gives you easy ways to format your tables and to sort the information in them.

Finally, I'll show you how to design your documents by using Word's themes. Themes let you quickly apply a whole different look to a document in moments. You can also dig deeper and change just the colors, the fonts, or the graphical effects the document uses.

Creating Bulleted, Numbered, and Multilevel Lists

To present information clearly, it's often helpful to create lists. Word makes it easy to create bulleted lists for presenting non-sequential information, numbered lists for presenting sequential information, and multilevel lists that feature two or more levels of bullets, numbering, or both.

Understanding How Word Creates Bulleted and Numbered Lists

When you create bulleted, numbered, or multilevel lists, Word applies the bullets or numbering as part of the paragraph formatting rather than as a bullet character or an actual number in the text. This means that Word can automatically apply the formatting to the next paragraph in the list and can automatically keep the sequence of numbers.

■ **Note** If you want, you can create bulleted and numbered lists by inserting actual bullet characters or numbers in your documents. Normally, it's best not to do this for documents you'll handle in Word, but you may want to use actual characters for documents you plan to export as plain text. When you create bulleted lists or numbered lists manually, you will need to turn off the Automatic bulleted lists feature and the Automatic numbered lists feature on the AutoFormat As You Type tab of the AutoCorrect dialog window (see Chapter 4 for details)—otherwise, Word automatically applies formatted bullets and numbers for you.

Creating Bulleted Lists

In Word, you can create bulleted lists in several different ways, from using AutoFormat to using styles. This section shows you the different ways and explains their advantages and disadvantages.

Creating Bulleted Lists by Using AutoFormat

If you leave Word with its default AutoFormat As You Type settings, you can quickly create a bulleted list by typing a bullet-like character and a space or tab at the beginning of a paragraph. For example:

- Type * or o and a space or tab to create a solid round bullet.
- Type > and a space or tab to create a triangular-arrow bullet.
- Type - and a space or tab to create a hyphen bullet.

You can then type the rest of the paragraph. When you press the Enter key to start the next paragraph, Word automatically continues the bulleting to the new paragraph.

To end a bulleted list that AutoFormat has started, press the Enter key twice in succession.

■ **Note** Creating a bulleted list by using AutoFormat can be convenient for quick work, but it leaves the paragraph using the same style as before—Word simply applies bulleted list formatting to the paragraph. To handle bulleted lists consistently, it's better to create bulleted lists by using a style, as discussed in the section "Creating Bulleted Lists by Applying a Style," later in this chapter.

Creating Bulleted Lists by Applying Bullet Formatting

If you choose not to use AutoFormat to create bulleted lists, or when you need to apply bullets to existing paragraphs, you can use the Bullets command in the Paragraph group on the Home tab of the ribbon. Select the text, and then choose either Home ➤ Paragraph ➤ Bullets (clicking the Bullets button itself) to apply a default solid round bullet or Home ➤ Paragraph ➤ Bullets (clicking the drop-down button) and then click the bullet type on the Bullets gallery (see Figure 5–1).

The Bullet Library section of the Bullets gallery shows all the predefined bullets available for the document. The Document Bullets section shows the bullets the document is already using (to help you avoid choosing a similar but different bullet by mistake).

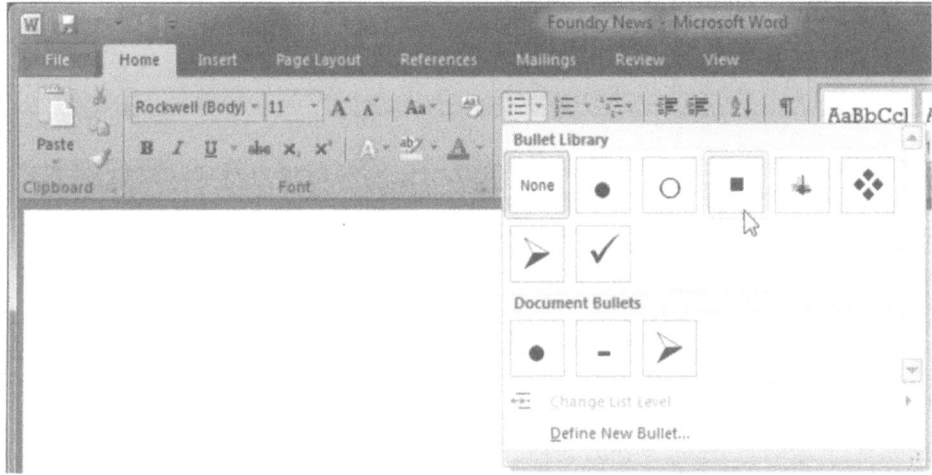

Figure 5–1. To choose which type of bullet to apply, open the Bullets gallery, and then pick from the Bullet Library list or the Document Bullets list. The Document Bullets list shows the bullets you've already used in this document.

■ **Note** Applying bullets from the Bullets gallery is easy, but, for consistency, it's better to create bulleted lists by using a style, as discussed in the following section.

Creating Bulleted Lists by Applying a Style

The best way to create a bulleted list is by applying a style that includes bullets as part of the paragraph formatting. When you do this, you create a bulleted list that you can manipulate through the style rather than just through direct formatting. For example, if you need to change the look of all of a document's bulleted lists, you can modify the style, and Word will apply the change to each of the bulleted lists automatically.

Most Word templates, including the Normal template used for blank documents, include several styles of bulleted list. If any of these styles suits you, simply use it as is. If not, you can customize one of the existing styles or create a new style from scratch.

To apply a style, click in the paragraph (or select multiple paragraphs), and then use one of the methods explained in Chapter 3:

- **Quick Style gallery:** If the style appears in the Quick Style gallery on the Home tab of the ribbon, apply it from there.

- **Apply Styles pane**: Choose Home ➤ Styles ➤ More ➤ Apply Styles to display the Apply Styles pane. You can then open the Style Name drop-down list and click the style you want.

- **Styles pane**: Choose Home ➤ Styles ➤ Styles (clicking the little button in the lower-right corner of the Styles group) or press Ctrl+Alt+Shift+S to display the Styles pane. You can then click the style in the list.

■ **Note** In many templates, Word hides the list styles until you tell it to display them. To do so, choose Home ➤ Styles ➤ Styles (clicking the little button in the lower-right corner of the Styles group) to display the Styles pane, and click the Options link at the bottom to display the Style Pane Options dialog window. In the "Select styles to show" drop-down list, choose All styles, and then click the OK button.

Customizing the Bullet Used on a List

If none of the bullets in the Bullets gallery is suitable, click the Define New Bullet item at the bottom of the gallery to display the Define New Bullet dialog window (see Figure 5–2).

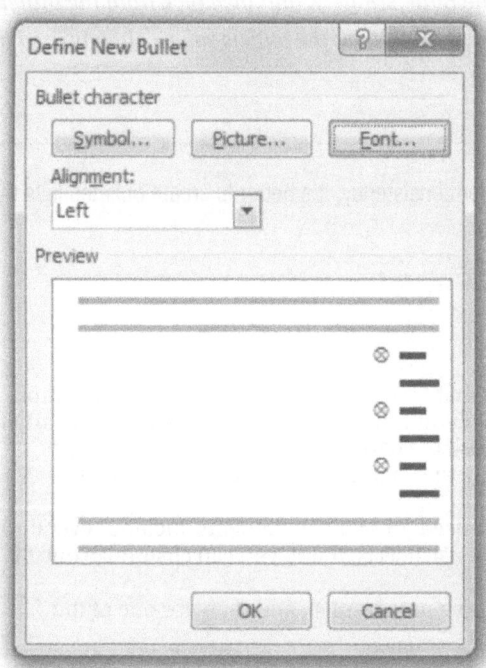

Figure 5–2. Use the Define New Bullet dialog window when you want to create a custom bullet for your document.

From here, you can create a new bullet based on a symbol or a picture. Here are the details:

- **Symbol:** Click the Symbol button to open the Symbol dialog window. Navigate to the symbol you want, changing font in the Font drop-down list if necessary. Click the bullet character, and then click the OK button. If you want to change the font or font formatting used for the symbol, click the Font button to display the Font dialog window, choose the formatting you want, and then click the OK button. For example, you may want to increase the symbol's size or change its color.

- **Picture:** Click the Picture button to display the Picture Bullet dialog window (see Figure 5–3). Make sure the "Include content from Office.com" check box is selected if you want to search for bullet pictures on Microsoft's Office.com site as well (usually a good idea). Then either browse the bullets that the dialog window displays automatically, or type a search term (for example, **nature**) in the Search text box, and press the Enter key or click the Go button. Select the bullet you want, and then click the OK button.

■ **Note** If you have a picture you want to use as a bullet, click the Import button in the Picture Bullet dialog window, select the picture in the Add Clips to Organizer dialog window that opens, and then click the Add button. The bullet then appears in the Picture Bullet dialog window, already selected so that you can click the OK button and start using it. Word automatically shrinks the image for you, so you'll want to start with a picture that has a subject distinct enough to be clear when reduced to bullet size.

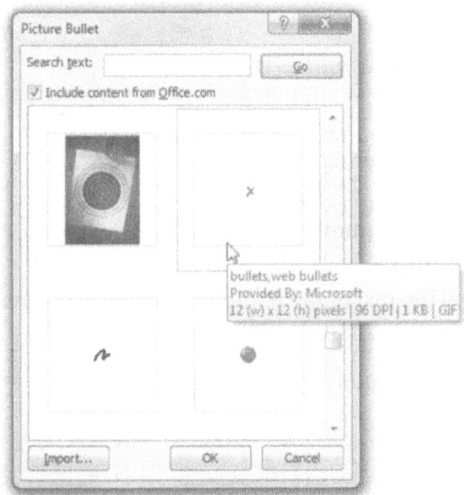

Figure 5–3. In the Picture Bullet dialog window, you can select from a wide variety of graphical bullets. Hold the mouse pointer over a bullet to display a ScreenTip of information about it.

Removing Bullets from a Paragraph

You can remove bullets from a paragraph in either of two ways:

- **Apply a style that doesn't include bullets**. If you're formatting with styles, this is the best way of removing bullets.

- **Remove the bullets from the paragraph**. To remove the bullets but leave the paragraph with the same style, click in the paragraph (or select multiple paragraphs), and then choose Home ➤ Paragraph ➤ Bullets ➤ None.

Creating Numbered Lists

As with bulleted lists, Word lets you create numbered lists in several different ways, including with AutoFormat, by applying direct formatting, and by using styles. This section shows you each approach and tries to steer you toward using styles, which is the best approach for creating consistently formatted documents.

Creating Numbered Lists by Using AutoFormat

If you leave Word's default AutoFormat As You Type settings unchanged, you can quickly create a numbered list by typing a number or numbering letter and suitable punctuation at the beginning of a paragraph—for example:

- Type **1.** and a space or tab to start creating a list numbered with **1., 2., 3.**, and so on.

- Type **1)** and a space or tab to start creating a list numbered with **1), 2), 3)**, and so on.

- Type **a.** and a space or tab to start creating a list numbered with **a., b., c.**, and so on. Or type **A.** and a space or tab to start a list numbered with uppercase letters.

- Type **A)** and a space or tab to start creating a list numbered with **A), B), C)**, and so on. Or type **a)** and a space or tab to start lowercase numbering.

- Type **i.** and a space or tab to start creating a list with lowercase Roman numbering—**i., ii., iii**. Or type **I.** to use uppercase Roman numbering, or use a closing parenthesis instead of the period.

Once you've started the type of numbering you want, type the rest of the paragraph. When you press the Enter key to start the next paragraph, Word automatically continues the numbering with the next number.

To end a numbered list that AutoFormat has started, press the Enter key twice in immediate succession.

Note Creating a numbered list by using AutoFormat As You Type is easy but leaves the paragraph using the same style as before—Word simply applies numbered list formatting to the paragraph. To handle numbered lists consistently, it's better to create them by applying a numbered list style. See the section "Creating Numbered Lists by Applying a Style," later in this chapter, for details.

Creating Numbered Lists by Applying Number Formatting

You can also create numbered lists by applying number formatting as direct formatting. When you do this, the paragraph keeps its existing style rather than changing to a style that has the numbered list formatting built in.

To apply numbering, select the text, and then choose either Home ➤ Paragraph ➤ Numbering (clicking the Numbering button itself) to apply default numbering, or Home ➤ Paragraph ➤ Numbering (clicking the drop-down button) and then click the desired numbering type on the Numbering gallery (see Figure 5–4).

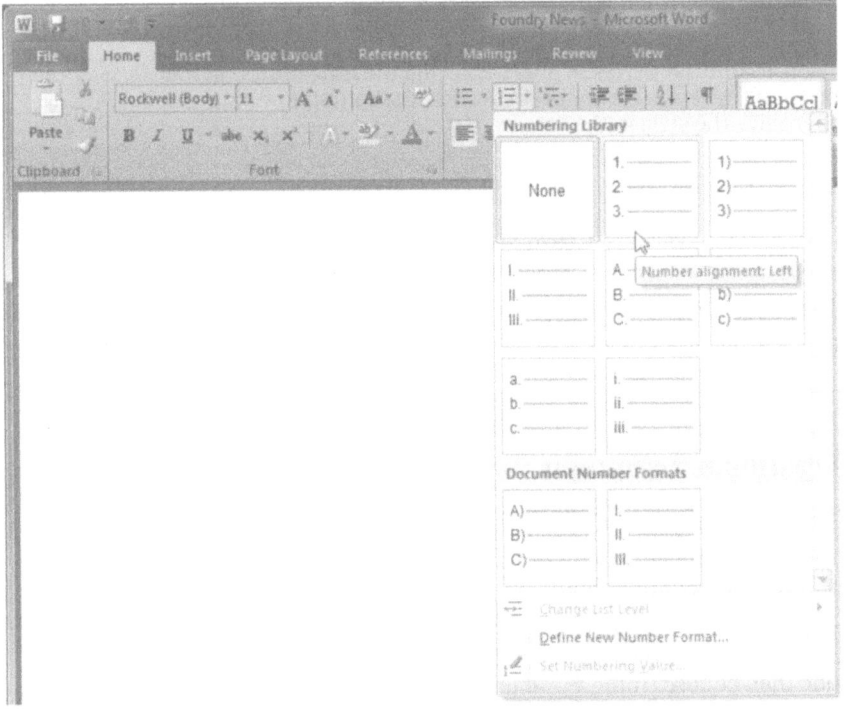

Figure 5–4. When creating a numbered list, you can choose the format from the Numbering gallery. The Document Number Formats area shows the number formats the document already uses.

Note The Numbering Library section of the Numbering gallery shows all the predefined numbering types available for the document. The Document Number Formats section shows the number formats you've used so far in this document.

Creating Numbered Lists by Applying a Style

The most efficient way to create a numbered list is by applying a style that includes the numbering as part of the paragraph formatting. You can then reformat all the numbered list paragraphs (if necessary) by changing the list style—for example, switching to a different numbering format.

Most Word templates, including the Normal template used for blank documents, include several styles of numbered list, usually named List Number, List Number 2, and so on. You can use these styles if they're suitable or modify them if they're not. You can also create numbered list styles of your own.

To apply a style to a single paragraph, click anywhere in it. To apply a style to multiple paragraphs, select all of them (or parts of all of them). Then apply the style in one of these ways:

- **Quick Style gallery**: If the style appears in the Quick Style gallery on the Home tab of the ribbon, apply it from there.

- **Apply Styles pane**: Choose Home ➤ Styles ➤ More ➤ Apply Styles to display the Apply Styles pane. You can then select the style in the Style Name drop-down list.

- **Styles pane**: Choose Home ➤ Styles ➤ Styles (clicking the little button in the lower-right corner of the Styles group) or press Ctrl+Alt+Shift+S to display the Styles pane. Then click the style in the list.

Note If the List Number styles don't appear in the Apply Styles pane or the Styles pane, Word may be hiding them. To reveal the styles, choose Home ➤ Styles ➤ Styles. In the Styles pane, click the Options link at the bottom to display the Style Pane Options dialog window. In the "Select styles to show" drop-down list, choose All styles, and then click the OK button.

Removing Numbering from a Paragraph

You can remove numbering from a paragraph in either of two ways:

- **Apply a style that doesn't include numbering**. If you're formatting with styles, this is the best way of removing numbering.

- **Remove the numbering from the paragraph**. To remove the numbering but leave the paragraph with the same style, click in the paragraph (or select multiple paragraphs), and then choose Home ➤ Paragraph ➤ Numbering ➤ None.

Restarting or Changing the Numbering on a Numbered List

In theory, keeping your list numbering straight is easy enough. When you finish creating a list, and apply a style that doesn't use numbering, Word stops numbering the paragraphs. Then, when you start a new numbered list, Word starts the numbering from 1.

Tip If you need to restart a numbered list after several intervening paragraphs without numbering, type the next number in the sequence, a period, and a tab.

But sometimes you may need to move material from one list to another. Other times, you may need to stop a list temporarily, so that you can have a few non-list paragraphs, and then resume the numbering on the list.

To change the numbering, right-click the list paragraph, and then make the appropriate choice from the context menu:

- **Continue the numbering from the previous list**. Click the Continue Numbering item.

- **Restart the numbering at 1**. Click the "Restart at 1" item.

- **Set a custom value**. Click the Set Numbering Value item to display the Set Numbering Value dialog window (see Figure 5–5). Select the "Start new list" option button, set the starting value in the "Set value to" box, and then click the OK button.

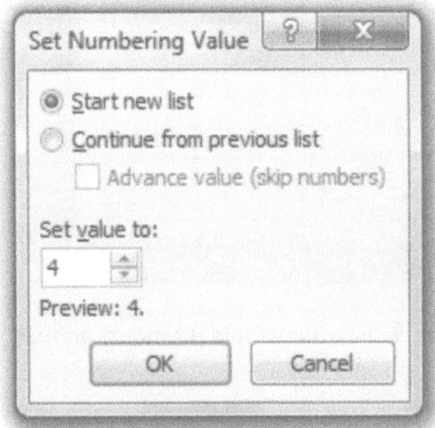

Figure 5–5. Use the Set Numbering Value dialog window to set a custom value for a numbered paragraph.

Creating Multilevel Lists

As you've seen in the previous sections, straightforward bulleted and numbered lists are easy enough to create. But what you'll often need to create is multilevel lists—ones that use both numbers and bullets, or that use two or more levels of numbers or of bullets.

To create a multilevel list, select the existing paragraphs you will turn into a list or (if you're just starting the list) click in the paragraph where you want to start it. Then choose Home ➤ Paragraph ➤ Multilevel List to open the Multilevel List gallery (see Figure 5–6). Hold the mouse pointer over a multilevel list template if you want to see the details of its levels, and then click the list type you want.

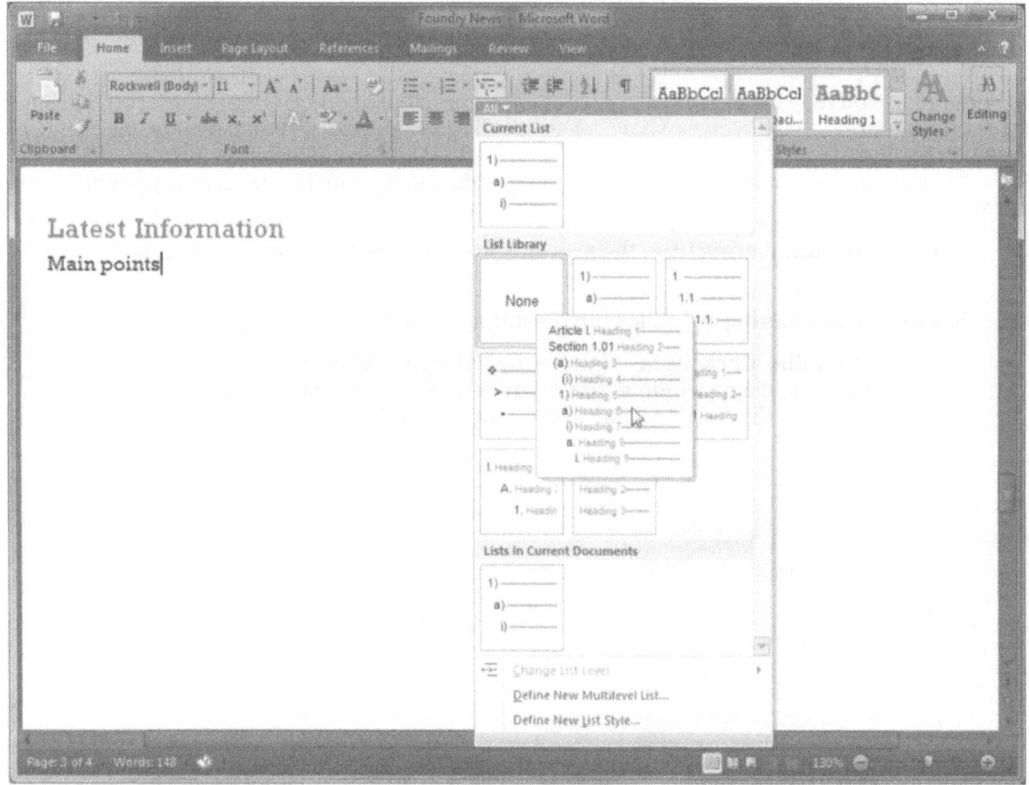

Figure 5–6. *Choose the multilevel list you want from the Multilevel List gallery. Hold the mouse pointer over a list type to see a preview of the list's contents.*

You can then type the rest of the list. To move the current paragraph to the next level down the list, place the insertion point at the beginning of the paragraph, and then press the Tab key. To move the current paragraph to the next level up the list, place the insertion point at the beginning of the paragraph, and then press Shift+Tab.

Note To remove multilevel list formatting from text, select the text, and then choose Home ➤ Paragraph ➤ Multilevel List ➤ None.

Laying Out Information with Tables

When you need to lay out data in a regular grid, create a table. A table is a structure consisting of cells, rectangular areas formed by the intersection of rows and columns. Each table can contain one or more rows and one or more columns.

You can create either regular tables that have the same number of cells in each row or column, or irregular tables that have different numbers of cells in the rows or columns. You can choose whether to display the borders for a table; by hiding the borders, you can use a table to create a complex layout in which the underlying table isn't apparent.

Understanding How You Create Tables

You can create tables in four ways:

- **Insert a Quick Table**. Word includes various pre-built tables that you can quickly insert and then adapt to your needs. Using a Quick Table can save you plenty of layout and formatting, so it's worth looking through the selection of Quick Tables before building a custom table.

- **Insert a custom table**. Use this method when creating a table that has a regular layout—for example, a table based on the same number of cells in each row.

- **Draw a custom table**. When you need to create an irregular table or a complex layout, you can draw the table instead of inserting it.

- **Convert existing text to a table**. If the document already contains the text you want to create the table from, you can convert the text into a table, as discussed next.

In the following sections, I'll show you how to create tables in these ways. I'll also show you how to insert one table inside another table.

Inserting a Quick Table

When you need to add a table swiftly to a document, look first to Word's selection of Quick Tables—pre-built tables that you can change as needed.

To insert a Quick Table, position the insertion point where you want the table to appear. Then choose Insert ➤ Tables ➤ Table ➤ Quick Tables to display the Quick Tables gallery, and click the table you want (see Figure 5–7).

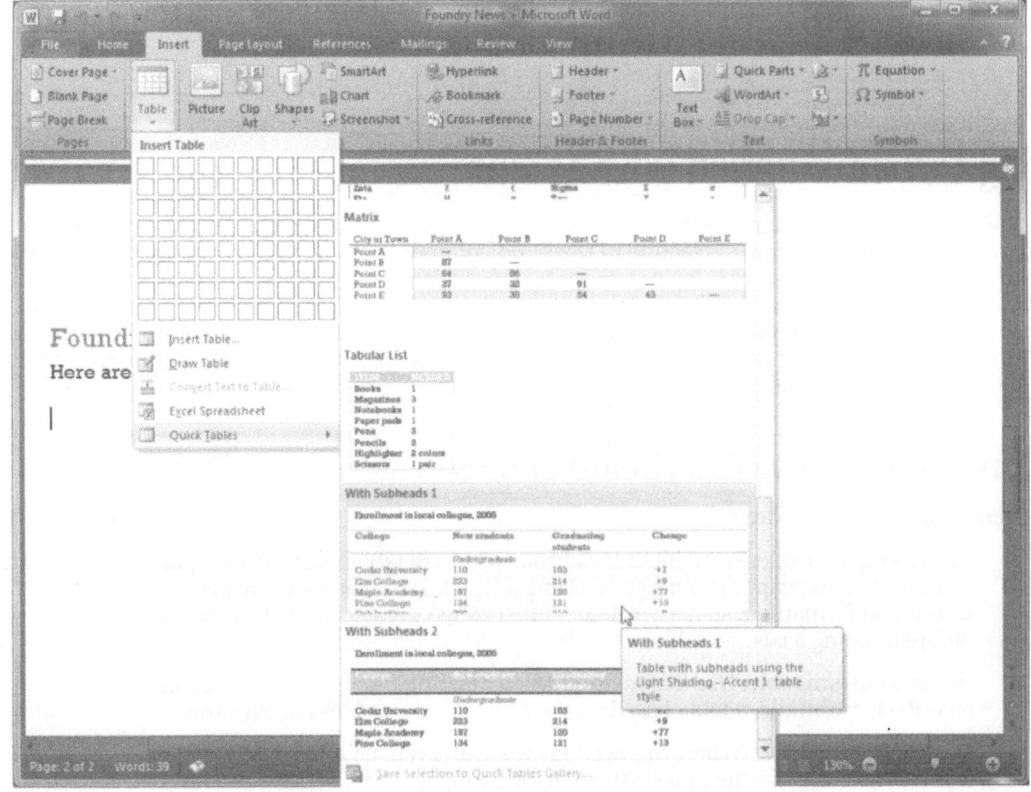

Figure 5–7. You can often save time and effort by inserting a pre-built Quick Table and then customizing it.

Word inserts the table (see Figure 5–8). You can then replace the sample caption and sample data with your own caption and data.

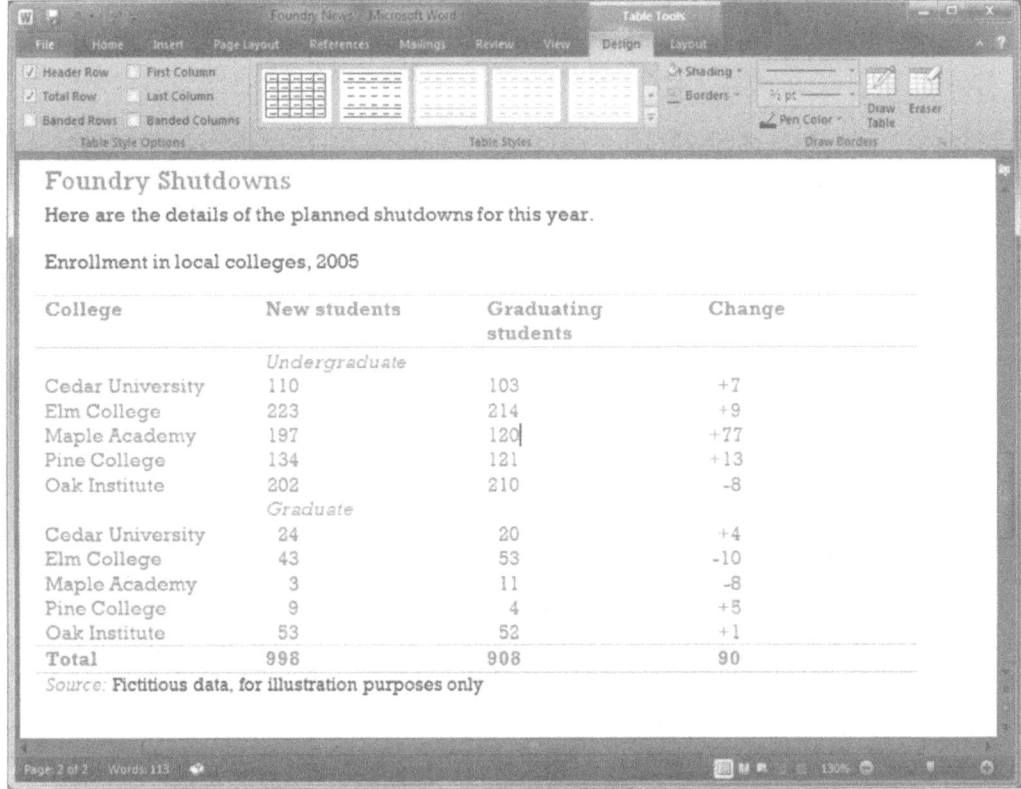

Figure 5–8. *After inserting a Quick Table, replace the sample caption and sample data with your own caption and data.*

Inserting a Custom Table

When none of the Quick Tables will do, and you need a regular table, insert it and specify the number of rows and columns you want.

To insert a table, follow these steps:

1. Position the insertion point where you want the table to appear.

2. Choose Insert ➤ Table ➤ Table to open the Table gallery (see Figure 5–9).

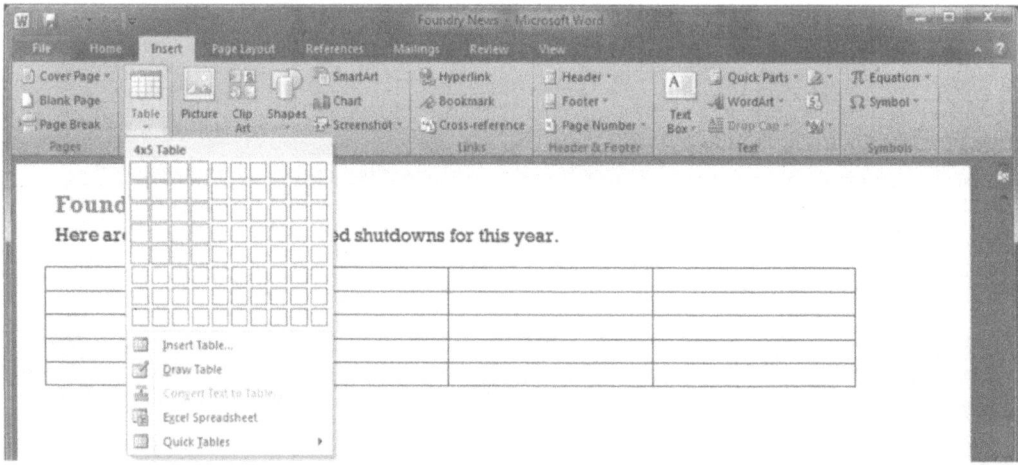

Figure 5–9. Move the mouse pointer over the grid in the top part of the Table gallery to display a preview of the table, then click the square for the table you want to insert.

3. Move the mouse pointer over the grid in the Insert Table area. Word shows a preview of the type of table—for example, five rows of four columns.

4. When the preview shows the number of rows and columns you want, click the square the mouse pointer is over. Word inserts the table and adds the Table Tools section to the ribbon (see Figure 5–10).

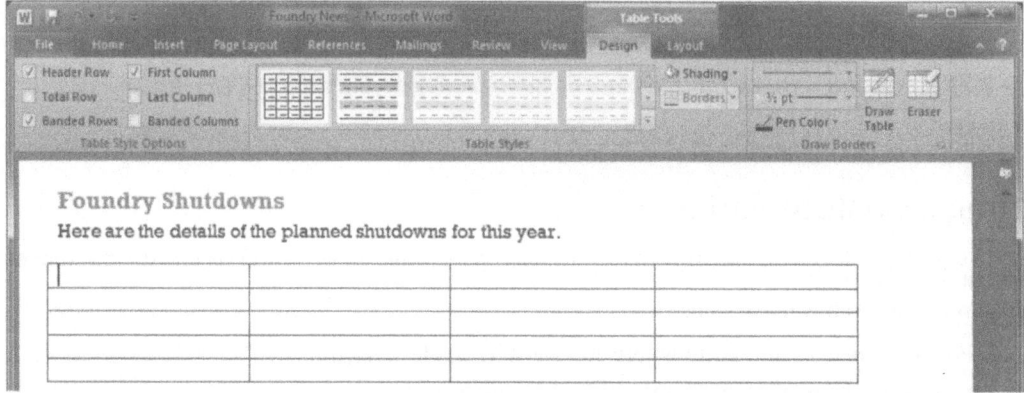

Figure 5–10. Word inserts the table in the document and displays the Table Tools section of the ribbon.

Instead of using the grid on the Table gallery to choose the size of table, you can use the Insert Table dialog window. This method is useful when you need to change the way Word fits the table's columns to its contents or to the window. Follow these steps:

1. Position the insertion point where you want the table to appear.

2. Choose Insert ➤ Table ➤ Table ➤ Insert Table to display the Insert Table dialog window (see Figure 5–11).

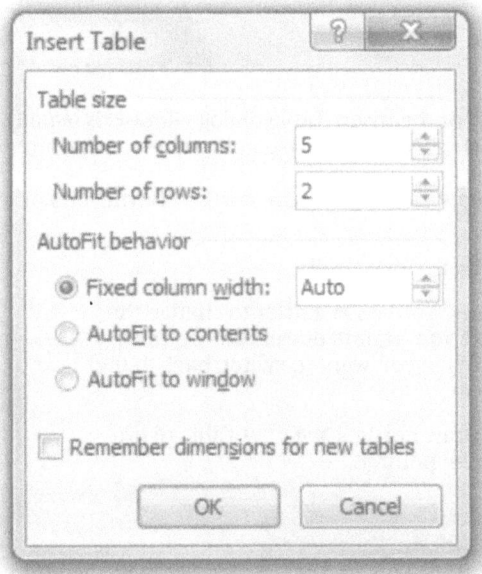

Figure 5–11. *The Insert Table dialog window lets you set the AutoFit behavior for the table. You can select the "Remember dimensions for new tables" check box to apply the same dimensions to future tables you create.*

3. Specify the number of columns in the "Number of columns" box.

4. Specify the number of rows in the "Number of rows" box.

5. In the AutoFit behavior area, choose how you want Word to automatically fit the table:

   - **Fixed column width**: Select this option button if you want each column to have a fixed width. Choose the Auto item in the "Fixed column width" box to have Word allocate column width automatically. Otherwise, set the measurement you want Word to apply to each column.

   - **AutoFit to contents**: Select this option button to make Word automatically adjust each column's width to fit its contents. This is often a good choice.

   - **AutoFit to window**: Select this option button to make Word automatically adjust each column's width to suit the document window. This option is useful for tables you expect people to view on-screen at different window widths.

6. Select the "Remember dimensions for new tables" check box if you want Word to store these settings for future use.

7. Click the OK button to close the Insert Table dialog window. Word inserts the table you specified.

You can now add contents to the table as discussed later in this chapter.

Drawing a Custom Table

Inserting a table using either the grid on the Tables gallery or the Insert Table dialog window is usually the easiest way of creating a regular table, but you may also need to create irregular tables and complex layouts. In this case, you may prefer to draw a table.

To draw a table, choose Insert ➤ Table ➤ Table ➤ Draw Table, and then use the drawing cursor to draw the table layout you want (see Figure 5–12).

- **Draw a cell**. Click with the pen pointer and drag to draw a cell.

- **Erase a line**. Choose Table Tools Design ➤ Draw Borders ➤ Eraser to change the pen pointer to an eraser, and then click the line you want to erase. Choose Table Tools Design ➤ Draw Borders ➤ Draw Table when you want to switch back to the pen for drawing more cells.

- **Stop drawing**. Choose Table Tools Design ➤ Draw Borders ➤ Draw Table to un-press the Draw Table button and turn off the pen pointer.

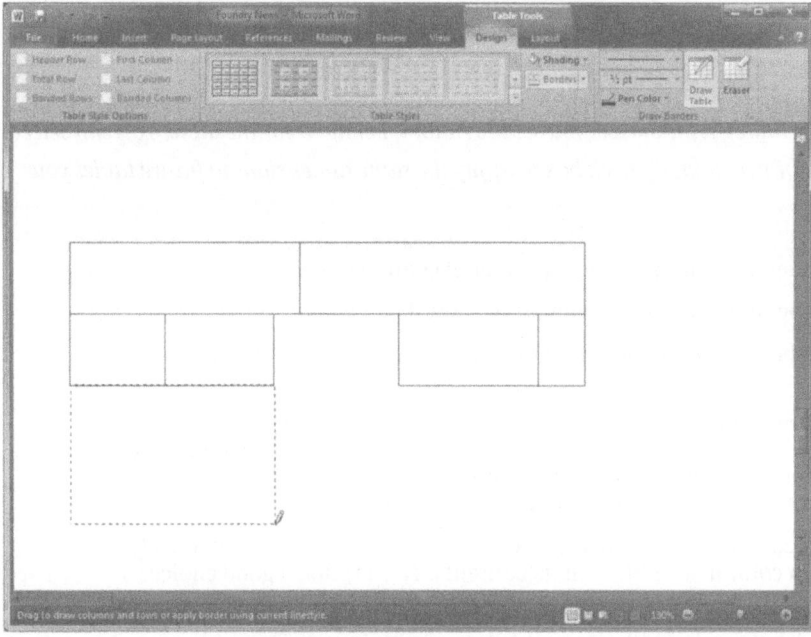

Figure 5–12. When you need an irregular table, give the Draw Table command, and then use the pen pointer to draw the table layout you need.

Merging and Splitting Cells in a Table

To change the layout of a table, you can merge cells together to form a larger cell or split a cell into several smaller cells. Merging is useful when you need to create a single large cell from two or more smaller cells, while splitting lets you create multiple cells within a single existing column.

Merging Multiple Cells into a Single Cell

To merge cells together, select the cells, and then choose Table Tools Layout ➤ Merge ➤ Merge Cells. Word turns the selected cells into a single cell. Any contents of the previous cells appear as separate paragraphs in the merged cell. If you want to make them into a single paragraph, delete the extra paragraph marks between them.

Splitting One or More Cells into Multiple Cells

To split one or more cells into multiple cells, follow these steps:

1. Click in the cell you want to split. If you want to split multiple cells the same way, select each of the cells.

2. Choose Table Tools Layout ➤ Merge ➤ Split Cells to display the Split Cells dialog window (see Figure 5–13).

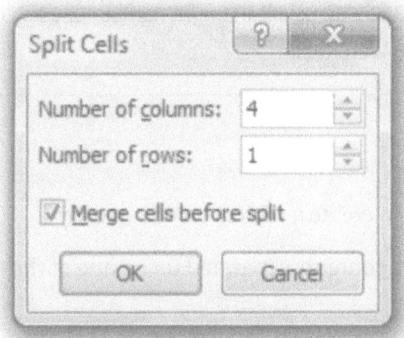

Figure 5–13. Use the Split Cells dialog window to split an existing cell into two or more new cells. If you select multiple cells before opening this dialog window, you can choose whether to merge the cells before splitting them.

3. In the "Number of columns" box, enter the number of columns you want to create within the cell.

4. In the "Number of rows" box, enter the number of rows you want to create, and then click the OK button.

5. If you selected multiple cells in Step 1, select the "Merge cells before split" check box to make Word treat them all as one cell. For example, if you select two cells, select the "Merge cells before split" check box, and specify four columns, you get four columns total. If you select two cells, clear the "Merge cells before split" check box, and specify four columns, you get four columns from each cell, giving eight columns altogether.

6. Click the OK button to close the Split Cells dialog window. Word splits the cells as you specified.

Adding Content to a Table

After inserting a table in a document, you can add content to it by typing or by other means.

To add text by typing, click the cell in which you want to enter it, and then type the text. Press the Tab key to move the insertion point to the next cell, or press Shift+Tab to move the insertion point to the previous cell.

You can also paste text into a table you've created. Simply click in the cell, and then paste the text (for example, choose Home ➤ Clipboard ➤ Paste or press Ctrl+V).

■ **Tip** If you copy text that's laid out with a tab between each separate item, you can paste it into multiple cells at once. Copy the text from the source, select the appropriate number of cells in the table, and then give the Paste command. This also works with cells you've copied from an Excel spreadsheet: select the right number of cells in the table, and you can paste one Excel cell into each selected cell in the Word table.

Converting Existing Text into a Table

If your document already contains the text from which you want to create a table, you can quickly convert it to a table.

First, make sure that the material is laid out regularly, with its contents separated using one of these four items:

- **Tabs:** This is usually the easiest way of separating material, as you can see the different columns that the table will create. Figure 5–14 shows an example of text laid out with tabs.

Coach·Name·Destination→ Departs → **Arrives¶**

Great·Northern → Redding → 4:40·AM → 1:00·PM¶

Western·Roller → Santa·Cruz → 8:30·AM → 11:00·AM¶

Old·Sal → San·Francisco·(Mission·District) → 9:30·AM → 10:30·AM¶

Southern·Stroller → San·Francisco·(Golden·Gate) → 10:00·AM → 11:30·AM¶

Figure 5–14. If you have text laid out with tabs between items, you can quickly convert it to a table. What's important is that there's only one tab between items, not that the items are aligned.

■ **Note** When converting tabbed material into a table, you must make sure of two things. First, check that each item is separated by only one tab, not by two or more tabs—otherwise, you'll get the wrong number of columns. Second, check that the material for each cell is not broken onto multiple lines—otherwise, you'll get the wrong number of rows.

- **Paragraphs**: If each cell's data appears in a separate paragraph, you can quickly convert it to a table. Make sure the data contains no unnecessary blank paragraphs. Word then lets you specify the number of columns you want to create, as you'll see in a moment.

- **Commas**: If you have data separated by commas, such as a comma-separated values export from a spreadsheet, you can use a comma as the separator character for a table.

- **Other character**: If your data is separated consistently by another character (for example, * or |), you can specify that character as the separator character. You need to make sure that this character doesn't appear as part of the regular text, only as the separator character.

When you've made sure the data is laid out regularly, convert it to a table like this:

1. Select the paragraphs of data. Select right from the start up to the paragraph mark at the end of the last paragraph. (If Word is hiding paragraph marks, you'll appear to have selected a chunk of blank space at the end of the last paragraph.)

2. Choose Insert ➤ Table ➤ Table ➤ Convert Text to Table to display the Convert Text to Table dialog window (see Figure 5–15).

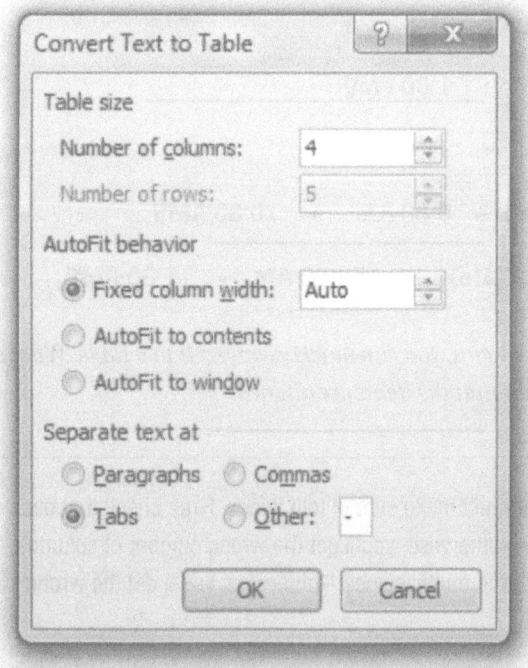

Figure 5–15. *In the Convert Text to Table dialog window, make sure that Word has chosen the right separator character (for example, tabs), and choose the AutoFit behavior you want.*

3. In the "Separate text at" area, make sure that Word has picked the right separator character. If not, select the Paragraphs option button, the Commas option button, the Tabs option button, or the Other option button as appropriate; for the Other option button, type the separator character in the text box.

4. In the Table size area, make sure that the number of columns is right:

    •   If you're using tabs as the separator character, and the number of columns is wrong, one or more of the paragraphs contains an extra tab (or is missing a tab). Click the Cancel button, find and remove the extra or missing tab, and then start the conversion again.

    •   If you're using paragraphs as the separator character, you must tell Word how many paragraphs to use for each row. Enter this number in the "Number of columns" box.

5. In the AutoFit behavior area, choose whether to fit the column widths automatically to their contents:

    •   **Fixed column width:** Select this option button to use a fixed width for each column. You can then choose Auto to have Word allocate the space equally among the columns or type the fixed width you want.

- **AutoFit to Contents**: Select this option button to let Word adjust each column's width to fit its contents. You may need to adjust the widths afterward.

- **AutoFit to Window**: Select this option button to have Word make the table automatically fit the window's width.

6. Click the OK button to close the Convert Text to Table dialog window. Word converts the text to a table. Figure 5–16 shows the sample text converted to a table.

Coach·Name¤	Destination¤	Departs¤	Arrives¤	¤
Great·Northern¤	Redding¤	4:40·AM¤	1:00·PM¤	¤
Western·Roller¤	Santa·Cruz¤	8:30·AM¤	11:00·AM¤	¤
Old·Sal¤	San·Francisco· (Mission·District)¤	9:30·AM¤	10:30·AM¤	¤
Southern·Stroller¤	San·Francisco· (Golden·Gate)¤	10:00·AM¤	11:30·AM¤	¤

Figure 5–16. After converting text to a table, you will often need to change the column widths.

Creating Table Headings

Many tables need one or more rows of headings at the top of the columns. To distinguish the headings, you can apply different formatting, either by simply using boldface or by applying a table style and selecting the Header Row check box in the Table Style Options group on the Table Tools Design tab of the ribbon.

When a table runs from one page to the next, you'll normally want the headers to repeat at the top of the second page. To make Word do this automatically for you, select the row or rows you want to repeat, and then choose Table Tools Layout ➤ Data ➤ Repeat Header Rows.

Nesting One Table Inside Another Table

When you need to create a complex layout, you can nest one table inside another, so that one cell of the outer table contains the whole of the inner table. Figure 5–17 shows an example of a nested table.

To nest a table, click in the cell in which you want to nest the table, and then insert the table as usual.

Department	Coverage		Contact Information
Anthropology	Biological Anthropology	1-8	
	Cultural Anthropology	1-4	
	Linguistic Anthropology	5-12	
	Social Anthropology	1-12	
Biology			
Chemistry			

Figure 5–17. You can nest one table inside another table to create complex layouts.

■ **Tip** You can nest tables several levels deep if necessary, but the further you nest tables, the more confusing working with them tends to become. If you're considering several levels of nesting, see if merging and splitting cells could give you a similar result with less trouble.

Converting a Table to Text

Word also lets you convert a table back to text. This move is useful when you've received material in table form that you need to convert to a different layout.

To convert a table to text, follow these steps:

1. Click anywhere in the table. You don't need to select the table.

2. Choose Table Tools Layout ➤ Data ➤ Convert to Text to display the Convert Table to Text dialog window (see Figure 5–18).

Figure 5–18. When converting a table back to text, you can separate the cells with paragraph marks, tabs, commas, or another character of your choice.

3. In the "Separate text with" area, choose the character with which to separate the cell contents. Select the Paragraph marks option button, the Tabs option button, the Commas option button, or the Other option button (and type the character in the text box).

4. Select the "Convert nested tables" check box if you want to convert nested tables as well. This check box is available only when you're using paragraphs as the separator character.

Note Word converts a nested table to paragraphs of text like the rest of the table. The nested table's paragraphs appear in their cell order between the paragraphs for the table cells that surround them.

5. Click the OK button to close the Convert Table to Text dialog window and perform the conversion.

Formatting a Table

To make a table look the way you want, you format it. You can apply formatting either quickly by using a table style or manually by applying only the formatting the table needs.

To apply a table style, click anywhere in the table, and then choose Table Tools Design ➤ Table Styles ➤ Quick Styles, choosing the style from the Quick Styles gallery (see Figure 5–19).

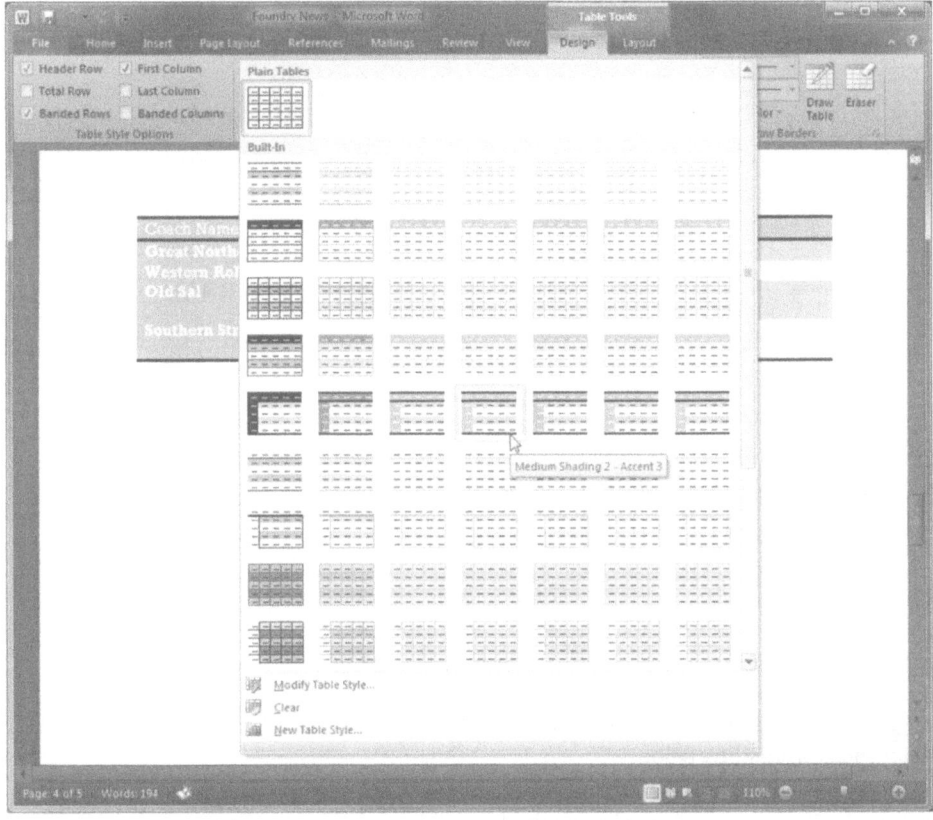

Figure 5–19. You can quickly format a table by applying a table style from the Table Styles gallery on the Design tab of the ribbon.

After applying a table style, you can customize it by selecting or clearing the check boxes in the Table Style Options group on the Design tab of the ribbon. For example, select the Header Row check box to apply different formatting to the table's first row so that it looks like a header, or select the first Column check box to apply different formatting to the first column if it contains headings.

If you prefer not to use a table style, you can format a table manually. These are the main techniques you'll need:

- **Borders**: Click the table, choose Table Tools Design ➤ Table Styles ➤ Borders, and then click the border style you want. The Borders gallery shows a highlight on each item that's currently applied, as you can see in Figure 5–20.

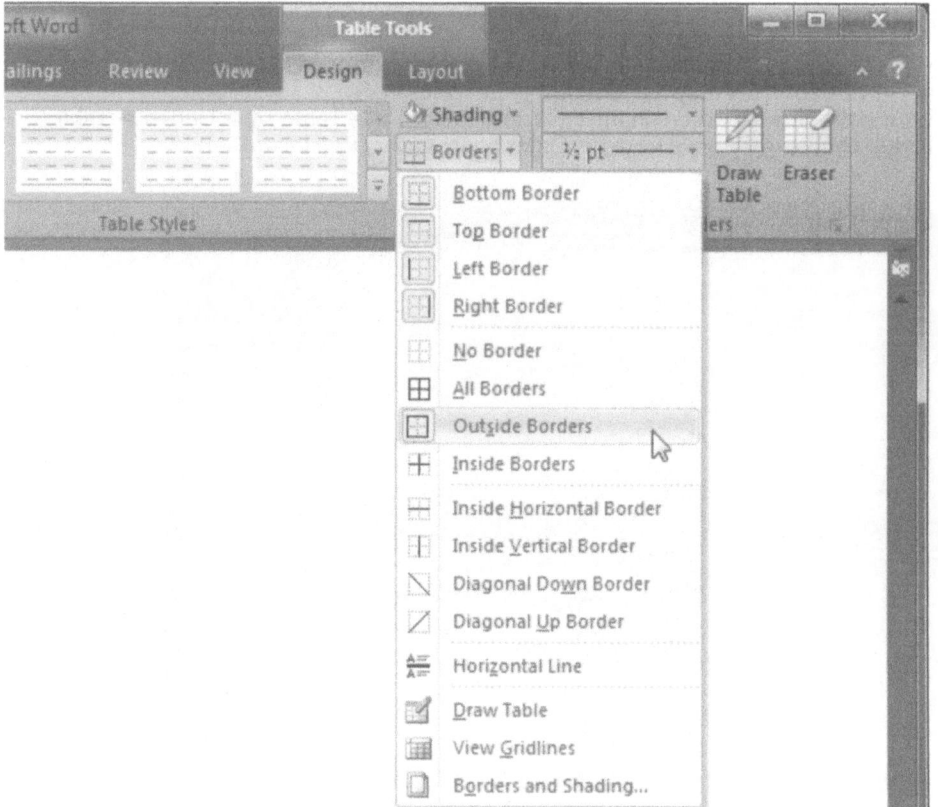

Figure 5–20. Use the Borders gallery to apply exactly the border formatting your table needs.

- **Shading**: Click the table, choose Table Tools Design ➤ Table Styles ➤ Shading, and then click the shading color.

- **Font formatting**: Select the cell or cells you want to format, and then use the controls in the Font group of the Home tab of the ribbon as for other text.

Sorting a Table

After you've added your data to a table, you can sort it by one, two, or three columns to get the rows into the right order. For example, if you create a table of names and addresses, you may want to sort them by state, by city, and then by name.

To sort a table, follow these steps:

1. Click in the table to select it.

2. Choose Table Tools Layout ➤ Data ➤ Sort to display the Sort dialog window (shown in Figure 5–21 with settings chosen).

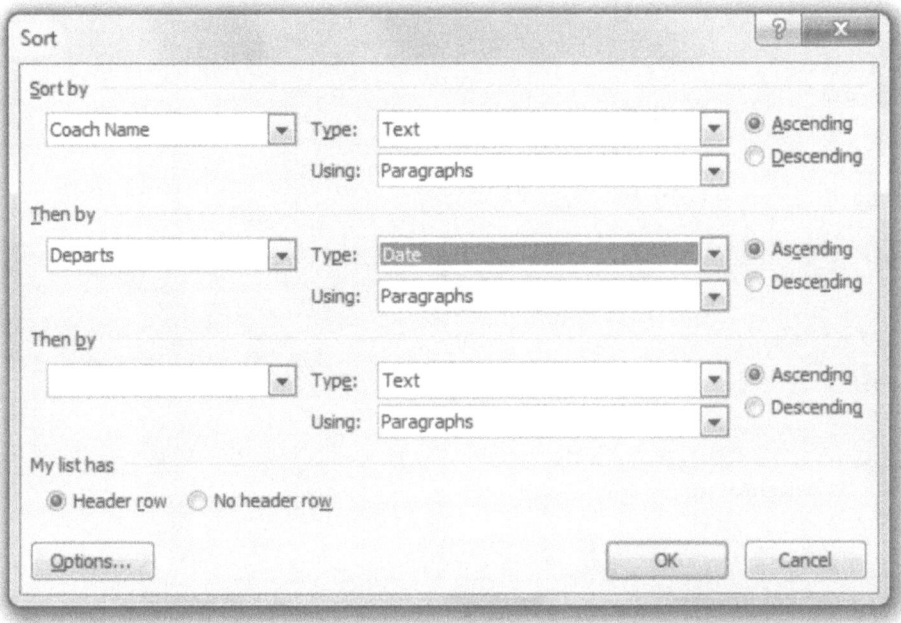

Figure 5–21. Use the Sort dialog window to sort a table by one, two, or three columns.

3. In the "Sort by" area, set up the first sort like this:

   - Choose the appropriate column heading in the left drop-down list. If the table doesn't have column headings, the drop-down list shows Column 1, Column 2, and so on.

   - In the Type drop-down list, choose the type of sort. Choose Text to sort normally. Choose Number to sort by numbers. Choose Date to sort by dates and times.

   - In the Using drop-down list, make sure Paragraphs is selected.

   - On the right side, select the Ascending option button if you want an ascending sort (A to Z, low numbers to high, early dates and times to later ones). Select the Descending option button if you want a reverse sort.

4. In the upper "Then by" area, set up the second sort using the same techniques.

5. In the lower "Then by" area, set up the third sort using the same techniques.

6. In the "My list has" area, make sure the "Header row" option button is selected if your table has a header row. If not, select the "No header row" option button.

7. If you need to make the sort case-sensitive, so that lowercase letters appear before their uppercase equivalents, click the Options button to display the Sort Options dialog window (see Figure 5–22). Select the "Case sensitive" check box, and then click the OK button to close the dialog window.

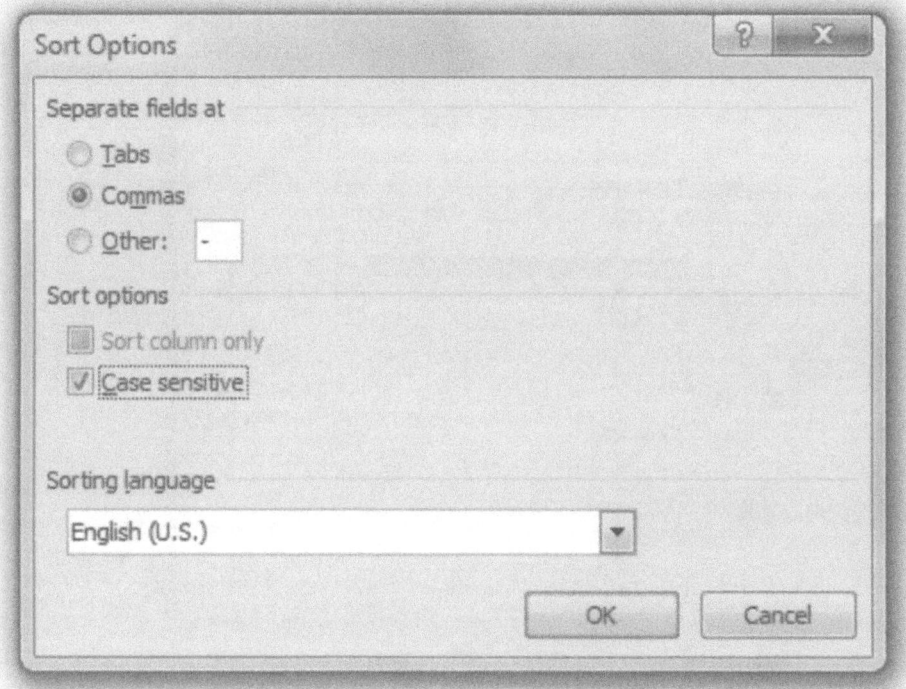

Figure 5–22. To make the sort case-sensitive, select the "Case sensitive" check box in the Sort Options dialog window.

8. Click the OK button to close the Sort dialog window. Word sorts the table as you specified.

Designing Your Documents with Themes

You can change a document's overall look by applying a different theme to it. A *theme* is an overall look for a document, including a set of colors, a set of fonts, and a set of visual effects for graphical objects such as arrows.

When you create a document, Word automatically applies the theme assigned to its template. For example, when you create a blank document, Word applies the Office theme, which is assigned by default to the Normal template (on which Word bases blank documents).

Changing the Theme Applied to a Document

To change the document's overall look, you can change its theme. To change the theme, choose Page Layout ➤ Themes ➤ Themes, and then click the theme on the Themes gallery (see Figure 5–23).

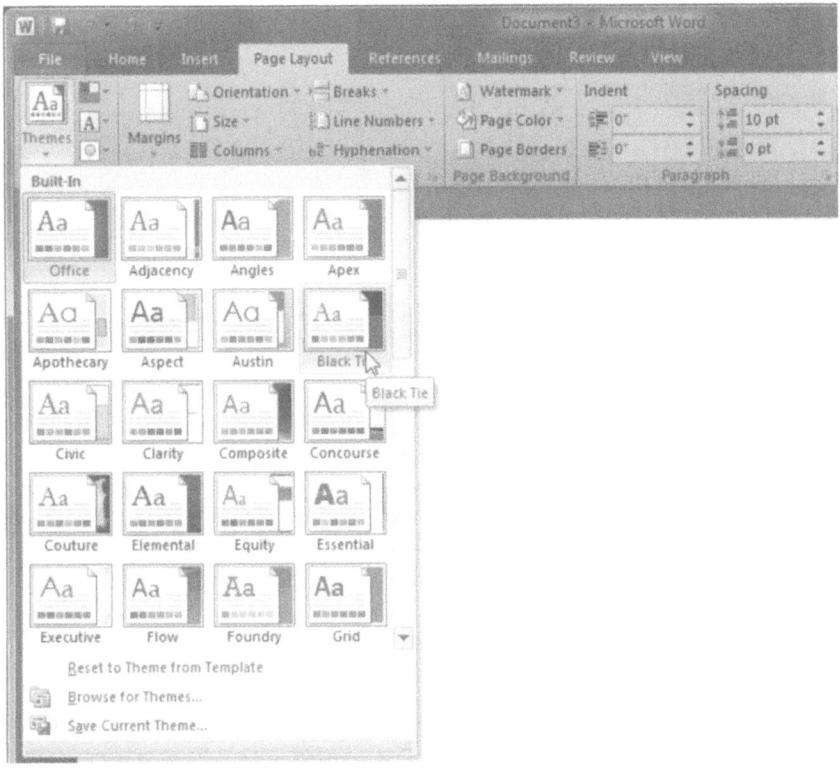

Figure 5–23. *You can change a document's overall look by applying a different theme to it from the Themes gallery on the Page Layout tab of the ribbon.*

When you've applied the theme you want, you can change the colors, fonts, or effects, as described in the following sections.

■ **Note** To go back to the original theme used for the document, choose Page Layout ➤ Themes ➤ Themes ➤ Reset to Theme from Template.

Changing the Colors Used for the Document

To change the colors used in the document, choose Page Layout ➤ Themes ➤ Colors, and then click the color set you want to use on the Colors gallery (see Figure 5–24).

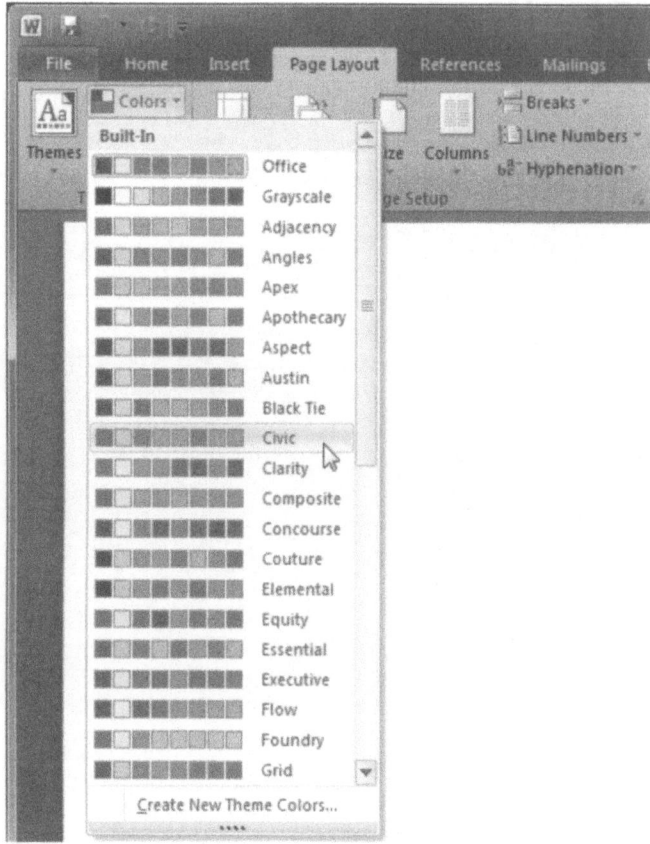

Figure 5–24. You can use the Colors gallery on the Page Layout tab of the ribbon to apply a different set of colors to the document without changing the rest of the theme.

Changing the Fonts Used for the Document

You can change the fonts used in the document by choosing Page Layout ➤ Themes ➤ Fonts, and then click the fonts set on the Fonts panel (see Figure 5–25).

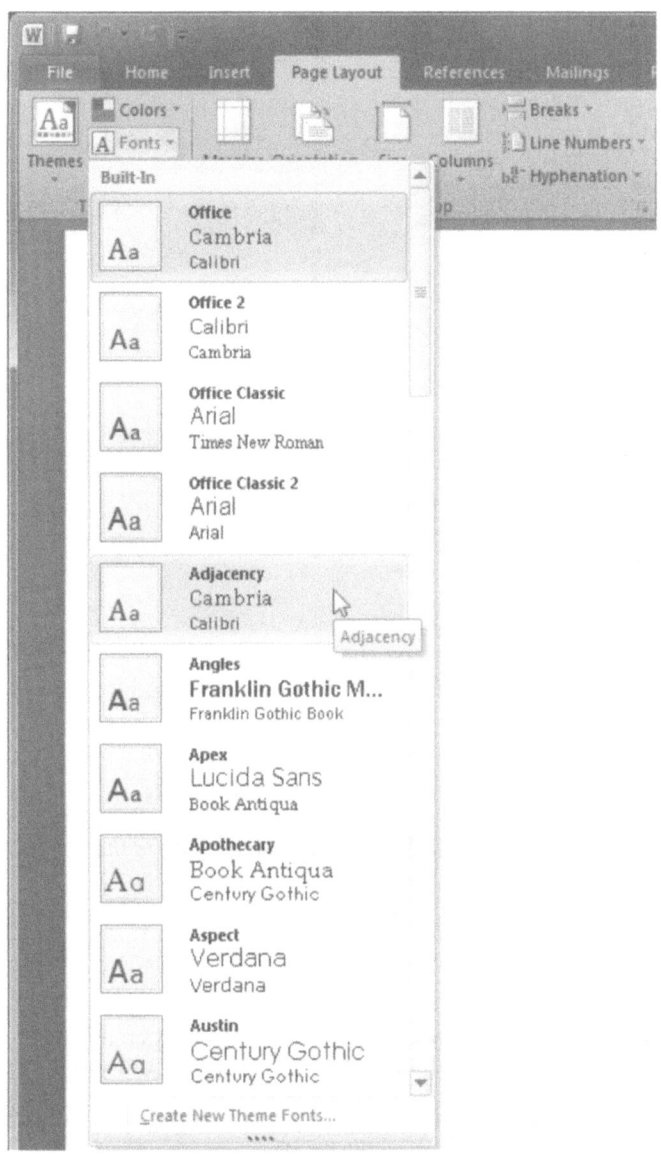

Figure 5–25. Use the Fonts gallery when you want to switch the document to a different set of fonts.

Changing the Visual Effects Used for the Document

To change the visual effects used in the document, choose Page Layout ➤ Themes ➤ Effects, and then click the effect on the Effects gallery (see Figure 5–26).

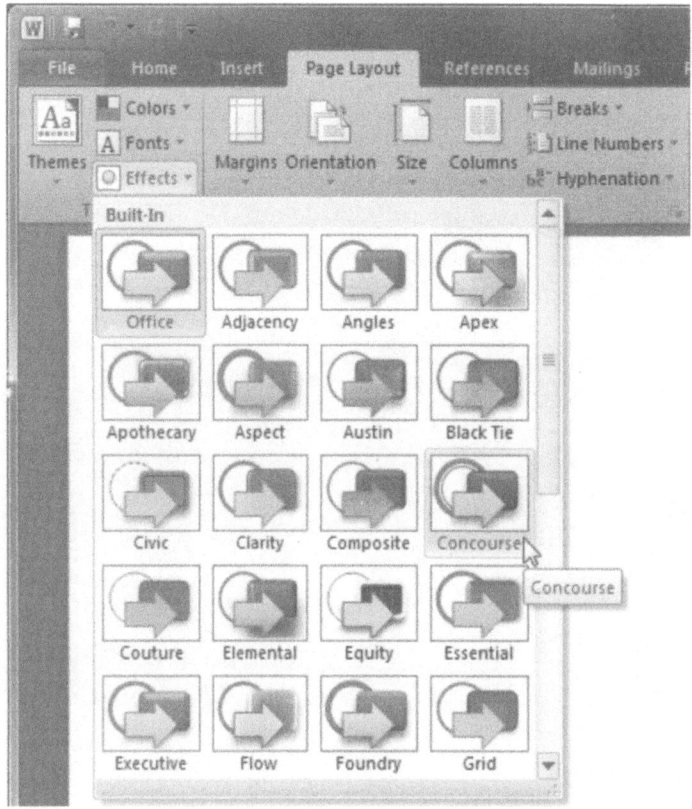

Figure 5–26. From the Effects gallery, you can instantly apply a different set of visual effects to the document.

Summary

In this chapter, you've learned to make your documents display information effectively by creating bulleted, numbered, and multilevel lists; by using tables to lay out information, format it, and sort it; and by using Word's graphical themes and their components.

In the next chapter, I'll show you how to complete a document by giving it a cover page and table of contents, customizing its print layout and margins, and securing it if necessary.

CHAPTER 6

Completing a Document

In this chapter, I'll show you how to complete a document you've created.

We'll start by going through how to add a cover page to a document quickly and easily from Word's Cover Pages gallery and how to add a table of contents to a document that will benefit from one. After that, I'll show you how to customize the page layout and the margins to make the document look the way you want.

Once the document is in shape, we'll look at how to finalize it and secure it. You can ensure that the document contains no sensitive information, mark it as final, and encrypt it with a password if necessary. You can even use Information Rights Management (IRM) to control which people can open the document, edit it, and print it. And you can sign a document with a digital signature to prove that it hasn't changed since you marked it as being final.

Lastly, you'll learn how to print all of a document, print only some parts of it, or print only special features such as a list of document properties or styles.

Let's get started.

Adding a Cover Page to a Document

To give your document a finished and professional appearance, it's often useful to add a cover page. Word makes it easy to add cover pages from its Cover Page gallery. You can also create custom cover pages of your own and add them to the Cover Page gallery so that you can quickly insert them in documents.

Adding a Cover Page from the Cover Page Gallery

To add a cover page to the document, choose Insert ➤ Pages ➤ Cover Page, and then click the design you want on the Cover Page gallery (see Figure 6–1).

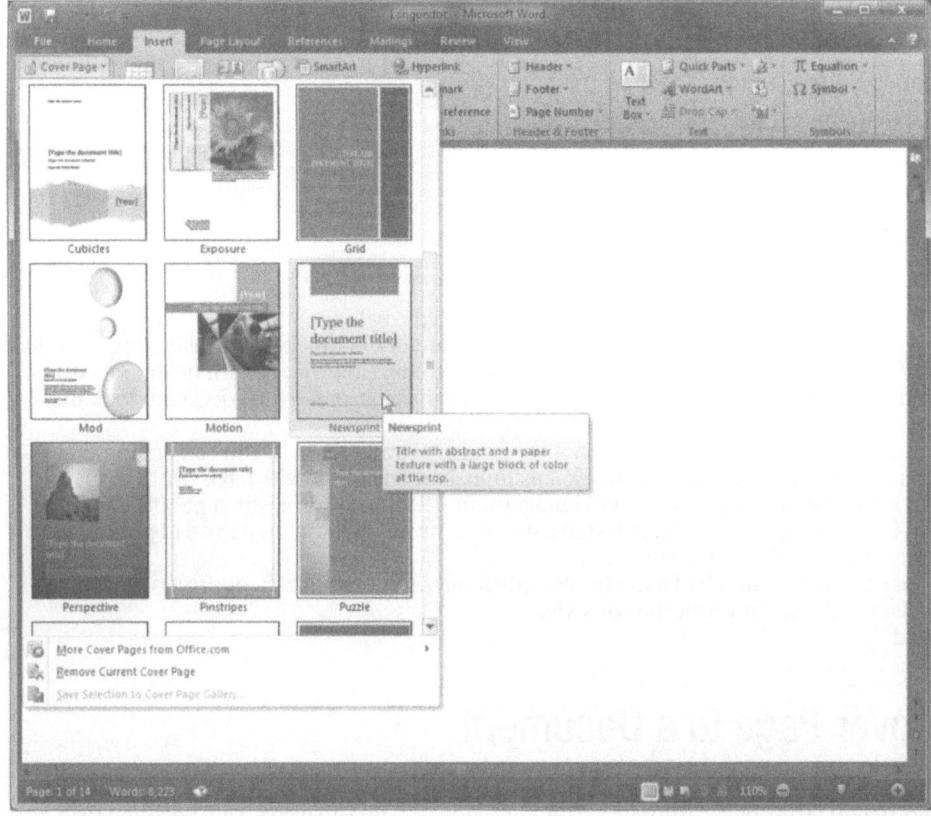

Figure 6–1. Use the Cover Page Gallery on the Insert tab of the ribbon to quickly insert a cover page in a document. Hold the mouse pointer over a cover page design to display a ScreenTip of notes on its layout.

After inserting a cover page, you can quickly enter the information it needs. For example, if the cover page has a "Type the document title" placeholder, click in the placeholder, and then type the document's title. If the cover page has an image placeholder, add your own image, such as a corporate logo.

Removing the Cover Page from a Document

To remove the cover page from the document, choose Insert ➤ Pages ➤ Cover Page ➤ Remove Current Cover Page. Word removes the cover page without further confirmation.

Instead of removing a cover page, you can replace it with a different design. To do so, choose Insert ➤ Pages ➤ Cover Page, and then click the design you want. Word removes the previous cover page and inserts the new one.

Creating a Custom Cover Page of Your Own

What's often most useful is to create one or more custom cover pages of your own. You can create a cover page either from scratch or by basing it on one of Word's built-in cover pages.

Once you've created your cover page, add it to the Cover Pages gallery like this:

1. Select the cover page.

2. Choose Insert ➤ Pages ➤ Cover Page ➤ Save Selection to Cover Page Gallery. Word displays the Create New Building Block dialog window with the Cover Pages gallery already selected in the Gallery drop-down list (see Figure 6–2).

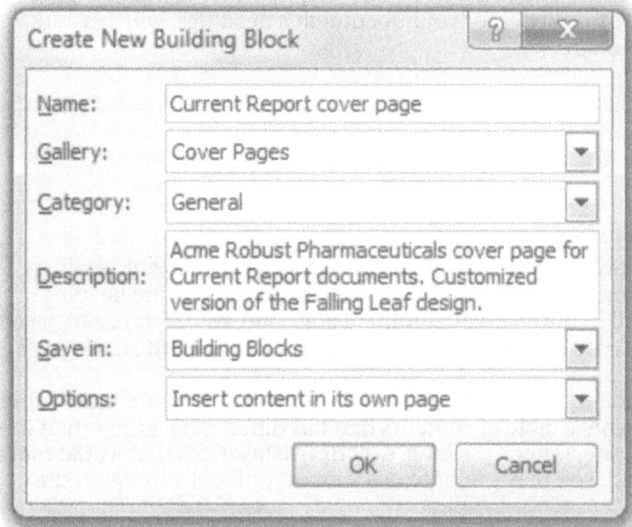

Figure 6–2. *Use the Create New Building Block dialog window to add a custom cover page to the Cover Pages gallery.*

3. In the Name box, type the name you want to give the cover page.

4. In the Category drop-down list, optionally select a different category than General.

5. In the Description box, type a description of the cover page to help you and your colleagues identify it in the Cover Pages gallery.

6. In the "Save in" drop-down list, make sure that Building Blocks is selected.

7. In the Options drop-down list, make sure that "Insert content in its own page" is selected.

8. Click the OK button to close the Create New Building Block dialog window. Word adds the cover page to the gallery.

You can now add your custom cover page to a document by choosing Insert ➤ Pages ➤ Cover Page, and then clicking the cover page at the bottom of the Cover Pages gallery.

Adding a Table of Contents to a Document

To give the reader an easy way to navigate a document, you can add a table of contents to it—a list of the major headings in the document, usually with their page numbers. Having a table of contents is particularly important for documents that are long, formal, or both.

Getting Your Document Ready for Adding a Table of Contents

To create a table of contents, you need to format the document consistently with styles. Normally, you'll use Heading styles for the headings in your document—for example, Heading 1 style for the top-level headings, Heading 2 style for the next level down, and so on—so Word makes it easy to include these styles in the table of contents. But if you use other styles for your document's headings, you can add those styles to the table of contents easily enough.

■ **Note** See Chapter 3 for instructions on formatting a document with styles.

When you create a table of contents this way, Word automatically picks up the relevant headings from the document and inserts them in the table of contents. If you then change any of the headings, you can update the table of contents and pull in the changes automatically. Similarly, if you change your document so that the page numbers change, you can update the table of contents with the latest page numbers.

You can also create a table of contents manually by typing the appropriate information into a table of contents structure. This enables you to create a table of contents that has different headings than the document actually uses. For example, if your document has long, descriptive headings that would make the table of contents lengthy and hard to read, you may prefer to use shorter, pithier headings in the table of contents.

Inserting an Automatic Table of Contents

The easiest way to create a table of contents is to have Word generate it automatically from the headings. To add a table of contents to your document, follow these steps:

1. Position the insertion point where you want to put the table of contents. If you want the table of contents to appear on a separate page at the beginning of the document, choose Insert ➤ Page Setup ➤ Breaks ➤ Page to insert a page break, and then click above it.

2. Choose References ➤ Table of Contents ➤ Table of Contents to open the Table of Contents gallery (see Figure 6–3), and then click one of the Automatic Table styles—for example, Automatic Table 1.

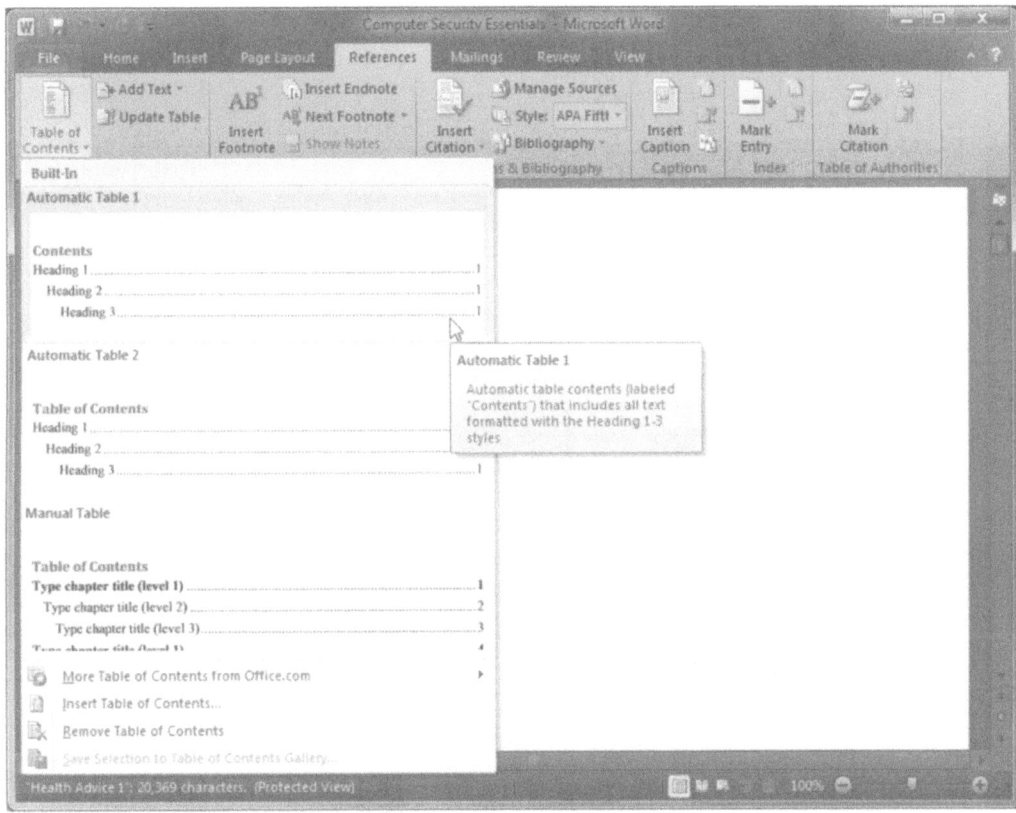

Figure 6–3. Insert one of the Automatic Table designs of tables of contents from the Table of Contents gallery.

Word inserts the table of contents (see Figure 6–4) consisting of the levels of heading set in the table design (usually Heading 1, Heading 2, and Heading 3 styles), a tab leader, and the page numbers.

Figure 6–4. Word inserts the table of contents as a field. When you need to update the table of contents with the latest headings and page numbers, click the Update Table button.

Sometimes you may need to add another entry to the table of contents without making that text a heading in the document. To do this, select the text, choose References ➤ Table of Contents ➤ Add Text, and then click the appropriate level on the Add Text gallery: Level 1, Level 2, or Level 3.

Inserting a Custom Table of Contents

Word's built-in table of contents designs are great for creating a table of contents quickly from paragraphs that use the Heading styles. But if your document uses different styles for its headings, you can create a custom table of contents that uses styles you choose.

To insert a custom table of contents, follow these steps:

1. Place the insertion point where you want the table of contents to appear.

2. Choose References ➤ Table of Contents ➤ Table of Contents ➤ Insert Table of Contents to display the Table of Contents tab of the Table of Contents dialog window (see Figure 6–5).

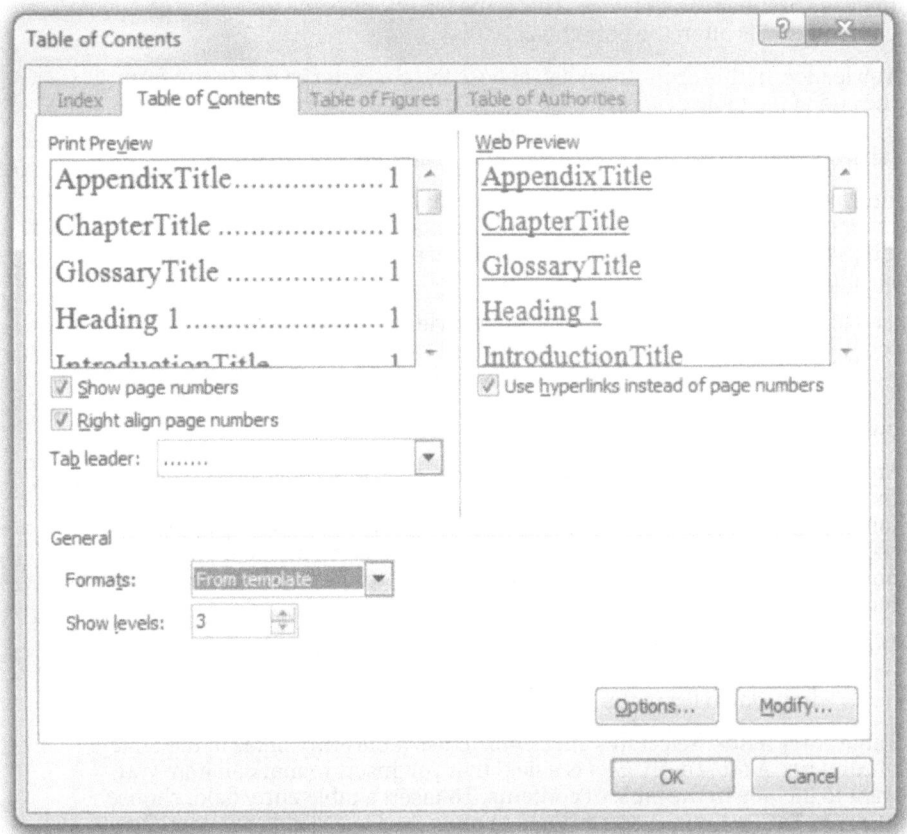

Figure 6–5. *Use the Table of Contents dialog window when you need to set up a custom table of contents for a document.*

3. In the General area, open the Formats drop-down list and choose the format you want to use. The default setting is "From template," which uses the styles in the document's current template, but you can also choose Classic, Distinctive, Fancy, Modern, Formal, or Simple. The Print Preview box and Web Preview box show how the current format will look.

4. In the "Show levels" drop-down list, set the number of heading levels you want to include. For example, select 2 to use Heading 1 and Heading 2 only.

5. Below the Print Preview box, choose whether and how to handle the page numbers:

   - **Show page numbers**. Select this check box to include page numbers in the table of contents. If you clear this check box, the "Right align page numbers" check box and the "Tab leader" drop-down list become unavailable.

- **Right align page numbers**. Select this check box if you want to right-align the page numbers on the page. This is the traditional style for a table of contents and is often the best choice.

- **Tab leader**. In this drop-down list, choose the character to use to run from the end of the table of contents entries to the page numbers. Your choices are (none), dots, dashes, or underlines. Usually, it's a good idea to include a tab leader character, as it makes the table of contents easier to read.

6. Below the Web Preview box, select the "Use hyperlinks instead of page numbers" check box if you want the table of contents to provide hyperlinks to the headings rather than their page numbers. If you plan to make the document available online, using hyperlinks is normally a good idea.

7. If you need to use styles other than the Heading styles as the source for the table of contents, click the Options button to display the Table of Contents Options dialog window (see Figure 6–6). You can then set up the table of contents to use styles, outline levels, table entry fields, or a mixture of them (see the following list). Click the OK button when you've finished.

- **Styles:** To use styles for the table of contents, select this check box. Then, in the TOC level column, go to the style you want to use, and type the number for the level this style represents in the table of contents. For example, to use the Special style as the second level in the table of contents, scroll the list down to the Special style, and then type 2 in its box. Repeat this procedure for each other style you want to use.

- **Outline levels:** Select this check box to use the outline levels defined in the paragraph formatting. You then choose the number of levels in the "Show levels" drop-down list in the Table of Contents dialog window.

- **Table entry fields:** Select this check box to use table entry fields in the table of contents. A *table entry field* is a field that you insert to mark an item you want to include in the table of contents. To insert a table entry field, choose Insert ➤ Text ➤ Quick Parts ➤ Field to open the Field dialog window. Open the Categories drop-down list and click Index and Tables, then click the TC item in the Field names box. In the Text entry box, type the text you want to appear in the table of contents. Select the "Outline level" check box and type in the box the level at which you want the field to appear—for example, 1 for a top-level heading. Click the OK button to close the Field dialog window.

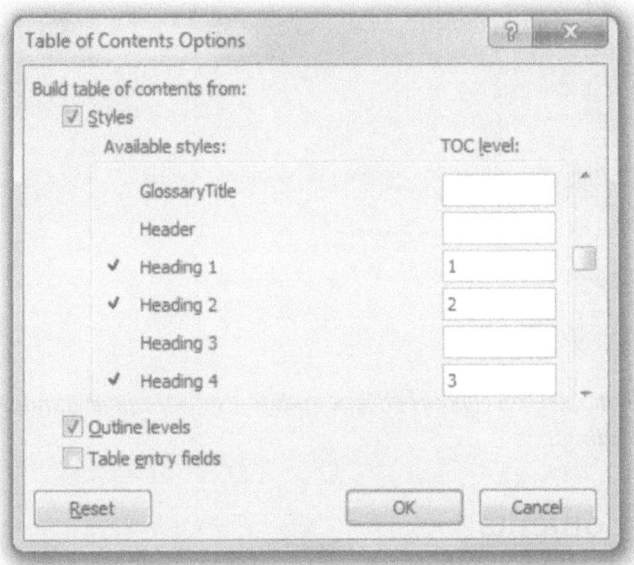

Figure 6–6. In the Table of Contents Options dialog window, choose the styles or outline levels to include in the table of contents.

8. Click the OK button to close the Table of Contents dialog window. Word inserts the table of contents.

■ **Note** After creating a custom table of contents, you can save it for future use. Select the table of contents, and then choose References ➤ Table of Contents ➤ Table of Contents ➤ Save Selection to Table of Contents Gallery. Word displays the Create New Building Block dialog window with the Table of Contents item selected in the Gallery drop-down list. Type the name for the table of contents in the Name box, type a description in the Description box, and then click the OK button.

Updating an Automatic Table of Contents

To make sure your table of contents is current, update it in either of these ways:

- Click in the table of contents, and then click the Update Table button.
- Choose References ➤ Table of Contents ➤ Update Table.

Whichever way you give the Update Table command, Word displays the Update Table of Contents dialog window (see Figure 6–7). Select the "Update page numbers only" option button if you want to update only the page numbers, or select the "Update entire table" option button if you want to update the headings as well as the page numbers. Then click the OK button.

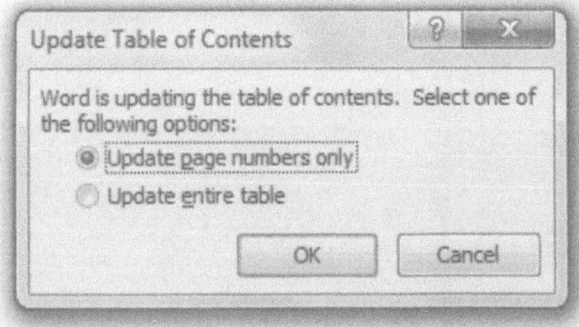

Figure 6–7. When you update a table of contents, you can choose between updating only the page numbers or updating the entire table, including the headings.

Inserting a Manual Table of Contents

For some documents, you'll want to show different information in the table of contents than the headings in the document. For example, you may want the table of contents to show only some of the many headings of the same level that appear in the document, or the table of contents may need shorter and snappier versions of the headings.

In this case, you can insert a manual table of contents, and then add the information you want to it. Follow these steps:

1. Position the insertion point where you want the table of contents to appear.

2. Choose References ➤ Table of Contents ➤ Table of Contents, and then click the Manual Table item in the Table of Contents gallery. Word inserts a table of contents with boilerplate text and sample page numbers instead of the real headings and page numbers (see Figure 6–8).

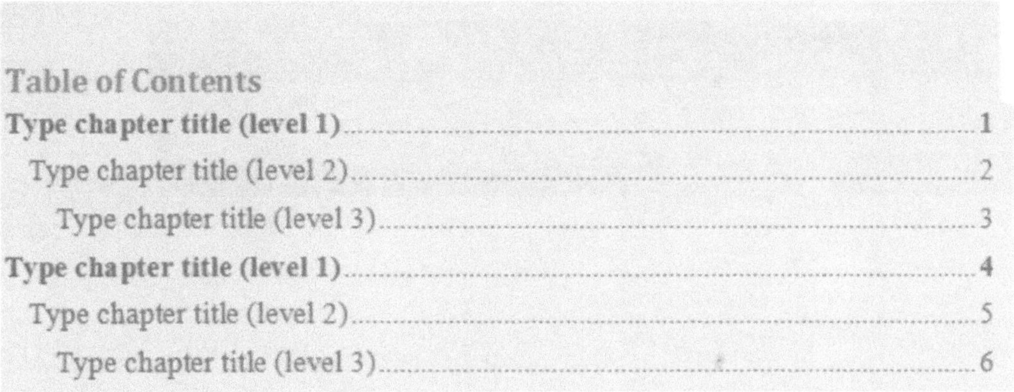
Table of Contents
Type chapter title (level 1) 1
Type chapter title (level 2) 2
Type chapter title (level 3) 3
Type chapter title (level 1) 4
Type chapter title (level 2) 5
Type chapter title (level 3) 6

Figure 6–8. *To create a table of contents that features only the text you want, insert the Manual Table item from the Table of Contents gallery, and then type the text and page numbers.*

3. Click each of the boilerplate items in turn, and then type the appropriate information. To add further entries, you can create new paragraphs by pressing Enter, and then apply the TOC style you want (for example, TOC 1 for a top-level heading). But it's usually easier to copy an existing paragraph, and then type the new information over it.

Customizing the Page Layout and Margins

To make your documents appear the way you want them to, you'll often need to customize the page layout and margins. To do so, you work with the controls in the Page Setup group on the Page Layout tab of the ribbon.

Choosing the Page Size and Orientation

What you'll usually want to do first is set the page size and orientation if you haven't set them already (for example, by picking a template that has the basic layout you want for the document).

To set the page size, choose Page Layout ➤ Page Setup ➤ Size, and then click the appropriate size on the Size gallery (see Figure 6–9)—for example, Letter for standard-size 8.5" × 11" paper.

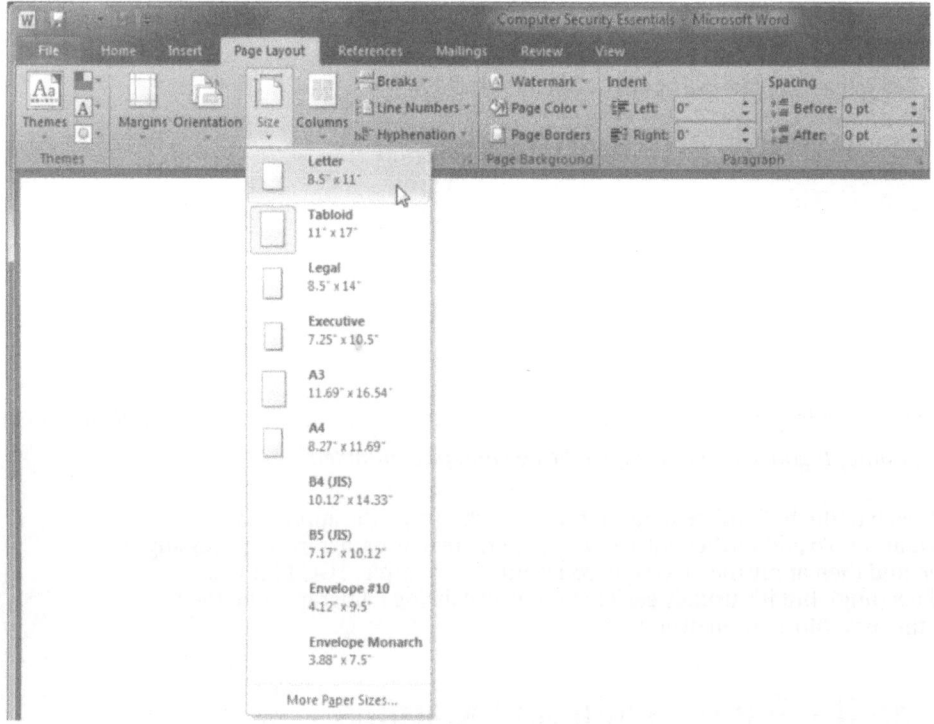

Figure 6–9. Your first step in customizing a document's layout is to choose the page size.

If the Size gallery doesn't contain the size you want, click the More Paper Sizes item at the bottom to display the Paper tab of the Page Setup dialog window (see Figure 6–10). Choose the size in the Paper size drop-down list, or create a custom size by entering the measurements in the Width box and the Height box. Then click the OK button to close the Page Setup dialog window.

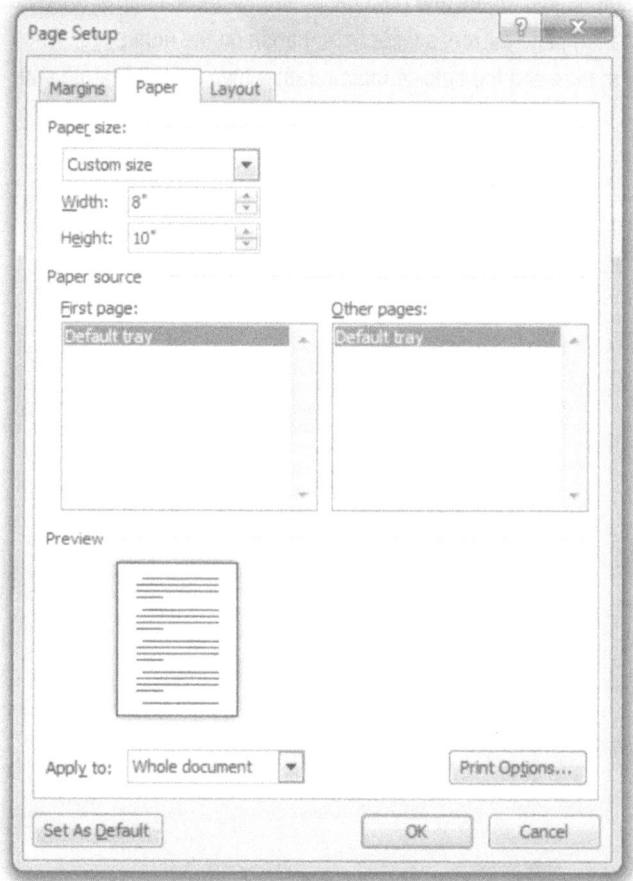

Figure 6–10. If Word doesn't have a preset for the page size you need, use the Paper tab of the Page Setup dialog window to set a custom page size.

After setting the page size, choose Page Layout ➤ Page Setup ➤ Orientation, and then click Portrait or Landscape in the Orientation gallery, as needed. Portrait is taller than it is wide, while Landscape is wider than it is tall.

Setting the Margins

After you've set the page size and orientation, set the margins by using the Margins gallery (see Figure 6–11). Choose Page Layout ➤ Page Setup ➤ Margins, and then click the type of margins you want: Normal, Narrow, Moderate, Wide, Mirrored, or Office 2003 Default. The Office 2003 Default settings have wider margins than the other settings.

■ **Note** Mirrored margins are ones in which the left page margins and right page margins form a mirror image of each other—for example, a wide left margin on the left page mirrors a wide right margin on the right page. When working with mirrored margins, you set the inside margin and the outside margin rather than the left margin and the right margin.

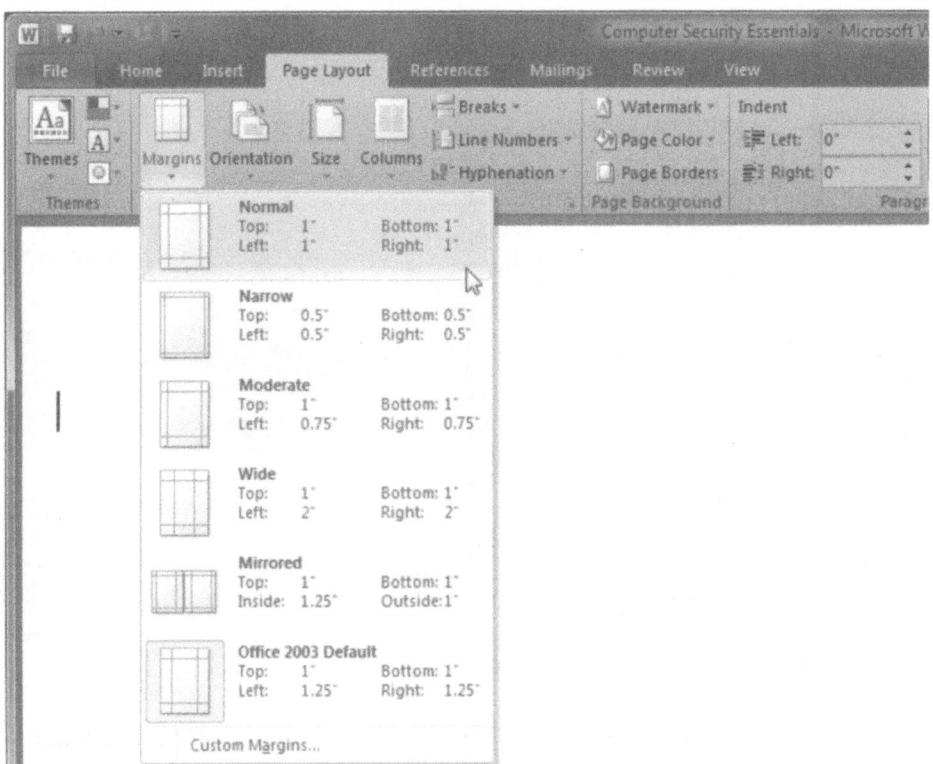

Figure 6–11. From the Margins gallery, you can quickly apply preset margins to the document. Click the Custom Margins item if you need to set custom margins.

If none of the margin presets is suitable, click the Custom Margins item at the bottom of the Margins gallery to display the Margins tab of the Page Setup dialog window (see Figure 6–12). You can then type the margin measurements in the Top box, Bottom box, Left box, and Right box. To allow extra space for binding the pages, enter the measurement in the Gutter box. If you need to place the gutter at the top of the page rather than on the left side, choose Left instead of Top in the Gutter position drop-down list.

Note If you want to create facing pages with symmetrical margins, open the Multiple pages drop-down list, and then choose Mirror margins. Word changes the Left box to an Inside box and the Right box to an Outside box; in these boxes, enter the inside and outside margins for the pages.

Figure 6-12. You can set custom margins using the Margins tab of the Page Setup dialog window.

When you've finished setting margins, click the OK button to close the Page Setup dialog window.

Finalizing and Securing a Document

When you have finished creating, editing, and reviewing a document, you can make it final and secure it. Finalizing a document has three main parts:

- Removing sensitive or surplus information from the document
- Marking the document as being final
- Signing the document with a digital signature to prove it hasn't been altered

You may also need to encrypt the document with a password or otherwise limit the people who can open, edit, or print the document. We'll look at these topics along the way.

Removing Sensitive Information from a Document

Even if a Word document's contents aren't confidential, the document can include sensitive information about who worked on it, who last saved it, and who added and deleted which parts of it. Before you distribute a document, use Word's tools for cleaning up a document to remove information that could come back to haunt you.

To remove potentially sensitive information from a document, follow these steps:

1. Save the document. For example, click the Save button on the Quick Access Toolbar.

2. Click the File button to open the Backstage view. Word displays the Info pane in the Backstage view.

3. Click the Check For Issues button, and then click Inspect Document on the drop-down menu to open the Document Inspector dialog window (see Figure 6–13).

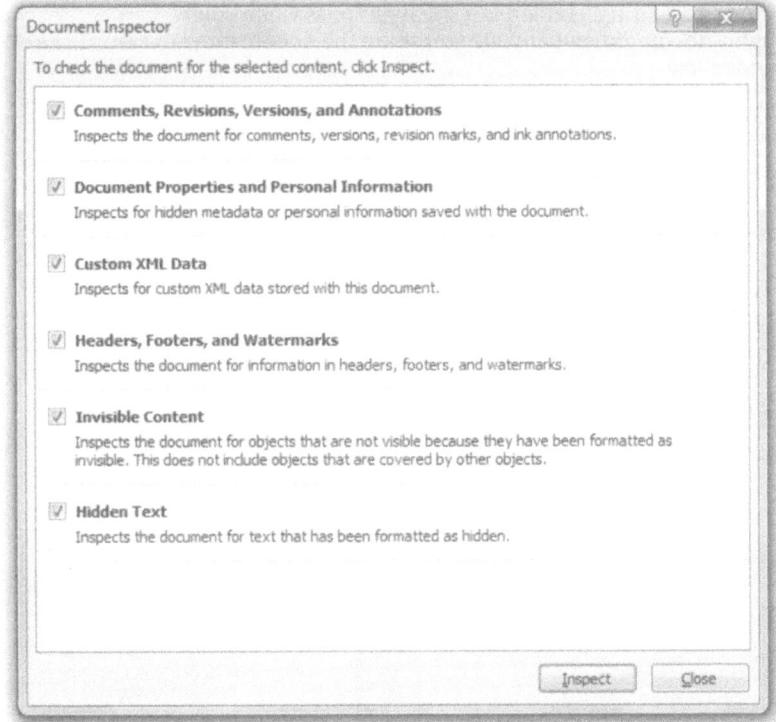

Figure 6–13. The Document Inspector dialog window lets you scan the document for various types of metadata and hidden content.

4. Select the check box for each content type you want to scan the document for:

- **Comments, Revisions, Versions, and Annotations**: Makes Word scan for comments, tracked changes, earlier versions of the document, and ink annotations.

- **Document Properties and Personal Information**: Makes Word scan for potentially sensitive document properties and personal information about you or other people who have worked on the document.

- **Custom XML Data**: Makes Word scan for custom XML tags and mappings. (XML is an advanced feature used for manipulating data automatically.)

- **Headers, Footers, and Watermarks**: Makes Word check the headers, footers, and any watermarks you've applied. These may contain information that you want to remove or update before sharing the document. For example, you may need to remove a Draft watermark or add a Confidential watermark.

- **Hidden Text**: Makes Word scan for text formatted to be hidden from view using hidden font formatting. Hidden text is easy to miss when you're looking through a document, but anyone you share the document with can display the hidden text.

5. Click the Inspect button to run the inspection for the items you chose. Word then updates the Document Inspector with details of what it found (see Figure 6–14).

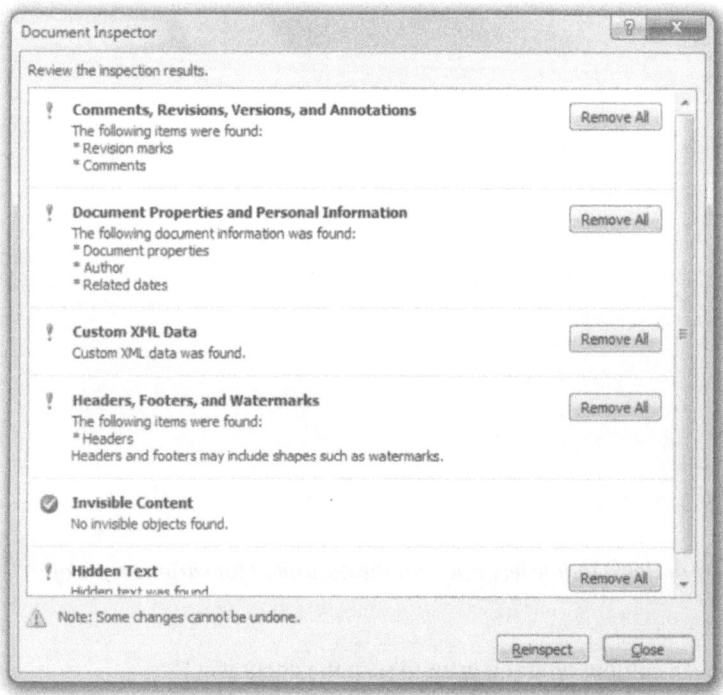

Figure 6–14. The Document Inspector shows each category of potentially sensitive data. You can remove all the items in a category by clicking the Remove All button next to it.

■ **Note** If you want to find out what the inspection results involve, click the Close button in the Document Inspector dialog window, and then look in the appropriate area in the document. For example, to see headers and footers, switch to Print Layout view; to see document properties, choose File ➤ Info and look in the Properties area in the Backstage View; to see hidden text, choose Home ➤ Paragraph ➤ Show/Hide ¶.

6. For each category of items, read through what the Document Inspector has found, and click the Remove All button if you want to remove those items. Word then removes that Remove All button and places a blue circle with a check mark to the left of the category.

■ **Tip** When you're cleaning up a document, you'll normally want to remove most of the items the Document Inspector checks for—but you may well want to leave the headers and footers in place if you've added them manually. The Document Inspector warns you about headers and footers because they're hidden if you use Draft view or Outline view; don't feel obliged to remove them if the document actually needs them.

---

7. If you want to check the document again, click the Reinspect button. This shouldn't be necessary, but you may want to make doubly sure.

8. When you're satisfied with the results the Document Inspector produces, click the Close button to close the dialog window.

9. Go through your document visually to check that the items you've removed haven't left any holes.

■ **Note** If you find that the actions you've taken in the Document Inspector have deleted vital portions of the document, close the document without saving it, and then reopen the saved version. Then manually deal with whichever sensitive data caused the problem (for example, accept or reject revisions manually) before you run the Document Inspector again.

---

10. Save the document, and then finalize it as described next.

Marking a Document as Final

To indicate that a document is finished rather than being in draft, you can mark it as finished. Doing so makes the document read-only, so nobody can make changes to the document without deliberately opening it up for editing rather than for reading.

To mark a document as final, follow these steps:

1. Click the File button to open the Backstage view. Word displays the Info pane.

2. Click the Protect Document button, and then click Mark as Final on the drop-down menu. Word displays a confirmation dialog window (see Figure 6–15).

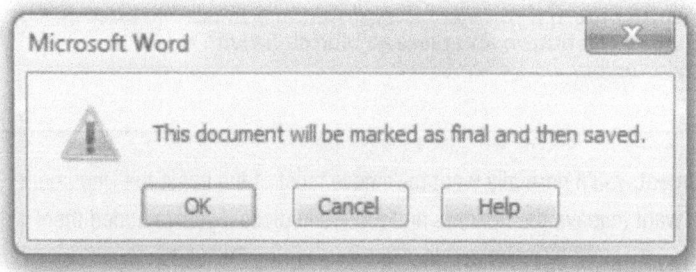

Figure 6–15. *You can mark a document as final to make sure that anyone who opens it knows it is finished.*

3. Click the OK button to close the dialog window. Word marks the document as final and read-only, and then saves it.

Word displays a yellow bar across the top of the window to warn you that the document is marked as final (see Figure 6–16). Click the Edit Anyway button if you want to open the document for editing anyway. When you've finished editing the document, repeat the above process to mark it as final again.

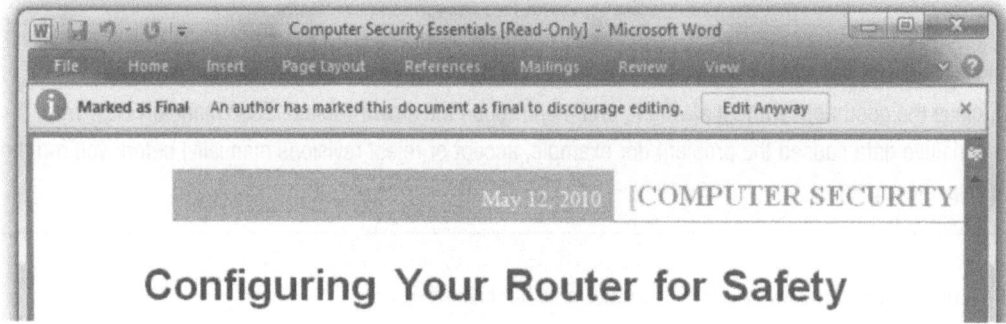

Figure 6–16. *After you mark a document as final, Word makes it read-only. If you need to change the document, click the Edit Anyway button on the Marked as Final bar.*

Encrypting a Document with a Password

If you need to keep other people out of a document, or let only approved people open it, you can encrypt the document with a password.

> ■ **Caution** Word's encryption is effective only against casual snoopers. An attacker who uses a password-cracking program (which are widely available on the Internet) can open an encrypted document with minimal effort.

To encrypt a document with a password, follow these steps:

1. Click the File button to open the Backstage view. Word displays the Info pane by default.

2. Click the Protect Document button, and then click Encrypt with Password on the drop-down menu to display the Encrypt Document dialog window (see Figure 6–17).

Figure 6–17. To protect a document against casual snooping, encrypt it with a password.

3. Type the password you want to use; the dialog window shows dots rather than characters, in case someone's looking over your shoulder. To give the most protection, use eight or more characters, using both capitals and lowercase, and including numbers and symbols. Memorize the password, or write it down somewhere safe.

4. Click the OK button. Word displays the Confirm Password dialog window, which is almost exactly the same as the Encrypt Document dialog window.

5. Type the password again (this is to check you've typed the password you intended), and then click the OK button to close the Confirm Password dialog window. Word changes the Permissions readout in the Info pane in Backstage to show that the document is protected (see Figure 6–18).

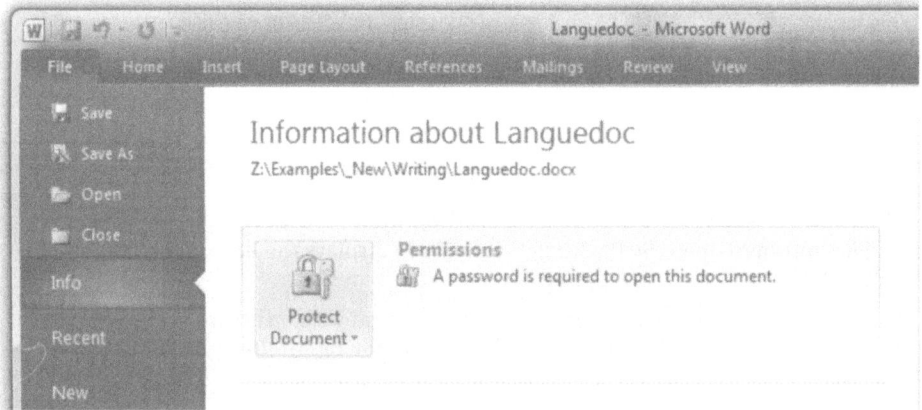

Figure 6–18. After you encrypt a document with a password, the Permissions readout in the Backstage view shows that the document is protected with a password.

6.   Save the document. For example, press Ctrl+S.

After you password-protect a document, it behaves as normal, except that when you try to open it, Word displays the Password dialog window demanding the password. If you type the password and click the OK button (or press Enter), Word opens the document; otherwise, Word displays a dialog window saying that it can't open the document.

■ **Note** To remove the password, click the File tab to open Backstage, click the Protect Document button in the Info pane, and then click Encrypt with Password. In the Encrypt Document dialog window, delete the password from the Password text box, and then click the OK button. Word removes the password. Save the document (for example, press Ctrl+S).

Limiting the People Who Can Open, Edit, and Print the Document

Instead of protecting a document by requiring a password to open it, you can set permissions on a document so that only specified people can open it. To make sure only authorized people open the document, Word uses Microsoft's Information Rights Management (IRM) tools, which attempt to verify the identity of each user who tries to open a document.

If you're working for a company or organization that has implemented Microsoft's Information Rights Management (IRM), you can use the company's IRM server to authenticate people's credentials. Otherwise, you can sign up to Microsoft's free IRM service, which uses a Windows Live ID for authentication.

Signing Up for Microsoft's IRM Service

If you want to sign up for Microsoft's IRM service, follow these steps:

1. Click the File button to open the Backstage view. Word displays the Info pane by default.

2. Click the Permissions button, click the Restrict Permission by People item on the drop-down menu, and then click Manage Credentials. Word displays the Service Sign-Up dialog window for the IRM service.

3. Select the "Yes, I want to sign up for this free service from Microsoft" option button, and then click the Next button. Follow through the Information Rights Management Configuration Wizard, either providing your existing Windows Live ID or signing up for a new one to use.

4. When you reach the Select User dialog window, in which you identify the user account for creating or opening IRM-protected content, select your user name, and then click the OK button. Word then displays the Permission dialog window, which you normally reach as described in the next section, so that you can set permissions on the document.

Setting Permissions on a Document

When you've set up your IRM credentials as described in the previous section, you can set permissions on a document like this:

1. Click the File button to open the Backstage view. Word displays the Info pane.

2. Click the Permissions button, click the Restrict Permission by People item on the drop-down menu, and then click Restricted Access to display the Permission dialog window (shown in Figure 6–19 with settings chosen).

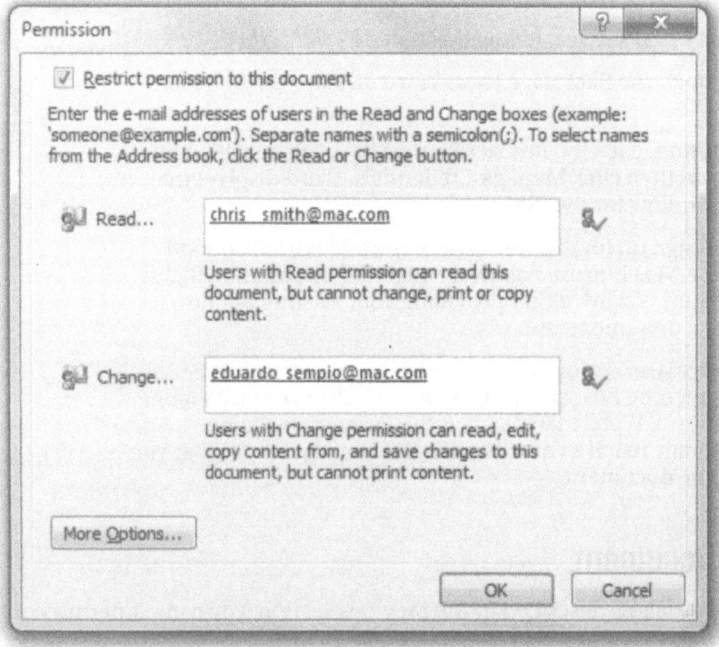

Figure 6–19. Use the Permission dialog window to set Information Rights Management to control which people can read a document and which can change it.

3. Select the "Restrict permission in this document" check box.

4. In the Read text box, enter the e-mail address for each person allowed to open the document but not change it, print it, or copy material from it.

   • You can either type in the addresses, separating them with semicolons, or click the Read button and pick the addresses from your address book.

■ **Tip** To add multiple people at once, add a group from your address book.

   • Click the checkmark button to the right of the Read box to check the addresses.

5. In the Change text box, enter the e-mail address for each person allowed to open the document, edit it, and save changes to it, but not print it.

   • As with the Read addresses, you can type the Change addresses, separating them with semicolons, or click the Change button and choose the addresses from your address book.

- Click the checkmark button to the right of the Change box to check the addresses.

6. If you want to let users print the document or copy content, or make the document expire automatically after a time, click the More Options button to display additional controls in the Permission dialog window (see Figure 6–20).

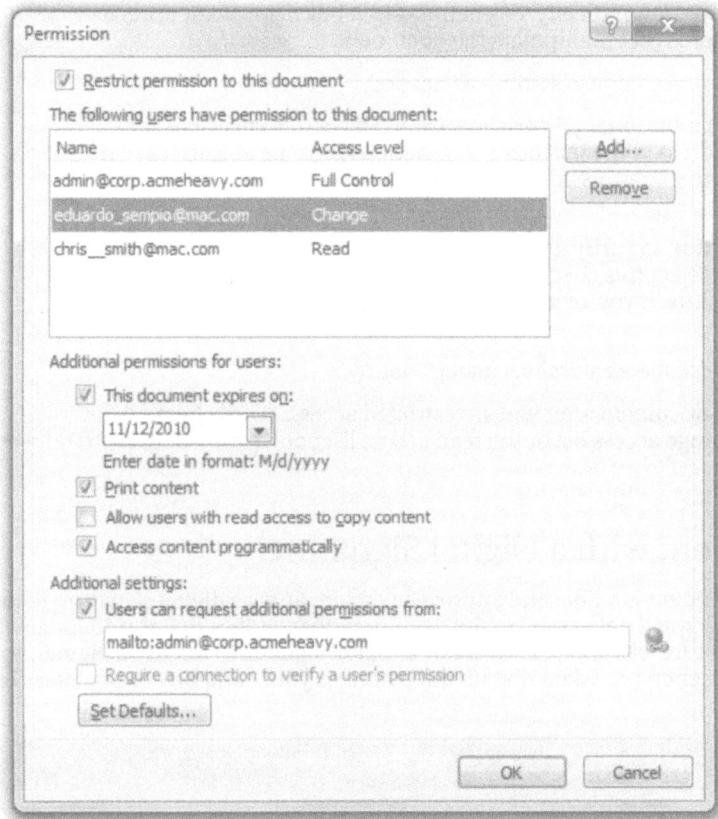

Figure 6–20. Expand the Permission dialog window to reveal extra options, including settings for making the document expire and allowing users to print the document.

7. Use the Add and Remove buttons to add users to the list box called "The following users have permission to this document."

8. In the "Additional permissions for users" area, choose permissions as needed:

- **This document expires on**. To make the document unavailable after a certain date, select this check box, open the date picker, and click the date. After that date, if someone tries to open the document, Word displays a dialog box explaining that it is unable to open it.

- **Print content.** Select this check box if you want users to be able to print the document. This applies to both users with read access and users with change access.

- **Allow users with read access to copy content.** Select this check box if you want users with read access to be able to copy document content (and paste it into other documents or programs).

- **Access content programmatically.** Select this check box if you want users to be able to run macros that manipulate the document.

9. In the Additional settings area, choose settings as needed:

    - **Users can request additional permissions from.** Select this check box and type an e-mail address in the text box if you want users to be able to request that you upgrade their permissions—for example, from read access to change access.

    - **Require a connection to verify a user's permission.** If you're using IRM on a network, you can select this check box to make Word check the user's authentication online. If you're using Microsoft's IRM service, this check box is unavailable.

10. Click the OK button to close the Permissions dialog window.

When anyone tries to open the document after you've restricted access, Word checks their credentials. If they're not on the change access list or the read access list you've provided, Word refuses to open the document.

Signing a Final Document with a Digital Signature

When you need to prove that a document is a final and approved version, apply a digital signature to the document. A *digital signature* is encrypted data saved in the document that verifies that the document hasn't been changed since the signature was applied. To create a digital signature, you use a digital certificate, which is a file containing encrypted data that identifies you or your company or organization.

GETTING A DIGITAL CERTIFICATE

To get a digital certificate, you apply to a certificate authority (CA). Commercial CAs, such as VeriSign (www.verisign.com) or Comodo (www.comodo.com), issue certificates to both companies and individuals. You can either take your browser directly to a CA's website or go via Microsoft's web site by selecting the "Get a digital ID from a Microsoft partner" option button in the Get a Digital ID dialog window (see Figure 6–21).

Figure 6–21. From the Get a Digital ID dialog window, you can either connect to a certificate authority partnered with Microsoft or create a self-signed digital ID of your own.

If you use Word at work, your company or organization may also run its own CA to provide digital certificates to its employees. In this case, you will normally get a digital certificate from a system administrator.

If you need a digital certificate for testing, you can create a self-signed certificate using tools that Office includes. When Word displays the Get a Digital ID dialog window, select the "Create your own digital ID" option button, and then click the OK button. In the Create a Digital ID dialog window (see Figure 6–22), type the information to use for the certificate, and then click the Create button. Word then displays the Sign dialog window, as described later in this chapter.

Figure 6–22. Use the Create a Digital ID dialog window to create a self-signed digital certificate containing the information you choose. A self-signed certificate is useful for testing, but other people will have no reason to trust it.

Signing a document with a digital signature authenticates the final document but doesn't protect it; to protect the document, you need to use a password or restrictions, as discussed earlier in this chapter. If somebody changes the document, Word removes the digital signature. If necessary, you can finalize the document again and then sign it once more.

To sign a document with a digital signature, follow these steps:

1. Click the File button to open the Backstage view.

2. On the Info screen that Word automatically displays, click the Protect Document button, and then click Add a Digital Signature on the drop-down menu to display the Sign dialog window (see Figure 6–23).

■ **Note** The first time you give the Add a Digital Signature command, Word displays a Microsoft Office Word dialog window explaining briefly what digital signatures are and what they're useful for. Click the Signature Services from the Office Marketplace button if you want to browse options for getting a digital certificate. Otherwise, select the "Don't show this message again" check box, and then click the OK button to dismiss the dialog window. If your PC doesn't have a digital certificate installed, Word then displays the Get a Digital ID dialog window.

Figure 6–23. Use the Sign dialog window to apply a digital signature to a document to prove it hasn't been changed since you last worked on it.

3. Check that the certificate that appears in the "Signing as" box is the right one. If not, click the Change button to open the Windows Security: Select a Certificate dialog window, click the right certificate, and then click the OK button. The certificate you chose appears in the "Signing as" box.

4. If you need to double-check what you're signing, click the "See additional information about what you are signing" link to display the Additional Information dialog window. Figure 6–24 shows an example of this dialog window. Click the OK button when you have read the warnings and information.

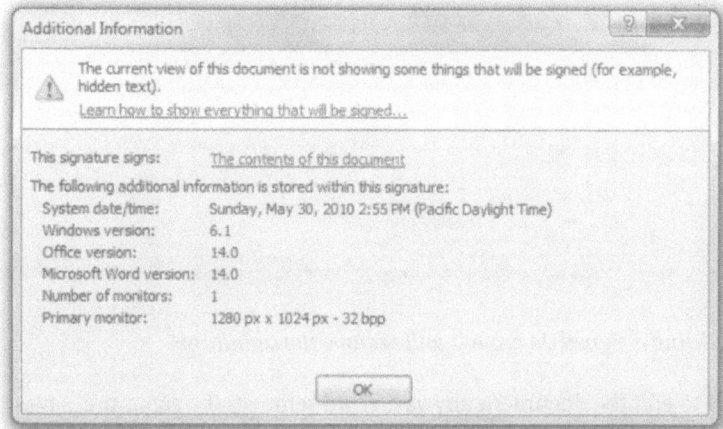

Figure 6–24. *Use the Additional Information dialog window to show any warnings about document contents that don't appear in the current view (such as hidden text or markup) and the information the signature will contain.*

5. Click the Sign button. Word signs the document, saves it, and displays the Signature Confirmation dialog window (see Figure 6–25).

Figure 6–25. *Word displays the Signature Confirmation dialog window to confirm that you have applied a digital signature to the document.*

6. Click the OK button to close the Signature Confirmation dialog window. You can select the "Don't show this message again" check box first if you want to suppress this dialog window in future, but usually it's useful to see.

The document remains signed until you change it. If you go to edit the document, Word warns you that editing will remove the signature (see Figure 6–26).

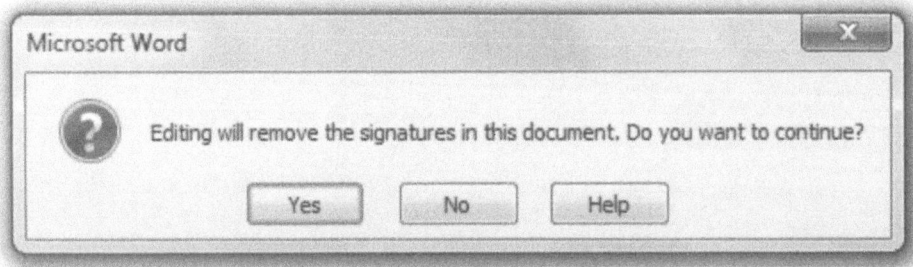

Figure 6–26. Word warns you that editing a signed document will remove the signatures.

Click the Yes button if you need to edit the document anyway. Word removes the signature, saves the document, and then displays the Signature Removed dialog window to make sure you're aware of the change.

Click the OK button to close the Signature Removed dialog window. You can then edit the document freely. When you have finished, you can finalize and sign the document again if necessary.

Printing a Document

When you need to share a document as a hard copy, you can print it out. Word makes the process of getting the printouts you need as easy as possible. First, Word integrates the print preview function directly into the Print place in the Backstage view, so you don't have to remember to preview the document separately. Second, Word provides a wide range of printing options to make the printout look the way you want it to.

Opening the Print Place in Backstage

To start printing or to choose options for it, open the Print place in the Backstage view in one of these ways:

- Press Ctrl+P. This standard keyboard shortcut works in Word as in most Windows programs.

- Click the File button to open the Backstage view, and then click the Print item in the left pane.

Figure 6–27 shows the Print place in the Backstage view.

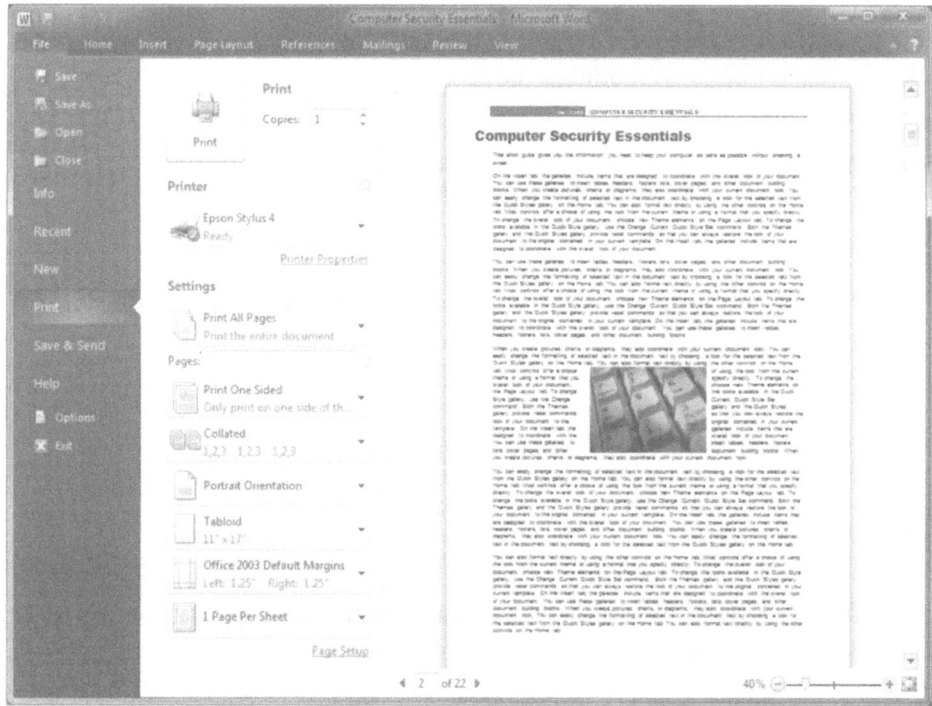

Figure 6–27. The Print place in the Backstage view includes a built-in preview of the document.

Previewing the Document in the Print Place

From here, check the preview on the right side to make sure the document looks the way you want it to:

- **Move from page to page**. Click the Previous Page button or Next Page button at the bottom left corner of the preview to move to the previous page or next page. To jump to a page by its number, type the number in the text box and press the Enter key. You can also scroll up and down the document as needed.

- **Zoom in or out**. Use the Zoom Out (–) button or the Zoom In (+) button to zoom by increments, or drag the Zoom slider to zoom freely.

- **Display the whole page**. Click the Zoom to Page button in the lower-right corner of the window.

Choosing Standard Printing Options

If the preview looks right, choose options for printing the document:

- **Print**: Click this button to print the document with its current settings.

- **Copies**: In this box, enter the number of copies you want. Either click the spin buttons to adjust the number, or simply type in the number.

■ **Note** If you need to change the print quality, paper size, paper orientation, or other printer settings, click the Printer Properties link, and then work in the Properties dialog window for the printer.

- **Printer**: In this drop-down list, select the printer you want to print to. If the list shows no printer you want to use, you can click the Add Printer item to start the process of adding another printer.

■ **Note** If you need to create a print file for printing the document on a different printer (for example, at a print shop), click the Print to File item at the bottom of the Printer drop-down list. If you need to create a file in Adobe's widely used Portable Document Format (PDF), choose File ➤ Save & Send, click the Create PDF/XPS Document item, and then click the Create PDF/XPS button.

- **Print What**: In this drop-down list (see Figure 6–28), choose the item you want to print. Choose the Print All Pages item to print all the pages, Print Selection to print only what you've selected, Print Current Page to print the current page, or choose Print Custom Range to print the range of pages you enter in the Pages box (as discussed in the section "Printing a Range of Pages," later in this chapter).

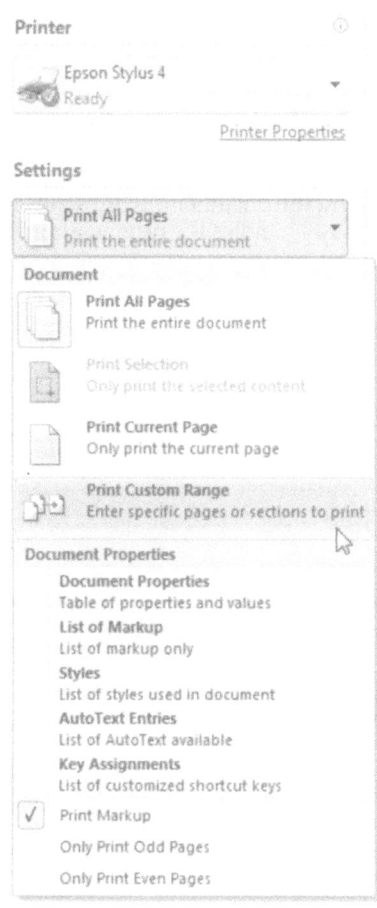

Figure 6–28. From the Print What drop-down list, you can choose to print a custom range of pages, a table of document properties, a list of key assignments, or other items.

- **Sides**: In this drop-down list, choose Print One Sided to print on one side of the paper only. Choose Manually Print on Both Sides if you want to print on one side of the paper, and then reinsert the paper in the printer to print on the other side.

- **Collated**: When you're printing multiple copies, choose Collated from this drop-down list to print each copy in order, or choose Uncollated to print all the copies of the first page together, all the copies of the second page together, and so on.

- **Orientation**: In this drop-down list, choose Portrait Orientation to print with the paper's longer dimension vertical. Choose Landscape Orientation to print with the longer dimension horizontal.

- **Margins**: Choose the type of margins from this drop-down list. For a quick change, choose one of the presets, such as Normal, Wide, or Narrow. To adjust the margins manually, choose Custom Margins, and then work on the Margins tab of the Page Setup dialog window.

When you choose a change that affects how the document looks, the preview shows the change. (By contrast, the preview can't show changes such as the number of copies or whether they're set for collation.)

When you've finished choosing settings, click the Print button to print the document. Word sends it to the Windows print queue that serves the printer you chose, and Windows handles the print job from there.

Printing Extra Items

From the Print What drop-down list, you can choose to print a custom range of pages or to print a specific item, such as printing only odd pages or even pages, printing the markup in the document, or printing a list of document properties.

Printing a Custom Range of Pages

After correcting a document, you may need to print a custom range of pages from it—for example, pages 3, 5, 8–10, 15, and 20. To do so, open the Print What drop-down menu, click Print Custom Range, and then type the details of the range in the Pages box

To specify the range, use the conventions shown in Table 6–1. For example, "3,5,8–10,15,20" prints the pages mentioned in the previous paragraph. Then click the Print button.

Table 6–1. Specifying a Custom Range of Pages to Print

To Print These Pages	Type This	Example
Consecutive pages	Starting page number, hyphen, ending page number	8–10
Individual pages	Page number, comma, page number	7,11,15
Sections	s and section number	s1,s3
Range of sections	s and starting section number, hyphen, s and ending section number	s1–s3
Pages within sections	p and page number, s and section number	p3s5–p8s7

■ **Note** Printing by sections is most useful if you've split up a document into different sections, each of which starts on a new page. See Chapter 3 for information on sections.

Choosing Whether to Include Markup—Or Printing Only Markup

When you print a document, you can choose whether to print any markup and comments it contains or whether to print the document as it appears without the markup and comments.

To tell Word which you want, open the Print What drop-down menu in the Print place in the Backstage view. At the bottom, click the Print Markup item, placing a check mark next to it, if you want to print the markup. If you don't want the markup, make sure the Print Markup item has no check mark next to it.

Other times, you may need to print only the markup for a document. To do so, open the Print What drop-down menu in the Print place in Backstage, click List of Markup, and then click the Print button.

Printing Only Odd Pages or Even Pages

Sometimes when you need to handle a document in a special way, it's useful to print the odd pages separately from the even pages. To do so, open the Print What drop-down menu and select the Only Print Odd Pages item or the Only Print Even Pages item, as needed. Print the document, select the other item on the Print What drop-down menu, and then print it again.

Printing Document Properties, Styles, AutoText Entries, and Key Assignments

You can also print four other items by choosing them on the Print What drop-down menu in the Print place in Backstage:

- **Document Properties**: Select this item to print a page showing the document's properties—the filename, directory (folder), template, title, subject, author, and so on.

- **Styles**: Select this item to print pages listing the styles used in the document and their formatting.

- **AutoText Entries**: Select this item to print a list of the AutoText entries stored in the document's template.

- **Key Assignments**: Select this item to print a list of the custom key assignments in the document (there may not be any).

Summary

In this chapter, you've learned how to complete a document by adding a cover page, inserting a table of contents, and customizing the page layout and margins to look the way you need them. You've also learned various skills for finalizing and securing a document, ranging from removing sensitive information from it to locking it down with Information Rights Management. You've also learned to print a full document, part of it, or only particular aspects of it.

In the next chapter, I'll show you how to work with Word's powerful tools for improving pictures.

■ ■ ■

CHAPTER 7

Editing Pictures within Word

In this chapter, I'll show you how to use Word's powerful features for editing pictures to make them look just the way you need them to. With just a few clicks, you can transform a picture's aspect, feeling, and even its content so that it suits your document.

We'll start with inserting a picture the quick and easy way, to make sure that you have a picture to work with. (Chapter 8 shows you the other ways of inserting a picture.) I'll then show you how to resize a picture, crop it to show only the part you want, compress it to save space if necessary, and how to correct its color balance, contrast, and brightness. Finally, you'll learn how to remove the background from a picture, making the subject stand out clearly and eliminating visual distractions.

Inserting a Picture

To work through this chapter, first open a new document (or an existing document in which you want to insert a picture), and then insert a picture in it. Follow these steps:

1. Press Ctrl+N to create a new blank document. Or, if you prefer, open an existing document of your own that you're happy to use for testing.

2. Position the insertion point where you want to insert the picture.

3. Choose Insert ➤ Illustrations ➤ Picture to display the Insert Picture dialog window (see Figure 7–1).

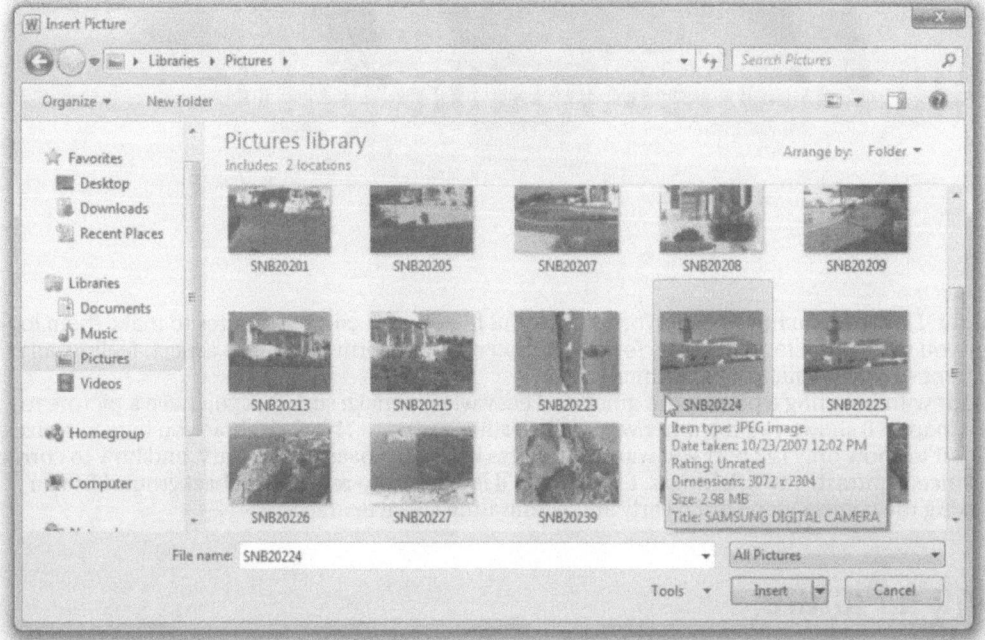

Figure 7–1. *In the Insert Picture dialog window, select the picture you want to insert, and then click the Insert button. You can hold the mouse pointer over a picture to display a ScreenTip showing its info.*

4. Navigate to the folder that contains the picture. For example, if you're using Windows 7, expand the Libraries item in the left pane of the Insert Picture dialog window, and then click the Pictures item to display the contents.

___

■ **Tip** If you want to see the details of a picture, hold the mouse pointer over it in the Insert Picture window until Word displays a ScreenTip. To see each picture at a larger size, open the View drop-down list near the upper-right corner of the dialog window, and then choose Extra Large Icons or Large Icons on the View slider.

___

5. Click the picture to select it.

6. Click the Insert button to close the Insert Picture dialog window. Word inserts the picture in the document.

■ **Note** The drop-down button that appears to the right of the Insert button in the Insert Picture dialog window enables you to link the picture to the document instead of inserting it. Chapter 8 explains how linking works and when to use it.

Making the Picture Float Instead of Appearing Inline

When you insert a picture, Word places it inline with the text by default. This means that the picture appears as a character in the text rather than as a separate object that you can move freely. Having the picture appear inline is useful when you need to include pictures as icons in the document, but usually, you'll want to have a picture appear as a separate object.

To make the picture appear as a separate object, follow these steps:

1. Click the picture to select it. Word adds the Picture Tools section to the ribbon.

2. Click the Picture Tools Format tab of the ribbon if it's not already displayed.

3. Choose Picture Tools Format ➤ Arrange ➤ Wrap Text ➤ Square to position the picture with text wrapping around it.

■ **Note** You'll notice that the Wrap Text gallery provides several wrapping choices apart from In Line with Text and Square. See Chapter 8 for information on these wrapping options.

You'll notice that the picture now appears with selection handles around it and with a green rotation handle at the top (see Figure 7–2).

Figure 7–2. When you move a picture from being inline to being a floating object, Word displays sizing handles around it and a green rotation handle above it.

■ **Tip** To control how Word inserts pictures by default, choose File ➤ Options. In the left pane of the Word Options dialog window, click the Advanced category to display the Advanced options. Scroll down to the Cut, copy, and paste heading, open the "Insert/paste pictures as" drop-down list, and choose your preferred placement: In line with text (the default), Square, Tight, Behind text, In front of text, Through, or Top and bottom. Click the OK button to close the Word Options dialog window.

Resizing and Cropping a Picture

Now that you've inserted a picture and turned it into a floating object, you can resize it to the size needed to make it work in the document. You can also crop the picture so that the document displays only the parts you want to show.

Resizing a Picture

The quickest way to resize a picture is by clicking it and then dragging one of its sizing handles. Here's how to do this:

- **Resize the picture proportionally.** Drag a corner sizing handle until the picture becomes the size you want.

■ **Tip** If you want to resize the picture about its center point, Ctrl+drag one of the corner handles. This trick is useful when the picture is in the right place but is the wrong size.

- **Resize the picture in one dimension only.** Drag a side handle to resize the picture only horizontally, or drag the top handle or bottom handle to resize the picture only vertically. Because you're resizing the picture in one dimension only, you distort the picture.

■ **Note** If you need to resize a picture in only one dimension but don't want to distort it, crop the picture instead, as described in the next section.

Resizing a picture by dragging its handles is quick and easy, but to create consistent layouts, you may need to make the picture a precise size. You can do this by using either the Size controls on the ribbon (see Figure 7–3) or the Size tab of the Layout dialog window.

To resize using the size controls, click the picture to select it, and then click the Picture Tools Format tab of the ribbon if it's not already displayed.

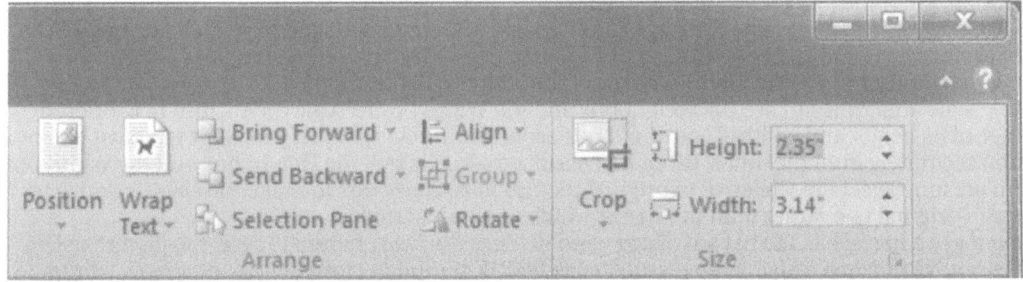

Figure 7–3. You can use the Height box and the Width box in the Size group of the Picture Tools Format tab to set the exact dimensions you need for a picture.

The Size controls are great for setting precise dimensions, but you may also need to set the size as a percentage of the page or one of the margins. For example, you may need to set a picture to be 50 percent of the width of the page.

To set relative dimensions, click the picture, and then choose Picture Tools Format ➤ Size ➤ Advanced Layout ➤ Size, clicking the tiny button in the lower-right corner of the Size group. Word displays the Size tab of the Layout dialog window (see Figure 7–4).

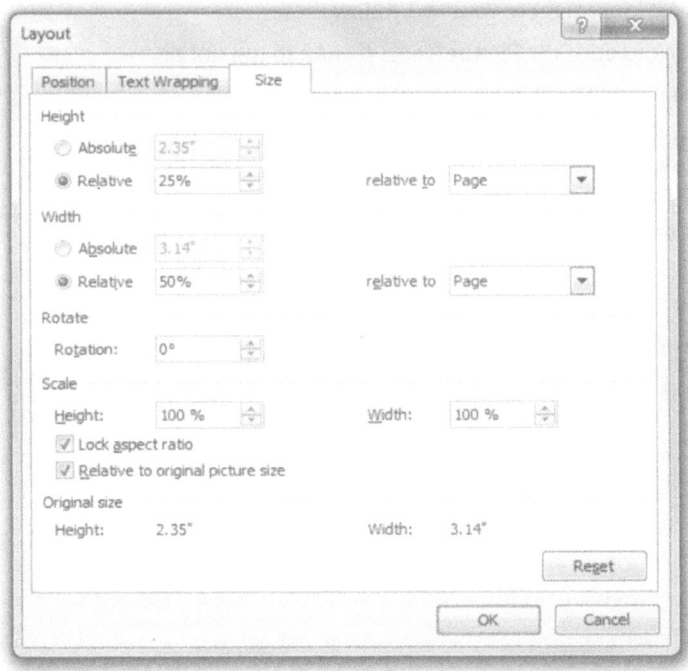

Figure 7–4. Use the Size tab of the Layout dialog window when you need to set relative dimensions for a picture.

Use the controls in the Height area to set the height of the picture. For example, select the Relative option button, enter the percentage in the box next to it, then open the "Relative to" drop-down list and choose Margin, Page, Top Margin, Bottom Margin, Inside Margin, or Outside Margin. Page tends to be the most useful.

Next, use the controls in the Width area to set the width in the same way.

In the Scale area, you can use the Height box and the Width box to scale the picture to a different percentage of its height and width. Clear the "Lock aspect ratio" check box if you want to adjust one dimension separately from the other; when this check box is selected, the Height box and the Width box change in unison. Select the "Relative to original picture" size check box to make the sizing relative to the picture's original size rather than the size at which you've inserted it.

If you make a mistake in the Layout dialog window, click the Reset button to reset the picture's size. When you've finished resizing the picture, click the OK button to close the Layout dialog window.

Cropping a Picture

If you need the document to show only part of a picture rather than the whole picture, you can crop off the parts you don't want.

Word lets you crop a picture freely, crop it to a particular shape, or crop it to a particular aspect ratio. Each capability can be useful, so we'll look at them in turn.

Cropping a Picture Freely

When you need to crop a picture so that it looks right to your eye, follow these steps:

1. Click the picture to select it. Word adds the Picture Tools section to the ribbon.

2. Click the Picture Tools Format tab if Word doesn't display it automatically.

3. Choose Picture Tools Format ➤ Size ➤ Crop, clicking the top part of the Crop button rather than the drop-down button. Word displays crop handles on the picture (see Figure 7–5).

4. Drag the crop handles to make the cropping area contain the part of the picture you want to show:

   • Shift+drag to crop the image proportionally.

   • Ctrl+drag to crop the image evenly about its center point.

   • Ctrl+Shift+drag to crop the image proportionally about its center point.

Figure 7–5. *The quick way of cropping is to drag the crop handles to select the part of the picture you want to show. Word darkens the parts of the picture that you're cropping off.*

■ **Tip** If you make the crop area exactly the size you need, you can click within the crop area and drag to make a different part of the picture appear in the crop area. Dragging like this doesn't move the crop area, which stays in place, but it moves the picture behind the crop area—as if you were reaching through a window and moving the landscape until the right part of it appeared in the window.

5. Click the Crop button again to turn off the Crop tool, or click elsewhere in the document to deselect the picture. Word applies the cropping to the picture, hiding the parts you've cropped off.

■ **Caution** The parts you've cropped off the picture are still there, just hidden. If you find you've cropped off the wrong part of the picture, you can easily restore it by changing the cropping. But if you distribute your Word documents electronically to others, make sure that the cropped areas of pictures don't contain any sensitive information, because other people can easily change the cropping too. If you need to remove the cropped areas, see the section "Compressing the Pictures in a Document," later in this chapter.

■ **Note** For more cropping options, choose Picture Tools ➤ Format ➤ Size ➤ Crop, clicking the Crop drop-down button rather than the top part of the button. On the drop-down menu that appears, choose Crop to Shape if you want to make the picture fit into a shape; choose Aspect Ratio if you want to crop the picture to a specific aspect ratio, such as 4:3 or 3:5.

Cropping a Picture to a Shape

Sometimes it's useful to crop a picture to a shape. For example, instead of cropping a picture to a conventional rectangle, you can crop it to a circle, a triangle, an arrow, or even a thought bubble (see Figure 7–6).

Figure 7–6. To create interesting visual effects, you can crop a picture to a shape.

To crop a picture to a shape like this, click the picture, choose Picture Tools Format ➤ Size ➤ Crop ➤ Crop to Shape, and then click the shape on the gallery that opens.

Cropping a Picture to an Aspect Ratio

When you need a picture to be a particular aspect ratio, such as 2:3 (two units wide by three units high), use Word's Aspect Ratio command. Click the picture, choose Picture Tools Format ➤ Size ➤ Crop ➤ Aspect Ratio, and then click the aspect ratio you want. Word applies the aspect ratio to the picture and displays crop marks so that you can select the part you want.

Once you've applied the aspect ratio cropping, you need to Shift+drag a corner handle when resizing the crop area if you want to maintain the aspect ratio.

■ **Note** If you need to remove cropping or other formatting from a picture, choose Picture Tools Format ➤ Adjust ➤ Reset Picture (clicking the main part of the Reset Picture button).

Correcting a Picture's Sharpness, Brightness, and Contrast

To make a picture look just right in a document, you may need to adjust its sharpness, brightness, or contrast. You can do so either in Word or in an image editor program such as the Microsoft Picture Manager program that comes as part of Office. (To launch Microsoft Picture Manager, choose Start ➤ All Programs ➤ Microsoft Office ➤ Microsoft Office Tools ➤ Microsoft Picture Manager.)

This section shows you how to make the corrections in Word. The advantage of this approach is that the underlying file remains unaffected, so you can use it in its original state in other programs. But if the original file needs correction to make it usable at all, you're better off applying the correction in an image editor program. You can then use the picture in Word or in other programs without making further changes.

To adjust the sharpness, brightness, or contrast in a picture, click the picture to select it, then choose Picture Tools Format ➤ Adjust ➤ Corrections to open the Corrections gallery (see Figure 7–7). Hold the mouse pointer over a correction to preview its effect on the picture, and then click the correction you want to apply.

- **Sharpen and Soften**. The top part of the gallery contains five different sharpness settings: Soften 50%, Soften 25%, Sharpen 0%, Sharpen 25%, and Sharpen 50%. Sharpen 0% has no effect unless you've already softened or sharpened the picture.

- **Brightness and Contrast**. The main part of the gallery contains five rows of combinations of brightness and contrast settings, from the lowest in both brightness and contrast (Brightness: –40%, Contrast: –40%) in the upper-left corner to the highest in both brightness and contrast (Brightness: +40%, Contrast: +40%) in the lower-right corner.

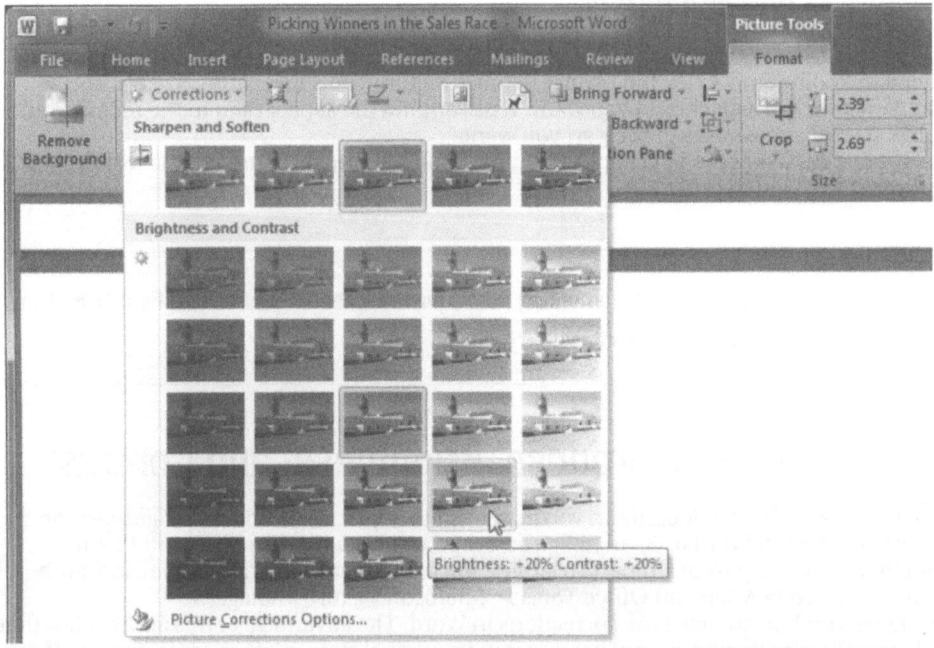

Figure 7–7. To fix problems with a picture's sharpness, brightness, or contrast, open the Corrections gallery, preview the effects by holding the mouse pointer over them, and then click the correction you want.

If you need greater control than the Corrections gallery's preset corrections provide, click the Picture Corrections Options item at the bottom of the gallery to display the Picture Corrections category in the Format Picture dialog window (see Figure 7–8). You can then use the Soften–Sharpen slider, the Brightness slider, and the Contrast slider to set exactly the correction your picture needs. Reposition the Format Picture dialog window so that you can see the picture as well, because Word makes the changes while the dialog window is open. Click the Close button when you've finished.

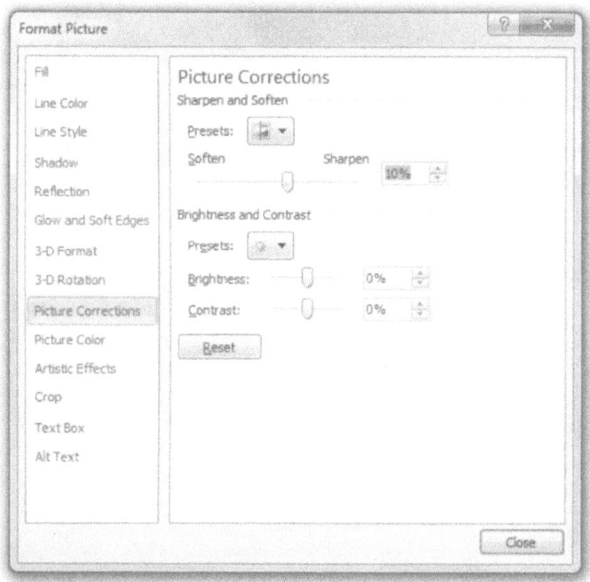

Figure 7–8. *Use the controls in the Picture Corrections category of the Format Picture dialog window when you need to make more precise changes to the sharpness, softness, brightness, and contrast of a picture.*

Changing the Colors in a Picture

To change the colors in a picture, click it, choose Picture Tools Format ➤ Adjust ➤ Color, and then click the effect you want. The Color gallery (see Figure 7–9) has three separate sections:

- **Color Saturation**. This section contains seven presets ranging from 0% saturation (which turns a color picture into monochrome) to 400% saturation, which makes the colors as rich as Warren Buffett.

- **Color Tone**. This section contains seven presets ranging from a low color temperature (giving a "cool" or bluish tone to the picture) to a high color temperature (giving a "warm" or golden tone).

- **Recolor**. This section contains 21 presets starting with No Recolor (which you use to restore normality to a picture) through Sepia, Washout, and Black and White to different accents (for example, Aqua accent).

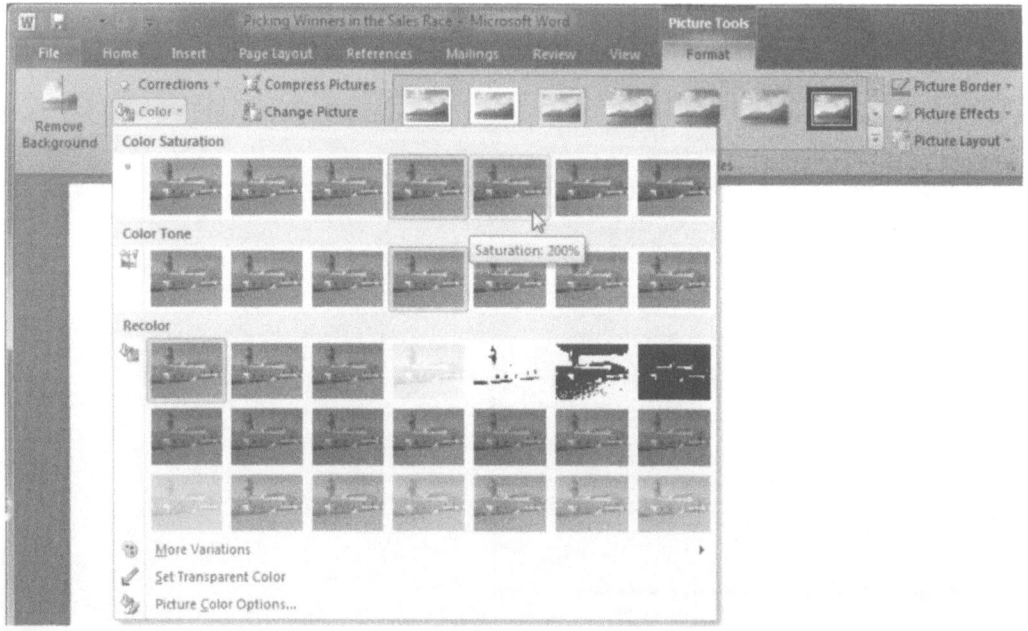

Figure 7–9. The Color gallery lets you change the color saturation and color tone of a picture. You can also choose to recolor it—for example, by turning it sepia.

You can preview any of these color changes by holding the mouse pointer over it and watching how the picture changes. Click the color change you want to apply to the picture.

If you want to apply a particular color to the picture, click the More Variations item in the Color gallery, and then click the color you want on the panel. Again, you can preview the effect to see which color works best.

If you want to make a color in the picture transparent, click Set Transparent Color in the Color gallery. The mouse pointer changes to a color-picker pen. Click the color in the picture that you want to make transparent, and Word knocks it out of the picture. This feature works best when the whole area you want to remove uses the same color.

If you want to adjust the colors in the picture manually, click Picture Color Options at the bottom of the Color gallery. Word displays the Picture Color category in the Format Picture dialog window (see Figure 7–10). Here, you can adjust the color saturation by using the Saturation slider and spin box, and the color temperature by using the Temperature slider and spin box. You can also choose a preset for saturation, color tone, or recoloring, but chances are that if you wanted to use a preset, you'd have done so from the Color gallery rather than open the Format Picture dialog window.

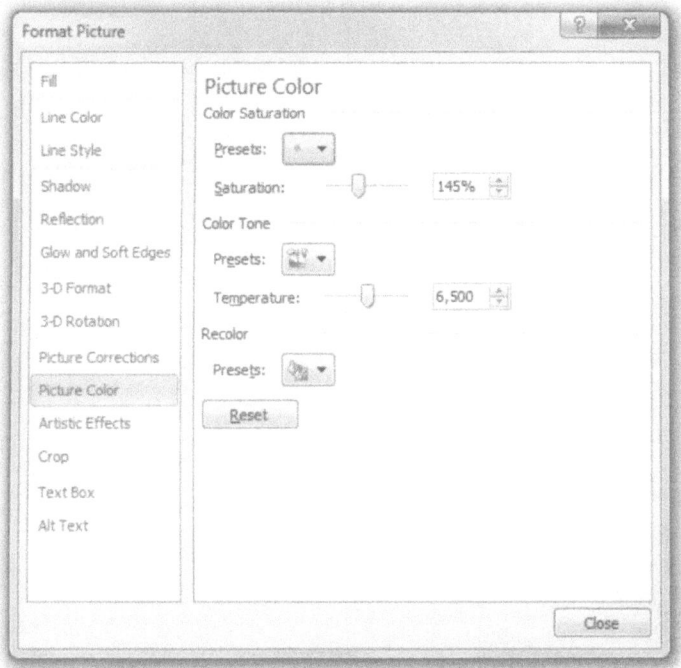

Figure 7–10. Open the Picture Color category in the Format Picture dialog window when you want to adjust the saturation and color temperature manually.

Applying an Artistic Effect to a Picture

To apply an artistic effect such as paint strokes or a light screen to a picture, click the picture, choose Picture Tools Format ➤ Adjust ➤ Artistic Effects, and then click the effect you want on the Artistic Effects gallery (see Figure 7–11).

Figure 7–11. To make a picture look different, you can apply an artistic effect to it from the Artistic Effects gallery.

■ **Note** The Artistic Effects Options item at the bottom of the Artistic Effects gallery opens the Format Picture dialog window with the Artistic Effects category displayed. This category contains only an Artistic Effect gallery that gives you the same choices as the Artistic Effects gallery on the ribbon, so there's little point in opening the dialog window unless you want to make other formatting choices in it.

Compressing the Pictures in a Document

When you insert pictures in a document (rather than linking them, as discussed in Chapter 8), Word saves a copy of each picture in the document. This can greatly increase the file size of the document.

To keep the document's file size down, you can compress the pictures and delete the cropped areas of them. To do so, follow these steps:

1. Click a picture to make Word add the Picture Tools section to the ribbon.

2. Choose Picture Tools Format ➤ Adjust ➤ Compress Pictures to display the Compress Pictures dialog window (see Figure 7–12).

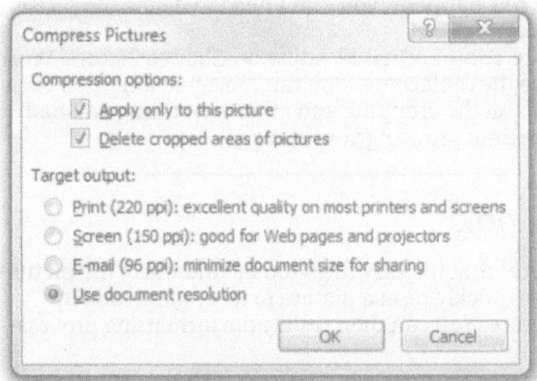

Figure 7–12. Use the Compress Pictures dialog window when you want to reduce the file size of one or more pictures or when you want to delete the cropped areas of pictures.

3. In the Compression options area, select the "Apply only to this picture" check box if you want to affect only the picture you've selected. Normally, you'll want to clear this check box to make Word compress all the pictures in the document.

4. Also in the Compression options area, select the "Delete cropped areas of pictures" check box if you want to get rid of the areas you've cropped off. This is a good security measure provided you don't need to adjust the cropping of any pictures in the document to reveal more.

5. In the Target Output area, select the appropriate option button to tell Word how severely to compress the pictures:

   • **Print (220 ppi): excellent quality on most printers and screens**. Compresses the pictures only a bit, leaving them high enough quality for most purposes.

   • **Screen (150 ppi): good for web pages and projectors**. Compresses the pictures a bit further, but leaves them looking good enough for use on-screen.

   • **E-mail (96 ppi): minimize document size for sharing**. Compresses the pictures to the extent that they start to look bad but are okay for viewing on-screen at small sizes.

   • **Use document resolution**. Changes the resolution of the pictures to match that of the document. The default setting is 220 dpi (print quality). To change the resolution, choose File ➤ Options, click the Advanced category, and scroll down to the Image Size and Quality area (about halfway down). In the "Set default target output to" drop-down list, choose the resolution you want (220 ppi, 150 ppi, or 96 ppi), and then click the OK button.

6. Click the OK button to close the Compress Pictures dialog window.

Replacing One Picture with Another Picture

Sometimes you may insert a picture, size and crop it, and maybe apply effects—and then realize you need to use another picture that looks similar. When this happens, you don't need to delete the picture, insert the new picture, and make all the adjustments again.

Instead, click the picture, and then choose Picture Tools Format ➤ Adjust ➤ Change Picture. Word displays the Insert Picture dialog window. Navigate to the replacement picture, select it, and then click the Insert button. Word inserts the picture and retains all the cropping and other formatting you had applied to the first picture, so you don't have to waste time retracing your steps.

Resetting a Picture to Its Original Look

Word gives you so many options for formatting pictures that it's easy to go too far and make the picture look odd—or even awful. When this happens, you can quickly reset a picture to its original look by choosing Picture Tools Format ➤ Adjust ➤ Reset Picture. You can then restart the formatting process—perhaps a little more carefully this time.

Removing a Picture's Background

Word includes a clever tool for removing the background from a picture. This is great when you need to remove extraneous elements from the picture to draw the viewer's eye to the subject.

For many pictures, Word's Remove Background tool can remove all the background needed with only minimal help. For other pictures, you may need to draw around the areas you want to keep and those you want to remove.

You'll probably want to start by seeing what the Remove Background tool can remove on its own. To do so, follow these steps:

1. Select the picture to make Word add the Picture Tools section to the ribbon.

2. Choose Picture Tools Format ➤ Adjust ➤ Remove Background. Word adds the Background Removal tab to the ribbon and displays its controls. At the same time, Word colors purple those parts of the picture it deems to be background and displays an outline around the area to keep (see Figure 7–13).

Figure 7–13. The first step in removing the background is to select the target area.

3. Drag the handles to resize and reposition the rectangle around the part of the picture you want to keep—in the example, the woman's face.

4. Choose Background Removal ➤ Close ➤ Keep Changes. Word hides the Background Removal tab and removes the background. Figure 7–14 shows the result with the sample picture.

If the Background Removal tool takes out all the background you want to lose, you're all set. Otherwise, click the Undo button on the Quick Access Toolbar to display the Background Removal tab again. You can then use the commands in the Refine group to mark which areas to keep and which to remove. The following examples use a different picture, as the Background Removal tool did a good job on the first picture.

Drag the handles on the rectangle to tell Word which parts of the picture you're most interested in (see Figure 7–15).

Figure 7–14. The sample picture with its background removed

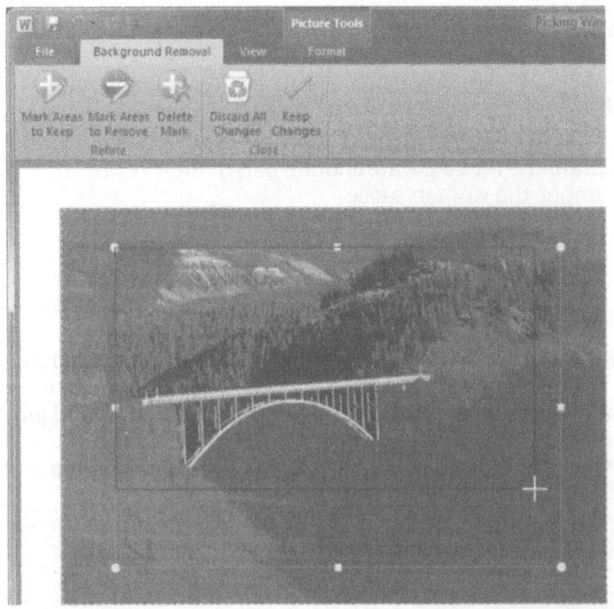

Figure 7–15. Drag the rectangle to mark the area of the picture that contains the parts you want to keep.

If Word applies purple shading to anything you want to keep, choose Background Removal ➤ Refine ➤ Mark Areas to Keep. Word changes the mouse pointer to a pen. Click and drag across each area you want to keep (see Figure 7–16). Word removes the purple shading from that area and displays a + sign to indicate that you've added the area. When you finish marking these areas, click the Mark Areas to Keep button again to turn off the tool.

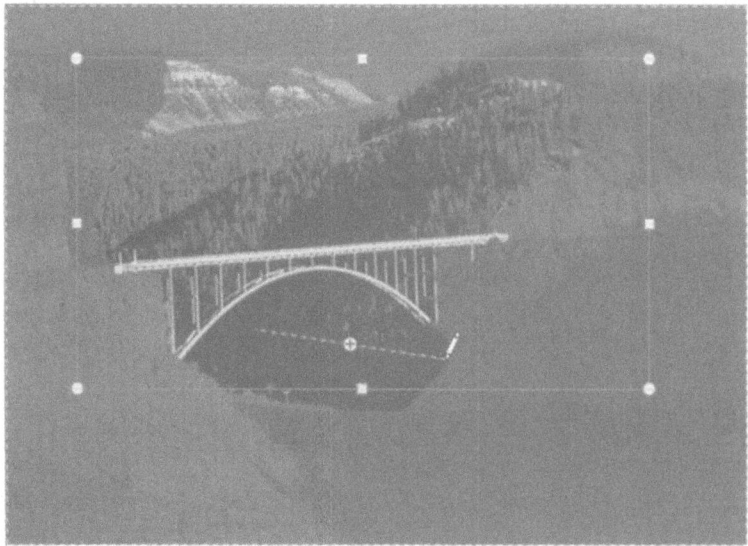

Figure 7–16. Drag the Mark Areas to Keep pen across purple-shaded areas you want to keep when removing the background. Word removes the shading from the areas you mark.

If the unshaded area of the picture contains background areas you want to remove, choose Background Removal ➤ Refine ➤ Mark Areas to Remove. Again, Word turns the mouse pointer to a pen. Drag with this pen across each area you want to remove. Word applies purple shading to it and displays a – sign to indicate that you've marked the area for removal. When you finish selecting these areas, click the Mark Areas to Remove button again to turn off the tool.

If you need to remove a particular area you've marked for keeping or for removal, choose Background Removal ➤ Refine ➤ Delete Mark, and then click the area's + sign or – sign. Click the Delete Mark button again when you want to turn off the Delete Mark tool.

■ **Note** If you get the background marking wrong and want to start again, choose Background Removal ➤ Close ➤ Discard All Changes. And if your background is all the same color, it's worth using the Color tool, as discussed earlier in this chapter.

When you've arranged the background to your satisfaction, choose Background Removal ➤ Close ➤ Keep Changes.

Summary

In this chapter, you've learned how to insert pictures in your documents and resize and crop them as needed. You also know how to correct the color balance, contrast, and brightness of a picture, and how to remove a picture's background.

In the next chapter, I'll show you how to use other graphical objects in your documents—everything from clip art items that come with Word to custom illustrations that you create.

■■■

CHAPTER 8

Using Media with Word

A document that consists of nothing but text may be well written and persuasive, but it runs the risk of being boring to look at.

In this chapter, I'll show you how to spice up your documents by adding graphical objects to them. The easiest way to start is by using Word's Clip Art task pane to insert clip art from the extensive collection that Microsoft provides, but you can also insert pictures of your own quickly and effortlessly.

After that, we'll look at how to add shapes (such as arrows or callouts), SmartArt illustrations (such as flow charts and organization charts), and charts (such as column charts or pie charts) to your documents. I'll also show you how to use Word's Screenshot feature to insert windows or other parts of computer screens in your documents, and how to resize and reposition graphical objects exactly as you need them. You'll even learn to insert video files and audio files in your documents.

Inserting Clip Art and Pictures

To add life to a document, you can quickly insert a clip art item or a picture in it. We'll start with inserting clip art items, and then look at how to insert pictures.

Inserting Clip Art in a Document

When you install Microsoft Office on your PC, you normally include its selection of clip art pictures, photographs, videos, and sounds. You can quickly add any of these items to a document, and you can also add items from the much larger selection of clip art at the Office.com web site.

To insert a clip art item in a document, follow these steps:

1. Position the insertion point where you want to insert the item.

2. Choose Insert ➤ Illustrations ➤ Clip Art to display the Clip Art task pane (shown in Figure 8–1 after a search that has found some results).

Figure 8–1. Use the Clip Art task pane to insert clip art items, photos, movies, or sounds in your Office documents. Hold the mouse pointer over a search result to see its keywords, size, resolution, and other details.

3. In the "Search for" box, type your search term or terms—for example, **dog**.

4. Open the "Results should be" drop-down list, and then select the check box for each file type you want to find: Illustrations, Photographs, Videos, and Sounds. Select the "All media types" item if you want to find everything that matches the keywords.

5. Select the "Include Office.com content" check box if you want to search online as well. As long as you have an Internet connection, this is usually a good idea.

6. Click the Go button to start the search.

7. Browse through the clip art items that appear in the Clip Art task pane, and then click the one you want to insert in the document. The program inserts the clip art item at its default size; you can resize it as described later in this chapter.

Making a Collection of Clip Art

Inserting a clip art item in a document is easy and straightforward, but you may also want to build up a collection of clip art to use at a later point. For example, when you're planning a document about a particular topic, you can gather a collection of clip art images that you may want to use. When the time comes to put the document together, you'll have the images on hand to drop right in rather than having to search for them.

For managing your clip art, Microsoft Office provides a program called the Microsoft Clip Organizer. You can add clip art to your collection from the Clip Art task pane or by working directly in the Microsoft Clip Organizer.

Adding Clip Art Items to Your Collections from the Clip Art Task Pane

When you're browsing clip art in the Clip Art task pane and you find a clip art item that you want to keep for future use, move the mouse pointer over the clip art item so that a drop-down button appears. Click this button to produce the drop-down menu shown in Figure 8–2.

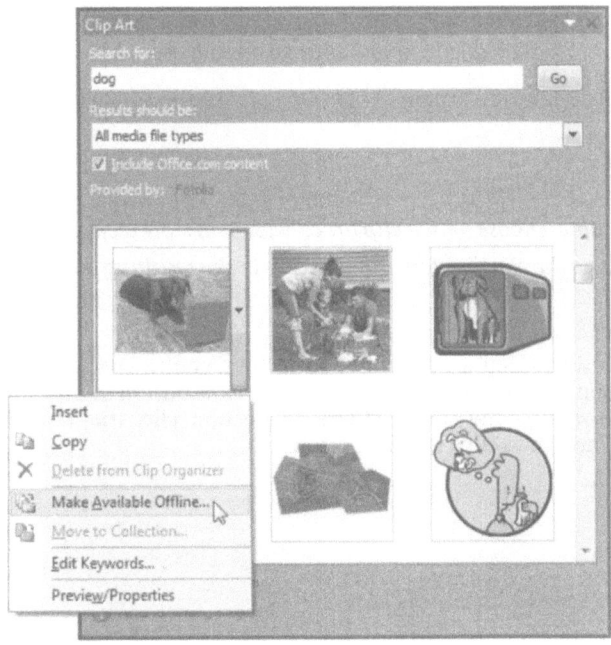

Figure 8–2. Use the drop-down menu to make a clip art item available offline, copy it to a collection, edit its keywords, or examine it more closely.

As you can see, the drop-down menu contains several commands. Some of the commands are available only for clip art items that you've added to your clip art collection; for other items, such as those on the Office.com web site, these commands are grayed out.

What you'll normally want to do here is click the Make Available Offline menu item. Word then displays the Copy to Collection dialog window (see Figure 8–3).

Figure 8–3. In the Copy to Collection dialog window, choose which clip art collection to store a clip art item in. You can create a new collection by clicking the New button and working in the resulting dialog window.

If the Copy to Collection dialog window shows a suitable collection for the item you're saving, click that collection. (The Favorites collection is a good catch-all.) Otherwise, click the New button to display the New Collection dialog window (see Figure 8–4), type the name for a new collection, click the collection in which to place the new collection, and then click the OK button.

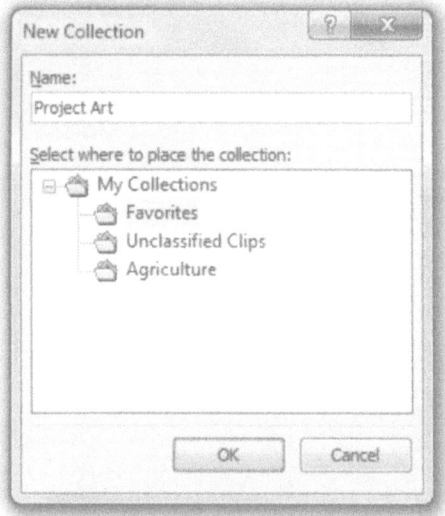

Figure 8–4. You can quickly create a new collection to keep your clip art neatly organized.

Once you've selected the collection in the Copy to Collection dialog window, click the OK button. Word closes the dialog window and copies the clip art item to the collection. Depending on how big the item is and how fast your Internet connection, this may take a few seconds.

You may also want to use some of the other commands on the drop-down menu:

- **Insert**: Inserts the item in the document—the same as clicking the item, which is usually easier.

- **Copy**: Copies the clip art item to the Clipboard so that you can paste it into another program.

- **Delete from Clip Organizer**: Deletes an item you've added to the Clip Organizer. You can't delete the items that come with the Clip Organizer.

- **Move to Collection**: Displays the Move to Collection dialog window, which you use for moving one of your clips (rather than one of Office's clips) to a different collection. The Move to Collection dialog window box is a renamed version of the Copy to Collection dialog window.

- **Edit Keywords**: Displays the Keywords dialog window (see Figure 8–5), in which you can add or edit keywords for a clip you've added to the Clip Organizer. You can't edit the keywords for the Office clips. Once you've opened the Keywords dialog window, you can move from one clip art item to another by clicking the Previous button and Next button.

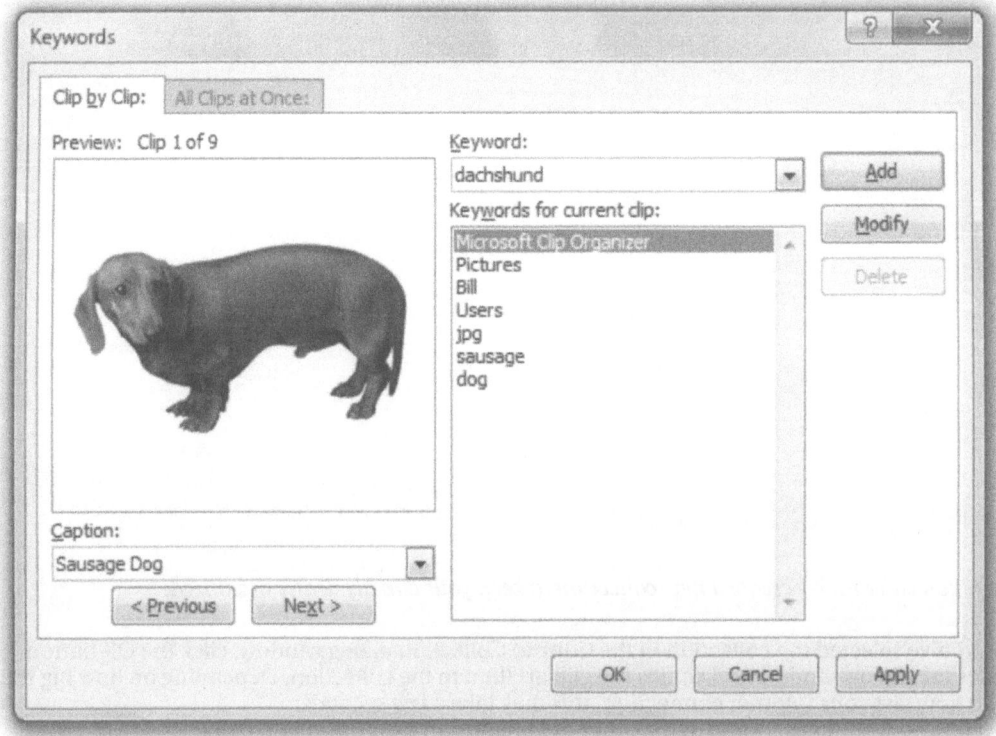

Figure 8–5. *Use the Keywords dialog window to add keywords to a clip you've added to the Clip Organizer.*

- **Preview/Properties**: Click this item to display the Preview/Properties dialog window showing the clip art item (see Figure 8–6). Use this dialog window to get a better look at an image. You can click the Previous button or the Next button to move from image to image, and you can click the Edit Keywords button to open the Keywords dialog window.

Figure 8–6. Open the Preview/Properties dialog window when you want to get a closer look at an image.

Using the Microsoft Clip Organizer

As you saw in the previous section, you can start collecting and organizing a clip art collection from the Clip Art pane in Word. But when you need more space to really dig into the collection, open the Microsoft Clip Organizer (see Figure 8–7) by choosing Start ➤ All Programs ➤ Microsoft Office ➤ Microsoft Office Tools ➤ Microsoft Clip Organizer.

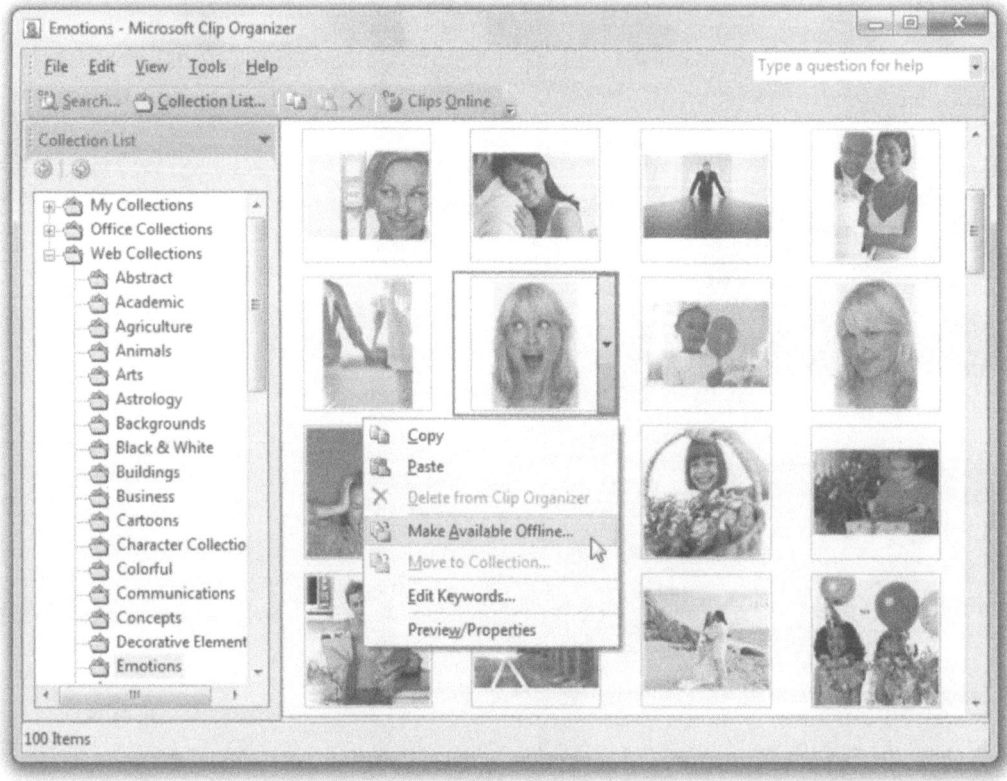

Figure 8–7. *Use the Microsoft Clip Organizer when you want to browse the various collections and gather clip art for use in your projects.*

You can search for clip art items by clicking the Search button on the toolbar and then using the Search pane that opens, but you may also simply want to browse the contents of the Office Collections (on your PC's hard drive) and Web Collections (on Office.com).

When you find an item you want to store, move the mouse pointer over it, click the drop-down button that appears, and then make your choice from the drop-down menu. For example, click the Make Available Offline button, and then choose the destination collection in the Copy to Collection dialog window that opens.

Inserting Pictures in Your Documents

As we saw in Chapter 7, if you have pictures of your own that you want to use in your documents, you can easily insert them, but there are also some more advanced options that we didn't cover:

1. Position the insertion point where you want to insert the picture.

2. Choose Insert ➤ Illustrations ➤ Picture to display the Insert Picture dialog window.

3. Navigate to the folder that contains the picture, and then click the picture to select it.

4. Choose how to insert the picture:

- **Save the picture in the document**: Click the Insert button in the Insert Picture dialog window. Word saves the picture in the document, so the picture is always available even if you move the document to another computer.

■ **Tip** If you will need to move the document to another computer, either save the picture in the document or use the Insert and Link command. If you expect to use the document only on your PC, you can keep the document's size down by linking the picture file.

- **Link the picture to the document**: Click the drop-down button to the right of the Insert button, and then click Link to File on the drop-down menu (see Figure 8–8). Word adds a link to the picture file to the document rather than saving a copy of the picture in the document. When you open the document, Word loads the picture from the file. But if you move the document to a different computer, the link will no longer work, because the program will be unable to find the picture file.

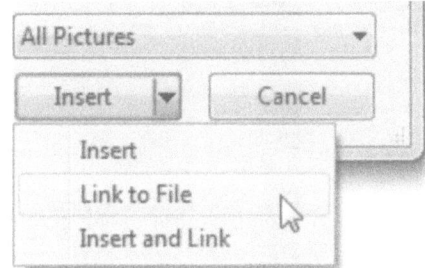

Figure 8–8. To link a picture to the document, click the Insert drop-down button in the Insert Picture dialog window, and then click Link to File.

- **Link the picture and save a copy**: Click the drop-down button to the right of the Insert button, and then click Insert and Link on the drop-down menu. Word inserts a copy of the picture in the document and links it back to the original picture. When you open the document, Word checks to see if the linked version is available. If so, Word loads the linked picture; if not, it displays the version saved in the document. Either way, the document shows the most up-to-date version of the picture available.

After inserting a picture, you can resize, reposition, or format it as discussed later in this chapter.

Inserting Shapes in a Document

If a document needs a drawing, you can create it from scratch by using Office's shapes. Office provides a wide variety of shapes, from arrows and basic shapes through to stars, banners, and callouts.

To insert a shape in a document, follow these steps:

1. Display the page on which you want to add the shape. Word places shapes in the graphics layers, so you don't need to position the insertion point.

2. Choose Insert ➤ Illustrations ➤ Shapes to display the Shapes gallery (see Figure 8–9), and then click the type of shape you want to insert.

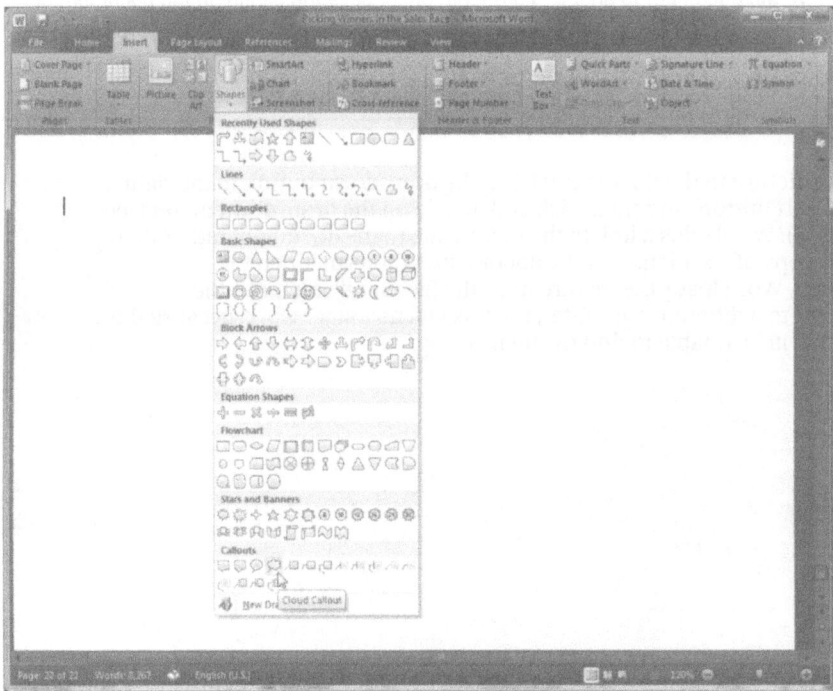

Figure 8–9. *Choose the type of shape from the Shapes gallery in the Illustrations group of the Insert tab of the ribbon. Hold the mouse pointer over a shape to see a ScreenTip showing its description.*

3. When you click the shape, Word changes the mouse pointer to a crosshair. With this crosshair, click where you want to place one corner of the shape, and then drag to the opposite corner (see Figure 8–10). It doesn't matter which corner you place first, as you can drag in any direction, but placing the upper-left corner first and dragging down and to the right is usually easiest.

Figure 8–10. Click and drag with the crosshair to place and size the shape you're inserting.

When you release the mouse button, the shape appears with selection handles around it and a green rotation handle at the top (see Figure 8–11), so you can resize or reposition it as described later in this chapter. When the shape is selected, the program adds the Drawing Tools section to the ribbon, which gives you access to the controls on the Format tab.

Figure 8–11. Word displays the shape with selection handles around it and a green rotation handle at the top.

Applying a Style to a Shape

After inserting a shape, you can apply a style to it from the Shape Styles gallery in the Shape Styles group on the Drawing Tools Format tab of the ribbon. If the style you want appears in the Shape Styles gallery box, click it; otherwise, click the More button (the drop-down button at the right side of the Shape Styles gallery), and then click the style in the gallery (see Figure 8–12).

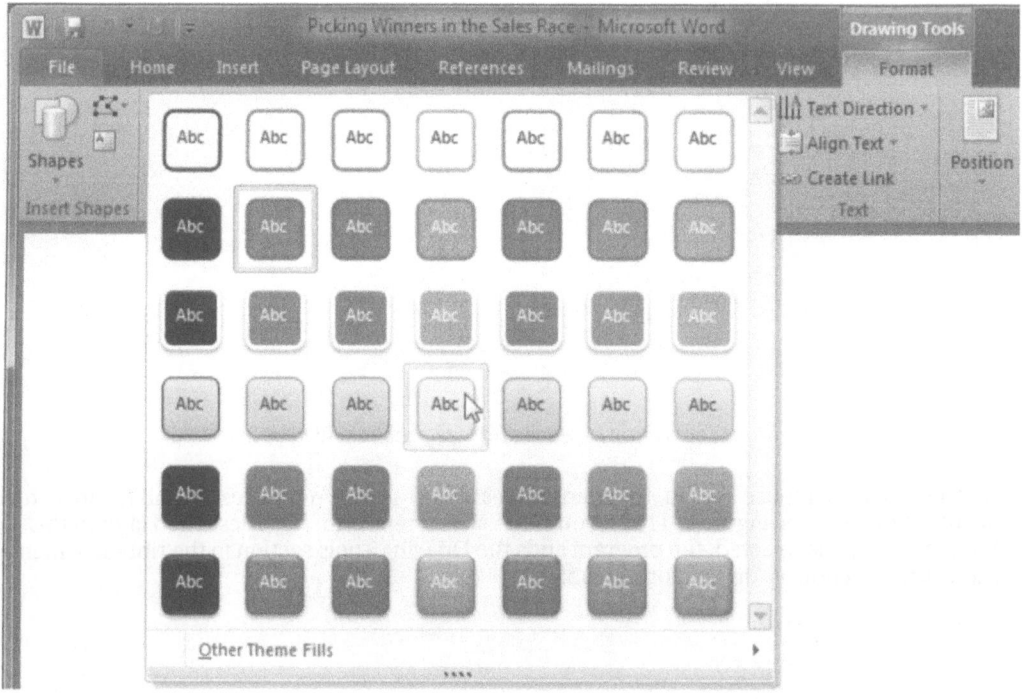

Figure 8–12. *To apply a style to a shape, open the Shape Styles gallery on the Drawing Tools Format tab,
and then click the style you want.*

After choosing the style that's nearest the look you want, you can refine the shape further as needed
by using the other controls in the Shape Styles group on the Drawing Tools Format tab:

- **Change the shape's fill**: Open the Shape Fill gallery, and then choose the color,
  picture, gradient, or texture you want.

- **Change the shape's outline**: Open the Shape Outline gallery, and then choose the
  color, weight, or style. For example, if you want to give the shape a dashed outline,
  click the Dashes submenu in the Shape Outline gallery, and then click the type of
  dashes.

- **Apply an effect to the shape**: Open the Shape Effects gallery, and then choose the
  effect you want. For example, click the 3-D Rotation submenu in the Shape Effects
  gallery, and then choose the rotation from the gallery that opens (see Figure 8–13).

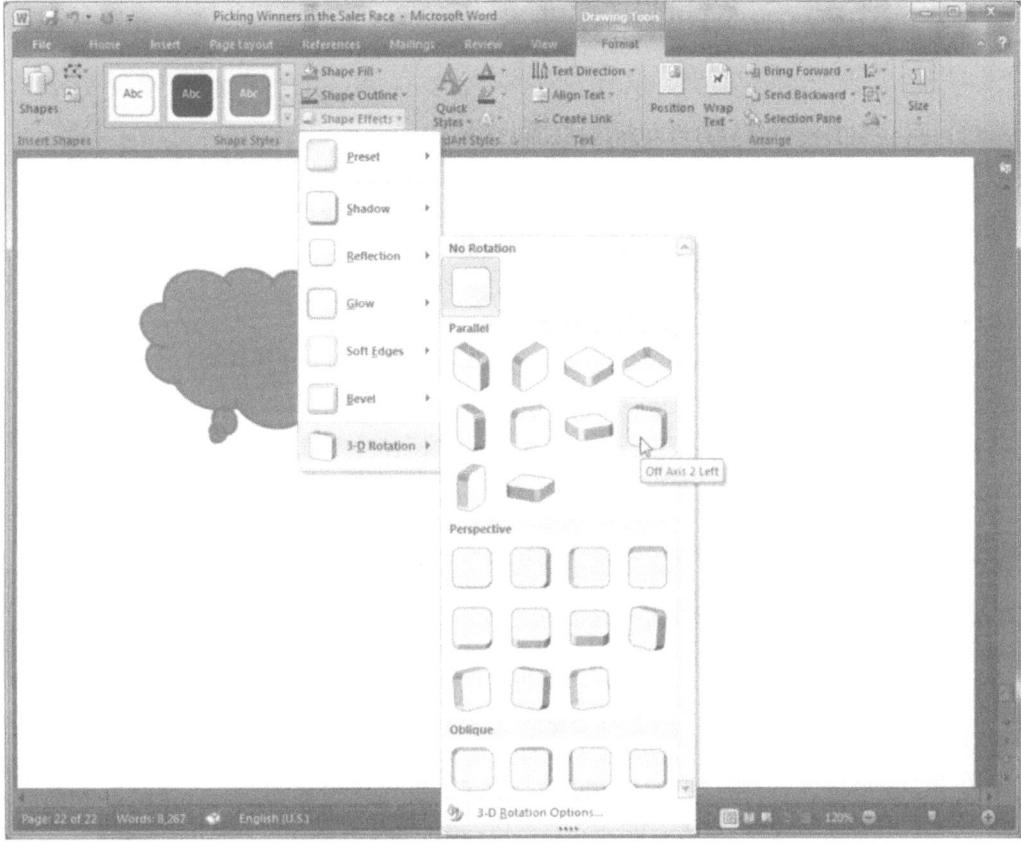

Figure 8–13. *After inserting a shape, use the galleries in the Shape Styles group of the Drawing Tools Format tab of the ribbon to customize the shape.*

Creating Illustrations with SmartArt

SmartArt is a tool for creating illustrations that include text, such as flow charts, organization charts, or cycle charts. The name contains "smart" because the feature helps you create the illustrations easily, automatically entering text for you and resizing it as needed.

To insert a SmartArt illustration, follow these steps:

1. Position the insertion point where you want to insert the SmartArt object.

2. Choose Insert ➤ Illustrations ➤ SmartArt to display the Choose a SmartArt Graphic dialog window (shown in Figure 8–14 with settings chosen).

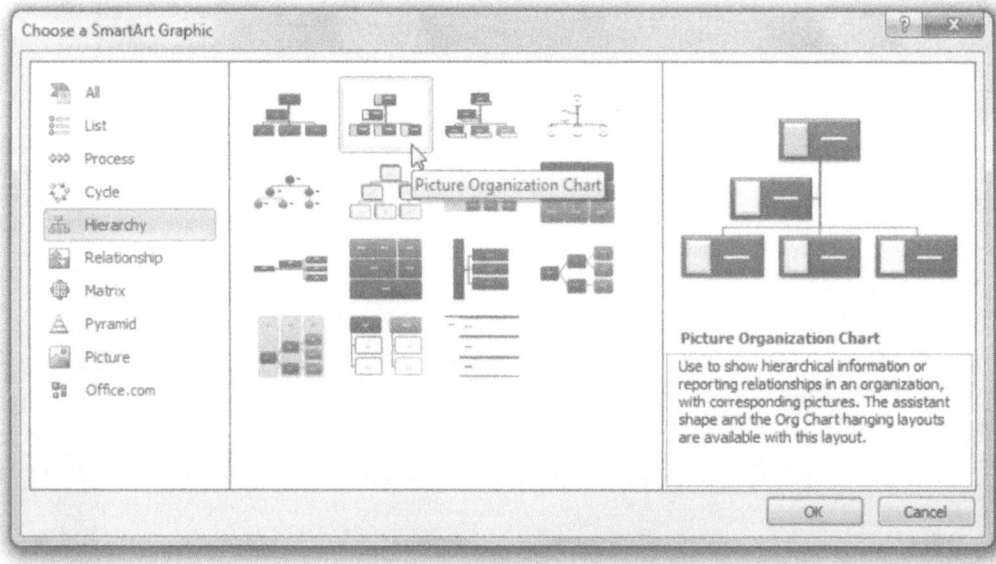

Figure 8–14. *In the Choose a SmartArt Graphic dialog window, choose the type of SmartArt graphic you want to create.*

3. In the left list box, click the category of graphic you want—for example, choose Hierarchy if you want to create an org chart.

4. In the main pane, click the type of graphic—for example, Picture Organization Chart.

5. Click the OK button to close the Choose a SmartArt Graphic dialog window. Word inserts the SmartArt graphic, displays the "Type your text here" window next to it, and adds the SmartArt Tools section to the ribbon (see Figure 8–15).

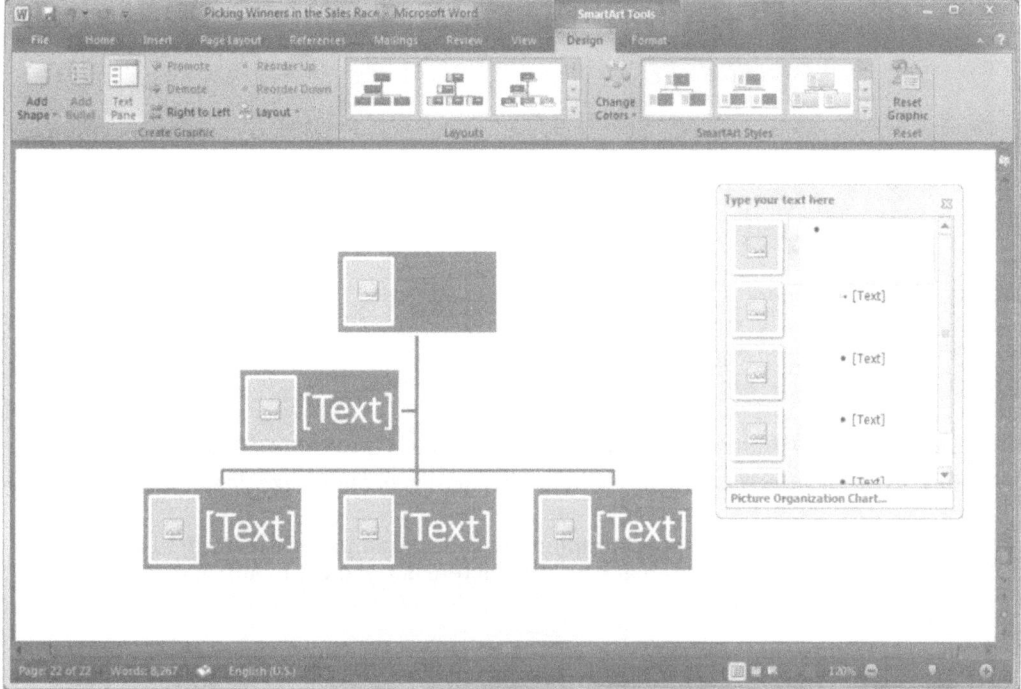

Figure 8–15. *When you insert a SmartArt graphic, Word displays the "Type your text here" window next to it and adds the SmartArt Tools section to the ribbon.*

■ **Note** If Word doesn't display the "Type your text here" window, choose SmartArt Tools ➤ Design ➤ Create Graphic ➤ Text Pane to display it.

---

6. Type the text for each item in the "Type your text here" window. As you do, Word adds the text to the SmartArt graphic (see Figure 8–16).

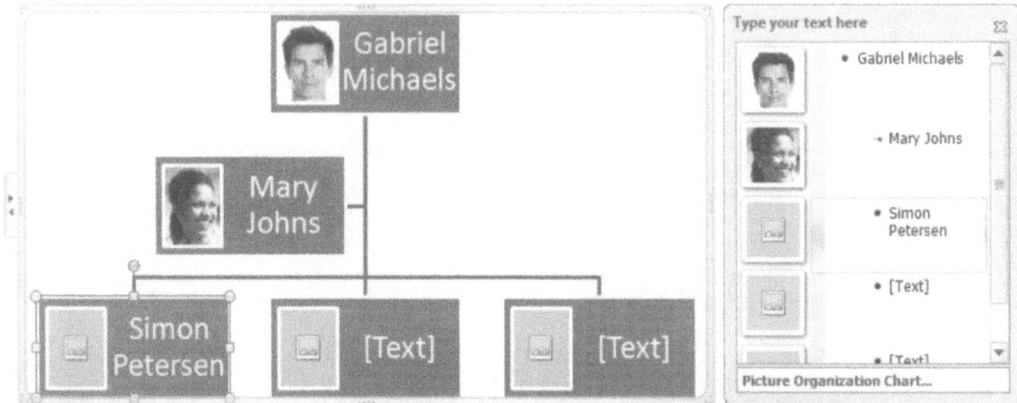

Figure 8–16. Add the text to the SmartArt graphic by typing in the "Type your text here" window. To add other items, such as the pictures shown here, click the placeholder and use the dialog window that opens.

7. Add any other items the SmartArt graphic needs. For example, add pictures to a Picture Organization Chart by clicking each picture placeholder in turn and then, in the Insert Picture dialog window that opens, selecting the picture to use.

■ **Note** To open the Insert Picture dialog window, you can either click the picture placeholder in the "Type your text here" window once or double-click the picture placeholder in the SmartArt graphic itself.

---

8. Use the controls in the Create Graphic group on the SmartArt Tools Design tab to adjust the SmartArt graphic as needed:

- **Add a shape:** Click the shape you want to use as a starting point for the new shape, choose SmartArt Tools Design ➤ Create Graphic ➤ Add Shape, and then click Add Shape After, Add Shape Before, Add Shape Above, Add Shape Below, or Add Assistant.

- **Add a bullet:** Choose SmartArt Tools Design ➤ Create Graphic ➤ Add Bullet.

- **Move an item:** Click the item you want to move, and then click the Promote button, Demote button, Right to Left button, Reorder Up button, or Reorder Down button, as needed.

- **Change the branch layout:** Chose SmartArt Tools Design ➤ Create Graphic ➤ Layout, and then click the branch layout you want.

9. If necessary, resize the SmartArt graphic to suit your document.

10. If you need to change the overall layout of the SmartArt graphic, choose SmartArt Tools Design ➤ Layouts ➤ Change Layout, and then click the layout on the gallery (see Figure 8–17).

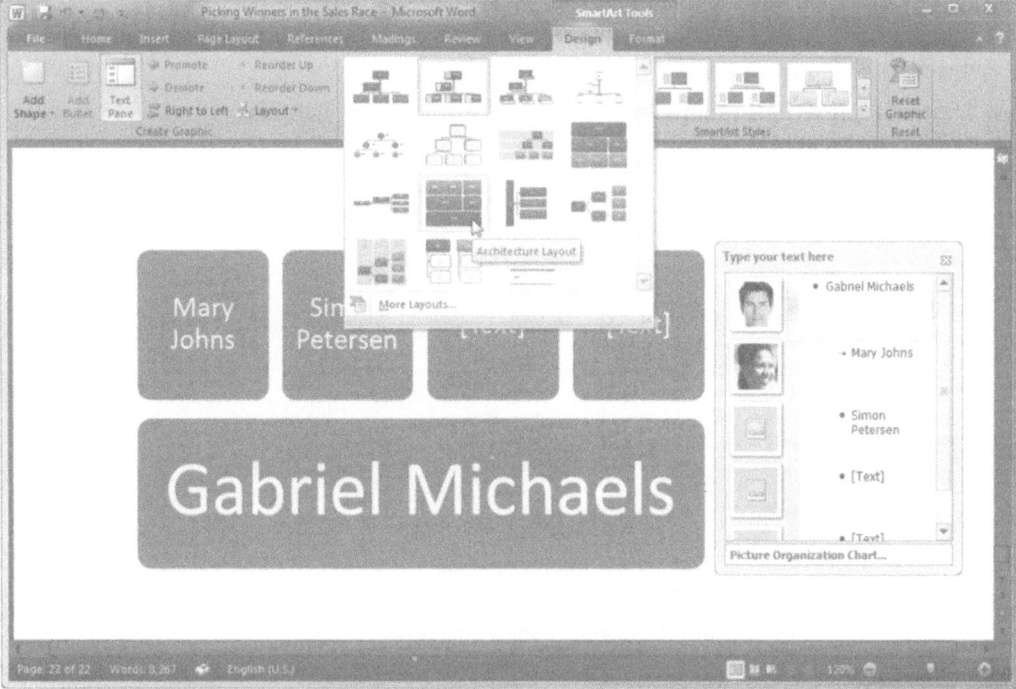

Figure 8–17. You can quickly change the layout of a SmartArt graphic by using the Change Layout gallery on the SmartArt Tools Design tab of the ribbon.

11. Apply a style to the SmartArt graphic by choosing a style from the Quick Styles gallery in the SmartArt Styles group of the Design tab.

Adding Charts to Your Documents

When you need to illustrate a point in a document, adding a chart can often help. For charts, Word harnesses the full power of Microsoft Excel, the spreadsheet program that's part of Office. This enables you to create attractive and convincing charts with a minimum of effort.

You can add a chart in either of two ways:

- Create a new chart in an Excel workbook embedded in the Word document.

- Paste an existing chart (and maybe its workbook) into the Word document.

We'll look at each approach in turn.

Creating a New Chart in a Word Document

To create a new chart in a Word document, you insert an Excel workbook to contain the data. Word handles all the details of the process, so it's easy.

To create a new chart in a Word document, follow these steps:

1. In Word, open the document and display the page on which you want to insert the chart.

2. Choose Insert ➤ Illustrations ➤ Chart to display the Insert Chart dialog window (see Figure 8–18).

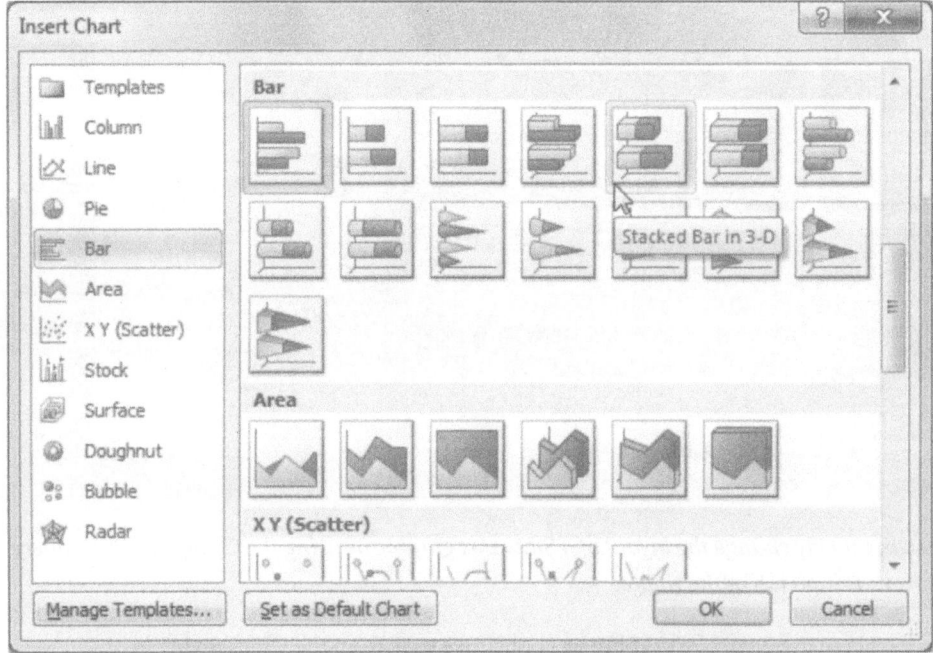

Figure 8–18. In the Insert Chart dialog window, choose first the type of chart and then the subtype. If you're not sure which type of chart you want, scroll down the list of charts until you find the right type.

3. In the left pane, click the type of chart you want to insert. For example, click the Bar item in the left pane to display the selection of bar charts in the main list box.

4. In the main list box, click the chart subtype you want. For example, Excel includes bar charts such as Clustered Bar, Stacked Bar, 100% Stacked Bar, Clustered Horizontal Pyramid, and other variations. Hold the mouse pointer over a chart picture to display a ScreenTip showing its subtype.

5. Click the OK button to close the Insert Chart dialog window. Word opens Excel, which creates a workbook named Chart in Microsoft Word and enters sample data in it (see Figure 8–19).

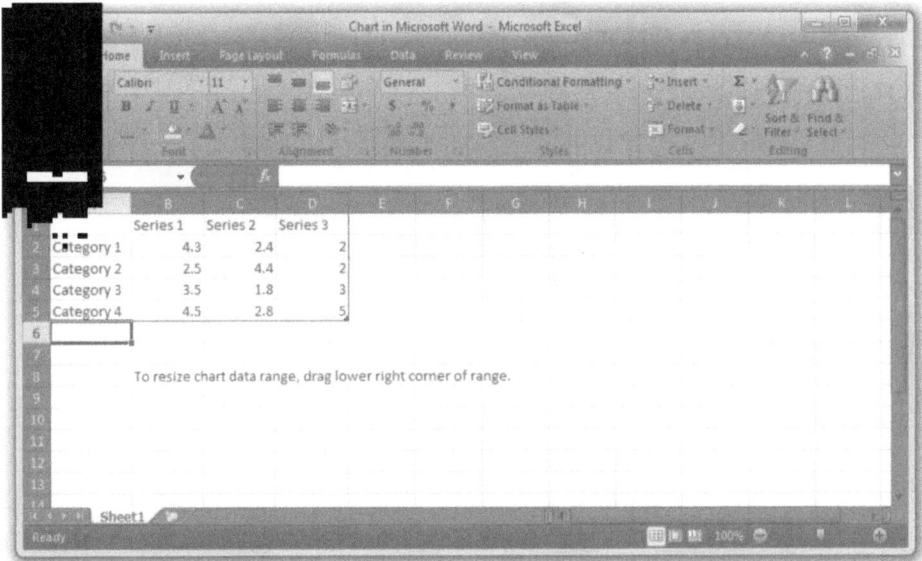

Figure 8–19. Replace the sample data in the Excel worksheet with the data you want in the chart.

6. Type your own data for the chart over the sample data, replacing the category labels (Category 1 through Category 4) and the series labels (Series 1 through Series 3) with the labels you want on the chart. As you change the data, Excel updates the chart in the Word document (see Figure 8–20).

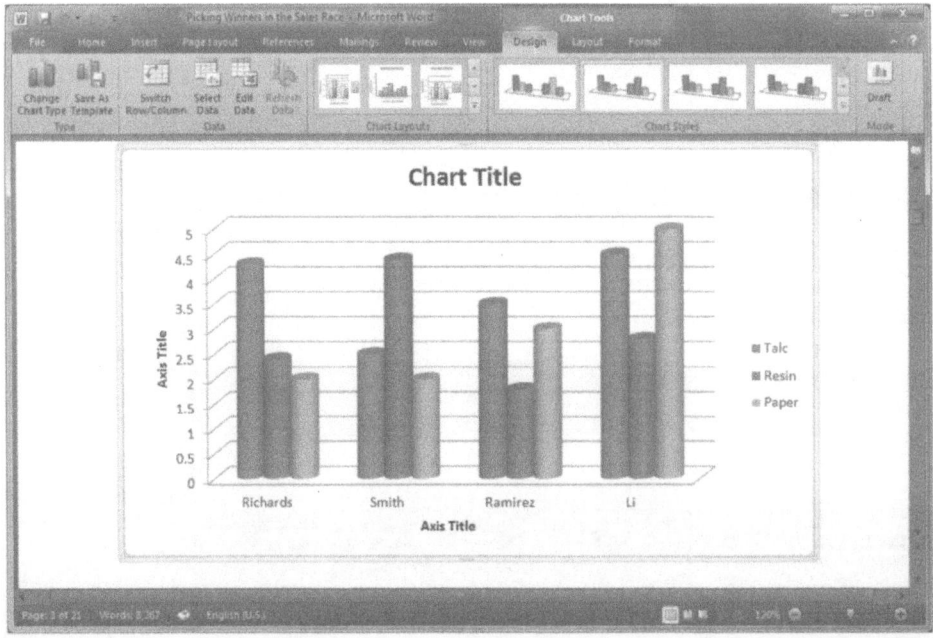

Figure 8–20. *As you work in the embedded workbook, Excel updates the chart in the Word document with the new data.*

7. If you need to make the data area larger or smaller, click the sizing handle in its lower-right corner and drag until the data area is the size you need. For example, if you need to add another column to the data area, drag the sizing handle one column to the right.

8. When you have finished changing the data, close Excel. For example, choose File ➤ Close. You don't need to save the data in the Excel workbook, because Word saves it automatically for you.

9. Format the chart as discussed later in this chapter.

10. Save the Word document. Word saves the embedded Excel workbook in the document.

Pasting a Chart from Excel into a Word Document

If you have a chart already created in Excel, or if you have a workbook containing the data from which you will create the chart, you can paste the chart into a Word document. When you do this, you must choose whether to embed the chart's workbook in the Word document or merely link the chart to the document. There's a big difference between the two:

- **Embed a workbook**: Embedding the chart's workbook produces a Word document that contains not only the chart but also all the data in the workbook. This enables you to move the Word document to another PC and still be able to edit the chart, but it makes it almost impossible to keep the Word document's copy of the workbook and your main copy synchronized.

- **Link a workbook**: Linking the chart's workbook produces a Word document that contains a version of the chart that you can easily update as long as the workbook is present. If you keep the document and workbook on the same PC, this is the best choice. If you move the Word document to another PC, you won't be able to update the chart, because the workbook won't be available.

To paste a chart from Excel into a Word document, follow these steps:

1. Launch Excel, and then open the workbook that contains the chart or the data.

2. If you need to create the chart, select the data, and then create the chart. For example, click the Insert tab of the ribbon, go to the Charts group, click the button for the chart type you want (for instance, Column), and then click the chart subtype on the gallery that opens.

3. Click the chart to select it.

4. Copy the chart to the Clipboard. For example, choose Home ➤ Clipboard ➤ Copy, or right-click the selected chart and then click Copy on the context menu.

5. Switch to the Word document, and then display the page on which you want to paste the chart.

6. Right-click the page, and then click the appropriate icon in the Paste Options section of the context menu (see Figure 8–21):

   - **Keep Source Formatting & Embed Workbook**: Click this item to insert the chart using an embedded workbook, but to retain the chart's current formatting.

   - **Use Destination Theme & Embed Workbook**: Click this item to insert the chart using an embedded workbook, changing the chart's formatting to match the presentation's current theme.

   - **Keep Source Formatting & Link Data**: Click this item to link the chart back to the Excel workbook and retain the chart's current formatting.

   - **Use Destination Theme & Link Data**: Click this item to link the chart back to the Excel workbook, changing the chart's formatting to match the document's current theme.

   - **Picture**: Click this item to insert the chart as a picture, without embedding the workbook or linking the chart back to the Excel workbook.

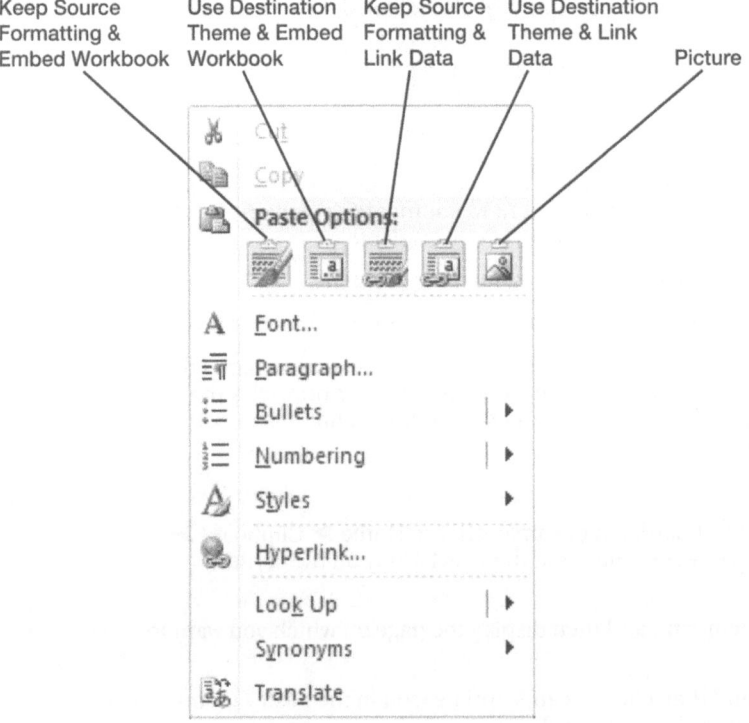

Figure 8–21. When pasting a chart from Excel into a Word document, choose how to paste the chart by clicking the appropriate icon in the Paste Options section of the context menu.

7. Use the controls in the Chart Tools section of the ribbon to format the chart the way you want it.

Formatting a Chart in a Word Document

When you've inserted a chart in a Word document either by embedding its workbook or by linking the chart, you can format the chart in Word so that it looks the way you want. To format the chart, you use the controls on the three contextual tabs that appear on the Chart Tools section of the ribbon when you select a chart—the Design tab, the Layout tab, and the Format tab.

Changing the Overall Chart Type and Appearance

You'll probably want to start your formatting on the Chart Tools Design tab (which you can see in Figure 8–20, earlier in this chapter), which you use to control the overall chart type and appearance. These are the changes you're most likely to need to make here:

- **Change the chart type:** If you need to change the chart to a different type, choose Chart Tools Design ➤ Type ➤ Change Chart Type, and then work in the Change Chart Type dialog window that opens. Apart from its title bar, this dialog window is the same as the Insert Chart dialog window that you met earlier in this chapter.

- **Switch the rows and columns:** If the chart is the wrong way around, choose Chart Tools Design ➤ Data ➤ Switch Row/Column. Word causes Excel to switch over the rows and columns, which is far preferable to you having to retype the data.

- **Change the layout:** To choose a different layout for the chart, its title, and its legend, choose Chart Tools Design ➤ Chart Layouts ➤ Quick Layout, and then click the layout you want on the Quick Layout gallery. If none of the layouts suits you, click the element you want to move (for example, the chart title), and then drag it to where you want it to appear.

- **Change the chart style:** Choose the style you want from the Chart Styles gallery. This gallery provides a wide range of different designs.

Note The Draft gallery in the Mode group on the Chart Tools Design tab of the ribbon enables you to switch to Draft mode to display complex charts more quickly than Normal mode does. Try using Draft mode if Word takes ages to display a chart. If Word displays charts quickly enough, stick with Normal mode.

Changing the Layout of the Chart

After you've sorted out the basics of the chart by using the controls on the Chart Tools Design tab, click the Chart Tools Layout tab to display its controls (see Figure 8–22), and then use them to change the chart as needed:

- **Select part of the chart:** If the chart is cluttered, you can use the Chart Elements drop-down list at the top of the Current Selection group to select the part of the chart that you want to affect. Otherwise, simply click the part of the chart.

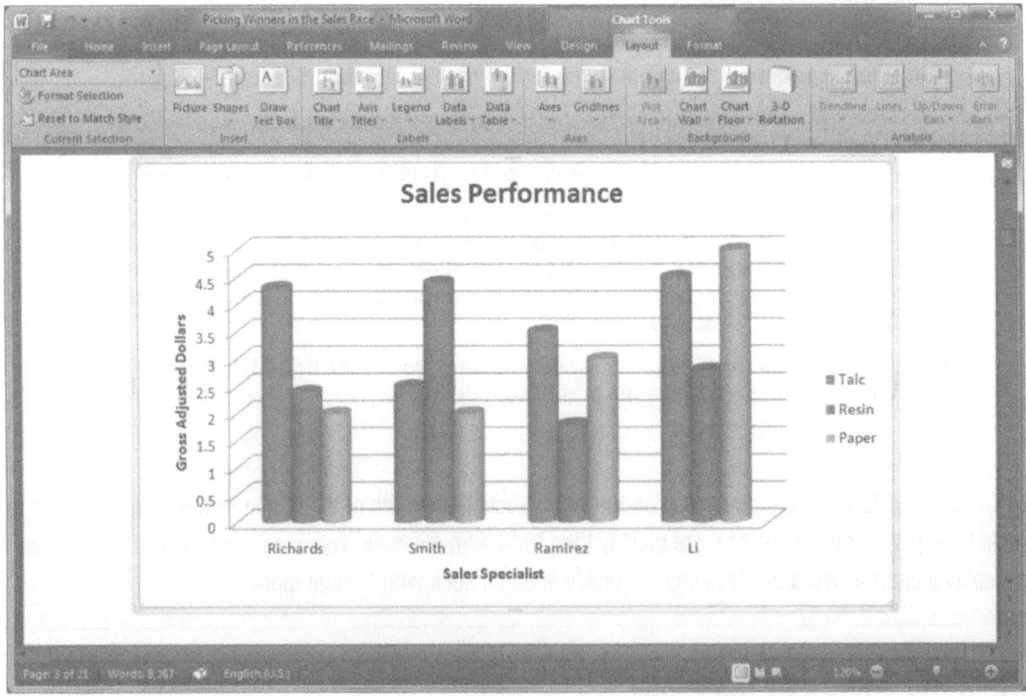

Figure 8–22. *Use the controls on the Chart Tools Layout tab to format the chart's labels, axes, and background areas.*

- **Add a chart title:** Choose Chart Tools Layout ➤ Labels ➤ Chart Title to display the Chart Title gallery, and then choose the title placement you want: None (to suppress the chart title), Centered Overlay Title (to display the title overlaid at the top of the chart), or Above Chart (to reduce the chart's height and display the title above it).

- **Add axis titles:** Choose Chart Tools Layout ➤ Labels ➤ Axis Titles, click the axis title you want to affect (for example, Primary Horizontal Axis Title or Primary Vertical Axis Title), and then choose the axis titles you want—for example, Title Below Axis for the primary horizontal axis.

- **Add a legend.** Choose Chart Tools Layout ➤ Labels ➤ Legend, and then click the legend option you want: None, Show Legend at Right, Show Legend at Top, Show Legend at Left, Show Legend at Bottom, Overlay Legend at Right, or Overlay Legend at Left.

- **Add data labels:** Data labels are text items that give the values of the data points in the chart. Data labels are useful if readers need to see the exact values rather than using the chart to get a general idea of them. To add data labels, choose Chart Tools Layout ➤ Labels ➤ Data Labels ➤ Show; to turn data labels off, choose Chart Tools Layout ➤ Labels ➤ Data Labels ➤ None.

- **Add a data table**: If you need the Word document to show the data from which the chart is derived as well as the chart itself, choose Chart Tools Layout ➤ Labels ➤ Data Table ➤ Show Data Table. You can also choose Chart Tools Layout ➤ Labels ➤ Data Table ➤ Show Data Table with Legend Keys to include legend keys for the data table. This is sometimes helpful for complex charts.

- **Choose whether and how to display the axes**: Some charts don't need axes, but others are clearer with them. To control whether and how axes appear, choose Chart Tools Layout ➤ Axes ➤ Axes, click the axis you want to affect (for example, Primary Horizontal Axis or Primary Vertical Axis), and then click the display option. For example, to display the default category axis for a chart, choose Chart Tools Layout ➤ Axes ➤ Axes ➤ Primary Horizontal Axis ➤ Show Default Axis.

- **Add gridlines if needed**: To make the values of the chart's data points easier to gauge, you can add gridlines that run across the chart from the axes. To add gridlines, choose Chart Tools Layout ➤ Axes ➤ Gridlines, click the axis you want to affect, and then click the gridlines type: None, Major Gridlines, Minor Gridlines, or Major & Minor Gridlines.

- **Format the chart background if needed**: The controls in the Background group of the Layout tab enable you to apply a color, fill, or picture to the plot area, the chart wall, or the chart floor. For example, you can insert a photograph on the chart wall to give the chart a visual backdrop.

Changing How the Chart Shape Appears in the Document

If you need to change the way the shape that contains the chart appears in the document, click the Chart Tools Format tab, and then use its controls. We'll look at resizing and repositioning graphical objects later in this chapter. For example, you can use the Position gallery in the Arrange area to control whether the chart appears in line with the document's text or with text wrapping, or you can use the Wrap Text gallery to position the chart behind the text or in front of the text.

Editing or Updating a Chart in a Word Document

If you need to edit the data for the chart, click the chart to select it, and then choose Chart Tools Design ➤ Data ➤ Edit Data. Word opens Excel, which displays the embedded workbook, and you can start working with the data again.

If you've linked the chart to the document rather than embedding the chart's workbook in the document, you can update the document with the latest version of the chart. To do so, choose Chart Tools Design ➤ Data ➤ Refresh Data. As I mentioned before, the linked workbook must be available for this to work.

Creating Documentation by Using Screenshots

If you create documentation about using computers, you may need to insert screenshots to illustrate what you're explaining. Word's Screenshot feature gives you an easy way of inserting screenshots of either full windows or partial screens that you capture using the Screen Clipping feature.

To insert a screenshot, follow these steps:

1. Open the program or window that you want to capture, and set it up the way you want. For example, make the window show the relevant content, or resize it to the size at which you want to capture it.

2. In Word, display the page on which you want to insert the screenshot. You can move the screenshot after inserting it, but you might as well start in the right place.

3. Choose Insert ➤ Illustrations ➤ Screenshot to display the Screenshot gallery (see Figure 8–23). This gallery automatically displays a screenshot of each of the open windows apart from Word's own window.

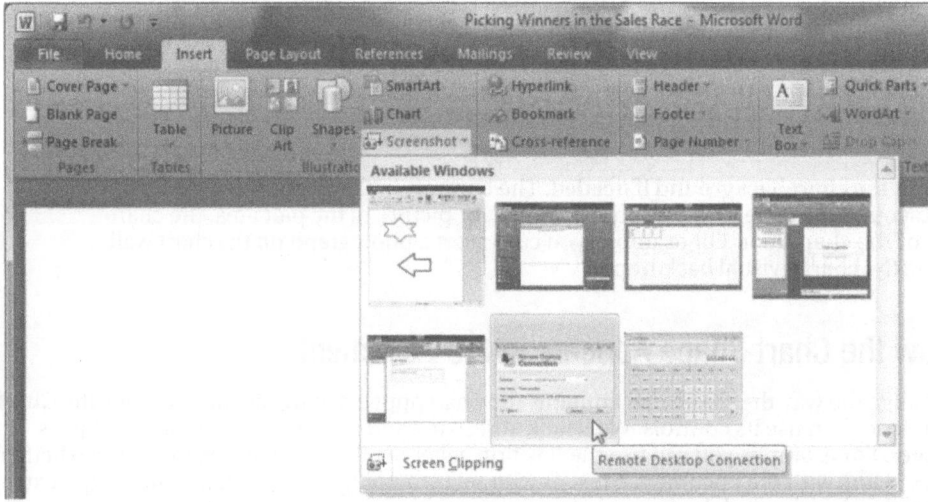

Figure 8–23. To insert a screenshot of one of the open windows, click that window in the Screenshot gallery. Click the Screen Clipping item if you want to capture a different area of the screen.

4. Click the window you want to take the screenshot of. Word inserts a screenshot of the window at the position of the insertion point (see Figure 8–24). You can than resize and reposition the screen capture as needed.

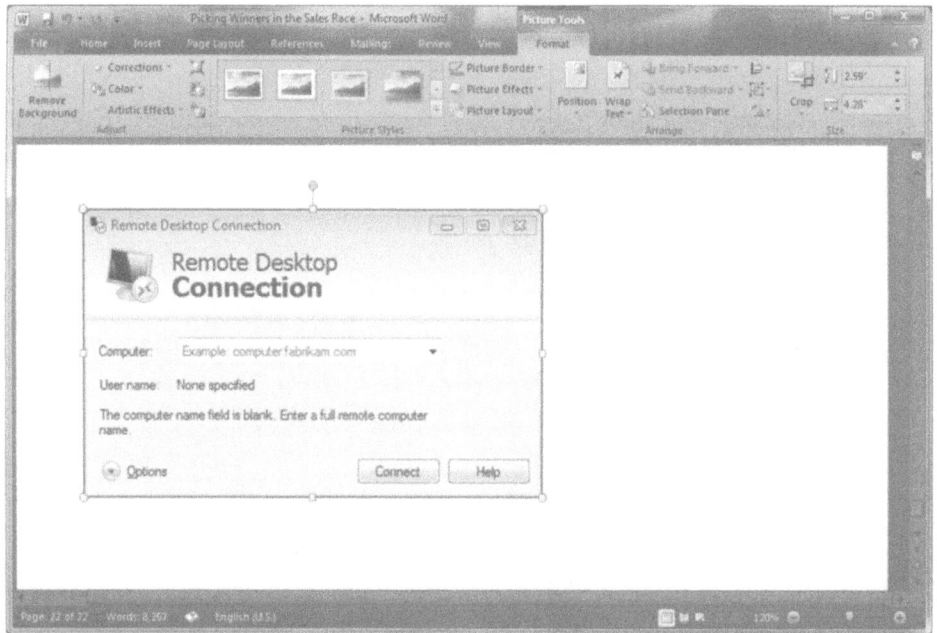

Figure 8–24. After inserting a screenshot, you can resize, reposition, or format it like any other picture.

If you want to capture a particular area of a window or of the screen rather than an entire window, choose Insert ➤ Illustrations ➤ Screenshot ➤ Screen Clipping. Word hides its own windows and changes the mouse pointer to a crosshair. Click and drag with this crosshair (see Figure 8–25) to capture the part of the window or of the screen you want. When you release the mouse button, Word inserts the captured part of the screen in the document.

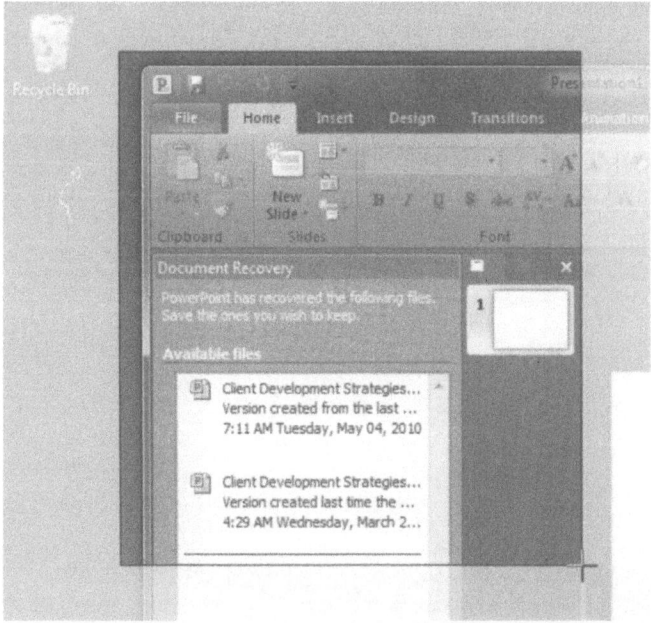

Figure 8–25. Click and drag with the crosshair to capture just part of a window.

■ **Tip** If you need to edit a screen capture before inserting it, run Snipping Tool outside Word. Choose Start ➤ All Programs ➤ Accessories ➤ Snipping Tool to launch Snipping Tool. Create a new snip by clicking the New drop-down button, clicking the type of snip (for example, Full-screen Snip), and save the file. You can then open the file in Microsoft Picture Manager (choose Start ➤ All Programs ➤ Microsoft Office ➤ Microsoft Office Tools ➤ Microsoft Picture Manage) and crop it as needed (choose Picture ➤ Crop).

Resizing and Positioning Graphical Objects

After you insert a graphical object such as a picture, a clip art item, or a screenshot, you'll often need to resize it, move it to a different position, or both. This section explains what you need to know to position graphical objects exactly where you want them in your documents.

Understanding How You Position Graphical Objects

A Word document appears to be flat when you look at it on-screen, but it actually consists of multiple separate layers. One of the layers is for the document's main text—the paragraphs that flow from one page to the next. Another layer contains the headers, footers, and any other objects you set to repeat on every page—for example, a watermark. Other layers contain any graphical objects that you add to the document.

Having these multiple layers enables you to position graphical objects either in front of the text layer or behind the text layer. You can also position one graphical object in front of another graphical object—for example, to superimpose one graphical object on another.

Word lets you position graphical objects either inline in the text layer or as free-floating objects in the graphics layers. When you place a graphical object inline, Word treats the graphical object like a character in the document's text. If you then insert text before the graphical object, it moves further down the document.

Selecting a Graphical Object

The easiest way to select a graphical object is to click it with the mouse. But if you've added several graphical objects to the same area and layered them on top of each other, it can be difficult to click the objects that are behind other objects.

To solve this problem, Word provides the Selection and Visibility task pane (see Figure 8–26). You display this pane by clicking a graphical object, and then choosing Format ➤ Arrange ➤ Selection Pane.

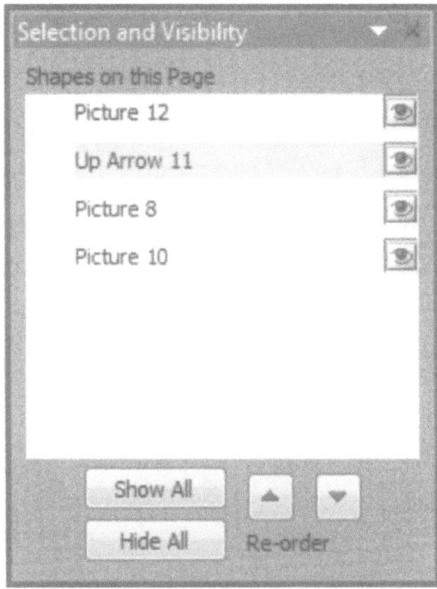

Figure 8–26. Use the Selection and Visibility task pane to select objects easily when you have layered them over each other. You can hide particular objects, hide them all, or change their order.

Here's how to use the Selection and Visibility task pane:

- **Select an object**: In the list of objects, click the object you want to affect.

- **Hide an object**: To turn off the display of an object, clear the check box to the right of it. Select the check box again when you want to see the object once more.

- **Hide all objects**: To hide all the current objects (for example, so that you can work with a new object or edit the text), click the Hide All button. Click the Show All button when you're ready to bring the objects back.

- **Change the order of the objects**: Click an object, and then click the Up button or the Down button to move it up or down the order.

You can leave the Selection and Visibility task pane open as long as you need. To close it, click the Close button (the × button) or choose Format ➤ Arrange ➤ Selection Pane again.

Placing a Graphical Object Inline or in the Graphics Layers

The key decision when placing a graphical object is whether to place it inline with the text or place it in the graphics layers.

In most cases, it's best to place your graphical objects in the graphics layers so that you can move them freely. Only when you need to treat a graphical object as a character in the text should you place the object inline with the text.

To change how the object appears in Word, click the object, choose Format ➤ Arrange ➤ Position, and then click the position you want in the Position gallery (see Figure 8–27).

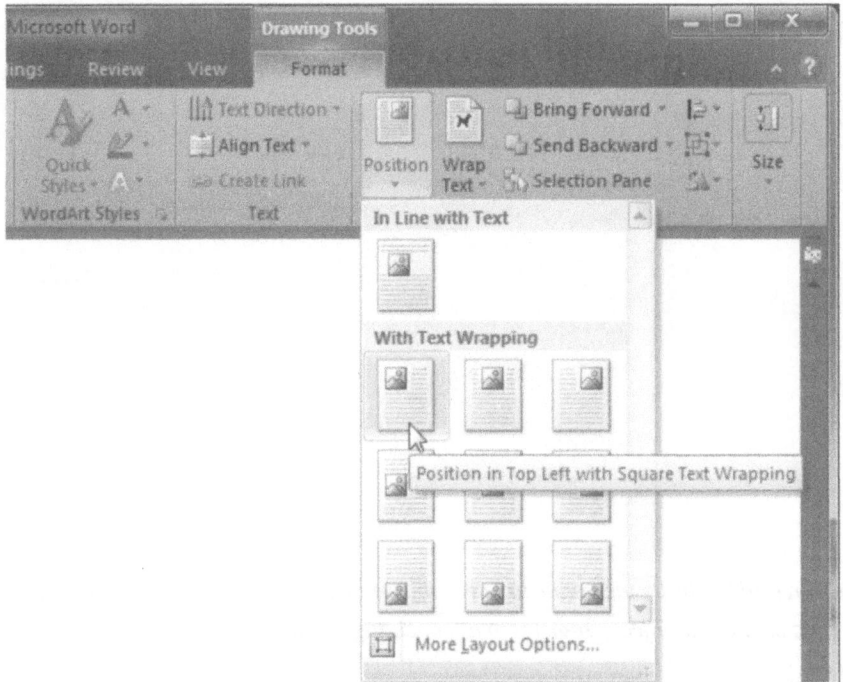

Figure 8–27. Use the Position gallery on the Format tab to control whether an object appears in line with text or with text wrapping.

You can then choose Format ➤ Arrange ➤ Wrap Text, and then click the appropriate option in the Wrap Text gallery (see Figure 8–28): In Line with Text, Square, Tight, Through, Top and Bottom, Behind

Text, or In Front of Text. Click Edit Wrap Points to set up custom text wrapping by placing your own wrap points around the object.

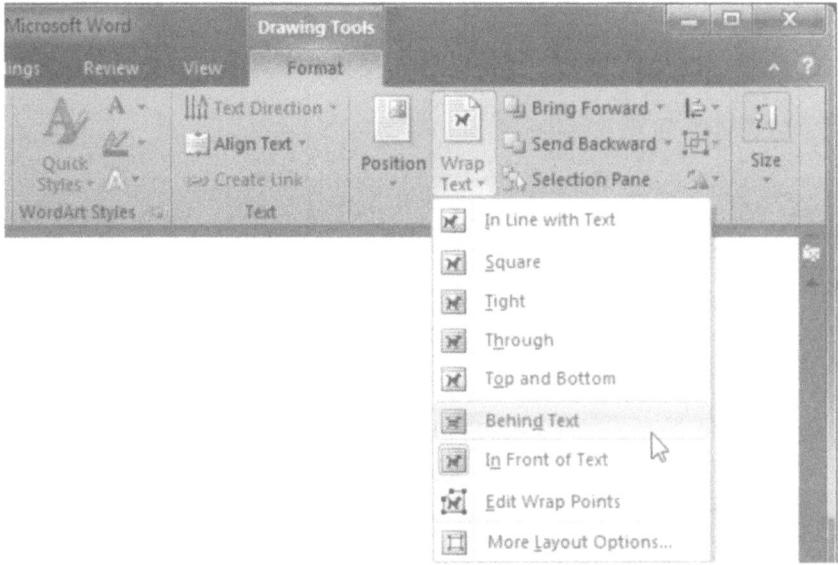

Figure 8–28. Use the Wrap Text gallery to choose how to wrap text around a graphical object.

When you click the Edit Wrap Points item, Word displays an outline around the object showing the wrap points as black squares. You can then drag a wrap point to change the wrapping (see Figure 8–29). Editing the wrap points is useful for wrapping text tightly around an irregular object, but you can also use it to create special effects with regularly shaped objects.

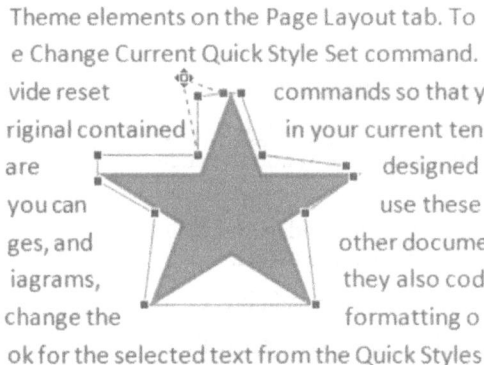

Figure 8–29. Give the Edit Wrap Points command if you want to position the wrap points exactly where you need them.

When you need to take precise control of the wrapping, click the More Layout Options item at the bottom of the Wrap Text gallery to display the Text Wrapping tab of the Layout dialog window (see Figure 8–30).

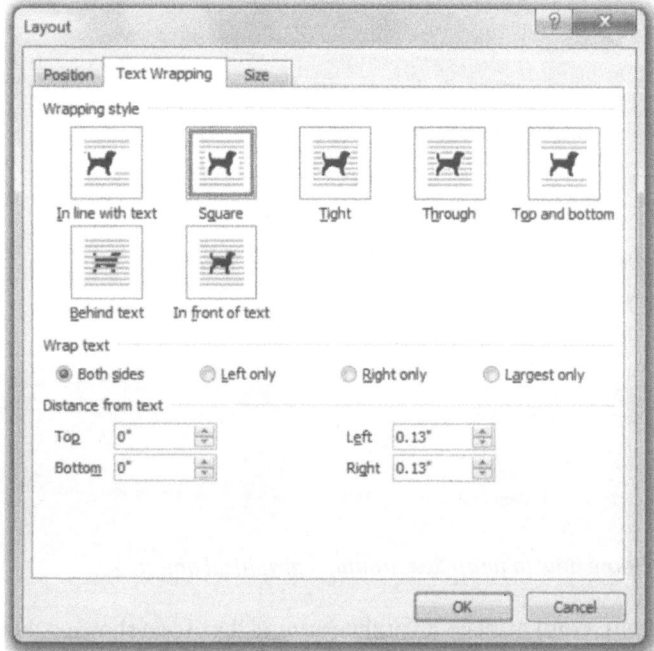

Figure 8–30. Use the Text Wrapping tab of the Layout dialog window to take precise control of how Word wraps text around an object.

In the Wrapping style box, click the wrapping style you want:

- **In line with text:** Places the graphical object as an inline character.

- **Square:** Wraps the text around the graphical object with straight edges as a square or rectangle, leaving a modest amount of space between the text and the edges of the object.

- **Tight:** Wraps the text around the graphical object with straight edges, leaving a minimal amount of space between the text and the edges of the object.

- **Through:** Wraps the text through any white spaces in the graphical object.

- **Top and bottom:** Wraps the text above and below the graphical object without placing any text to its left and right.

- **Behind text:** Places the graphical object behind the text, so that the text appears to be on top of the object.

- **In front of text:** Places the graphical object in front of the text, so that the object obscures the text (unless you make the object transparent).

Next, go to the Wrap text section of the Text Wrapping tab, and then select the appropriate option button: Both sides, Left only, Right only, or Largest only. These options are easy to understand.

Now go to the "Distance from text" section at the bottom of the dialog window. Here, you can use the Top box, Bottom box, Left box, and Right box to set the distance between the text and the object. Depending on the wrapping choices you've made, all these boxes may be available, only some may be available, or none may be available.

Once you've finished choosing settings on the Text Wrapping tab, click the OK button to close the Layout dialog window.

Positioning a Graphical Object

When you insert a graphical object, you normally try to put it in the right place straight away. But often you'll need to move it afterward—for example, because you've changed the layout of the document. You can either position the graphical object quickly by clicking and dragging it, or move it more precisely by using the drawing grid.

Positioning a Graphical Object Quickly

When you need to reposition a graphical object quickly, click it and drag it to the new position.

If you need to move a graphical object only a short distance, nudge it into place. Click the graphical object to select it, and then press the Left arrow key, the Right arrow key, the Up arrow key, or the Down arrow key to nudge the object a short distance in the right direction.

Displaying and Adjusting the Drawing Grid

When you nudge a graphical object, Word moves it by one unit on its underlying drawing grid. Word normally hides this grid, but you may find it helpful to display the grid temporarily when you're arranging graphical objects. You may also want to adjust the settings for the grid even if you don't display it.

To display the drawing grid, click a graphical object, and then choose Format ➤ Arrange ➤ Align ➤ View Gridlines. Word displays the drawing grid in the text area of the page (see Figure 8–31), making it easier to align objects by eye.

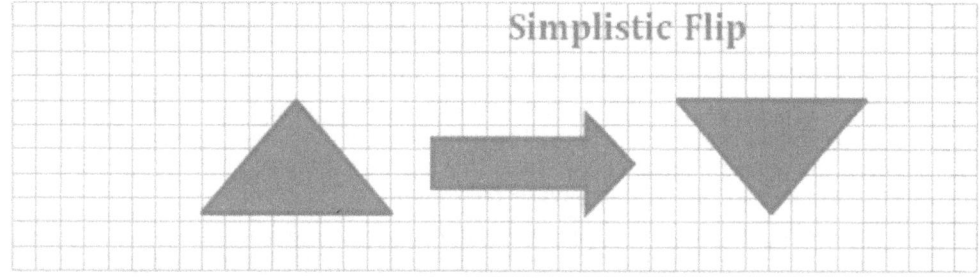

Figure 8–31. Display the drawing grid when you need help aligning objects by eye.

233

To adjust the drawing grid, follow these steps:

1. Select a graphical object in the document.

2. Choose Format ➤ Arrange ➤ Align ➤ Grid Settings to display the Drawing Grid dialog window (see Figure 8–32).

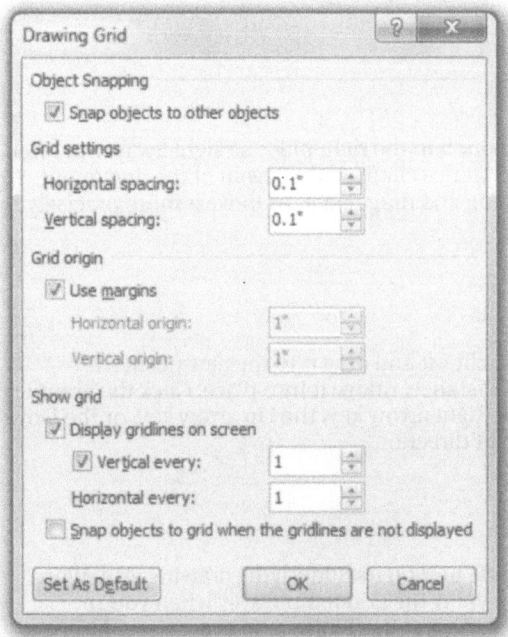

Figure 8–32. Open the Drawing Grid dialog window when you need to adjust the grid settings or control how Word snaps objects to the grid or to other objects.

3. In the Object Snapping area, select the "Snap objects to other objects" check box if you want Word to automatically snap an object to another object when you bring it close. This setting is often useful when you're creating drawings composed of different objects, but you may prefer to turn it off when you need to place objects near each other but not touching.

4. In the Grid settings area, you can adjust the size of the grid squares by changing the measurements in the Horizontal spacing box and the Vertical spacing box. When you're snapping objects to the grid, you may want to make the grid squares smaller to allow more precise placement.

5. In the Grid origin area, choose where the grid appears on screen. Select the "Use margins" check box if you want Word to keep the grid within the page margins. Otherwise, clear this check box, and then set the starting measurements in the Horizontal origin box and the Vertical origin box. For example, you may want the grid to extend outside the text area so that you can position objects there.

6. In the Show grid area, select the "Display gridlines on screen" check box if you want Word to display gridlines on-screen. You can then select the "Vertical every" box if you want to see vertical gridlines, and enter the number in the box—for example, set 1 if you want to see a gridline every unit of the grid, or set 2 if you want to see a gridline every other unit. In the "Horizontal every" box, set the corresponding number for horizontal gridlines.

7. Select the "Snap objects to grid when the gridlines are not displayed" check box if you want to use snapping to position objects even when the gridlines are hidden. This feature is useful provided you know about it; if you don't, Word's apparent refusal to position objects exactly where you drag them can be infuriating.

8. Click the Set As Default button if you want to use these grid settings as your defaults in Word.

9. Click the OK button to close the Drawing Grid dialog window.

Positioning a Graphical Object Exactly Using the Layout Dialog Window

When you need to control exactly where a graphical object appears, choose Format ➤ Arrange ➤ Position ➤ More Layout Options to display the Position tab of the Layout dialog window (see Figure 8–33).

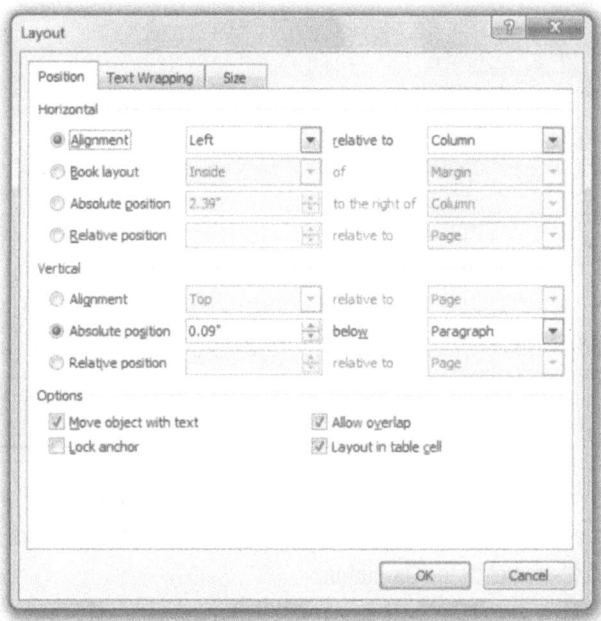

Figure 8–33. Use the options on the Position tab of the Layout dialog window when you need to position a graphical object precisely and when you need to choose what its positioning is relative to.

Before you can come to grips with the options on the Position tab of the Layout dialog window, you need to understand how Word positions items and what object anchors are. When you place a graphical object in a graphics layer, Word attaches it to the text layer using an object anchor and positions it relative to an object in the text. This object can be the margin, the page, the column, or a character.

The easiest way to make object anchors visible is to choose Home ➤ Paragraph ➤ Show/Hide ¶ (so that the ¶ button appears pressed in). This makes Word display all formatting marks, including spaces, tabs, paragraph marks, and object anchors. When you click a graphical object positioned in the graphics layer, Word displays the object anchor that secures the object. Figure 8–34 shows an example of a graphical object and its object anchor.

The·quick·brown·fox·jumped·over·the·barking·dog. ¶

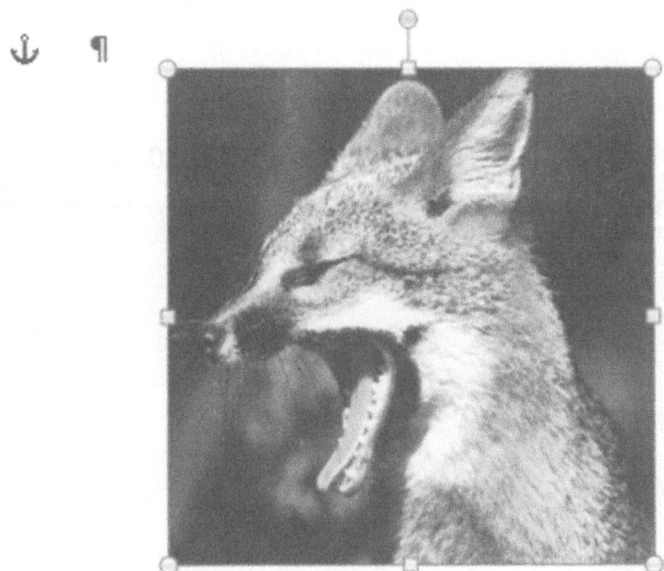

Figure 8–34. Choose Home ➤ Paragraph ➤ Show/Hide ¶ to reveal all formatting marks including the object anchor for a graphical object you select.

■ **Note** If you want to display object anchors all the time, choose File ➤ Options to display the Word Options dialog window. Click the Display category in the left pane, select the "Object anchors" check box in the "Always show these formatting marks on the screen" area, and then click the OK button.

To set a graphical object's position using the Position tab of the Layout dialog window, follow these steps:

1. In the Horizontal area, choose the appropriate option button and set the horizontal position:

- **Alignment**: Select this option button if you want to align the object relative to a text object. In the first drop-down list, choose Left, Centered, or Right, as needed. Then in the "Relative to" drop-down list, choose the object: Margin, Page, Column, Character, Left Margin, Right Margin, Inside Margin, or Outside Margin.

- **Book layout**: Select this option button if you're creating a facing-page layout—where the left page is designed to face the right page. In the first drop-down list, choose Inside or Outside as needed. In the "Of" drop-down list, choose Margin or Page. For example, you can anchor an object to the inside margin or the outside margin.

- **Absolute position**: Select this option button when you want to set an absolute position. In the text box, set the distance, and then choose the object in the "To the right of" drop-down list. Your choices are Margin, Page, Column, Character, Left Margin, Right Margin, Inside Margin, or Outside Margin; setting an absolute position by the page is often the easiest option.

- **Relative position**: Select this option button when you want to set the position using a percentage of the object you specify. In the text box, set the distance—for example, 10%. Then in the "Relative to" drop-down list, choose Margin, Page, Left Margin, Right Margin, Inside Margin, or Outside Margin, as needed.

2. In the Vertical area, choose the appropriate option button and set the vertical position:

- **Alignment**: Select this option button when you want to align the object relative to a text object. In the first drop-down list, choose the alignment: Top, Centered, Bottom, Inside, or Outside. Then in the "Relative to" drop-down list, choose the object: Margin, Page, Line, Top Margin, Bottom Margin, Inside Margin, or Outside Margin.

- **Absolute position**: Select this option button when you want to set an absolute position. In the text box, set the distance, and then choose the object in the Below list box: Margin, Page, Paragraph, Line, Top Margin, Bottom Margin, Inside Margin, or Outside Margin.

- **Relative position**: Select this option button when you want to set the position using a percentage of the object you specify. In the text box, set the distance—for example, 50%. Then in the "Relative to" drop-down list, choose Margin, Page, Top Margin, Bottom Margin, Inside Margin, or Outside Margin, as needed.

3. In the Options area, choose the options you want to use for the position:

- **Move object with text**: Select this check box to allow Word to move the object with the text. When you position an object relative to part of the text, you will most likely want it to move like this. But when you position an object relative to the page, you may want to clear this check box so that Word keeps it in place even when the text moves.

- **Lock anchor**: Select this check box when you want to prevent the anchor from moving. Do this when you've placed the object exactly where you want it and you need to make sure you don't move it by accident.

- **Allow overlap:** Select this check box to allow other objects to overlap this object. Clear this check box to prevent overlap. If you then drag another object onto this one, Word repositions the objects so there's no overlap. It's like putting the negative poles of magnets together.

- **Layout in table cell:** Select this check box when you're positioning a graphical object in a table. This setting makes Word force the object into a cell rather than allowing it to cross a cell border. This setting works only with the Square, Tight, Through, and Top and Bottom wrappings, not with Behind Text or In Front of Text. If you're not using a table, selecting this check box has no effect.

4. Click the OK button to close the Layout dialog window. Word applies the layout to the graphical object.

Arranging Graphical Objects to Control Which Is Visible

When you have placed multiple graphical objects in the same area of a document, you may need to arrange the order in which they appear in the document's layers to control how they appear in relation to each other. For example, you may need to move a particular object to the front of the stack of document layers, so that it appears on top of the other objects, or move another object back so that it appears behind one of its companion objects.

To change where a graphical object appears in the layers, follow these steps:

1. Click the object to select it. Word adds the appropriate section to the ribbon— for example, the Drawing Tools section if you click a shape.

2. Make sure the Format tab of the ribbon is displayed. If not, click it.

3. Go to the Arrange group on the Format tab, and then click the appropriate control:

- **Bring Forward:** Click this button to bring the object forward by one layer. To bring it all the way to the front, click the Bring Forward drop-down button, and then click Bring to Front.

- **Send Backward:** Click this button to send the object backward by one layer. To send the object all the way to the back, click the Send Backward drop-down button, and then click Send to Back.

■ **Note** You can also move an object forward or back by right-clicking it and using the Bring to Front command and submenu and the Send to Back command and submenu on the context menu. For example, to send an object backward, right-click it and choose Send to Back ➤ Send Backward.

Rotating a Graphical Object

After inserting a graphical object, you can rotate it as needed. Click to select the object, and then drag the green handle to the left to rotate counterclockwise (see Figure 8–35) or to the right to rotate clockwise.

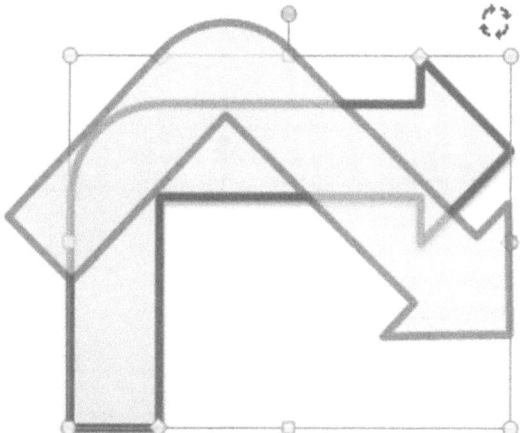

Figure 8–35. Drag the green rotation handle (at the top here) to the left or right to rotate a graphical object counterclockwise or clockwise.

Adding Sounds and Videos to Your Documents

When you're creating a document for online reading or distribution, you can include sounds and videos as well as static content. You can also include these items in printed documents if you want, but as paper doesn't yet have the multimedia capabilities to render them, there's little point.

Word's interface for playing sounds and videos is clumsy, as the sound file or video file opens in a separate Windows Media Player window rather than playing in the Word document, as you might want it to. But when you need to include a sound or video in a document, it works well enough.

To add a sound or video file to a document, follow these steps:

1. Place the insertion point where you want the sound to appear.

2. Choose Insert ➤ Text ➤ Object, clicking the Object button rather than the drop-down button to its right. Word displays the Object dialog window.

3. Click the Create from File tab to display it. Figure 8–36 shows the Create from File tab of the Object dialog window with a file ready for inserting.

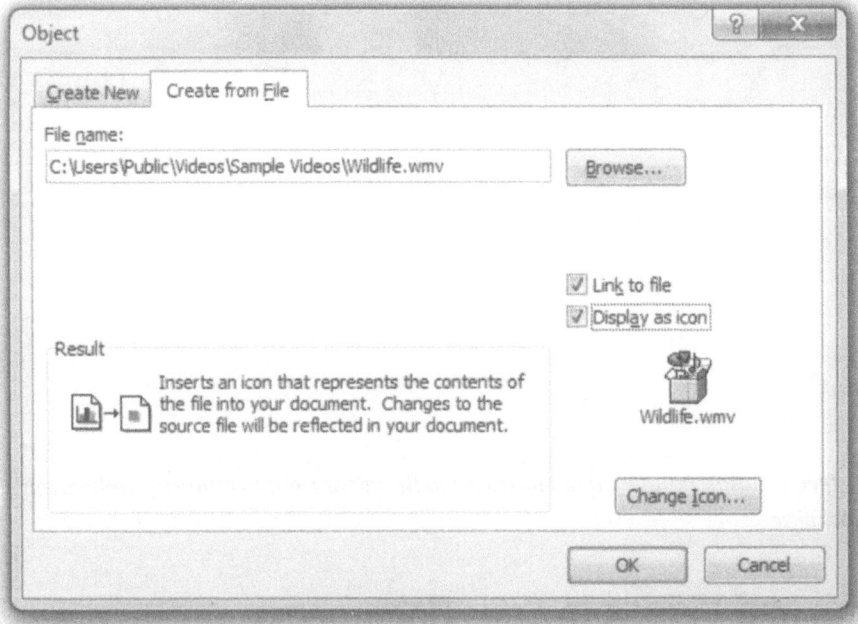

Figure 8–36. To insert a video or audio file in a document, enter its file name on the Create from File tab of the Object dialog window.

4. Click the Browse button to display the Browse dialog window, navigate to the folder that contains the file, click the file, and then click the Open button. Word closes the Browse dialog window and adds the filename to the File name box.

5. If you want to link the video or audio file rather than inserting a full copy of it in the document, select the "Link to file" check box.

6. Choose the icon and text that appear in the document to show the video or audio file's presence like this:

   • Select the "Display as icon" check box.

   • Click the Change Icon button to display the Change Icon dialog window (see Figure 8–37).

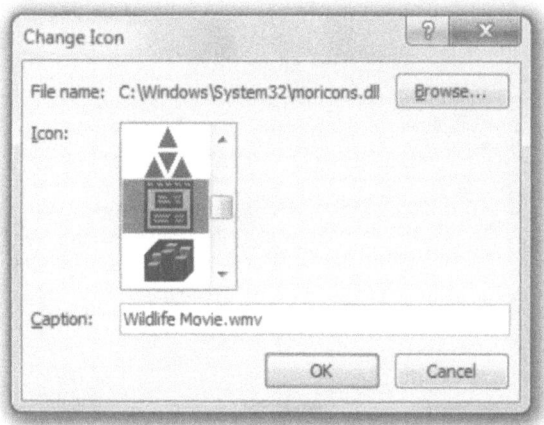

Figure 8–37. Use the Change Icon dialog window to choose the icon and caption Word displays for the video or audio file.

- In the Icon box, click the icon you want. To reach a different selection of icons, click the Browse button and use the resulting Browse dialog window to pick a file that contains icons. For example, the files `shell32.dll` and `moricons.dll` in the `Windows\System32` folder contain various icons.

- In the Caption box, change the text that Word displays for the file to what you want.

- Click the OK button to close the Change Icon dialog window.

7. Click the OK button to close the Object dialog window. Word inserts the video or audio file in the document.

The video file or audio file appears as an icon in the document (see Figure 8–38). To play the file, the user double-clicks the icon. This makes Word open a Windows Media Player window and start the video file or audio file playing in it.

Double-click this icon to play the song:

Sleep Away.mp3

Double-click this icon to play the movie:

Wildlife.wmv

Figure 8–38. The video file or audio file appears as an icon that the user can double-click to play the file.

Summary

In this chapter, you've learned how to add graphical objects to your documents. We started by looking at how to use the Clip Art task pane to insert clip art from Microsoft's collection, moved on to inserting your own pictures, and then went through drawing shapes, creating SmartArt illustrations, and adding charts created in Excel.

Along the way, you've also learned how to use Word's Screenshot feature, how to resize and reposition graphical objects, and how to insert video files and audio files in your documents.

In the next chapter, I'll show you how to use Word's powerful features for creating and editing documents with other people.

■ ■ ■

CHAPTER 9

Working with Others

In this chapter, you'll learn how to save time and effort by using Word's powerful features for working with other people on your documents.

We'll start with the Track Changes feature, which marks almost all the changes you and your colleagues make to a document. By tracking changes, you can not only eliminate any confusion about who made which change but also decide which changes you want to implement—and quickly accept them.

After that, we'll move on to comments, which you use to add notes to a document without changing its contents. I'll show you how to review both tracked changes and comments, accepting and rejecting changes as needed, and deleting comments when you no longer need to keep them.

Moving on, we'll look at how you can merge either marked or unmarked changes from two versions of the same document, giving you a document with the changes marked so that you can easily find them and deal with them. I'll also show you how to restrict edit rights on a document to prevent your colleagues from making changes you don't want them to make, and how to take notes in OneNote that are linked to documents in Word, which is useful when you need to keep track of what you're doing.

Tracking Changes in a Document

When you create or edit documents with other people, it's often useful to track the changes made to the document. To do so, turn on Word's Track Changes feature and configure it to display the changes you want to see. Track Changes can automatically track almost all the changes in the document so that you can review them, see who made which changes when, accept the changes you want to keep, and reject the rest.

You can choose which types of changes to track and which to ignore. For example, you may want to track only the edits to the text of a document and let your colleagues handle the formatting.

Choosing Which Changes to Track

To choose which types of changes Word tracks in a document, follow these steps:

1. Choose Review ➤ Tracking ➤ Track Changes ➤ Change Tracking Options to display the Track Changes Options dialog window (see Figure 9–1).

Figure 9–1. *In the Track Changes Options dialog window, choose how to show markup, track moves, and handle changes to table cells and formatting. You can also choose whether to use balloons to display changes.*

2. In the Markup area, choose how to mark insertions, deletions, changed lines, and comments:

- **Insertions**: Open the Insertions drop-down list, and then click the type of markup you want for inserted text. Your choices are (none), Color only, Bold, Italic, Underline, Double Underline, or Strikethrough. Use the "Color only" setting when you need a subtle indication of added text; use Underline or Double Underline when you need a stronger indication. Open the topmost Color drop-down list and choose "By author" if you want Word to use a different color for each reviewer's additions; to use a specific color or shading for all added text, click that color or shading.

- **Deletions**: Open the Deletions drop-down list, and then click the type of markup to use for deleted text. Your choices are (none), Color only, Bold, Italic, Underline, Double Underline, Strikethrough, Hidden, ^ (Word displays a single caret mark to show where text has been deleted), # (Word shows a single pound/hash sign where text has been deleted), or Double strikethrough. Open the middle Color drop-down list and choose "By author" if you want Word to use a different color for each reviewer's deletions; to use a specific color or shading for all deletions, click that color or shading.

■ **Tip** The (none) item can be a good choice for deletions, as it makes the deleted items disappear from the document, leaving only the text that hasn't been deleted and the text that has been added.

- **Changed lines**: Open the "Changed lines" drop-down list and choose whether and where you want Word to display a vertical line in the margin next to each line that has changed. These changed lines help you locate changes in documents that contain changes on only some lines, but if most every line has changed, the changed lines are of little use. Choose (none) to skip using changed lines, Left border to put them in the left margin, Right border to put them in the right margin, or Outside to put the lines in the left margin on left pages and the right margin on right pages. Open the third color drop-down list and choose the color or shading you want; the Auto item applies the default text color and is often the best choice.

- **Comments**: Open the Comments drop-down list and choose the color or shading to give to each reviewer's comments. Choose the "By author" item to have Word use different colors for each reviewer.

3. In the Moves area, select the "Track moves" check box if you want Word to track text you've moved within a document separately from insertions and deletions. If you select this check box, you can choose settings as follows:

- **Moved from**: Open the "Moved from" drop-down list and choose how to mark the text that is no longer there because it has been moved to a different location in the document. Your choices are the same as for Deletions, but you'll want to use a different marking so that you can identify moved text. For example, use Strikethrough for Deletions and Double Strikethrough for Moved From text. Open the Color drop-down list and choose "By author" or the color or shading you want.

- **Moved to**: Open the "Moved to" drop-down list and choose how to mark the moved text in its new location. Your choices are the same as for Insertions, but you'll want to use a different marking so that you can distinguish the moved text—for example, Underline for Insertions and Double Underline for Moved To text.

4. In the Table cell highlighting area, choose the colors with which to shade cells that have been inserted, deleted, merged, or split in a table. Usually, you'll want to use a different color for each of these changes to a table's structure so that you can easily identify each type of change.

> ⬛ **Caution** Word provides the "By author" setting for the four drop-down lists in the Table cell highlighting area of the Track Changes Options dialog window, but it's best not to use this setting. Otherwise, while you can see who changed the table's structure, you need to dig deeper to see exactly which changes that person made. Usually, it's easier to see how the table has changed, and then find out who made the changes only if you need to.

5. In the Formatting area, select the "Track formatting" check box if you want to track changes to formatting. This is usually a good idea. You can then open the Formatting drop-down list and choose the marking for formatting changes (for example, Bold or Italic), and open the Color drop-down list and choose the color.

6. In the Balloons area, choose whether to use balloons and the markup pane to display details of tracked changes and comments. The markup pane is a column on the right of the page that Word adds to display the balloons, little windows that contain the details of changes. These are the settings you can choose:

   - **Use Balloons (Print and Web Layout)**: Open the Use Balloons drop-down list and choose Always if you want to use balloons for all markup, Never if you don't want to use balloons, or "Only for comments/formatting" if you want to use balloons for comments and formatting but not for other tracked changes. If you choose Never, skip the rest of this sublist, as the options don't apply.

   - **Preferred width**: Set your preferred width for the markup pane, using the measurement type specified in the "Measure in" drop-down list—for example, 2" or 25 percent of the page width.

   - **Margin**: Choose Left to display the markup pane on the left, or Right to display it on the right (the default position).

   - **Show lines connecting to text**: Select this check box to make Word show a line connecting each balloon to the text it refers to. Usually, you'll want to show these lines unless the document is so full of markup that it's hard to follow the lines. If the document is that full of markup, clear this check box to turn the lines off. You can then click a comment to display a line connecting it to its reference, making the reference easy to see.

   - **Paper orientation in printing**. Choose the orientation to use when printing a document with its markup. Choose Auto to stay with Word's default orientation, Preserve to use the orientation set in this section of the document, or Force Landscape to print all the pages in landscape orientation.

> **Note** When printing a document containing markup, you must select the Print Markup check box on the Print What drop-down list in the Print Place in the Backstage View to make Word include the markup on the printout. See Chapter 6 for instructions on printing.

7.   Click the OK button to close the Track Changes Options dialog window.

Turning On Track Changes for a Document

To turn on Track Changes for a document, choose Review ➤ Tracking ➤ Track Changes, clicking the top part of the Track Changes button so that the button appears pressed in. (You can also click the bottom part of the button and then click Track Changes on the drop-down menu, but there's no advantage to doing so.)

> **Tip** To give yourself an easy way to turn Track Changes on and off, right-click the blank space on the status bar to display the Customize Status Bar menu. Click the Track Changes item to put a check mark next to it, and then click the status bar to close the menu. The status bar then displays a Track Changes readout that you can click to toggle Track Changes on or off. You can also press Ctrl+Shift+E to toggle Track Changes on or off.

When you need to turn Track Changes off again, choose Review ➤ Tracking ➤ Track Changes again, so that the button no longer appears pressed in.

> **Note** It's often a good idea to prevent your colleagues from turning Track Changes off for a document. To do so, restrict their edit rights, as discussed in the section "Restricting Edit Rights," later in this chapter.

Working in a Document with Track Changes On

After you turn on Track Changes for a document, you can work in it much as normal. Word tracks your insertions, deletions, and other changes and displays such markup as you've chosen to show.

For example, in Print Layout view, Web Layout view, and Full Screen Reading view, Word normally displays the markup pane (the shaded area on the right) and balloons, as shown in Figure 9–2.

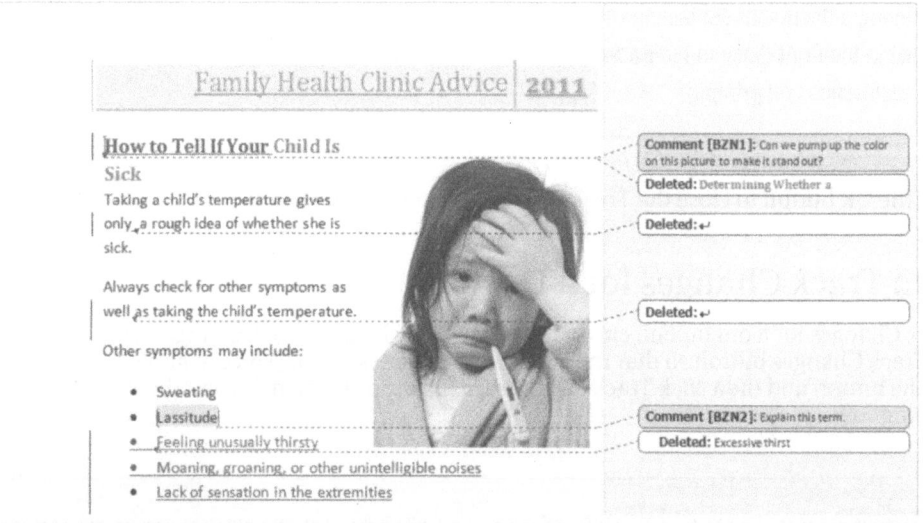

Figure 9–2. In Print Layout view, Web Layout view, and Full Screen Reading view, Word displays the markup pane with balloons on the right detailing the changes.

■ **Tip** To switch quickly among the settings for markup balloons, choose Review ➤ Tracking ➤ Show Markup ➤ Balloons, and then click the command you want: Show Revisions in Balloons, Show All Revisions Inline, or Show Only Comments and Formatting in Balloons.

In Draft view and Outline view, Word shows the changes inline, using the markup you set in the Track Changes Options dialog box—for example, applying an underscore to each insertion and strikethrough to each deletion, as shown in Figure 9–3.

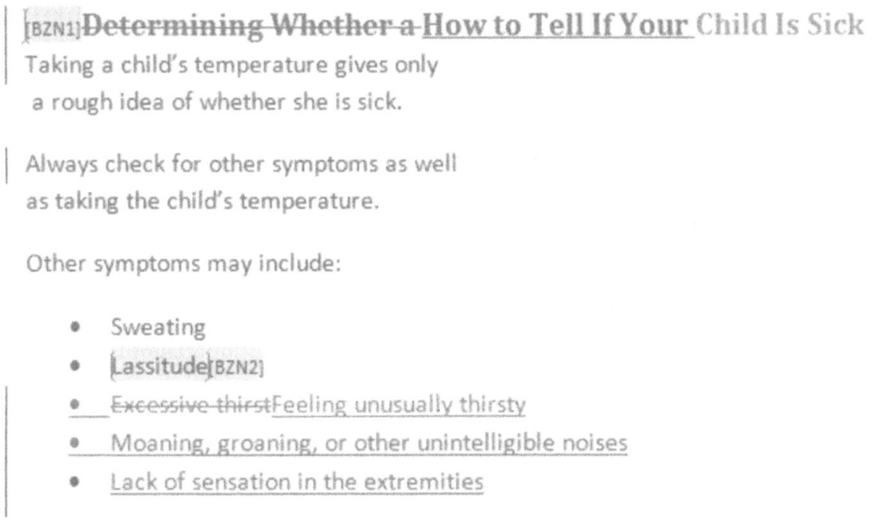

[BZN1]~~Determining Whether a~~ How to Tell If Your Child Is Sick

Taking a child's temperature gives only
a rough idea of whether she is sick.

Always check for other symptoms as well
as taking the child's temperature.

Other symptoms may include:

- Sweating
- Lassitude[BZN2]
- ~~Excessive thirst~~Feeling unusually thirsty
- Moaning, groaning, or other unintelligible noises
- Lack of sensation in the extremities

Figure 9–3. Depending on the markup options you've chosen and the view you're using, Word can mark insertions and deletions inline.

To see information about a change in Draft view or Outline view (or in one of the other views when you have chosen not to use the markup pane), hold the mouse pointer over the change. Word displays a ScreenTip showing the details of the change (see Figure 9–4).

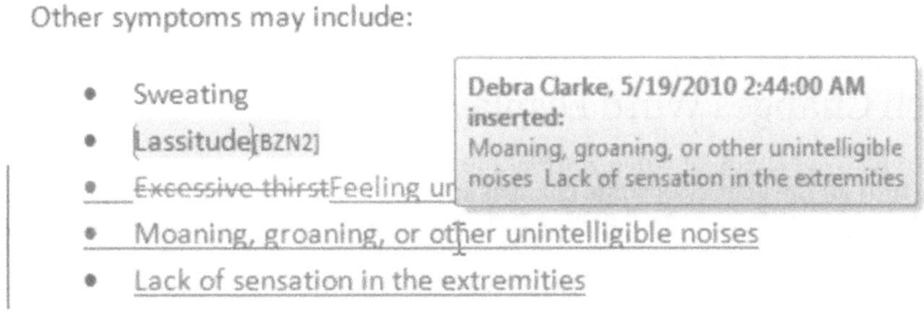

Other symptoms may include:

- Sweating
- Lassitude[BZN2]
- ~~Excessive thirst~~Feeling u...
- Moaning, groaning, or other unintelligible noises
- Lack of sensation in the extremities

> Debra Clarke, 5/19/2010 2:44:00 AM
> inserted:
> Moaning, groaning, or other unintelligible
> noises Lack of sensation in the extremities

Figure 9–4. Hold the mouse pointer over a tracked change to display a ScreenTip showing who made the change, the date and time, the type of change, and the material involved.

Choosing How to View the Document's Changes and Markup

As you work with Track Changes on, it's often useful to change the way that markup is displayed. For example, you can show the document as it will appear with all the markup accepted, or show the document's original version to see how it was.

■ **Note** The different markup views are most effective in the three layout views with balloons displayed. In Draft view and Outline view, the different markup views have much less effect, because of the way changes are displayed.

To choose how to view the document's markup, choose Review ➤ Tracking ➤ Display for Review, and then click the setting you want on the Display for Review drop-down menu:

- **Final: Show Markup**: Choose this item to see the document's final text with all the markup displayed. This is the default setting, and the one you'll probably want to use most of the time while marking up the document. In the layout views with balloons displayed, the insertions appear in the document's text without balloons; the deletions disappear from the document except for markers connected to balloons in the markup pane that show what was deleted.

- **Final**: Choose this item to see the document's final text with no markup appearing. Use this view when you want to read the document without the visual distraction of markup or when you want to see the true page count of the final version of the document.

- **Original: Show Markup**: Choose this item to see the document's original text with the markup displayed. Use this view when you want to focus on the changes made to the original text. In the layout views with balloons displayed, the deleted items appear in the document marked with strikethrough (or your chosen marking); the insertions appear only as markers connected to balloons in the markup pane that show what was inserted.

- **Original**: Choose this item to see the document's original text before any of the changes were made. This view is useful for reminding yourself of how the document was before the editors set about it.

Controlling Which Changes Word Displays

When a document contains many changes, or when you want to focus only on one aspect of the changes, you may want to turn off the display of some changes so that you see only others. To control which changes Word displays, choose Review ➤ Tracking ➤ Show Markup. On the Show Markup drop-down menu (shown in Figure 9–5 with the Reviewers submenu displayed), select the check box for each item you want to see, and clear the check box for each item you want to hide.

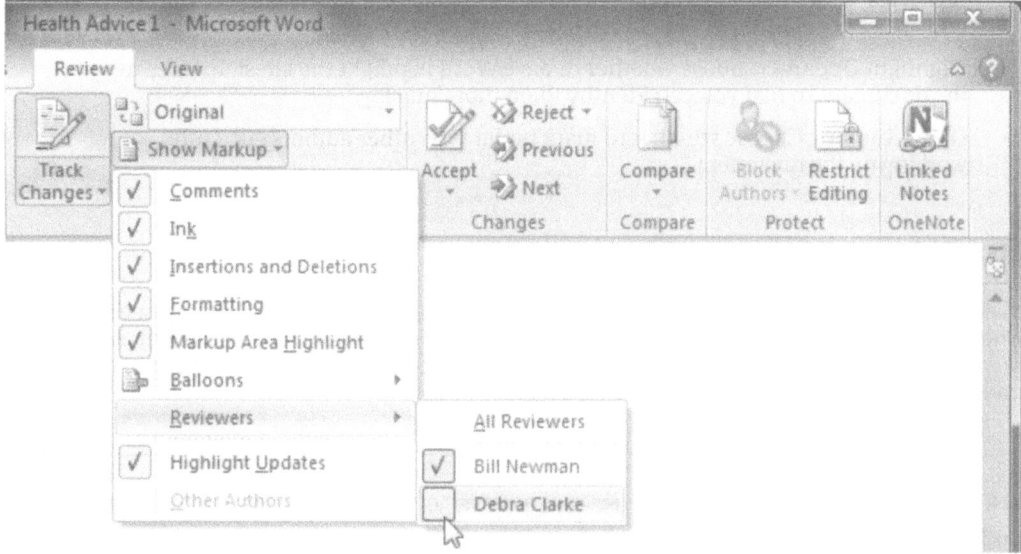

Figure 9–5. *Use the Show Markup menu to control which types of markup Word displays. For example, you can suppress the display of a particular reviewer's changes by clearing the appropriate check box on the Reviewers submenu.*

These are the options on the Show Markup submenu:

- **Comments**: Choose whether to show comments inserted in the document (as discussed later in this chapter).

- **Ink**: Choose whether to show ink markup added to the document using Windows' handwriting support.

- **Insertions and Deletions**: Choose whether to show text and other items inserted in the document, deleted from it, or moved from one place in the document to another.

- **Formatting**: Choose whether to show changes to formatting—for example, where someone applied a style or some direct formatting.

- **Markup Area Highlight**: Choose whether to show shading on the markup pane rather than displaying it as the document's normal background color. The shading is usually helpful.

- **Balloons**: In this submenu, choose whether Word uses balloons (Show Revisions in Balloons), displays revisions in the text (Show All Revisions Inline), or shows comments and formatting changes in balloons but all other changes inline (Show Only Comments and Formatting in Balloons). The menu uses check marks rather than option buttons, but these settings are mutually exclusive—you can choose only one at a time.

- **Reviewers**: In this submenu, choose All Reviewers to display comments from all reviewers. Otherwise, clear the All Reviewers check box, and select the check box only for each reviewer whose changes you want to see.

- **Highlight Updates**: Choose whether to have Word highlight the latest updates to the document so that you can identify them more quickly.

- **Other Authors**: Choose whether to mark updates by other authors currently working on the document.

Adding Comments to a Document

Tracked changes are great when you're editing a document, but at other times, you may need to provide input without actually changing the text. In this case, use Word's comments for your input. A *comment* appears in a floating balloon attached to a word or another object in text, enabling you to comment easily and clearly on a specific item.

■ **Note** If you need to force your colleagues to use comments rather than alter the text of a document, restrict them to using comments. See the section "Restricting Edit Rights," later in this chapter, for details.

To add a comment to a document, follow these steps:

1. Select the text or object you're commenting on. If you want to attach a comment to a single word, click anywhere in that word. When you insert the comment, Word selects the word and puts the comment parentheses around it.

2. Choose Review ➤ Comments ➤ New Comment. Word adds colored parentheses around the word or selection and displays the comment.

3. Type or paste the text of the comment in the comment balloon or in the Reviewing pane.

In Print Layout view, Web Layout view, and Full Screen Reading view, Word displays the markup pane at the right side of the page and opens a comment balloon for you to type the comment in. The comment balloon is attached to the comment markers by a thin line, so you can see which part of the document each comment belongs to. Figure 9–6 shows the markup pane open with two comments inserted.

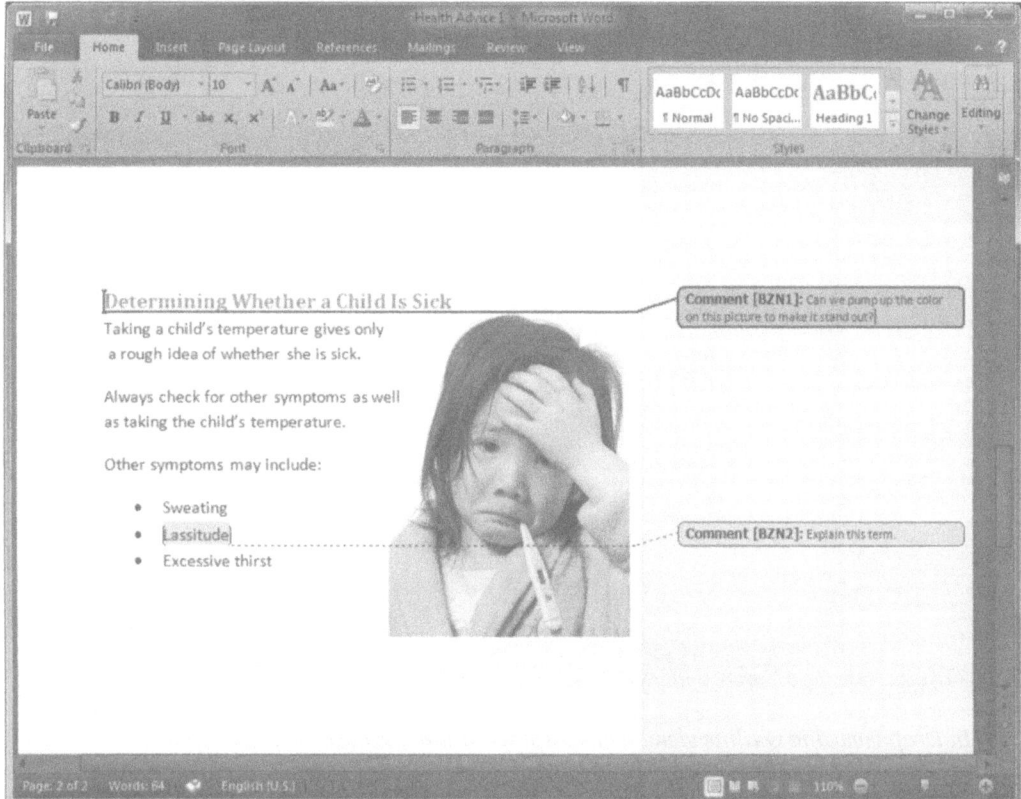

Figure 9–6. In Print Layout view, Web Layout view, or Full Screen Reading view, Word displays comments in the markup pane to the side of the document.

In Draft view or Outline view, Word opens the Reviewing pane when you add a comment. This is a pane you use for adding and reviewing comments and other markup. Figure 9–7 shows the Reviewing pane open in Draft view. When you're ready to close the Reviewing pane, click the Close button (the × button) at its upper-right corner or choose Review ➤ Tracking ➤ Reviewing Pane.

■ **Tip** If you prefer to have the Reviewing pane wide rather than tall, choose Review ➤ Tracking ➤ Reviewing Pane ➤ Reviewing Pane Horizontal to move the Reviewing pane to the bottom of the window. Choose Review ➤ Tracking ➤ Reviewing Pane ➤ Reviewing Pane Vertical to put it back.

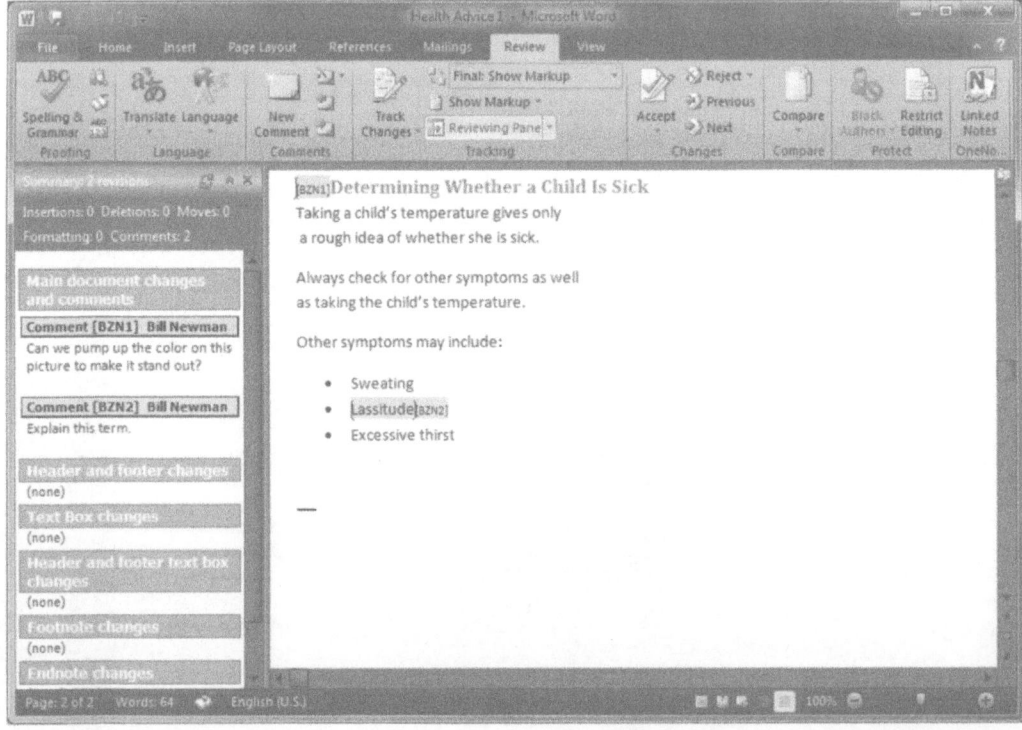

Figure 9–7. In Draft view and Outline view, Word displays comments in the Reviewing pane and shows the commenter's initials and the comment number in brackets after the commented item.

■ **Note** Word displays comments in a plain text font at first, but you can apply formatting to a comment if you want. For example, you can apply boldface or a style to a word that you want to emphasize. You can also insert elements such as tables and graphics in comments if you need to.

Reviewing Tracked Changes and Comments

After your colleagues have edited the document using tracked changes or comments (or both), you'll need to review the changes and comments. For tracked changes, you can quickly accept the changes you want to keep and reject those you don't. Comments are different, because you will normally want to delete each comment from the document after you have dealt with it.

Accepting and Rejecting Tracked Changes

As discussed earlier in this chapter, you can review changes and comments by using the comment balloons (in Print Layout view, Web Layout view, or Full Screen Reading view) or the Reviewing pane.

To go through the changes, use the controls in the Changes group on the Review tab. First, select a change by clicking the Next button or the Previous button, clicking the balloon in the markup pane, or clicking the change in the Reviewing pane.

You can then accept changes by using the Accept button and its drop-down menu:

- **Accept the selected change and select the next change:** Click the upper part of the Accept button (or click the lower part and then click Accept and Move to Next on the drop-down menu).

- **Accept the selected change:** Click the lower part of the Accept button, and then click Accept Change.

- **Accept all changes shown with your Show Markup options:** When you've chosen to show only some markup, click the lower part of the Accept button, and then click Accept All Changes Shown to accept all of that markup, but not markup that's hidden. For example, if you've chosen to show formatting but not show insertions and deletions, clicking Accept All Changes Shown accepts all formatting changes.

- **Accept all the changes in the document:** If the document contains changes light enough that you can review them all without dealing with individual changes along the way, click the lower part of the Accept button, and then click Accept All Changes in Document.

■ **Note** If you want to see the document without the revision marks just temporarily, choose Review ➤ Tracking ➤ Display for Review ➤ Final to hide the revision marks. You don't need to accept the revision marks to get a clean view of the document.

Similarly, you can reject one or more changes at once:

- **Reject the selected change and select the next change:** Click the upper part of the Reject button (or click the lower part and then click Reject and Move to Next on the drop-down menu).

- **Reject the selected change:** Click the lower part of the Reject button, and then click Reject Change.

- **Reject all changes shown with your Show Markup options:** When you've chosen to show only some markup, click the lower part of the Reject button, and then click Reject All Changes Shown to reject all of that markup, but not markup that's hidden.

- **Reject all the changes in the document:** To get rid of all the changes, click the lower part of the Reject button, and then click Reject All Changes in Document.

When you've finished accepting or rejecting changes, save the document. You may want to save it under a different name, or in a different folder, if the document is now ready for a different purpose (such as finalizing or approval by management).

■ **Tip** You can also accept or reject a change by using the context menu. Right-click the change in the text, in the markup pane, or in the Reviewing pane, and then click Accept Change or Reject Change on the context menu.

Reviewing and Integrating Comments

To review the comments in a document, you can use either the balloons or the Reviewing pane. As with tracked changes, the balloons work well when the document contains few enough balloons for each of them to fit on the page and display all of its contents. When there isn't enough space for all the balloons to fit, or when their contents are too long to appear completely, or both, you'll usually be better off using the Reviewing pane—and Word helpfully opens the Reviewing pane for you when the comments become too many or too long.

The easiest way to turn balloons off is to choose Review ➤ Tracking ➤ Show Markup ➤ Balloons ➤ Show All Revisions Inline. To go back to balloons, choose Review ➤ Tracking ➤ Show Markup ➤ Balloons ➤ Show Revisions in Balloons.

When you're using balloons, you can view a comment simply by looking at its balloon. If you can't see where the comment refers to, click anywhere in the balloon to display a heavier line to the comment marker.

Regardless of whether you're using comment balloons, you can also hold the mouse pointer over commented text (or the comment mark, when you're not using balloons) to display a ScreenTip showing the text of the comment, as shown in Figure 9–8.

■ **Caution** The disadvantage of reviewing comments via ScreenTips is that non-text content, such as graphics or tables, doesn't appear in the ScreenTip. If you see a ScreenTip that consists of a laconic "commented:" (after the editor's name and the date and time), you'll know there's content that you need to use the balloons or the Reviewing pane to see. If the comment contains text as well, you may not notice what you're missing.

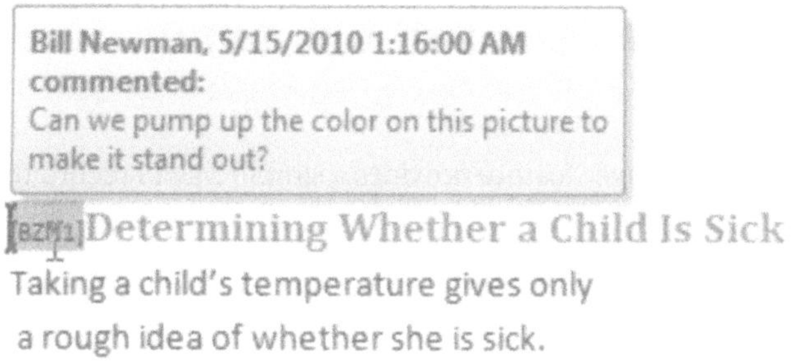

Bill Newman, 5/15/2010 1:16:00 AM
commented:
Can we pump up the color on this picture to
make it stand out?

[BZM1]Determining Whether a Child Is Sick

Taking a child's temperature gives only

a rough idea of whether she is sick.

Figure 9–8. Hold the mouse pointer over commented text or a comment mark to display a ScreenTip showing the commenter's name, the date and time of the comment, and its text.

Even when the markup pane is open, you can display the Reviewing pane by choosing Review ➤ Tracking ➤ Reviewing Pane. If any of the comments or changes contains more text than its balloon can display, the text in the balloon ends with an ellipsis (…) button that you can click to display the Reviewing pane, or you can hold the mouse pointer over the commented text to display a ScreenTip containing the full text.

■ **Tip** You can browse comments by using the browse object. Click the Select Browse Object button (the round button between the Previous button and Next button below the vertical scroll bar), and then click Comment on the panel that pops out. You can then click the Previous button and Next button to move from comment to comment. Generally, though, using the Previous button and Next button in the Comments group on the Review tab of the ribbon is easier.

Deleting Comments

When you've dealt with a comment—or simply decided to ignore it—you'll probably want to delete it rather than leave it in the document.

You can delete a single comment in either of these ways:

- **Use the context menu:** Right-click the comment in the text, in the markup pane, or in the Reviewing pane, and then click Delete Comment on the context menu.

- **Use the ribbon:** Click the comment in the text, in the markup pane, or in the Reviewing pane. Then choose Review ➤ Comments ➤ Delete (clicking the top part of the Delete button).

To delete all the comments from the document, choose Review ➤ Comments ➤ Delete ➤ Delete All Comments in Document. Word doesn't confirm the deletion, but you can use Undo if you give the command by accident.

Merging Changes Between Two Versions of the Same Document

As you've seen earlier in this chapter, Word's Track Changes feature provides a simple way to record the changes made in a document so that you can review them and decide which to keep. If you can circulate a single copy of a document around your colleagues in turn, you can gather all the changes into that single file, so that you can review them all together. This is normally the easiest way to perform group editing and review of a document, provided you have the time for each person to review the document in turn.

Other times, you may need to circulate a document to various colleagues at the same time—for example, to get the review done more quickly or to prevent your colleagues from seeing the previous edits. This method gives you multiple copies of the same document containing their different edits marked by Track Changes. To incorporate all the different edits into a single copy of the document, you can use Word's Document Combine feature.

You may also need to compare two copies of a document in which the changes haven't been tracked. For this, you can use the Document Compare feature. This feature isn't as good as Track Changes used consistently, but it's a huge improvement over spending hours poring over different document files and trying to integrate the best changes into a single version.

To use Document Compare to compare or combine two documents, follow these steps:

1. If the documents are open, close them. Starting with both documents closed is usually easier than starting with either or both open.

2. Give the command for comparing or combining, as appropriate:

   • **Compare:** Choose Review ➤ Compare ➤ Compare to display the Compare Documents dialog box (shown in Figure 9–9 expanded to display all its settings).

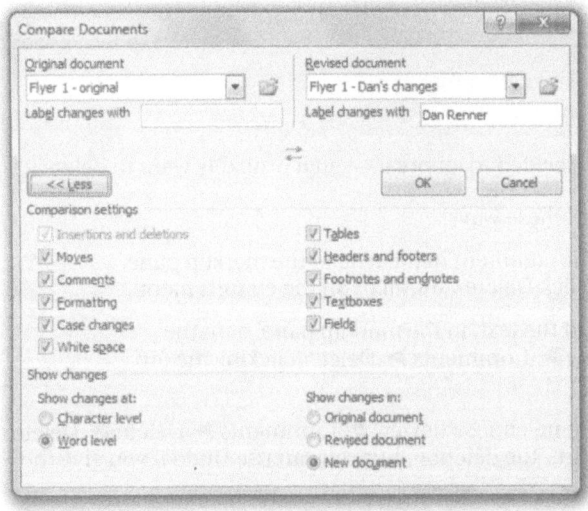

Figure 9–9. Use the Compare Documents dialog box or the similar Combine Documents dialog box to identify the changes between two documents based on the same document.

3. Choose the documents you want to compare:

    •   Either open the Original Document drop-down list and click the document in the list, or click the Open button next to the drop-down list, click the document in the Open dialog box, and then click the Open button.

    •   Similarly, either open the Revised Document drop-down list and click the document in the list, or click the Open button next to the drop-down list, click the document in the Open dialog box, and then click the Open button.

4. Tell Word how to label the changes to the document:

    •   The left Label Changes With text box shows the name of the original document's last reviewer who used revision marks. Type a different name if necessary. If the text box is blank and unavailable, the document contains no tracked changes. This will be the case if you're comparing the original document.

    •   The right Label Changes With text box shows the last reviewer of the revised document. Again, you may need to type a different name.

5. Click the More button to display the lower part of the dialog box so that you can choose comparison settings.

6. In the Comparison settings area, clear the check box for any items you don't want to integrate. For example, if you want to omit the changes to fields, clear the Fields check box. Usually, you'll want to leave most of the check boxes selected. You may want to omit formatting if you find your colleagues have made too many changes.

7. On the "Show changes at" side of the Show changes area, select the "Word level" option button to make Word analyze changes at the word level. If you need to dig deeper, you can select the "Character level" option button instead, but for many documents this produces more detail than you need.

8. On the "Show changes in" side of the Show changes area, select the "New document" option button if you want to merge the changes into a new document. This is usually clearest, but you can select the "Original document" option button or the "Revised document" option button instead if you prefer.

9. Click the OK button to close the dialog box and make Word analyze the changes.

10. If Word displays the dialog box shown in Figure 9–10, warning you that it will treat the tracked changes in the documents as having been accepted so that it can make the comparison, click the Yes button. (The alternative is to click the No button, go back into the documents, and accept or reject the revisions before you compare or combine the documents.) Word accepts the changes in the comparison document only, not in the original documents.

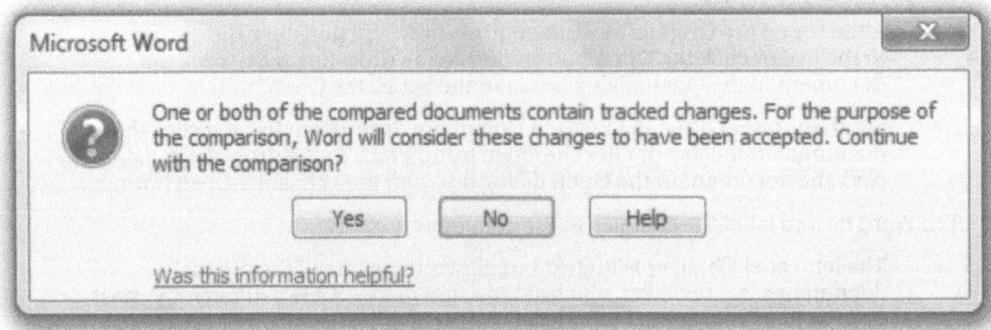

Figure 9–10. If Word displays this dialog box when you're comparing or combining documents, click the Yes button to proceed.

Word then displays the result of the comparison or combination—for example, a new compare document together with the source documents that produced it, with the Reviewing pane showing a list of the differences (see Figure 9–11).

If you don't need to see the source documents as you review the result of the comparison, click the Close button (the × button) on each of the source document panes or choose Review ➤ Compare ➤ Compare ➤ Show Source Documents ➤ Hide Source Documents. The Show Source Documents submenu also gives you commands for opening the compared document's source documents again if you need them.

Save the changes to the compared or combined document if you want to keep them.

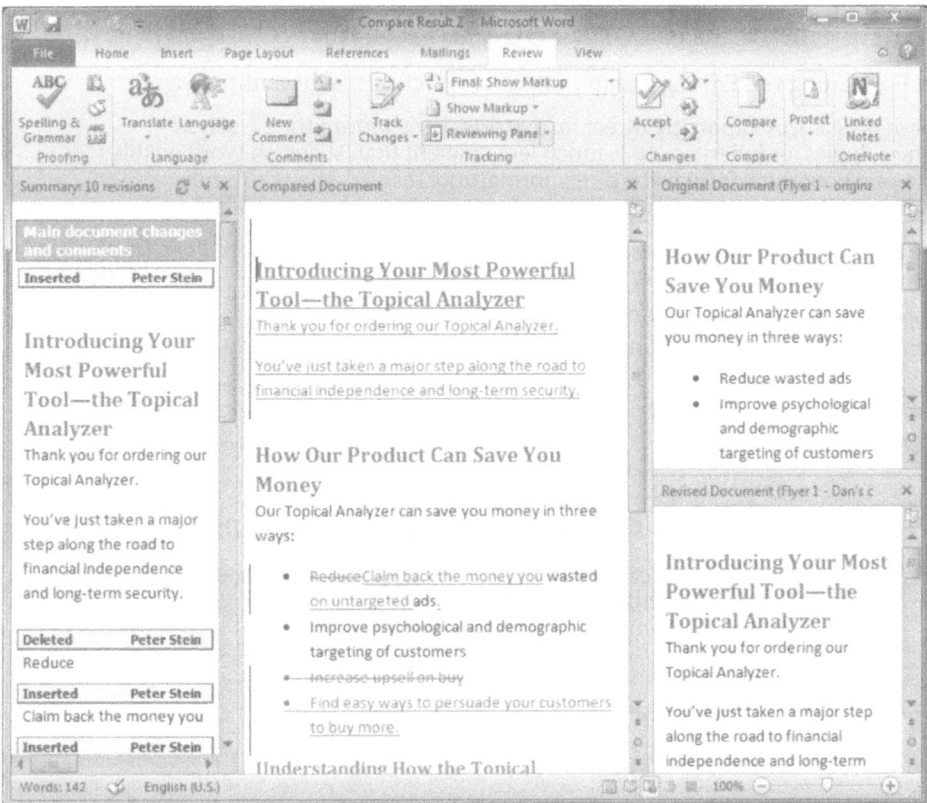

Figure 9–11. After you compare documents, Word displays the resulting document (the document named Compare Result 2 here) plus the source documents. The Reviewing pane (on the left here) shows a list of the changes.

Restricting Edit Rights to a Document

As you've seen earlier in this chapter, Track Changes can retain most of the changes you and your colleagues make to a document—but anyone can turn Track Changes off with the click of a button or the press of a key combination. To prevent this from happening, you can use Word's Restrict Formatting and Editing feature to restrict your colleagues' edit rights to the document.

Understanding the Restrictions You Can Apply

With the Restrict Formatting and Editing feature, you can restrict edit rights in three ways:

- **Prevent others from applying direct formatting**: Direct formatting (such as boldface, italics, or indentation) is much less efficient than styles, so Word enables you to prevent others from using direct formatting. Instead, they can apply formatting only using styles, and you can choose which styles are available.

- **Force others to use Track Changes**: If you need to track the changes, you can turn on the Track Changes and make sure nobody turns it off.

- **Force others to use comments**: When you need your colleagues to comment on the document rather than editing its text, you can make only comments available.

- **Enable others to change only form fields**: You can set up a Word document as an electronic form that contains fields the user fills in. (This book doesn't cover creating and using forms.)

Opening the Restrict Formatting and Editing Task Pane

To restrict edit rights, first open the Restrict Formatting and Editing Task pane (see Figure 9–12) by choosing Review ➤ Protect ➤ Restrict Editing.

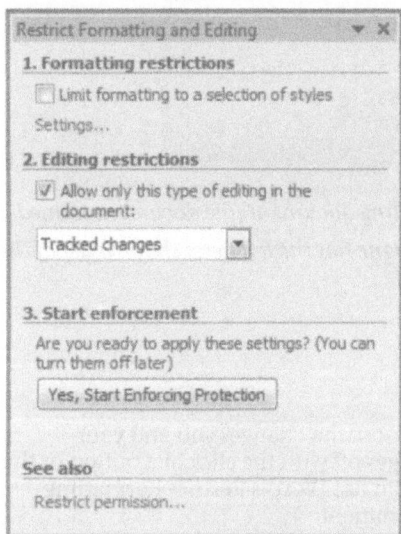

Figure 9–12. Use the Restrict Formatting and Editing pane to limit the changes your colleagues can make to a document. For example, you can force them to use Track Changes or limit them to applying styles rather than using direct formatting.

Preventing Others from Applying Direct Formatting

If you want to prevent others from applying direct formatting, follow these steps:

1. Select the "Limit formatting to a selection of styles" check box.

2. Click the Settings link to display the Formatting Restrictions dialog box (see Figure 9–13).

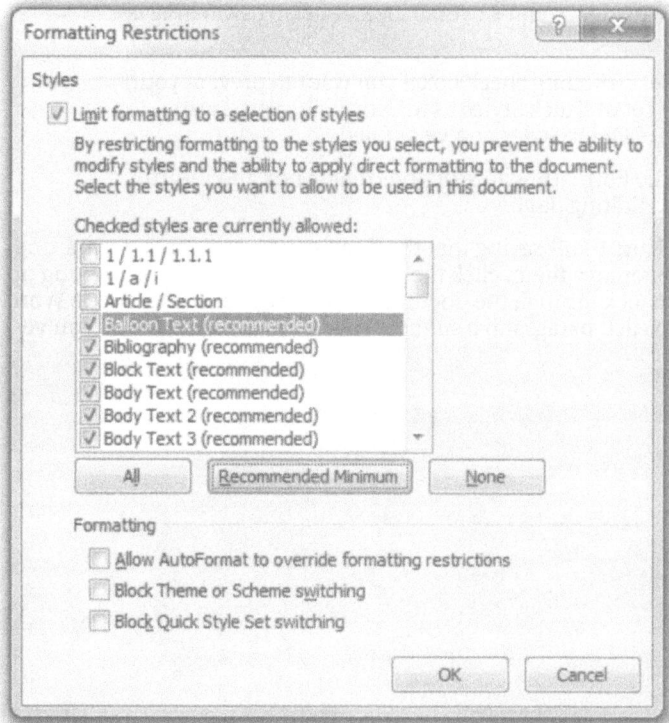

Figure 9–13. To prevent your colleagues from applying direct formatting to a document, use the Formatting Restrictions dialog box to limit them to applying the styles you choose.

3. Make sure the "Limit formatting to a selection of styles" check box is selected.

4. In the "Checked styles are currently allowed" list box, select the check box for each style you want to allow your colleagues to apply.

   • If you want to allow only a few styles, click the None button to clear all the check boxes, then select the allowed styles.

   • If you want to allow most styles, click the All button to select all the check boxes, then clear those you don't want.

- To allow the most widely used styles, click the Recommended Minimum button. You can then select or clear the check boxes for other styles as needed.

5.   In the Formatting area, clear the "Allow AutoFormat to override formatting restrictions" check box unless you want AutoFormat to apply any styles when formatting an unformatted document. This setting is relevant only if you use the AutoFormat feature.

6.   Select the Block Theme or Scheme switching check box if you want to ensure your colleagues don't change the document's overall look. Blocking switching is usually a good idea.

7.   Select the Block Quick Style Set switching check box if you want to prevent your colleagues from changing the set of Quick Styles used. Normally, you'll want your colleagues to use the set of Quick Styles you've applied.

8.   Click the OK button to close the Formatting Restrictions dialog box and return to the Restrict Formatting and Editing pane.

If Word displays a dialog box (see Figure 9–14) saying that the document may contain formatting or styles that aren't allowed and offering to remove them, click the Yes button. After you finish setting up the formatting and editing restrictions, check through the document for paragraphs whose style Word has replaced with Normal style. Apply to each paragraph a suitable style from the list of styles you've approved for the document.

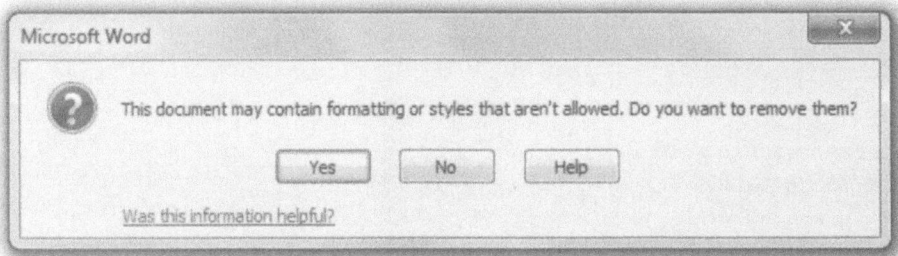

Figure 9–14. If Word warns you that the document may contain formatting or styles that aren't allowed, you'll normally want to click the Yes button to remove the formatting or styles.

To make the changes take effect, start enforcing protection, as discussed later in this chapter. Before that, though, you may want to apply editing restrictions as well, as discussed next.

Forcing Your Colleagues to Use Track Changes

To force your colleagues to use Track Changes, follow these steps:

1.   Select the "Allow only this type of editing in the document" check box.

2.   In the drop-down list, select the Track Changes item.

3.   Start enforcing protection, as discussed later in this chapter.

Limiting Your Colleagues to Using Comments

If you want to limit your colleagues to using comments when editing the document, follow these steps:

1. Select the "Allow only this type of editing in the document" check box.

2. In the drop-down list, select the Comments item. Word displays the Exceptions (optional) section in the Restrict Formatting and Editing task pane (see Figure 9–15). This section contains a Groups box and an Individuals box, but usually you'll see only the Groups box at first. Depending on how your PC is set up, the Groups box may show only the Everyone group, or it may show other groups too.

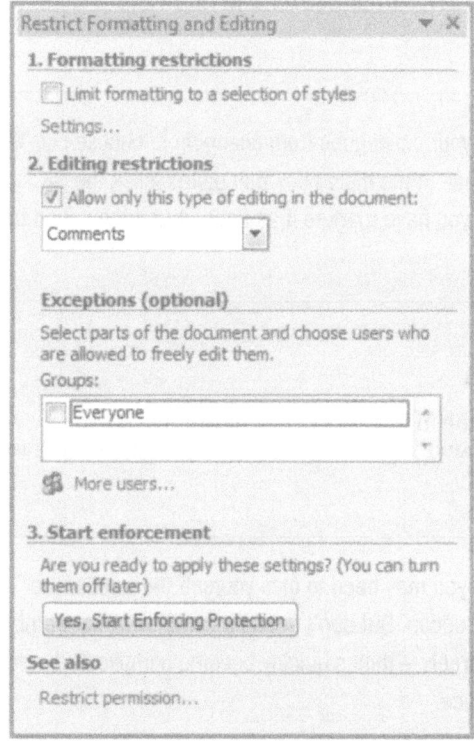

Figure 9–15. When you restrict your colleagues to using comments in the document, you can except specific users who need to be able to edit the document freely.

3. Use the controls in the Exceptions (optional) area to specify any parts of the document that people need to be able to edit, as discussed later in this chapter.

4. Start enforcing the restrictions, as discussed later in this chapter.

Preventing Your Colleagues from Making Any Changes at All

Sometimes you may need to prevent your colleagues from making any changes at all to the document. To do so, follow these steps:

1. Select the "Allow only this type of editing in the document" check box.

2. In the drop-down list, select the "No changes (Read only)" item. Word displays the Exceptions (optional) section in the Restrict Formatting and Editing task pane.

3. Use the controls in the Exceptions (optional) area, as discussed next, to specify any parts of the document that people need to be able to edit.

4. To make the protection take effect, start enforcing it, as discussed later in this chapter.

■ **Note** If you want to mark a document as final and discourage your colleagues from changing it, choose File ➤ Info, click the Protect Document button, and then click Mark as Final. In the dialog box that opens, click the OK button. When people open the document, they see a warning that you have marked it as final—but if they need to change it, they can remove that marking and edit it.

Adding Exceptions to Your Restrictions

When you restrict editing to the Comments setting, the "Filling in forms" setting, or the "No changes (Read only)" setting, you can except specific groups or individuals from the restrictions. Word doesn't let you make exceptions for Track Changes.

■ **Tip** Keep your exceptions as simple as possible. For example, you may need to give yourself the freedom to edit the whole document, and perhaps let your boss edit the introduction. But don't set up a complex structure of different areas that different people and different groups can edit freely—things quickly become complicated, and you undermine the point of imposing the restrictions in the first place.

To add exceptions to your restrictions, first add the groups or individuals you need to the Exceptions list. Follow these steps:

1. Click the "More users" link to display the Add Users dialog window (see Figure 9–16).

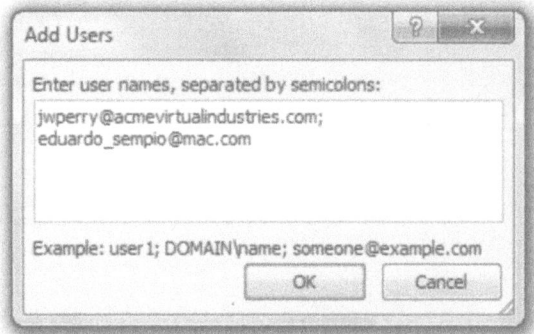

Figure 9–16. Type the user names for exceptions in the Add Users text box, separating the names with semicolons.

2. In the "Enter user names, separated by semicolons" box, type the names of the groups or users, separating them with semicolons. You can use these three formats:

    •   **Windows user names**: Type the name as it appears in Windows—for example, Bill Newman.

    •   **Active Directory names**: For example, CORP\jbraucher.

    •   **E-mail addresses**: For example, jwperry@acmevirtualindustries.com.

3. Click the OK button to close the Add Users dialog window. Word then displays the Individuals box (if it was hidden) with the user names in it (see Figure 9–17).

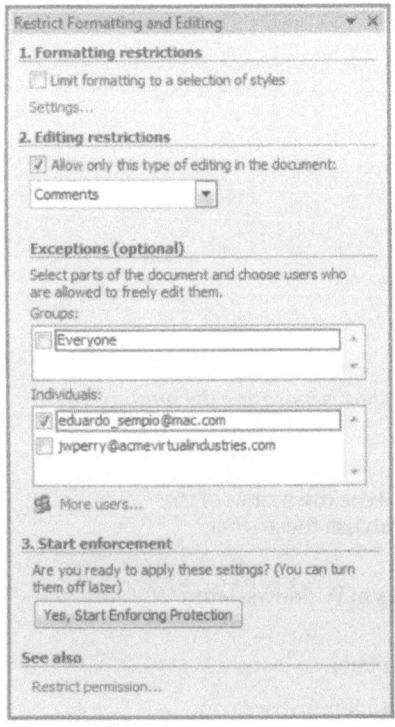

Figure 9–17. *Users you add to the Exceptions list appear in the Individuals box in the Restrict Formatting and Editing task pane.*

Now that you've set up the groups and users, specify the parts of the document each group or user can edit freely. Follow these steps:

1. Select the part of the document you want to let the group or user edit.

2. Select the group's or user's check box in the Exceptions area of the Restrict Formatting and Editing pane (see Figure 9–17).

3. Repeat this procedure for each document part on which you want to set special editing permissions.

For example, to enable all users to edit the first page of the document, select the first page, and then select the Everyone check box in the Groups box in the Restrict Formatting and Editing task pane.

To see which parts of the document a group or user can edit, click the group or user, and then click the drop-down button that appears. On the drop-down menu (see Figure 9–18), click the "Find next region this user can edit" item or the "Show all regions this user can edit" item, as appropriate. From this drop-down menu, you can also strip the group or user of editing permissions by clicking the "Remove all editing permissions for this user" item.

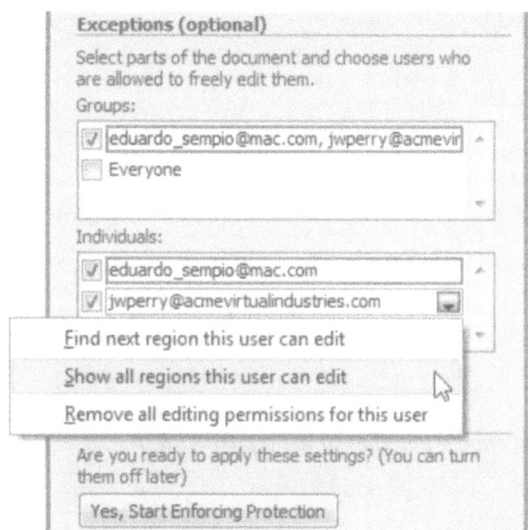

Figure 9–18. Use the drop-down menu to see which parts of the document a user or group can edit. You can also remove the editing permissions from the user or group.

After setting up your exceptions, you need to start enforcing the protection, as discussed next.

Starting to Enforce the Formatting and Editing Restrictions

When you've set up the formatting and editing restrictions you want, enforce them by taking the following steps:

1. In the "Start enforcement" area, click the Yes, Start Enforcing Protection button. Word displays the Start Enforcing Protection dialog box (see Figure 9–19).

Figure 9–19. In the Start Enforcing Protection dialog box, choose whether to use a password or user authentication to protect the document.

2. In the "Protection method" area, select the option button for the type of protection you want to use:

    - **Password:** To use password protection, select this option button, and then type a password in the "Enter new password" box and then in the "Reenter password to confirm" box. Make the password at least eight characters long, mix upper- and lowercase letters, and include numbers and symbols. Only users who enter the correct password will be able to remove the protection.

    - **User authentication:** To use user authentication (see the following note), select this option button. Any authenticated user will be able to remove the document protection.

■ **Note** User authentication uses Windows Live IDs or other e-mail addresses to uniquely identify users. To set up Word to use authentication, choose File ➤ Info, click the Protect Document button, click Restrict Permission by People, and then click Restricted Access. Word walks you through the process of setting up authentication for yourself and choosing which users can work with the document.

3. Click the OK button to close the Start Enforcing Protection dialog box. Word protects the document and updates the Restrict Formatting and Editing pane (see Figure 9–20).

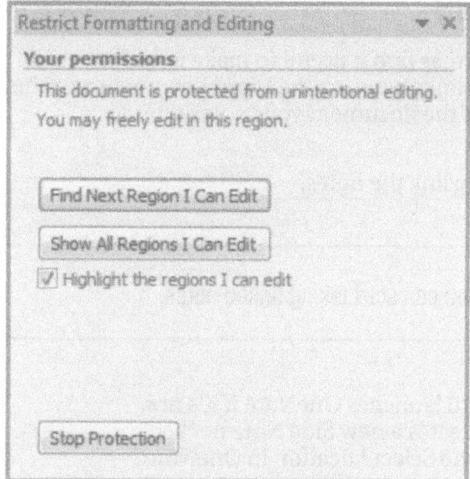

Figure 9-20. After you start enforcing protection, you can use the controls in the Restrict Formatting and Editing pane to find the document regions you can edit. You can also stop the protection by clicking the Stop Protection button and entering the password or authenticating yourself.

From here, you can take the following actions:

- Click the Find Next Region I Can Edit button to make Word select the next part of the document that you have permission to edit.

- Click the Show All Regions I Can Edit button to display all the document parts that you have permission to edit.

- Select the "Highlight the regions I can edit" check box to make Word apply a gray highlight to the areas you have permission to edit. This highlight is usually helpful for identifying the areas and seeing where they end.

If you're satisfied with the restrictions you've imposed, click the Close button (the × button) to close the Restrict Formatting and Editing pane. Then give a Save command (for example, click the Save button on the Quick Access Toolbar) to save the document with the protection in place.

Removing Formatting and Editing Restrictions from a Document

To remove formatting and editing restrictions from a document, follow these steps:

1. Choose Review ➤ Protect ➤ Restrict Editing to display the Restrict Formatting and Editing task pane.

2. Click the Stop Protection button.

3. If you enforced the protection with a password, Word displays the Unprotect Document dialog box. Type the password, and then click the OK button.

Using OneNote to Make Linked Notes

When you're working on a Word document, you may sometimes find it useful to make linked notes in OneNote. When you do this, OneNote automatically creates links between the Word document and the OneNote notebook, so that you can see exactly which part of the document your notes refer to.

To make linked notes, follow these steps:

1. In Word, open the document to which you want to link the notes.

■ **Note** If you create a new document, you must save it before you can start taking linked notes.

---

2. Choose Review ➤ OneNote ➤ Linked Notes. Word launches OneNote if it's not running, or activates it if it is running. OneNote creates a new Side Note docked to the side of the Windows desktop and displays the Select Location in OneNote dialog box (see Figure 9–21).

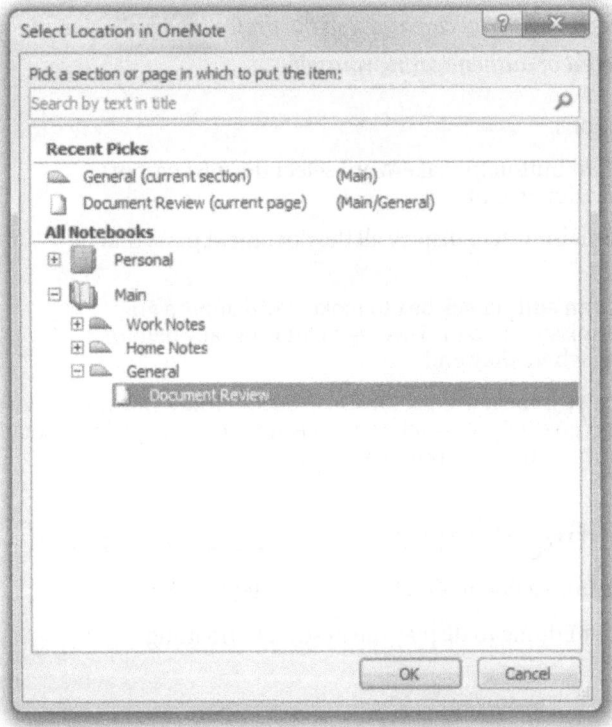

Figure 9–21. In the Select Location in OneNote dialog box, pick the section or page to which you want to add the linked notes.

3. Click the section or page to which you want to add the linked notes.

4. Click the OK button. OneNote creates the link to the Word document, and you can start taking notes in the Side Note window.

When you're ready to stop taking linked notes, click the link button in the Side Note window, and then click Stop Taking Linked Notes from the menu (see Figure 9–22). Alternatively, choose View ➤ Views ➤ Normal in the Side Note window in OneNote.

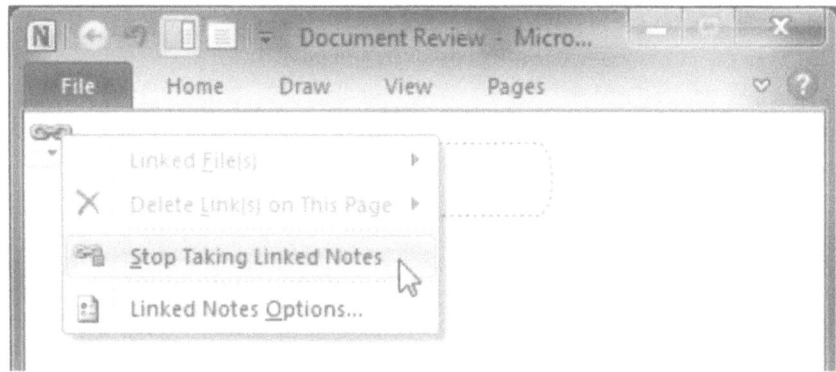

Figure 9–22. To stop taking linked notes, click the link icon in OneNote, and then click Stop Taking Linked Notes.

Summary

In this chapter, you've learned how to work productively with other people on documents.

First, you learned how to use the powerful Track Changes feature to mark, review, and integrate revisions in a document. Next, you picked up the skill of adding comments to a document to provide input without changing its text, reviewing comments, and deleting those you don't want to keep.

After that, I showed you how to merge marked or unmarked changes from two versions of the same document into another document, how to restrict edit rights on a document, and how to take linked notes in OneNote.

In the next chapter, I'll teach you to take your usage of Word to the next level, doing everything from customizing Word to suit your needs and preferences to automating repetitive actions with macros.

■ ■ ■

CHAPTER 10

Taking Your Use of Word to the Next Level

In this chapter, I'll show you how to take your use of Word to the next level—that of an advanced user. To this end, you'll learn skills you can use either in a business situation or at home.

We'll start by using the Word Options dialog window to configure the most important options in Word. By setting these options, you can control the way that Word appears and behaves, making it work the way you prefer.

After that, we'll move on to using Word's most exciting new feature—*coauthoring*, which means writing or editing a document at the same time as your colleagues are working on it. You'll also learn how to perform a mail merge to create personalized documents that you can print or e-mail, and how to customize the Word user interface to put the controls and information you need right at your fingertips.

Finally, I'll show you how to use the Visual Basic for Applications programming language (VBA) to automate your work by recording macros, sequences of commands that you can play back as needed. We'll even have a quick look at how you can edit a recorded macro to change what it does.

Configuring Word with the Word Options Dialog Window

To make Word work the way you prefer, you can change the settings in the Word Options dialog window.

This section explains the options you're most likely to benefit from changing. That means all the settings in the General category, the Display category, the Proofing category, and the Save category, and some of the settings in the Advanced category. We'll skip the Language category, as you probably won't need to change settings here, and many of the Advanced options that are less widely useful.

Start by choosing File ➤ Options to display the Word Options dialog window. The dialog window opens with the General category selected (see Figure 10–1). You can then switch to another category by clicking it in the left pane.

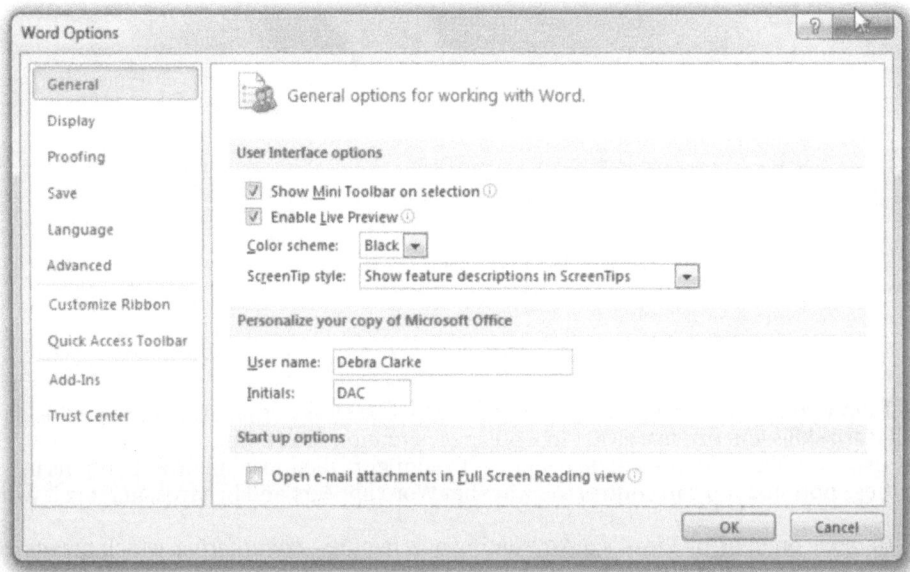

Figure 10–1. The Word Options dialog window at first displays the General category, which contains widely used options.

■ **Note** You can resize the Word Options dialog window by dragging the sizing handle (the dotted triangle) in its lower-right corner. The different categories contain widely varying numbers of options, and often it's useful to make the dialog window taller so that you can see more of them.

Choosing General Options

These are the options you can choose in the General category:

- **Show Mini Toolbar on selection**: Controls whether Word displays the Mini Toolbar when you hold the mouse pointer over a selection. If you don't find the Mini Toolbar useful, clear this check box.

- **Enable Live Preview**: Controls whether Word shows a preview of how the document will look when you hold the mouse pointer over an item in a gallery. For example, when you open the Quick Styles gallery and hold the mouse pointer over a style, Word shows the style applied to the current paragraph or selection. The Live Preview is a great feature that you'll probably want to use unless your PC struggles to show the previews—in which case, clear this check box.

- **Always use ClearType**: Controls whether Word always uses Microsoft's ClearType font-smoothing technology to make the edges of fonts look less jagged. This check box appears only if you're running Windows XP.

- **Color scheme**: In this drop-down list, choose the overall color scheme for Word and the other Office programs: Blue, Silver, or Black.

- **ScreenTip style**: In this drop-down list, choose the Show feature description in ScreenTips if you want ScreenTips that include a description of the command—usually useful when you're getting the hang of Word. Choose the "Don't show feature descriptions in ScreenTips" item if you want to see shorter ScreenTips with just the command name. Choose the "Don't show ScreenTips" item if you want to suppress ScreenTips altogether.

- **User name**: In this box, enter your name the way you want Word to display it. Word picks up the user name from Office during installation, so if Word thinks you're called Authorized User, it's not personal.

- **Initials**: In this box, enter your initials the way you want Word to display them.

- **Open e-mail attachments in Full Screen Reading view**: Select this check box if you want Word always to open e-mail attachments in Full Screen Reading view. This can be useful if you open attachments directly from Outlook, but usually it's best to save the files from Outlook and then open them from Word.

Choosing Display Options

Click the Display category in the left pane to show the Display options (see Figure 10–2). You can then choose settings for page display, formatting marks, and printing.

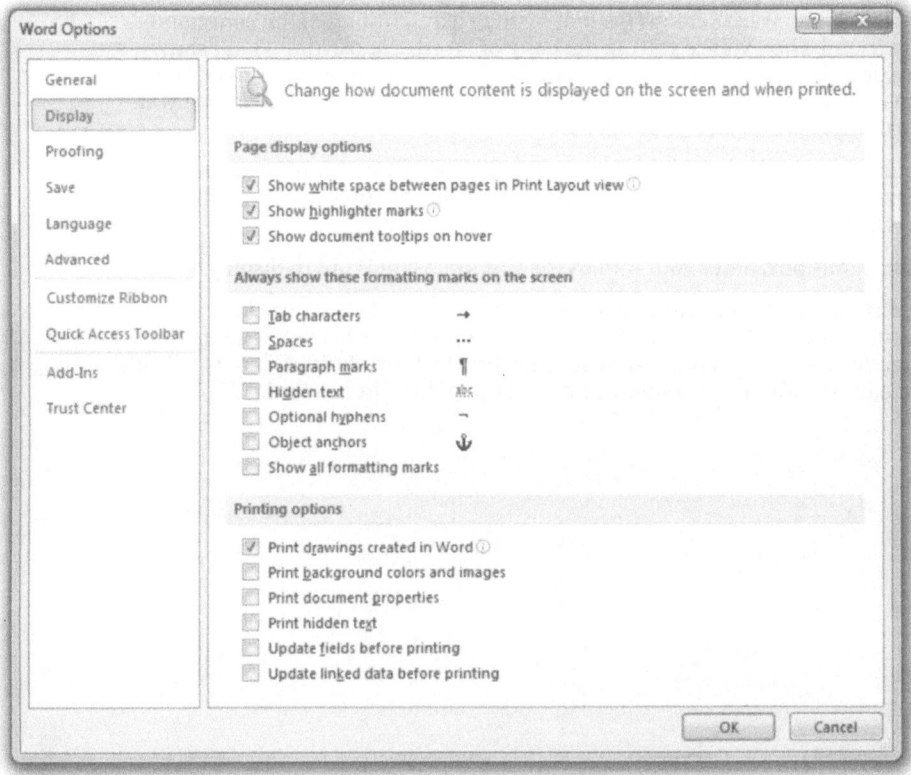

Figure 10–2. *Set the Display options to control how Word appears on screen and how it behaves when printing.*

Choosing Page Display Options

The three options in the "Page display options" section at the top of the Display category can make a big difference to how your documents look and act:

- **Show white space between pages in Print Layout view**: Controls whether Word displays the full amount of white space at the top and bottom of pages, including the headers and footers. Clear this check box if you want to hide these areas and show just a narrow line between pages.

■ **Tip** You can quickly change the "Show white space between pages in Print Layout view" setting by double-clicking the horizontal divider line between pages in a document. When you move the mouse pointer over the line, Word changes the mouse pointer to a pair of arrows pointing up and down, with the ScreenTip "Double-click to show white space" or "Double-click to hide white space" (as appropriate).

- **Show highlighter marks**: Controls whether Word displays highlighting you've applied with the Text Highlight tool on screen and on printouts. Clear this check box to hide highlighting without actually removing it.

- **Show document tooltips on hover**: Controls whether Word displays ScreenTips for document items such as comments when you hold the mouse pointer over them.

Choosing Formatting Marks Options

The options in the "Always show these formatting marks on the screen" section in the Display category let you control which invisible formatting items Word displays on screen:

- **Tab characters**: Select the check box to display a right-pointing arrow for a tab.

- **Spaces**: Select the check box to display a raised dot for each space.

- **Paragraph marks**: Select the check box to display a pilcrow (¶) at the end of each paragraph.

- **Hidden text**: Select the check box to display hidden text. Hidden text appears with a dotted underline.

- **Optional hyphens**: Select the check box to display a ¬ character where you've inserted an optional hyphen. (An optional hyphen is one you insert by pressing Ctrl+– to tell Word where it's okay to hyphenate a word if necessary.)

- **Object anchors**: Select the check box to display an anchor symbol for the object anchor for a selected graphical object.

- **Show all formatting marks**: Select this check box to display all the formatting marks. You can toggle all formatting marks on and off quickly from the Word UI by choosing Home ➤ Paragraph ➤ Show/Hide ¶ or pressing Ctrl+* (in other words, Ctrl+Shift+8).

■ **Note** Whether to display the formatting marks—and if so, which to display—is largely a matter of personal preference. Having the formatting marks displayed helps you avoid deleting invisible items by accident and is especially useful for hidden text and optional hyphens. Having all formatting marks displayed tends to be visually distracting—but you may disagree.

Choosing Printing Options

In the Printing options section of the Display category, choose how Word should handle printing:

- **Print drawings created in Word**: Controls whether your printouts include graphics you've created in Word (for example, shapes and SmartArt) and text boxes. Clear this check box if you're printing a draft and don't need to see the graphics. Word prints blank boxes instead to show where the graphics go.

- **Print background colors and images**: Controls whether printouts include background colors and background images. Clear this check box if you want to omit these items—for example, if you're printing to a monochrome printer and the background colors and images will look wretched in gray.

- **Print document properties**: Controls whether Word includes a page listing document properties at the end of the printout. Some companies require this setting, but if you need to print only the document properties, choose File ➤ Print to open the Print place, open the Print What menu, click Document Properties, and then click the Print button.

- **Print hidden text**: Controls whether Word prints hidden text in the document. Select this check box when you want to make sure you're seeing the full text of the document.

- **Update fields before printing**: Controls whether Word updates fields (such as dates, times, and cross-references) just before printing. To make sure your printout is up-to-date, select this check box.

- **Update linked data before printing**: Controls whether Word updates links to other documents before printing. This is usually a good idea provided that the linked documents are available; if you've moved the document away from its linked documents, clear this check box.

Choosing Proofing Options

Click the Proofing category in the left column to display the Proofing options (see Figure 10–3). The top section, AutoCorrect options, contains only the AutoCorrect Options button, which you click to open the AutoCorrect dialog window; Chapter 4 explains how to choose suitable options in this dialog window. The following sections discuss the other options.

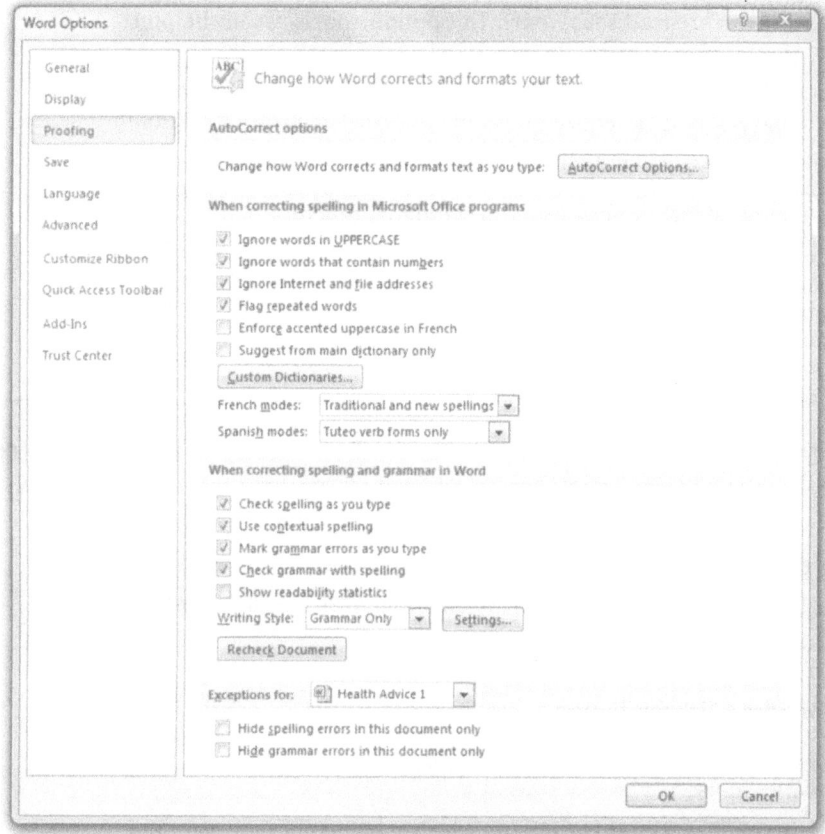

Figure 10–3. Set the options in the Proofing category in the Word Options dialog window to take control of the spelling checker and the grammar checker.

Choosing Spelling Options for All of the Office Programs

In the "When correcting spelling in Microsoft Office programs" section, you can choose the following options:

- **Ignore words in UPPERCASE:** Select this check box if you want the spelling checker to skip words that appear in uppercase. This is usually helpful, as it helps you avoid queries on technical terms.

- **Ignore words that contain numbers:** Select this check box to have the spelling checker skip any word that includes numbers (for example, IPv6). Clear this check box if you tend to get number typos in words.

- **Ignore Internet and file addresses**: Select this check box to make the spelling checker ignore any URLs (for example, www.apress.com) and file addresses (for example, \\server2\reference\manual.pdf). This option, too, is usually helpful.

- **Flag repeated words**: Select this check box to allow the spelling checker to query a word that appears twice in succession. This option is good at picking up useless duplication, though you may sometimes need to approve a deliberate repetition.

- **Enforce accented uppercase in French**: Select this check box if your documents use a French dialect (such as Canadian French) that retains accents on uppercase letters rather than removing the accents (as in standard French).

- **Suggest from main dictionary only**: Select this check box if you want spelling suggestions only from Office's main dictionary file, not from custom dictionaries you create. Usually, you'll want to clear this check box so that the spelling checker uses your custom dictionaries.

■ **Note** A *custom dictionary* is a file that Word uses to supplement the built-in dictionary file it uses for checking spelling. A custom dictionary contains a list of words that you've told the spell checker it should accept as being correctly spelled. Word starts you off with a custom dictionary named Custom.dic, but you can create other dictionaries as needed—for example, to keep different types of terms separate. You add words to the custom dictionary you're currently using by giving the Add to Dictionary command when checking spelling.

- **Custom Dictionaries**: Click this button to display the Custom Dictionaries dialog window, which you can use to create new custom dictionaries, import existing custom dictionaries (for example, ones your company uses), and choose which custom dictionaries to use.

- **French modes**: In this drop-down list, choose which spelling type you want the spelling checker to use: Traditional and new spellings, Traditional spelling, or New spelling.

- **Spanish modes**: In this drop-down list, choose whether to use the Tuteo verb forms, the Voseo verb forms, or both for the second person. The choices are Tuteo verb forms only, Tuteo and Voseo verb forms, and Voseo verb forms only.

Choosing Spelling and Grammar Options for Word

In the "When correcting spelling and grammar in Word" section, you can choose the following options:

- **Check spelling as you type**: Select the check box if you want the spelling checker to check spelling continually as you type. The spelling checker puts a wavy red underline under any word it queries. Clear this check box if you prefer to check spelling in a separate operation.

- **Use contextual spelling**: Select this check box if you want the spelling checker to try to check words in their contexts rather than just on their own. The spelling checker puts a wavy blue underline under a word that has a contextual spelling query.

■ **Note** Contextual spelling is worth using, but it doesn't work consistently because of the complexity of the English language, so don't rely on it. For example, if you write "She bought there car," the spelling checker correctly suggests replacing "there" with "their." But the spelling checker raises no query with "She wrecked there car," which has the same problem.

- **Mark grammar errors as you type:** Select this check box if you want the grammar checker to raise queries as you work. The grammar checker puts a wavy green underline under items it queries. On-the-fly grammar checking tends to be distracting, so you'll probably want to clear this check box.

- **Check grammar with spelling:** Select this check box if you want to use the grammar checker. Otherwise, clear it.

- **Show readability statistics:** Select this check box if you want the spelling checker to display the Readability Statistics dialog window when it finishes a spelling check.

■ **Tip** Don't bother with the readability statistics. The counts of words, characters, paragraphs, and sentences can be useful, but you can get the first three more easily in the Word Count dialog window (choose Review ➤ Proofing ➤ Word Count). The averages of sentences per paragraph, words per sentence, and characters per word have little relevance. The Passive Sentences, Flesch Reading Ease, and Flesch-Kincaid Grade Level are computed statistics that don't accurately assess how easy or hard the document is to read. If you want to know whether a document is hard to understand, ask a colleague to read it.

- **Writing Style:** In this drop-down list, choose Grammar Only to make the grammar checker check for grammatical problems such as fragments of sentences (rather than complete sentences), misused capitalization and punctuation, and verbs not agreeing with their subjects. Select Grammar & Style if you want the grammar checker to try to assess your document for clichés, gender-specific words, passive sentences, unclear phrasing, and a dozen or so other potential problems as well.

Choosing Grammar Options

If you choose to use the grammar checker, you choose the overall setting in the Writing Style drop-down list. To customize the grammar checking, click the Settings button. Word displays the Grammar Settings dialog window (see Figure 10–4).

***Figure 10–4.** Use the Grammar Settings dialog window to control which grammar and style issues the grammar checker raises when checking your documents.*

The "Writing style" drop-down list at the top shows the setting you chose in the Writing Style drop-down list in the Options dialog window. You can change it here if necessary. This acts as the master control for the check boxes in the Style area of the "Grammar and style options" list box (this area appears below the Grammar area, which you can see in the figure). When you choose Grammar & Style in the "Writing style" drop-down list, Word selects all the check boxes in the Style area; when you choose Grammar Only, it clears all the check boxes.

The most useful options here are the three in the Require area:

- **Comma required before last list item:** Choose the Always setting to make the grammar checker check for the serial comma always appearing (for example, "bacon, lettuce, and tomato"), as is widely used in U.S. English, or the Never command if you want Word to check that you never use serial commas (such as "bacon, lettuce and tomato"). Choose the "Don't check" setting if you don't want to check for this.

- **Punctuation required with quotes:** Choose the Inside setting to make the grammar checker check that punctuation appears inside quotes. Choose the Outside setting to make the grammar checker check that punctuation appears outside quotes. Or choose the "Don't check" setting to skip checking punctuation placement around quotes.

- **Spaces required between sentences**: Choose the 1 setting to make the grammar checker enforce one space between sentences, as is widely used. Choose the 2 setting to use two spaces between sentences, as some style guides recommend. Choose the "Don't check" setting to prevent the grammar checker from checking this.

In the Grammar area, clear the check box for any grammar item you don't want the grammar checker to check.

In the Style area, select the check box for each type of check you want to use, and clear the check box for each type of check you want to omit.

When you have finished choosing grammar and style options, click the OK button to close the Grammar Settings dialog window and return to the Grammar category in the Word Options dialog window.

Choosing Exceptions Options

In the "Exceptions for" area, you can choose to hide spelling or grammar errors in a particular document. This can be useful when you need to focus on the document's content without seeing the errors.

In the "Exceptions for" drop-down list, choose the document you want—Word selects the document that's active when you display the Word Options dialog window, but you can choose any other open document. Then select the "Hide spelling errors in this document only" check box or the "Hide grammar errors in this document only" check box, as needed.

Choosing Save Options

Click the Save category in the left pane to display the Save options (see Figure 10–5). You can then set options for the way you save documents, options for offline editing, and options for preserving the fidelity of documents.

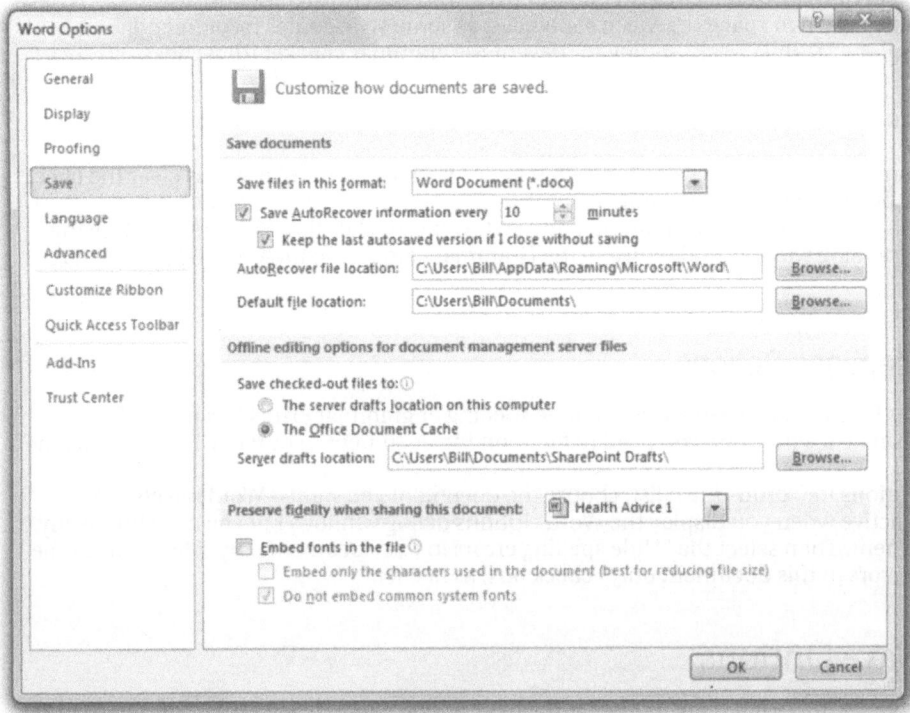

Figure 10–5. *In the Save category of the Word Options dialog window, you can set vital options such as the default document format and how often Word saves AutoRecover information to protect you against computer problems.*

Choosing Options for Saving Documents

In the Save documents section of the Save category, you can set the following options:

- **Save files in this format:** In this drop-down list, choose the default format for the documents you create in Word. Use the Word Document format if your colleagues have Office 2010, Office 2007 for Windows, or Office 2008 or Office 2011 for Mac. Otherwise, the Word 97–2003 Document format is a better choice for backward compatibility with older versions of Word and with other word processing programs.

Note People using Office 2003 for Windows or Office 2004 for Mac can install converter filters from the Microsoft web site to enable these versions of the Office programs to open files in the new formats, such as Word 2010's Word Document format. But because most people don't have these converters, it's safer to use the Word 97–2003 Document format for sharing with people using Office 2003 or Office 2004.

- **Save AutoRecover information every *N* minutes**: Select this check box if you want Word to create AutoRecover files. This is normally a good idea as a safety net. The default setting is 10 minutes, but if you work quickly and prefer not to save your documents manually, reduce the interval to 2 or 3 minutes.

- **Keep the last Auto Recovered file if I close without saving**: Select this check box if you want to prevent Word from deleting the last AutoRecover file it has saved when you close Word without saving changes. This setting is usually helpful.

Note AutoRecover is a safety net that automatically saves a copy of each open document every few minutes in case Word crashes and loses the changes you've made. After Word restarts automatically, or you restart it manually, it opens the latest AutoRecover files for you so that you can choose which versions to keep. If you save your documents and then exit Word, it gets rid of the AutoRecover files it has saved.

- **AutoRecover file location**: This box shows the folder in which Word is storing your AutoRecover files. This is usually a folder buried deep in your AppData folder, which itself is normally hidden. You don't need to open AutoRecover files manually, as Word automatically opens them for you after a crash, so normally there's no need to change this folder.

- **Default file location**: This box shows the folder that Word first displays in the Save As dialog window until you choose another folder. The default setting is your Documents folder, which often works well. To use a different folder, click the Browse button, select the folder in the Browse dialog window, and then click the OK button.

Choosing Offline Editing Options

In the "Offline editing options for document management server files" section of the Save category, choose where to store the SharePoint files you edit offline. You'll normally want to select the option button called The Office Document Cache, and leave the Server drafts location box unchanged. The Office Document Cache is SharePoint's standard location for storing files, so it's normally the best choice.

Choosing Options for Preserving Fidelity

In the "Preserve fidelity when sharing this document" area of the Save category, you can choose whether to embed fonts in the document so that it will display correctly on a PC that doesn't have all the fonts the document uses. These are the options:

- **Embed fonts in the file**: Select this check box to turn on embedding. Embedding the fonts is a good idea if you need your documents to display perfectly; if you're prepared to let Word substitute fonts as needed, don't bother with embedding. The main disadvantage to embedding fonts is that it increases the document's size; it's also possible to run into licensing issues, where you need permission to legally include the embedded fonts in the document you're sharing.

- **Embed only the characters used in the document**: Select this check box if you need to reduce the amount of embedded fonts. This works fine if whoever opens the file needs only to read it; but if they start editing the document, they may find some characters aren't available (because you hadn't used them, so Word didn't embed them).

- **Do not embed common system fonts**: Select this check box to prevent Word from embedding system fonts that most PCs have. Not embedding these fonts is usually a good idea when sharing with PCs, but if you're sharing with computers running other operating systems (for example, Macs or Linux boxes), you may want to include even the system fonts.

Choosing Advanced Options

Click the Advanced category in the left pane to display the Advanced options (see Figure 10–6). This category contains a long list of options broken up into several different topics. This section discusses only the options you're most likely to benefit from changing.

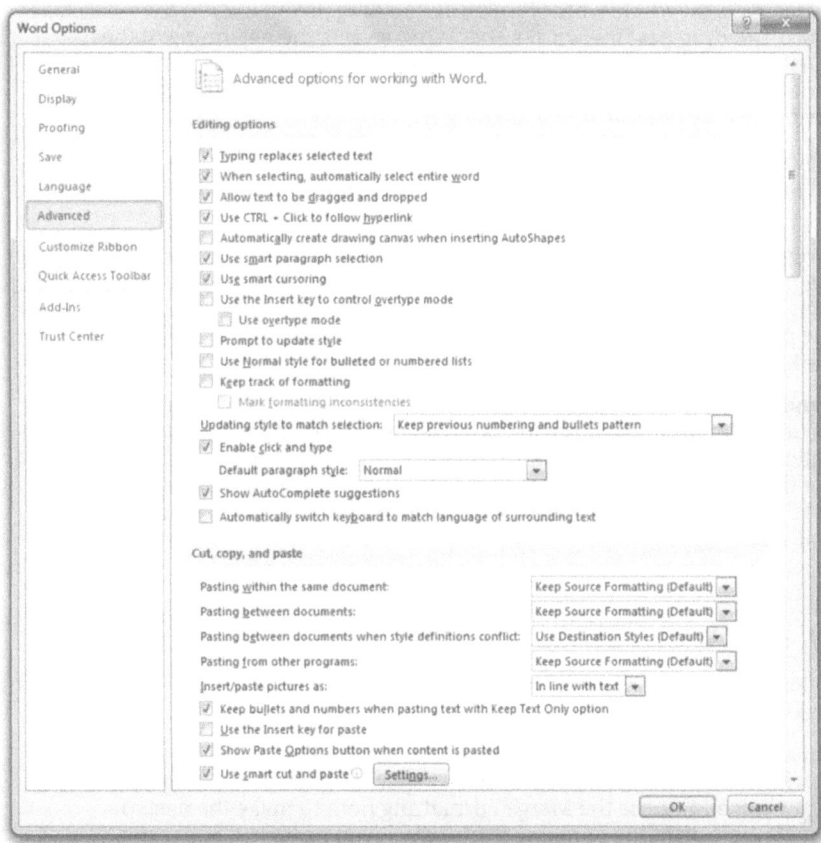

Figure 10–6. *The Advanced category in the Word Options dialog window contains a huge number of options—this screen shows just the top one-third of the list. Some options can make a big difference to the way you work, but others are obscure or specialized.*

Choosing Editing Options

Of the more than a dozen options in the "Editing options" area, these are the ones you'll most likely benefit from setting:

- **Typing replaces selected text**: Select this check box to allow yourself to select text and then type something over it. This is Word's default setting, and many people find it easy. If you tend to select material by accident and then type over it, clear this check box. When you start typing over a selection, Word moves the insertion point back to the beginning of the selection, so that what you type appears before the start of what was selected.

- **When selecting, automatically select entire word**: Select this check box to have Word automatically select whole words for you as you drag. If you click in the middle of a word and drag past the word's end, Word selects the beginning of the word as well. As you drag further, Word selects a whole word at a time. If you don't like this automatic selection, clear this check box. If you leave automatic selection on, you can override it by holding down the Alt key.

- **Allow text to be dragged and dropped**: Select this check box to enable drag and drop for text. If you find yourself dragging text unintentionally, clear this check box.

- **Use smart paragraph selection**: Select this check box to have Word automatically select the paragraph mark at the end of a paragraph for you when you select the rest of the paragraph. Unless you've displayed paragraph marks or all invisible characters, the paragraph mark will be hidden, so when Word selects the paragraph mark, it appears as selected white space at the end of the paragraph.

- **Enable click and type**: Select this check box if you want to be able to click after the end of the document to place the insertion point farther down the page, and have Word automatically insert extra paragraphs as needed up to that point. This feature is sometimes useful for laying out pages. If you use it, use the "Default paragraph style" drop-down list to set the style Word should use for the extra paragraphs it inserts.

Choosing Cut, Copy, and Paste Options

If you use Cut, Copy, and Paste in your documents, make sure the options in the "Cut, copy, and paste" section are set the way you want them:

- **Pasting within the same document**: In this drop-down list, choose the Keep Source Formatting item to make the pasted text keep its original formatting (this is usually the best choice). Choose the Merge Formatting item to make the pasted text receive the formatting of the paragraph into which you paste it. Choose the Keep Text Only item to paste the text without formatting.

- **Pasting between documents**: In this drop-down list, choose the Keep Source Formatting item to make the pasted text keep its original formatting. Choose the Merge Formatting item to make the pasted text take on the formatting of the destination paragraph (this is usually the best choice). Choose the Keep Text Only item to paste the text without formatting.

- **Pasting between documents when style definitions conflict**: In this drop-down list, choose the Keep Source Formatting item to make the pasted text keep its original formatting. Choose the Use Destination Styles item to make the pasted material take on the look of the document into which you paste it (this is usually the best choice). Choose the Merge Formatting item to make the pasted text pick up the style formatting from the destination document. Choose the Keep Text Only item to paste the text without formatting.

- **Pasting from other programs**: In this drop-down list, choose the setting you want for text you cut or copy from another program and paste into Word. The choices are Keep Source Formatting, Merge Formatting, and Keep Text Only. Usually, Merge Formatting is the best choice, but you may prefer Keep Text Only depending on the types of documents you work with.

- **Insert/paste pictures as**: In this drop-down list, choose the default wrapping method for pictures you insert or paste: In line with text, Square, Tight, Behind text, In front of text, Through, or Top and bottom. Choose the setting depending on how you usually position pictures in your documents.

- **Use the Insert key for paste**: Select this check box if you want to be able to give the Paste command by pressing the Insert key. Some people find this convenient, but many find the Insert key is easy to press by accident.

- **Show Paste Options button when content is pasted**: Select this check box if you want Word to display the Paste Options button so that you can choose a different Paste Option if needed. Usually this is helpful.

- **Use smart cut and paste**: Select this check box if you want Word to try to adjust sentence spacing, word spacing, paragraph spacing, and more when you paste material. For example, when you paste in a sentence straight after a period, Word adds a space automatically. This feature generally works pretty well. You can adjust specific smart cut and paste settings by clicking the Settings button and working in the Settings dialog window that opens.

Choosing Show Document Content Options

The "Show document content" section of the Advanced category in the Word Options dialog window contains several options you may want to change:

- **Show text wrapped within the document window**: Select this check box to make Word use the full width of the document window in Draft view and Outline view instead of sticking strictly to the ruler. This setting is normally helpful if you work extensively in either of these views.

- **Show picture placeholders**: Select this check box if your PC struggles to scroll through a document that's packed with pictures. This option makes Word display a placeholder box instead of each picture to improve scrolling performance.

- **Show bookmarks**: Select this check box to display visual indicators for bookmarks—a heavy I-beam for a bookmark that's a point in text, and a pair of brackets for a bookmark that has contents. Displaying bookmarks can help you avoid deleting them unintentionally. See the section "Creating a Bookmark" in Chapter 4 for instructions on creating bookmarks.

- **Field shading**: In this drop-down list, choose when Word should display shading for fields. Choose the Always item when you're laying out a document with fields and need to keep tabs on them all. Choose the "When selected" item to display shading only when you select a field (this is the default setting). Choose the Never item to turn off field shading entirely.

Choosing Display Options

In the Display section of the Advanced category, you may find it helpful to choose settings for the following options:

- **Show this number of Recent Documents**: Set the number of documents you want to appear in the Recent pane in the Backstage view. The default setting, 20, works well for a medium-height window, but you may want to increase the number if you have more space.

- **Show measurements in units of**: Choose Inches, Centimeters, Millimeters, Points, or Picas, as needed. (A *point* is 1/72 inch, and a *pica* is 1/6 inch, or 12 points.)

- **Style area pane width in Draft and Outline views**: If you use the style area to see which style is applied to which paragraph, set the width here. (Start with 1" and increase it if necessary.)

- **Show horizontal scroll bar**: Clear this check box if you don't need to see the horizontal scroll bar.

- **Show vertical scroll bar**: Clear this check box if you don't need to see the vertical scroll bar.

Choosing Print Options

In the Print section of the Advanced category, you may sometimes need to set these three options:

- **Use draft quality**: Select this check box to print at lower quality, using less ink or toner. This is the default setting for printing; when you want to print at higher quality, you can override it.

- **Print in background**: Select this check box to use background printing, which enables you to restart work in the document while Word is still sending the document to the printer.

- **Print pages in reverse order**: Select this check box to print the last page first. This can be useful when you're collating documents manually.

Choosing Save Options

In the Save section of the Advanced category, make sure you've chosen suitable settings for these three options:

- **Prompt before saving Normal template**: Select this check box if you want Word to ask your permission before saving the Normal template when you quit Word. Clear this check box if you want Word to go ahead and save changes to the Normal template without consulting you.

- **Always create backup copy**: Select this check box to have Word automatically retain the last saved copy of the document as a backup against disaster. When you select this check box, Word saves the document normally the first time. After that, Word renames the saved document under the name *Backup of* and the document name (for example, Backup of Relocation Report), and then saves the current document afresh under the main name. This option gives you an easy backup of the previous version; if you save your documents frequently, the backup version will be only a few changes behind the main version.

- **Allow background saves**: Select this check box if you want Word to save your documents in the background. This enables you to resume work in the document sooner than if Word performs a regular save, but unless you're saving huge documents across a slow network connection, the difference may not be perceptible.

Choosing General Options

The General section of the Advanced category contains several options you may want to set:

- **Provide feedback with sound**: Select this check box if you want Word to give you feedback using sounds to alert you when Word finishes doing something (such as saving or printing a document). This check box is cleared by default.

- **Provide feedback with animation**: Clear this check box (which is selected by default) if you want to prevent Word from giving you feedback using animation.

- **Update automatic links at open**: Select this check box to make Word update automatic links to other documents when you open a document. This setting is normally helpful because it makes sure you're looking at the latest content.

- **Allow opening a document in Draft view**: Select this check box if you want to be able to open documents in Draft view if they were displayed in Draft view when you closed them. If you clear this check box, Word switches the document to Print Layout view when you open it.

- **File Locations**: If you need to change the default location Word uses for documents, templates, or other items, click this button, and then work in the File Locations dialog window. See the section "Setting Your Templates Folders" in Chapter 4 for coverage of the File Locations dialog window.

Coauthoring or Editing a Document with Your Colleagues

In Chapter 9, you learned how to use powerful Word tools such as Track Changes, Comments, and Document Compare to work with your colleagues on a document. You also learned how to restrict edit rights to all or part of a document—for example, by restricting a document so that nobody can turn off Track Changes, or by limiting most of your colleagues to using comments when reviewing a document but letting privileged reviewers make edits in certain sections.

As well as these features, which give you great flexibility and control over the editing of your documents, Word also enables you to write or edit a document even while your colleagues are working in the same document. In this section, I'll show you how to use this terrific new tool for getting your documents created and finalized quickly.

Microsoft calls this process of multiple people working in the same document "coauthoring." To coauthor a document, you and your colleagues open the same copy of the document at the same time, and all work on it together. Here's what happens:

- **Create the document**: You create the document as normal (for example, by using a template) and store it on your SharePoint site or on Windows Live SkyDrive by choosing File ➤ Save & Send ➤ Save to SharePoint or File ➤ Save & Send ➤ Save to Web.

■ **Caution** Unless you have a fast and reliable Internet connection, simultaneous editing of a large document stored on Windows Live SkyDrive can be slow enough to make coauthoring difficult.

- **Open the document**: The first person opens the document as normal. When another person opens the document, he or she will see a pop-up message about the other people already editing the document (see Figure 10–7). The first person also receives a pop-up as soon as Word notices that other authors have opened the document.

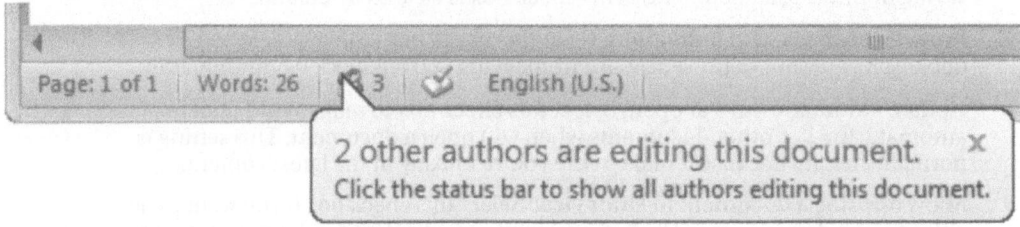

Figure 10–7. When you open a document that others are working on, Word displays a pop-up to let you know they're editing it.

- **See who's editing the document**: The status bar displays an icon showing the number of people editing the document. (This number includes you.) You can click the icon to see who the people are (see Figure 10–8). For more detail, click the File tab to open Backstage, and then look at the People Currently Editing readout at the top of the Info pane.

Figure 10–8. *To see who the other authors are, click the Authors icon on the status bar.*

▪ **Tip** In the People Currently Editing area of the Info pane in the Backstage view, there's a Send a Message button you can click to display a drop-down menu for sending either an e-mail message or an instant message to all the other people editing the document. For example, you could give them a ten-minute warning of the deadline by which you must finish the document, or you could tell them which section of the document you'll be working on next, so that they know they should leave it alone.

- **Edit the document**: You can work pretty much as normal in Word, except that only one person can edit a particular paragraph or other element at a time. As you work, Word shows you which parts of the document other authors are working on by placing a line to the left of the items and displaying a name box (see Figure 10–9).

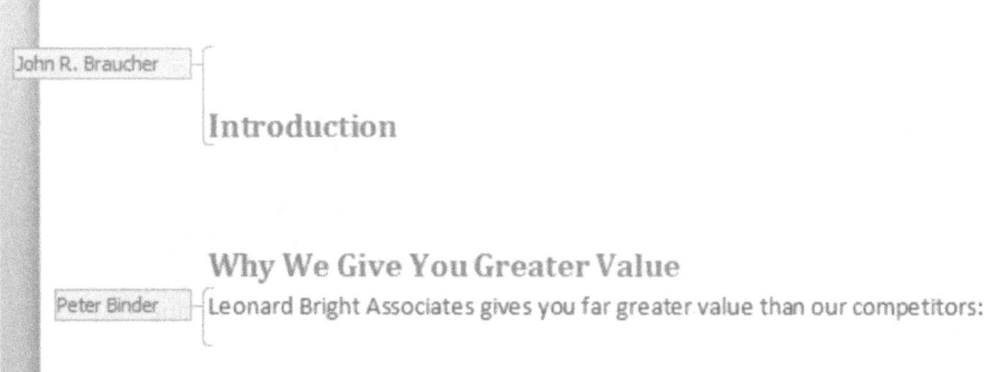

Figure 10–9. *Word shows you which parts of the document your coauthors are working on at the moment.*

■ **Note** The Updates Available button on the status bar lets you know when updates from your coauthors are available.

- **Update the document**: When you're ready to save changes and get any updates that are available, you press Ctrl+S or click the Save button on the Quick Access Toolbar as usual. The Save button displays a pair of curving arrows to indicate that it's acting as an Update button. Word then updates the copy of the document you're viewing with the changes the others have made (Figure 10–10 shows an example using the same document as before), applies shading to the changes to draw your attention to them, and makes your changes available to your coauthors.

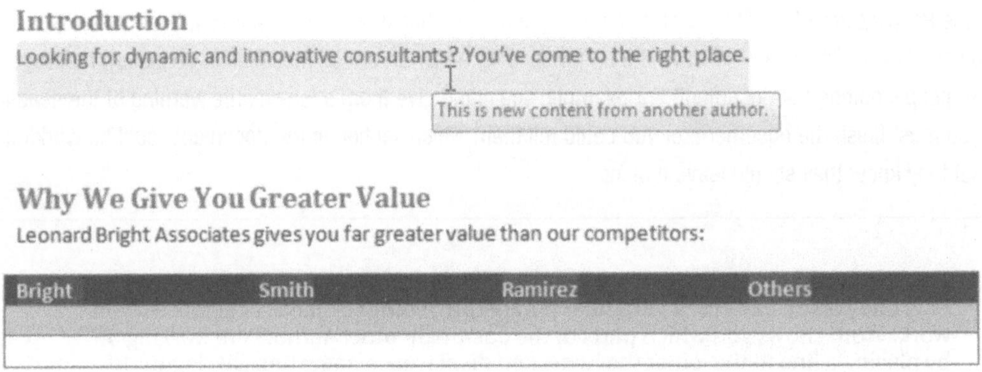

Introduction

Looking for dynamic and innovative consultants? You've come to the right place.

This is new content from another author.

Why We Give You Greater Value

Leonard Bright Associates gives you far greater value than our competitors:

Bright	Smith	Ramirez	Others

Figure 10–10. When you save your changes, Word merges in updates your coauthors have saved. Word displays the new items with shading (as in the paragraph under the Introduction heading here).

- **Resolve conflicts**: Word does its best to show you and your coauthors who's working where, but sooner or later, two or more of you may change the same part of the document in the same cycles of saving and updating. When this happens, Word displays the Upload Failed bar (see Figure 10–11) to the author who tried to save changes over changes another author had already saved. Click the Resolve button. In the "Conflicting changes" pane that Word displays, right-click the conflict, and then choose Accept Conflict or Reject Conflict, as appropriate. Word displays the Conflicts Resolved bar when you have resolved all the conflicts; click the Save and Close View button to save the changes and close the "Conflicting changes" pane.

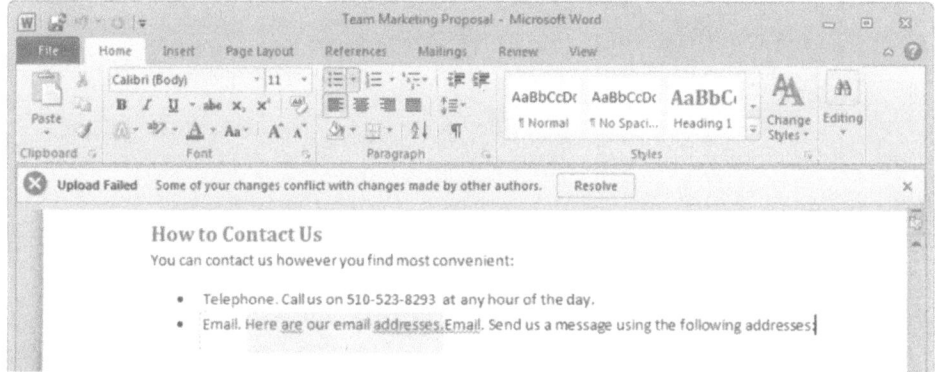

Figure 10–11. Word warns you of any conflicting changes when you try to save the document. Click the Resolve button on the Upload Failed bar to deal with the highlighted conflicts.

- **Close the document**: When you have finished working with the document, save any unsaved changes, and then close it as usual.

Performing a Mail Merge

When you need to create standardized documents such as form letters or mailing labels, use Word's Mail Merge feature. As you'll see in this section, you can quickly set up the main document for the mail merge, attach to it the data source that contains the records you want to use, and then merge the resulting documents either to a printer or to e-mail messages.

Creating the Main Document for the Mail Merge

The first step in performing a mail merge is to set up what Word calls the *main document*. This is the document that contains the standard part of the merge documents—for example, the boilerplate text and graphics to which you will add the customer names and addresses for a letter.

To create the main document for a mail merge, follow these steps:

1. Create a new document or open an existing document. For example, if you want to create a letter based on a template, choose File ➤ New, select the template, and then click the Create button. If you've opened a new document, save it as usual (for example, press Ctrl+S, and then specify the folder and filename).

2. Choose Mailings ➤ Start Mail Merge ➤ Start Mail Merge to open the Start Mail Merge gallery (see Figure 10–12).

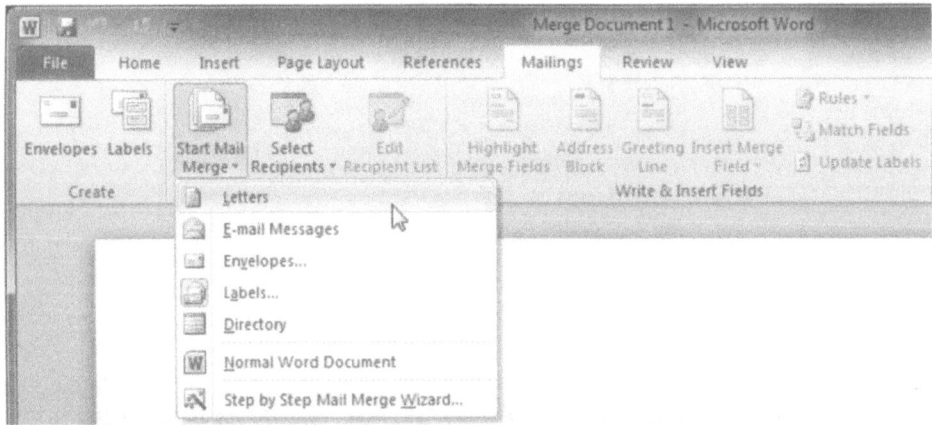

Figure 10–12. Choose the type of main document from the Start Mail Merge gallery.

3. Click the type of mail merge you want to perform:

    - **Letters**: Word changes the document to Print Layout view if it's currently in another view.

    - **E-mail messages**: Word changes the document to Web Layout view if it's currently in another view.

    - **Envelopes**: Word displays the Envelope Options dialog window (see Figure 10–13). On the Envelope Options tab, you can specify which type of envelopes you'll use. On the Printing Options tab, specify how to print them—for example, feeding them face up, lengthwise, in the middle of the default tray. Then click the OK button.

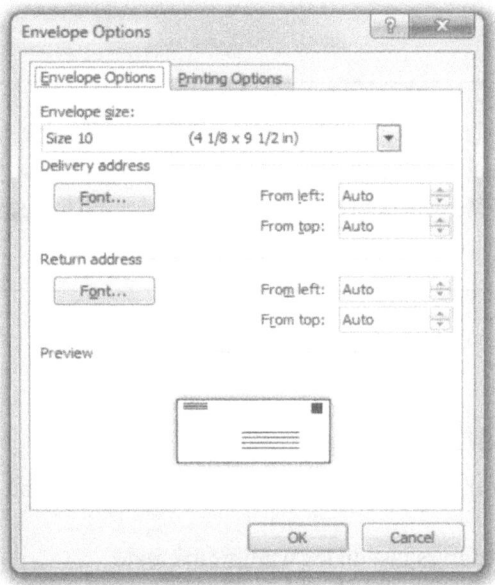

Figure 10–13. In the Envelope Options dialog window, choose the type of envelopes for the merge on the Envelope Options tab. On the Printing Options tab, tell Word how the printer will handle the envelopes.

- **Labels:** Word displays the Label Options dialog window (see Figure 10–14). Choose the type of labels you want to create, and then click the OK button.

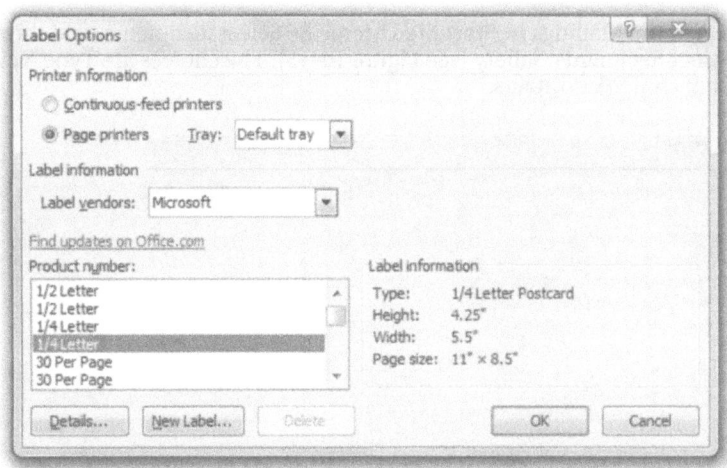

Figure 10–14. In the Label Options dialog window, choose the type of labels for the merge.

- **Directory**: Word changes the document to Print Layout view if it's currently in another view.

■ **Note** You use the Normal Word Document item on the Start Mail Merge gallery to disconnect a mail merge document from its data source and change it back into a normal Word document. The Step by Step Mail Merge Wizard item on the Start Mail Merge gallery launches the Mail Merge Wizard task pane, which walks you through the process of setting up a mail merge.

---

4. Save the main document again.

Attaching the Data Source for the Mail Merge

After you've created the main document, you attach to it the data source that contains the records you will use for the mail merge. You have three options here:

- **Create a new list in Word**: You use the New Address List dialog window to create an address list from Word. The process is somewhat clumsy, but it works in a pinch.

- **Use an existing list**: If you have a list containing your records (for example, an Excel worksheet containing details of your customers), you can use that list. This is usually the best choice unless all your records are in your Outlook contacts.

- **Use some of your Outlook contacts**: If you want to use some of your Outlook contacts (or all of them) in the mail merge, you simply choose the ones you want to include.

To pick the type of data source, choose Mailings ➤ Start Mail Merge ➤ Select Recipients, and then click the appropriate item on the Select Recipients Gallery (see Figure 10–15). The choices are Type New List, Use Existing List, and Select from Outlook Contacts.

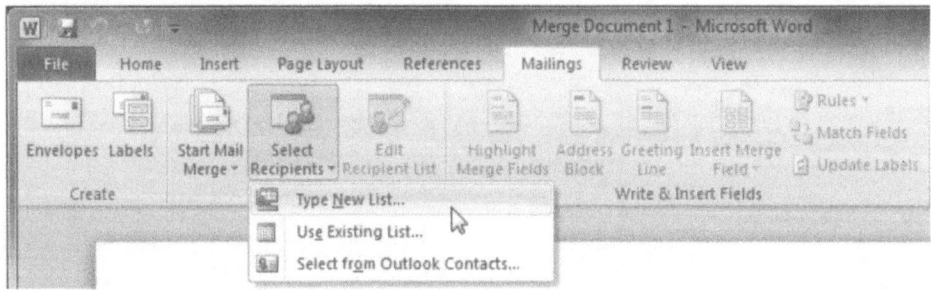

Figure 10–15. For your mail merge, you can create a new address list in Word, use an existing list, or use some or all of your Outlook contacts.

I'll show you how to use each of these options in turn.

Creating a New Data Source in Word

Sometimes you may need to create a new data source for the merge in Word. Create a new data source this way only when you have just a modest amount of data and you don't plan to use it in ways other than in mail merge. If you have a lot of data, or if you expect to use the data again for other purposes, you'll do better to set up the data source on a worksheet in Excel, and then attach the data source to the main document, as described in the next section.

To create a new data source in Word, follow these steps:

1. From your main document, choose Mailings ➤ Start Mail Merge ➤ Select Recipients ➤ Type New List. Word displays the New Address List dialog window (shown in Figure 10–16 with some data already added).

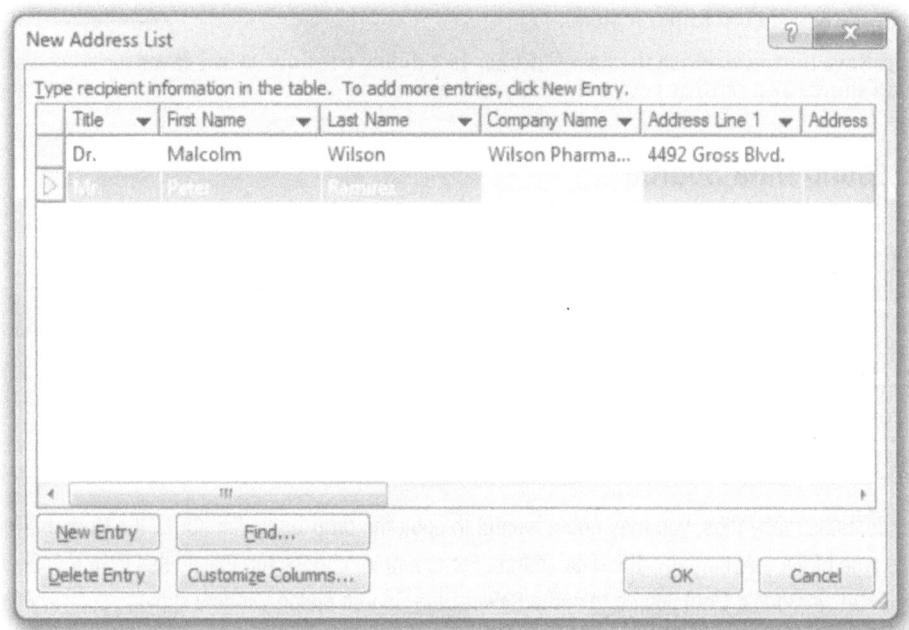

Figure 10–16. You can create a new data source by using the New Address List dialog window. Either use the existing selection of fields or click the Customize Columns button to customize them.

■ **Tip** The data source in the New Address List dialog window contains fields for a conventional address list: Title, First Name, Last Name, Company Name, Address Line 1, Address Line 2, City, and so on. If you need to store other types of data, click the Customize Columns button to display the Customize Address List dialog window. From here, you can add other fields, rename existing fields, or delete fields you don't need. You can also change the order in which the fields appear. Click the OK button when you've finished customizing the address list.

2. Type the data for the first record in the first line of fields. Press the Tab key to move to the next field (press Shift+Tab if you need to move backward).

3. Click the New Entry button when you're ready to create a new record, and then type the data for it.

4. When you've finished adding the entries to the list, click the OK button. Word displays the Save Address List dialog window.

5. In the "File name" box, type the file name you want to give this data source.

6. In the main part of the dialog window, choose the folder in which to store the data source. Word automatically selects the My Data Sources folder in your My Documents folder, which is a suitable location for a data source you will use only on your PC. If you need to share the data source with others, store the data source in a shared folder instead.

7. Click the Save button to close the Save Address List dialog window. Word saves the data source and returns you to the main document.

Opening an Existing Data Source

If you want to use an existing data source for the mail merge, follow these steps to connect the data source to the main document:

1. Choose Mailings ➤ Start Mail Merge ➤ Select Recipients ➤ Use Existing List to display the Select Data Source dialog window. This dialog window is a standard Open dialog window with a different name.

2. In the main area of the dialog window, navigate to the folder that contains the data source you want to use.

■ **Tip** If the folder contains many files, you may find it helpful to open the drop-down list above the Open button, and then choose the type of file that contains the data source. For example, choose the Excel Files item if your data is stored in an Excel workbook. Until you do this, the Select Data Source dialog window shows you every file that might possibly be a data source.

---

3. Click the file that contains the data source.

4. Click the Open button. Word closes the Select Data Source dialog window and attaches the data source to the main document. Word doesn't open the data source in the conventional sense, so you still see the main document, which looks the same as before—but the data source is now attached to it.

Selecting Outlook Contacts for the Merge

If you want to use some or all of your Outlook contacts as the data for the mail merge, follow these steps to choose the contacts:

1. Choose Mailings ➤ Start Mail Merge ➤ Select Recipients ➤ Select from Outlook Contacts.

2. If Word displays the Choose Profile dialog window (see Figure 10–17), choose the appropriate Outlook profile in the Profile Name drop-down list, and then click the OK button.

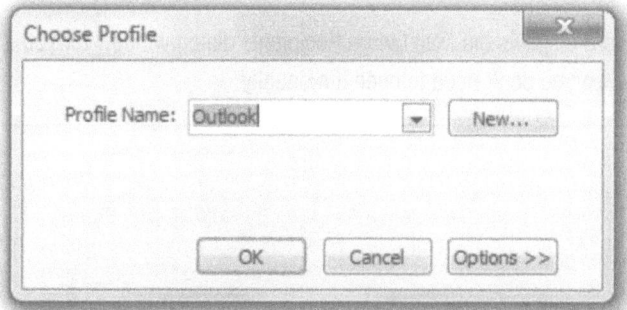

Figure 10–17. Select the appropriate profile in the Choose Profile dialog window, and then click the OK button.

3. In the Select Contacts dialog window that opens (see Figure 10–18), click the contact folder that contains the contacts you want, and then click the OK button.

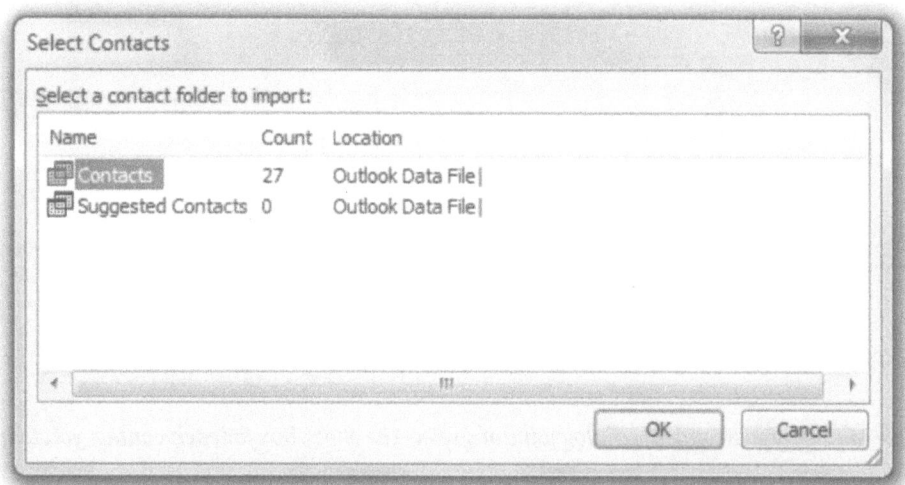

Figure 10–18. In the Select Contacts dialog window, choose the folder that contains the contacts.

Word now displays the Mail Merge Recipients dialog window, which you use to select the contacts, as described in the next section.

Choosing the Recipients from Your Data Source

At this point, you've connected the data source to the main document, but you haven't told Word which records in the data source to use. To do so, choose Mailings ➤ Start Mail Merge ➤ Edit Recipient list. Word displays the Mail Merge Recipients dialog window (see Figure 10–19).

■ **Note** When you're using Outlook contacts, Word displays the Mail Merge Recipients dialog window for you automatically after you select the contacts folder, so you don't need to open it manually.

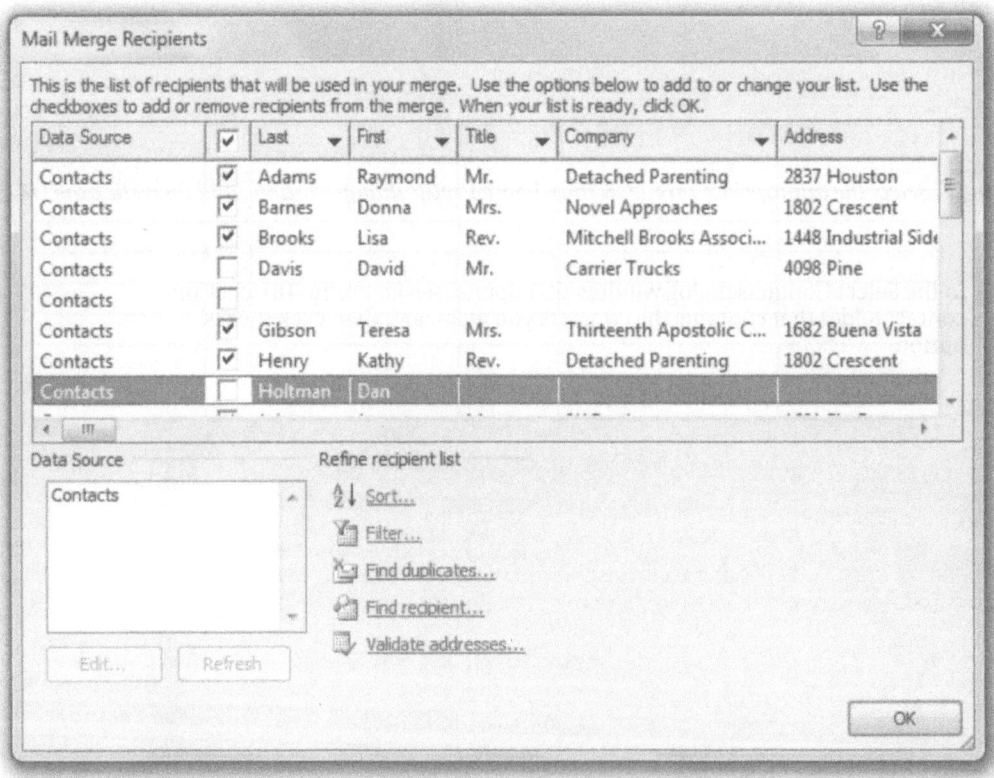

Figure 10–19. In the Main Merge Recipients dialog window, select the check box for each contact you want to include in the mail merge.

Now select the check box for each contact you want to include:

- You can clear all the check boxes by clearing the check box at the top of the check-box column, or select all the check boxes by selecting this check box.

- If you need to sort or filter the contacts, click the Sort link or the Filter link, and then work in the Filter and Sort dialog window that Word displays.

- To identify any duplicate records in your selection, click the "Find duplicates" link.

- To find a particular record, click the "Find recipient" link, and then work in the Find Entry dialog window that Word displays.

When you've selected all the appropriate check boxes, click the OK button to close the Mail Merge Recipients dialog window and return to the main document. Word stores the details of the recipients you've chosen but doesn't display them, so it may appear that nothing has happened.

At this point, it's a good idea to save the main document again, so press Ctrl+S or click the Save button on the Quick Access Toolbar when you have a moment.

Adding the Text and Merge Fields to the Main Document

Now that you've chosen the type of main document, attached the data source, and chosen the recipients, it's time to set up the main document with the text and the merge fields it needs. The text remains the same from one merged document to another, while the merge fields provide the text from your data source.

Adding the Text to the Main Document

Add the text to the main document using the skills you've learned in the earlier parts of this book. For example, position the insertion point where you want the text to appear, and then type the text—or create the main document quickly by using AutoText entries or other Building Blocks.

Adding the Merge Fields to the Main Document

To add merge fields to the main document, you use the controls in the Write & Insert Fields group on the Mailings tab of the ribbon. These are the key moves you'll need to make:

- **Insert an address block:** If your main document needs an address block (for example, for a letter, an envelope, or a mailing label), choose Mailings ➤ Write & Insert Fields ➤ Address Block, and then use the Insert Address Block dialog window (see Figure 10–20) to set up the address you want. When you're satisfied with the address format, click the OK button to insert the merge fields in the document.

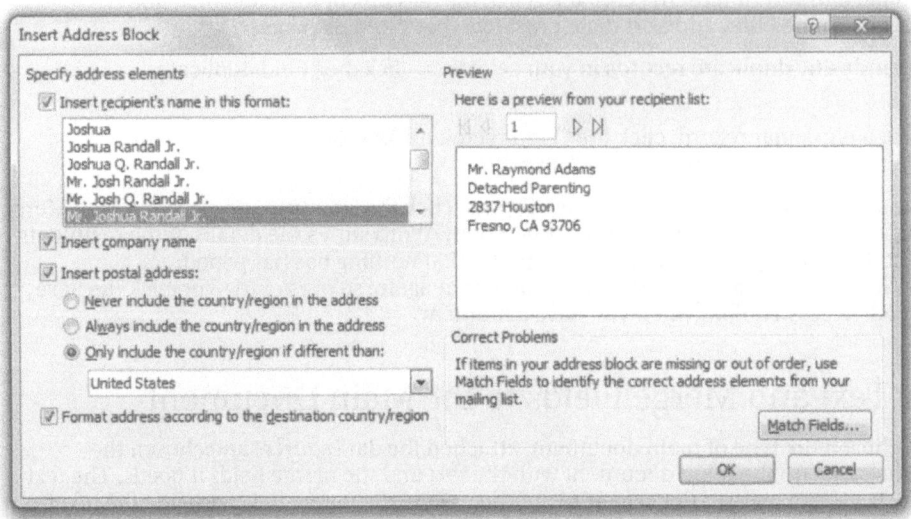

Figure 10–20. In the Insert Address Block dialog window, set up the address block with the contents and format you want for the merge documents.

- **Insert a greeting line**: If your main document needs a greeting line (for example, for a letter or flyer), choose Mailings ➤ Write & Insert Fields ➤ Greeting Line, and then use the Insert Greeting Line dialog window (see Figure 10–21) to set up the greeting. When you're satisfied, click the OK button to insert the merge fields in the document.

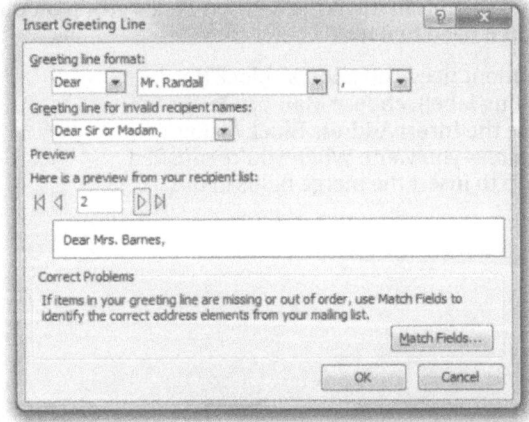

Figure 10–21. Use the Insert Greeting dialog window to set up a greeting for each named recipient of the merge. Use the "Greeting line for invalid recipient names" drop-down list to set the greeting for recipients whose names are missing from the data source.

- **Insert other merge fields**: For the other parts of the main document, you can insert a single field by choosing Mailings ➤ Write & Insert Fields ➤ Insert Merge Fields (clicking the bottom part of the Insert Merge Fields button), and then clicking the merge field on the gallery that Word displays. When you need to insert multiple fields, choose Mailings ➤ Write & Insert Fields ➤ Insert Merge Fields (clicking the top part of the Insert Merge Fields button) to display the Insert Merge Field dialog window (see Figure 10–22). You can then click a field, and click the Insert button to insert it. When you've finished, click the Close button to close the Insert Merge Field dialog window.

Figure 10–22. Use the Insert Merge Field dialog window to insert individual merge fields. At the top, select the Address Fields option button or the Database Fields option button to display the set of fields you want.

Each field appears inside double chevrons, as shown in Figure 10–23. Make sure the text around the fields is laid out with spacing and punctuation as usual.

«AddressBlock»

May 23, 2010

«GreetingLine»

Thank you for your order of «User_Field_1».

Figure 10–23. Word displays the merge fields inside double chevrons, like the <<AddressBlock>> and <<GreetingLine>> merge fields shown here.

To see how the document will look with the data in place, choose Mailings ➤ Preview Results ➤ Preview Results. Word inserts the first record of data (see Figure 10–24). You can then use the top line of controls in the Preview Results group to move from one record to another. For example, click the Next button to display the next record, or click the Last Record button to display the last record.

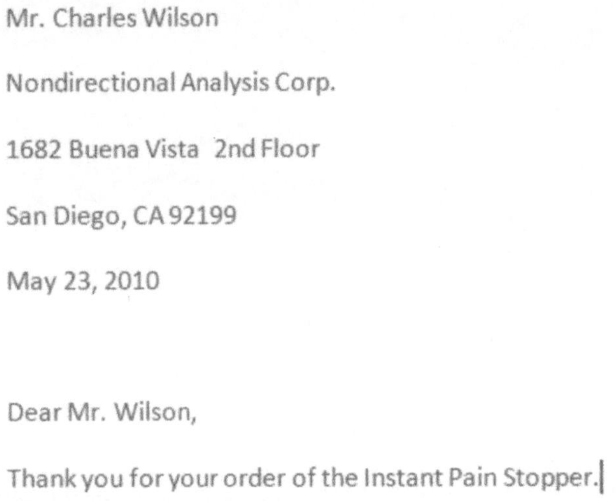

Mr. Charles Wilson

Nondirectional Analysis Corp.

1682 Buena Vista 2nd Floor

San Diego, CA 92199

May 23, 2010

Dear Mr. Wilson,

Thank you for your order of the Instant Pain Stopper.

Figure 10–24. Use the Preview Results command to see how the merge documents will look.

When you've got the fields in place, save the main document again.

Running the Mail Merge

When you have got the main document looking the way you want it, and you've previewed the data to make sure it appears correctly, you're ready to run the mail merge. You have three choices here:

- Create the merge documents so that you can edit them as needed.
- Merge the documents straight to the printer.
- Merge the documents straight to e-mail.

Creating Merge Documents That You Can Edit

To create merge documents that you can edit, follow these steps:

1. Choose Mailings ➤ Finish ➤ Finish & Merge ➤ Edit Individual Documents to display the Merge to New Document dialog window (see Figure 10–25).

Figure 10–25. In the Merge to New Document dialog window, choose whether to merge all the records or just some of them.

2. In the "Merge records" area, choose which records to merge:

    - *All.* Select this option button to merge all the records. If you've selected the records from the data source, this is what you'll often want.

    - *Current record.* Select this option button to merge just the selected record. This is useful when you've discovered a mistake in the merge documents and you need to fix just one of them.

    - *From… To.* Select this option button to merge the documents in the range you specify—for example, from 25 to 30.

3. Click the OK button. Word creates a new document containing all of the merged data.

4. Review the document, edit it as needed, and save it. You can then print it if necessary.

Merging the Documents Straight to the Printer

Instead of merging the documents to a document you can edit, you can send them straight to the printer. To do so, follow these steps:

1. Choose Mailings ➤ Finish ➤ Finish & Merge ➤ Print Documents to display the Merge to Printer dialog window (see Figure 10–26).

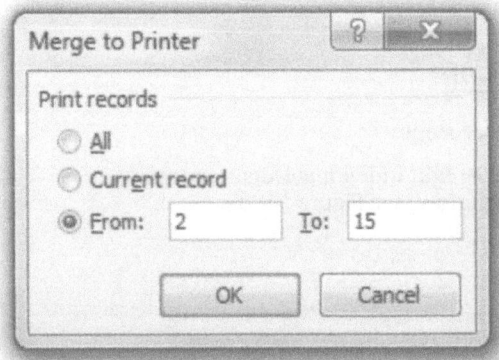

Figure 10–26. In the Merge to Printer dialog window, choose which records to merge and print.

2. In the "Print records" area, choose which records to merge to the printer:

   - **All**: Select this option button to merge all the records.

   - **Current record**: Select this option button to merge just the selected record.

   - **From... To**: Select this option button to merge the documents in the range you specify—for example, from 2 to 15.

3. Click the OK button. Word performs the merge and sends the results to the printer.

Merging the Documents Straight to E-mail

When you need to send the merged documents via e-mail, you can merge directly to messages. To do so, follow these steps:

1. Choose Mailings ➤ Finish ➤ Finish & Merge ➤ Send E-mail Messages to display the Merge to E-mail dialog window (see Figure 10–27).

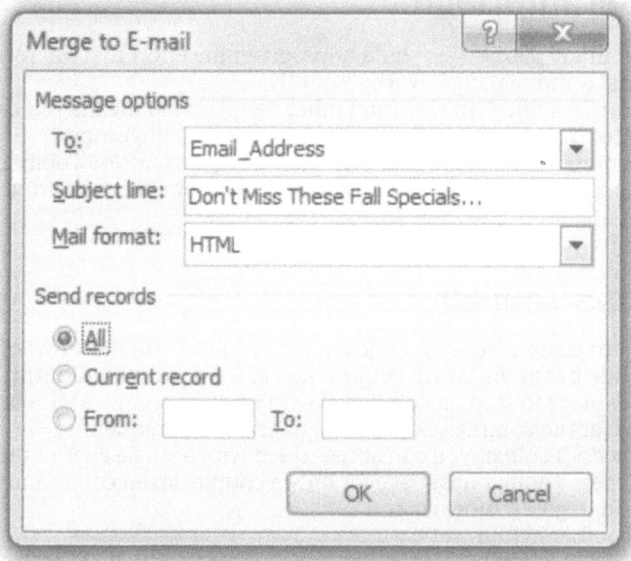

Figure 10–27. When merging to e-mail, choose the e-mail address field, enter the subject line, and choose the mail format in the Merge to E-mail dialog window.

2. In the "To" drop-down list, choose the field that contains the e-mail address you want to use.

3. In the "Subject line" box, type the subject line for the message.

4. In the "Mail format" drop-down list, choose the format in which to send the message:

    • **HTML**: Send the message as an HTML-formatted e-mail. This is usually the best choice.

    • **Plain text**: Send the message as a text-only message without formatting.

    • **Attachment**: Send the document as an attachment to a message. The recipient will then need to open the attachment to view its contents.

5. In the "Send records" area, choose which records to use:

    • **All**: Select this option button to merge all the records.

    • **Current record**: Select this option button to merge just the selected record.

    • **From… To**: Select this option button to merge the documents in the range you specify—for example, from 2 to 15.

6. Click the OK button. Word merges the records and sends the e-mail messages.

Customizing the Word User Interface

Word's out-of-the-box setup works well for many people—as you'd hope, given the effort that Microsoft has put into creating the Fluent User Interface and making it work smoothly.

That said, you almost certainly use Word in a different way from other people. That means you can benefit from customizing Word to put the controls and information you need at your fingertips.

Word lets you customize three major components of the user interface: the Quick Access Toolbar, the ribbon, and the status bar. You can also create custom keyboard shortcuts that enable you to run commands from the keyboard.

Customizing the Quick Access Toolbar

Normally, the first part of Word you'll want to customize is the Quick Access Toolbar, the short row of buttons that appears at the left end of the title bar in the Word window, just to the right of the control-menu icon. The Quick Access Toolbar is the place to start customizing Word because it comes with only a few icons so that you can easily add icons for the commands you want to give most frequently.

By putting commands on the Quick Access Toolbar, you can access them with a single click of the mouse. In its default position, the Quick Access Toolbar has space for only a couple dozen commands, but you can also move it to below the ribbon to give it more room.

You can customize the Quick Access Toolbar in four ways:

- **Add a frequently used button**: You can quickly add any of a dozen or so frequently used buttons to the Quick Access Toolbar.

- **Add any command from the ribbon**: Instead of choosing from the list of frequently used buttons, you can quickly add any command that's on the ribbon. This is useful when you find a ribbon command you want to use frequently.

- **Add any other command**: Some commands don't appear on the ribbon, but you can add them to the Quick Access Toolbar easily enough. You've used this technique already in this book—for example, in Chapter 4.

- **Move the Quick Access Toolbar to below the ribbon**: You can display the Quick Access Toolbar below the ribbon instead of in the title bar. This gives you plenty of room for extra buttons.

Adding Buttons for Frequently Used Commands to the Quick Access Toolbar

The fastest way to customize the Quick Access Toolbar is to add buttons for some of Word's most frequently used commands. Follow these steps:

1. Click the Customize Quick Access Toolbar button at the right end of the Quick Access Toolbar to display the Customize Quick Access Toolbar menu (see Figure 10–28).

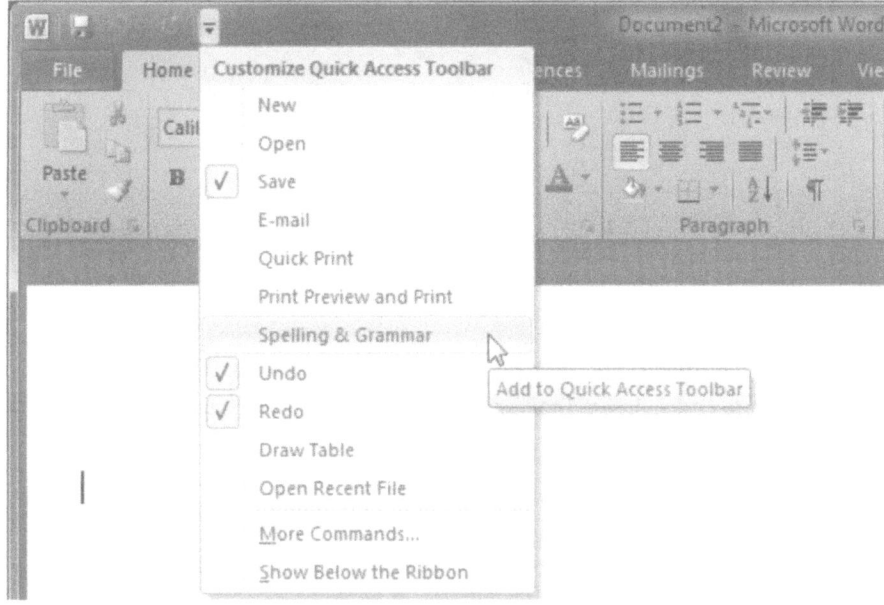

Figure 10–28. *Use the Customize Quick Access Toolbar menu to quickly add buttons for frequently used commands to the Quick Access Toolbar.*

2. Click the item you want to add to the menu or remove from it:

   - When you click an item that's not currently displayed, a check mark appears next to the item.

   - When you click an item that's on the Quick Access Toolbar, the check mark disappears from next to it.

3. If you need to add or remove other items, repeat Steps 1 and 2 until you've finished.

Adding a Ribbon Command to the Quick Access Toolbar

Adding commands with the Customize Quick Access Toolbar menu is easy but limited. What you'll likely want to do is add commands from the ribbon to the Quick Access Toolbar so that you can give the commands without having to display the right ribbon tab—or, if you've minimized the ribbon, without expanding the ribbon.

To add a ribbon command to the Quick Access Toolbar, right-click the command's button or control, and then click Add to Quick Access Toolbar on the context menu (see Figure 10–29). This move works for galleries as well as for individual commands—just click the Add Gallery to Quick Access Toolbar command on the context menu.

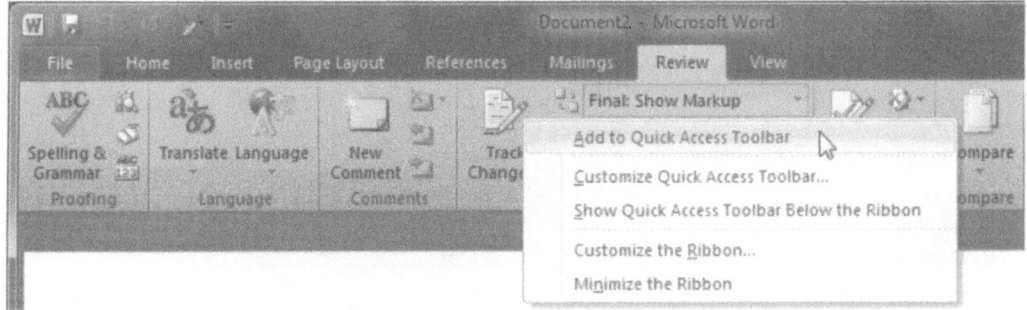

Figure 10–29. You can quickly add a ribbon command or gallery to the Quick Access Toolbar by right-clicking it and then choosing Add to Quick Access Toolbar or Add Gallery to Quick Access Toolbar from the context menu.

To remove a command or gallery you've added to the Quick Access Toolbar, right-click it, and then click Remove from Quick Access Toolbar on the context menu.

■ **Note** Customizing the Quick Access Toolbar using this technique makes the change for all documents rather than for just the active document. To make the change for just the active document, use the technique described in the following section.

Adding Buttons for Other Commands to the Quick Access Toolbar

To customize the Quick Access Toolbar with commands that don't appear on the ribbon or to rearrange the icons that appear on the Quick Access Toolbar, you need to open the Word Options dialog window. Follow these steps:

1. Right-click anywhere in the Quick Access Toolbar, and then click Customize Quick Access Toolbar on the context menu. Word displays the Word Options dialog window and selects the Quick Access Toolbar item in the left column (see Figure 10–30).

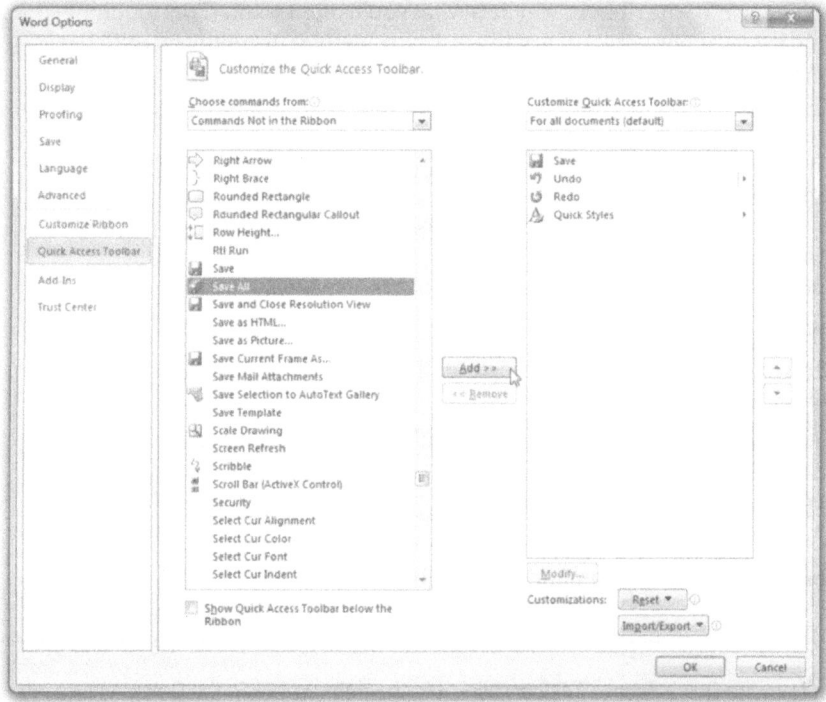

Figure 10–30. Open the Word Options dialog window when you want to customize the Quick Access Toolbar by adding commands that aren't on the ribbon or when you want to rearrange the toolbar's icons.

2. Click the Customize Quick Access Toolbar drop-down list in the upper-right corner of the Options dialog window, and then choose the item you want to affect:

    - **For all documents (default):** Select this item to make your changes apply to all the documents you create (except for documents that you customize separately). This setting makes Word save the customization in the Normal template, which is what you'll normally want to do.

    - **For document:** Select this item to make your changes affect only the active document. Customizing a document like this can be useful when you plan to distribute it on its own. For example, you may want to put all the commands the document needs on the Quick Access Toolbar so that readers don't need to use the ribbon.

3. Open the Choose commands from drop-down list and choose the category of commands you want to use:

    - **Popular Commands:** These are the commands that appear on the Customize Quick Access Toolbar menu. So if you've already used that menu to customize the Quick Access Toolbar, you'll probably want to select a different category.

- **Commands Not in the Ribbon**: This choice gives you access to commands that don't appear in the ribbon, which is what you'll often want. (For ribbon commands, it's usually easier to use the previous method of adding an item to the Quick Access Toolbar.)

- **All Commands**: This choice gives you the full range of commands available. The list is really long, but you can be sure the command you need is somewhere on it. Use this choice if you're not sure whether a command is on the ribbon.

- **Macros**: If you record or write your own macros, select this category when you want to put buttons on the Quick Access Toolbar that run the macros. See the section later in this chapter to learn about recording macros.

- **File Tab**: This category gives you access to the Backstage commands.

- **Home Tab and other tabs**: These categories display all the commands associated with these tabs.

4. In the left list box, click the command you want to add to the Quick Access Toolbar.

5. In the right list box, click the command you want to add the new command after.

6. Click the Add button to add the command to the right list box.

Note To remove an item from the Quick Access Toolbar, click it in the right list box in the Quick Access Toolbar category in the Word Options dialog window, and then click the Remove button.

7. If you want to position the Quick Access Toolbar below the ribbon rather than in the title bar, select the Show Quick Access Toolbar below the Ribbon check box.

8. If you want to rearrange the buttons on the Quick Access Toolbar, click a button in the right list box, and then click the up arrow button or the down arrow button until the button appears where you want it.

9. When you have finished customizing the Quick Access Toolbar, click the OK button to close the Word Options dialog window.

Resetting the Quick Access Toolbar to Its Default Buttons

If you need to restore the default set of buttons to the Quick Access Toolbar, follow these steps:

1. Right-click anywhere in the Quick Access Toolbar, and then click Customize Quick Access Toolbar on the context menu. Word opens the Word Options dialog window and selects the Quick Access Toolbar item in the left column.

2. In the lower-right corner, click the Reset drop-down button, and then choose Reset only Quick Access Toolbar from the menu. The program displays the Reset Customizations dialog window (see Figure 10–31).

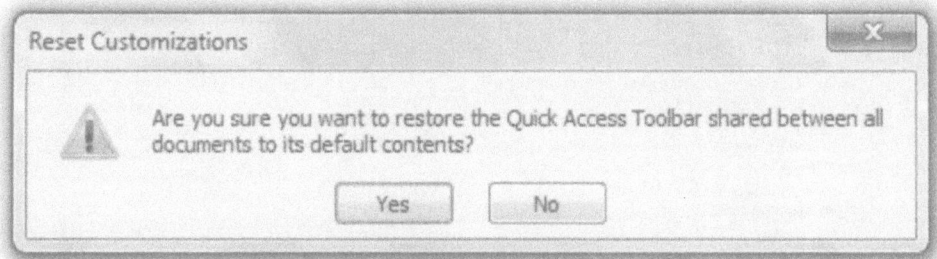

Figure 10–31. You can reset the Quick Access Toolbar to remove any customizations you've made to it.

3. Click the Yes button. Word resets the Quick Access Toolbar.

4. Click the OK button to close the Word Options dialog window.

Moving the Quick Access Toolbar to Below the Ribbon

When the Quick Access Toolbar appears in its default position at the left end of the title bar of the Word window, you need to keep down the number of buttons it contains so that it doesn't take over the title bar. To give yourself more space, you can move the Quick Access Toolbar to below the ribbon so that it stretches the full width of the Word window.

To move the Quick Access Toolbar, click the Customize Quick Access Toolbar button at the right end of the Quick Access Toolbar, and then click Show Below the Ribbon on the menu that appears.

To put the Quick Access Toolbar back in the title bar, click the Customize Quick Access Toolbar button again, but this time choose Show Above the Ribbon.

Customizing the Ribbon

Customizing the Quick Access Toolbar (as discussed in the previous section) is by far the easiest way to customize the selection of commands that Word presents—and it may be as far as you want to go. You can also customize the ribbon, as discussed in this section, but the process is clumsy compared to customizing the Quick Access Toolbar. This is because you can affect only a whole group of controls, or an entire tab of the ribbon, rather than customizing an individual button as you might want to.

If you do choose to customize the ribbon, follow these steps:

1. Right-click anywhere in the ribbon, and then click Customize the Ribbon on the context menu. Word displays the Word Options dialog window with the Customize Ribbon item selected in the left pane. Figure 10–32 shows the Word Options dialog window with customization underway.

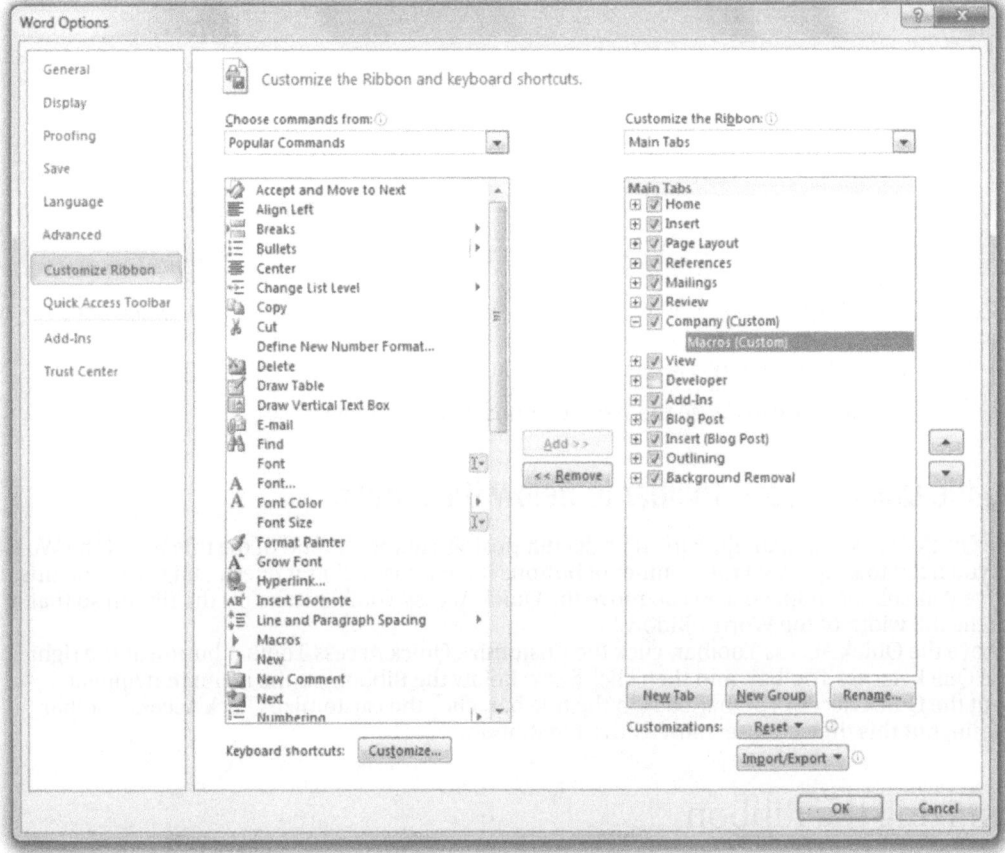

Figure 10–32. *Use the Customize Ribbon pane in the Word Options dialog window to create new ribbon tabs and ribbon groups.*

2. In the Customize the Ribbon drop-down list, choose the tabs you want to affect:

- **Main Tabs:** This is usually the best place to start, as it shows the regular set of tabs—Home, Insert, View, and so on.

- **All Tabs:** Choose this item to display the full list of tabs.

- **Tool Tabs:** Choose this item to display the list of tool tabs, such as the SmartArt Tools tab, the Chart Tools tab, and the Picture Tools tab.

3. To add a new tab, follow these steps:

- In the list of tabs in the large box on the right, click the tab after which you want to add the new tab.

- Click the New Tab button. The program adds the new tab, names it New Tab (Custom), and creates a new group in it called New Group (Custom).

- Click the New Tab (Custom) name, and then click the Rename button to display the Rename dialog window for tabs. Type the tab name in the "Display name" text box, and then click the OK button.

Note You can also add a new group to an existing tab. Double-click the tab to display its groups, and then click the group after which you want to add the new group. Click the New Group to add a new group named New Group (Custom), and then rename the group as described nearby.

- Click the New Group (Custom) name, and then click the Rename button to display the Rename dialog window for groups (see Figure 10–33).

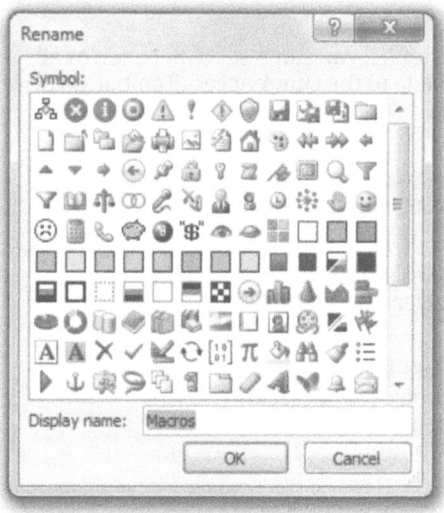

Figure 10–33. To rename a custom group, type the new name in the "Display name" text box in this Rename dialog window.

- If you want to assign an icon to the group, click it in the Symbol box.
- Type the name for the group, and then click the OK button.

4. To add items to the group, follow these steps:
   - In the "Choose commands from" drop-down list, choose the source of commands. For example, choose All Commands if you want access to every single command, or choose Macros if you want to add buttons for running macros.

- In the right list box, click your new group. If you've already added buttons to the group, click the command after which you want to add the new command.

- Click the command in the left list box.

- Click the Add button. The program adds the button to the group.

- If necessary, you can arrange buttons in a group by clicking the button and then clicking the up arrow button or the down arrow button, as appropriate.

5. To remove a group from a tab, click the group in the right list box, and then click the Remove button.

6. When you have finished customizing the ribbon, click the OK button to close the Word Options dialog window.

Resetting the Ribbon to Its Default Settings

If you find that your ribbon customization doesn't give good results, you can reset either a tab or all customizations. All customizations include changes you've made to the Quick Access Toolbar, so be prepared to lose these as well when you reset all of the ribbon.

To reset the ribbon, follow these steps:

1. Right-click anywhere in the ribbon, and then click Customize Ribbon on the context menu. Word displays the Word Options dialog window and selects the Customize Ribbon item in the left column.

2. To reset a tab, click it in the right list box, click the Reset drop-down button in the lower-right corner, and then click "Reset only selected Ribbon tab." Word resets the tab without confirmation.

3. To reset the whole of the ribbon and the Quick Access Toolbar, click the Reset drop-down button in the lower-right corner, and then click "Reset all customizations" on the drop-down menu. In the confirmation dialog window that Word displays (see Figure 10–34), click the Yes button.

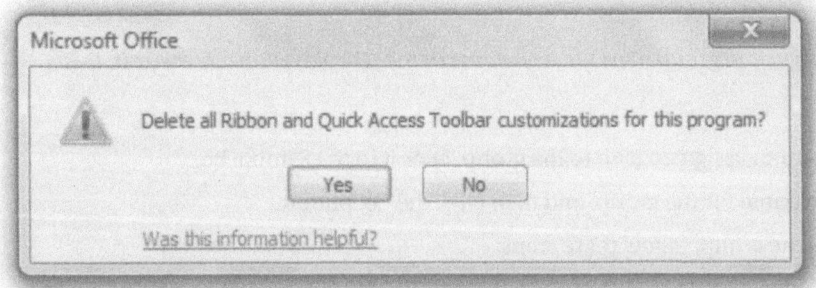

Figure 10–34. Resetting all the changes you've made to the ribbon also resets the Quick Access Toolbar.

4. Click the OK button to close the Word Options dialog window.

Sharing Customizations with Other PCs

After customizing the Quick Access Toolbar and ribbon in Word on one PC, you can easily share the customizations with another PC. To do so, follow these steps:

1. In Word on the customized PC, right-click anywhere in the ribbon, and then click Customize Ribbon on the context menu. Word displays the Word Options dialog window and selects the Customize Ribbon item in the left column.

2. In the lower-right corner, click the Import/Export drop-down button, and then click Export All Customizations to display the File Save dialog window.

3. Either accept the suggested name (for example, Word Customizations) or type another name over it.

4. Click the Save button to save the file.

5. Click the Cancel button to close the Word Options dialog window.

6. Transfer the customizations file to the other computer. For example, put it on a network drive or a USB stick, or send it via e-mail.

7. On the other computer, open Word, and then open the Customize Ribbon pane as described in Step 1.

8. Click the Import/Export drop-down button, and then choose Import Customization File. Word displays the File Open dialog window.

9. Choose the customizations file that you transferred to this new PC, and then click the Open button. Word displays a confirmation message box (see Figure 10–35).

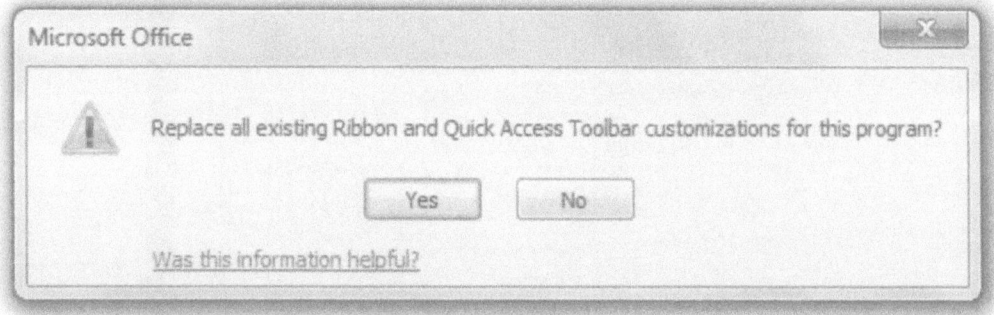

Figure 10–35. You can quickly import your Word customizations on another PC.

10. Click the Yes button to close the dialog window. Word imports the customizations.

11. Click the OK button to close the Word Options dialog window.

Customizing the Status Bar

The status bar at the bottom of the Word window shows a variety of useful information about the document and what you're currently doing to it. From left to right, the status bar shows the page readout (such as Page: 1 of 25), the number of words, the spelling status (whether the document contains spelling errors), and the language used. At the right end of the status bar, the View Shortcuts buttons let you quickly change views, and the Zoom controls provide a quick way of zooming in and out.

The status bar also displays further information as needed—for example, the details of any permission restrictions applied to the document.

You can change the selection of items that appear on the status bar like this:

1. Right-click anywhere in the status bar to open the Customize Status Bar menu (see Figure 10–36).

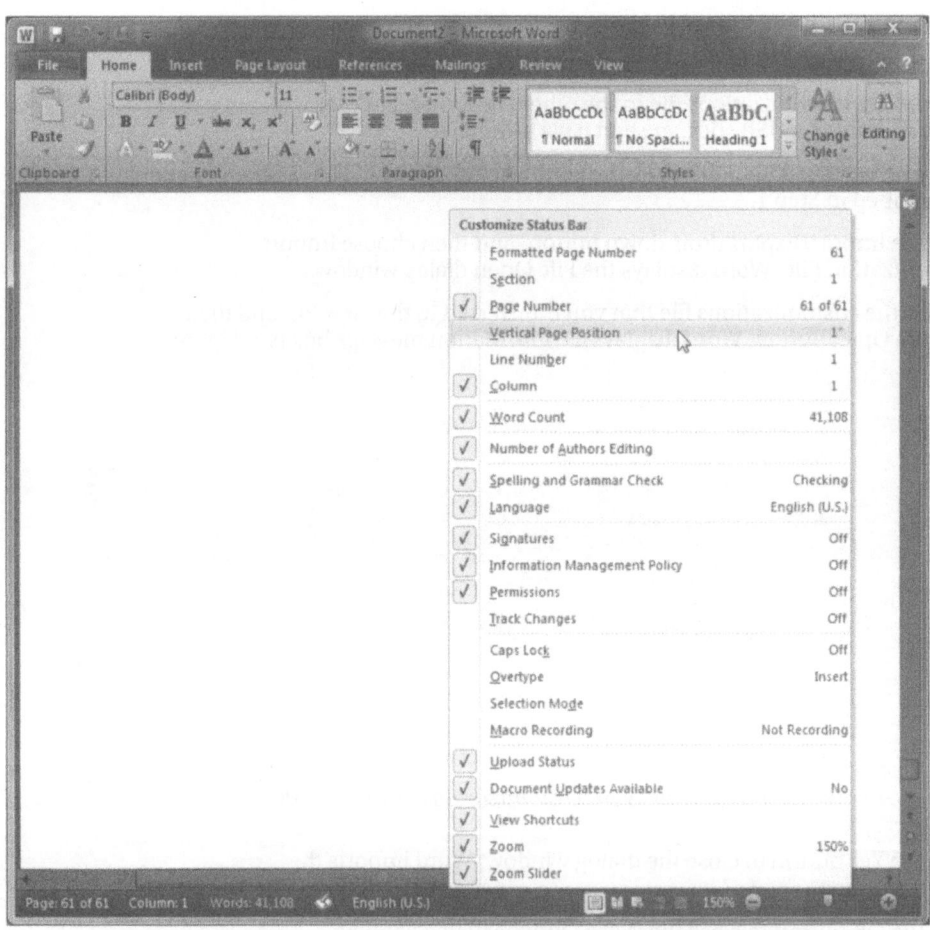

Figure 10–36. *Use the Customize Status Bar menu to control exactly which items appear in the Word status bar.*

Note Even when you select their check boxes, many of the items that you can display in the status bar appear only when the circumstances are right. For example, the Signatures item appears only if the document has a digital signature applied to it, and the Information Management Policy item appears only if the document has Information Rights Management (IRM) applied.

2. The check marks show which items are set to appear on the menu. Click an item to switch its check mark on or off. Table 10–1 explains the items.

3. When you're ready to close the menu, click the status bar, or click anywhere in the document area.

Table 10–1. Items on the Customize Status Bar Menu

Status Bar Item	What It Displays
Formatted Page Number	The current page number using the formatting applied to it (for example, "Page 3")
Section	The number of the section the insertion point is positioned in
Page Number	The page number in "Page X of Y" format—for example, "Page 5 of 15"
Vertical Page Position	The distance of the insertion point from the top of the page—for example, "At 2.5""
Line Number	The number of the line the insertion point is on for the current page—for example, 11 indicates the 11th line on this page.
Column	The number of characters (including spaces) between the insertion point and the left end of the line—for example, "Column: 8" means that eight characters appear between the insertion point and the left end of the line.
Word Count	The number of words in the document (for example, "Words: 250") or in the selected number of words out of the document's total (for example, "Words: 21/250")
Number of Authors Editing	The number of authors who have opened the same version of the document at the same time
Spelling and Grammar Check	The spelling and grammar status of the document—either a book icon with a green check to indicate no errors, or a book icon with a red cross to indicate one or more errors

Status Bar Item	What It Displays
Language	The text language Word is using—for example, "English (U.S.)"
Signatures	An indicator that looks like a seal (not the animal) to show that a digital signature is applied to the document; if the document has no digital signature, no indicator appears.
Information Management Policy	An indicator to show that an information management policy is applied to the document; this indicator appears near the left end of the status bar.
Permissions	An indicator to show that permission restrictions are applied to the document; this indicator appears near the left end of the status bar.
Track Changes	A readout that shows "Track Changes: On" or "Track Changes: Off"
Caps Lock	A readout that shows "Caps Lock" when the keyboard's Caps Lock is on
Overtype	A readout that shows "Insert" when the document is in normal editing mode (which is called Insert mode) or "Overtype" when the document is in Overtype mode (where a character you type overwrites a character to the right of the insertion point)
Selection Mode	A readout that shows "Extend Selection" when Extend mode is turned on
Macro Recording	An icon you can click to start recording a macro; when you're recording a macro, an icon you can click to stop recording
Upload Status	An icon that shows upload status when you're coauthoring a document
Document Updates Available	A readout that shows when document updates are available for a document you're coauthoring
View Shortcuts	The View buttons (Print Layout, Full Screen Reading view, Web Layout view, Outline, and Draft) that appear by default
Zoom	The Zoom Level readout that shows the zoom percentage
Zoom Slider	The Zoom slider and its – button and + button

Creating Custom Keyboard Shortcuts

If you prefer to keep both hands on the keyboard as you work rather than move a hand to the mouse, you'll probably want to make the most of Word's keyboard shortcuts. Word comes with a large number of keyboard shortcuts built in, but you can also create your own keyboard shortcuts to run other commands.

To customize Word's keyboard shortcuts, follow these steps:

1. Right-click any tab of the ribbon, and then click Customize the Ribbon on the context menu to open the Customize Ribbon pane in the Word Options dialog window.

2. Click the Customize button at the bottom to display the Customize Keyboard dialog window (shown in Figure 10–37 with settings chosen).

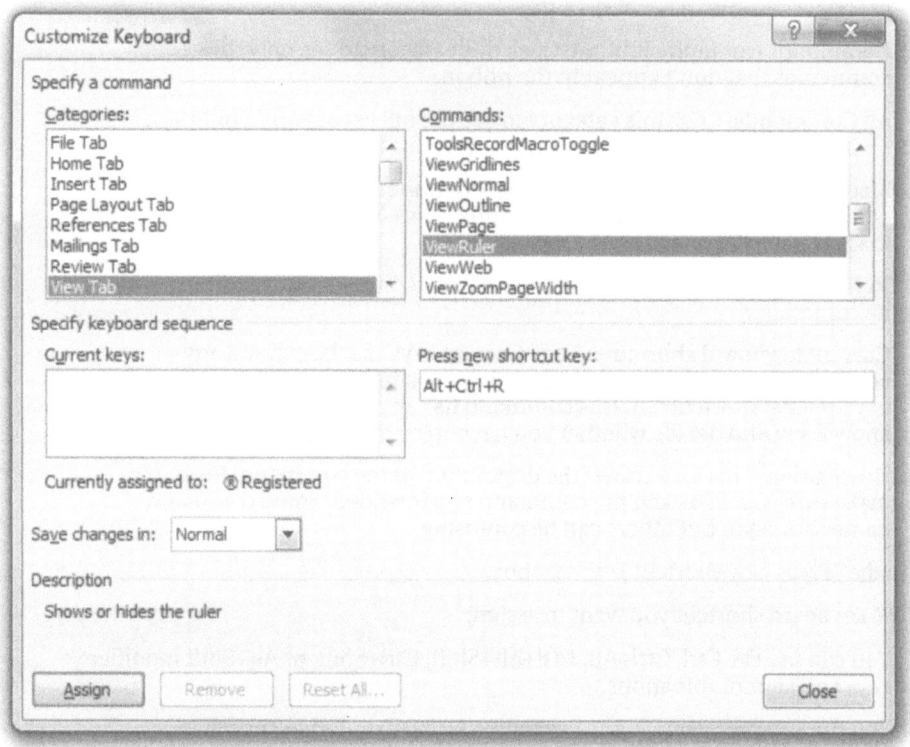

Figure 10–37. *Use the Customize Keyboard dialog window to create keyboard shortcuts for the commands you give most often.*

3. In the "Save changes in" drop-down list, choose the document or template to save the keyboard shortcuts in. These are your choices:

- **Normal**: Select this item to save the changes in Word's Normal template. Word loads Normal each time you start the program, making the keyboard shortcuts available in every document. Usually, this is the best choice.

- **Template attached to the active document**: Select the template's name that appears in the drop-down list—for example, Invoice (or Invoice.dot, if Windows is set to display file extensions). Keyboard shortcuts you store in the template are available when the template itself is open or when a document that has the template attached is open.

- **Active document**: Select the document's name that appears in the drop-down list. Keyboard shortcuts you save in a document are available only when that document is open.

4. In the Categories list box, click the category of command you want to create a keyboard shortcut for.

- **Ribbon tabs**: Click a ribbon tab to display its commands in the Commands list box.

- **Commands Not in the Ribbon**: Click this category to see only the commands that don't appear in the ribbon.

- **All Commands**: Click this category to see the full list of Word commands. There are more than 1,000, so working with this list is slow going.

- **Macros, Fonts, Building Blocks, Styles, Common Symbols**: Click the category for the type of item. For example, click Macros to display the list of macros in the Commands list box.

5. In the Commands list box, click the command. Word displays information about the command:

- **Current keyboard shortcuts**: The "Current keys" list box shows any keyboard shortcuts currently assigned to the command (some commands have several shortcuts). If this command has any shortcuts, check that you know them and decide whether you need to create another.

- **Description**: This area shows the description of the command. Read it to make sure you've picked the command you intended. Some command names are clear, but others can be confusing.

6. Click in the "Press new shortcut key" text box.

7. Press the keyboard shortcut you want to assign:

- You can use the Ctrl, Ctrl+Alt, Ctrl+Alt+Shift, Ctrl+Shift, or Alt+Shift modifier keys and key combinations.

- You can use pretty much any key on the keyboard—letters, numbers, function keys, and so on.

- A normal shortcut consists of a modifier or modifiers plus one key—for example, Ctrl+Alt+T. But you can also create modifiers that use two keys in sequence—for example, Ctrl+Alt+T, S—by pressing the extra key after the key combination. This lets you create many more keyboard shortcuts and is good for related commands—for example, using the "Ctrl+Shift+S, 1" keyboard shortcut for one style, the "Ctrl+Shift+S, 2" keyboard shortcut for another, and the "Ctrl+Shift+S,3" keyboard shortcut for a third.

8. Check the "Currently assigned to" area to see if the keyboard shortcut is currently used. If so, press another keyboard shortcut if you don't want to overwrite it.

9. Click the Assign button. Word assigns the keyboard shortcut to the command.

10. When you've finished assigning keyboard shortcuts, click the Close button to close the Customize Keyboard dialog window, and then click the OK button to close the Word Options dialog window.

At this point, you've created the keyboard shortcuts, but you haven't saved them in the document or template. Save them like this:

- **Normal template:** Close Word by choosing File ➤ Exit. If Word displays a dialog window telling you that "Changes have been made that affect the global template, Normal," click the Save button.

Note Word prompts you to save changes to the Normal template if you have cleared the Prompt Before Saving Normal Template check box in the Advanced category of the Word Options dialog window.

- **Document or template:** Save the document by pressing Ctrl+S or clicking the Save button on the Quick Access Toolbar. For a template, click the Yes button in the dialog window that prompts you to save the changes.

Using VBA to Automate Your Work

If you find yourself performing the same task over and over in Word, consider automating that task as much as possible. To automate a task, you can record a macro, as described in this section, or program in Visual Basic for Applications (VBA), a subject beyond the reach of this book. You can also combine the two approaches by recording a macro and then enhancing it by programming in VBA. This is a great way to get started using VBA, as you can use the recorded macro to identify the commands you need to work with.

VBA is a huge topic. In this section, we have only enough space to introduce you to it briefly—but you can save a huge amount of time by recording macros and running them.

Understanding What Macros Are and What You Can Do with Them

A *macro* is a sequence of commands that you create in Word. The easiest way to create a macro is by using Word's built-in Macro Recorder tool, but you can also write a macro from scratch by using the Visual Basic Editor (which is also built into Office).

When you record a macro, you can record any actions that you can perform in Word by using the keyboard and by giving commands with the mouse. For example, you can record yourself typing some text, selecting it, and formatting it; or you can record a macro that automatically replaces various words or phrases in a document with other phrases. You can then run the macro whenever you need to take that sequence of actions again.

You can record most of the actions you can take when working interactively with Word. The main exception is that you cannot select text or other objects (such as graphics or tables) with the mouse, as doing so doesn't give Word a workable point of reference when running the macro on another document. Instead, you need to select using the keyboard, so Word can tell where to start from.

Recording a Macro

You can record a macro with the Macro Recorder in moments—but before you start, plan what you'll do in the macro, and perhaps jot down the actions you'll take. This will help you get them right the first time around and avoid having to record the macro again.

When you're clear what the macro will do, follow these steps to record it:

1. Open Word (if it's not running) and set up the conditions the macro will need in order to run. For example, you may need to open a new document to work in, or open a particular existing document.

2. Choose View ➤ Macros ➤ Macros ➤ Record Macro to display the Record Macro dialog window (shown in Figure 10–38 with settings already chosen).

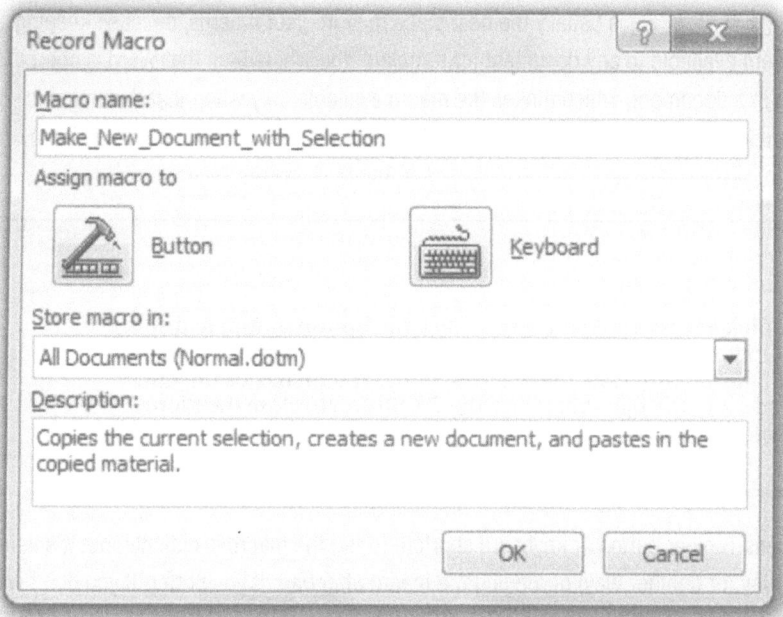

Figure 10–38. *In the Record Macro dialog window, type the name and description for the macro, and choose where to store it. You'll usually want to store your macros in the Normal template.*

3. In the "Macro name" box, type the name you want to give the macro. Word automatically names the macro Macro1 or the next available name (Macro2, Macro3), but you'll want to give it a descriptive name. These are the rules you have to work with:

    •   The name must start with a letter.

    •   After that, you can mix letters, numbers, and underscores at will.

    •   The name can't include spaces, symbols, or punctuation marks.

    •   You can use up to 80 characters, but long names are hard to distinguish from each other in the Macros dialog window that you use for running macros—so shorter names are usually better.

4. In the Description box, type a description of what the macro does. You may want to add your name and the date you recorded the macro.

5. In the "Store macro in" drop-down list, make sure that the All Documents (Normal.dotm) item is selected.

> ■ **Note** The Normal template (Normal.dotm) is usually the best place to store your macros, because keeping them in this template makes them available to any document (or template) the whole time that Word is open. Instead, you can store a macro in a document, which makes the macro available only when that document is open, or in a template, which makes the macro available when any document based on the template is open, or when the template itself is open.

6. Choose a way of running the macro:

   - **Create a Quick Access Toolbar button:** Click the Button button to display the Word Options dialog window with the Quick Access Toolbar category selected. In the left box, click the macro's name, and then click the Add button to add it to the right box. Click the OK button to close the Word Options dialog window.

> **Note** Creating a Quick Access Toolbar button or keyboard shortcut to run the macro is optional, but it's usually helpful. You can also assign a way (or another way) of running the macro afterward if you prefer. If you don't want to create a way to run the macro, click the OK button to close the Record Macro dialog window.

   - **Create a keyboard shortcut:** Click the Keyboard button to display the Customize Keyboard dialog window with the macro already selected for you and the focus in the "Press new shortcut key" box. Press the shortcut you want to use—for example, Ctrl+Alt+T. Check the "Current keys" box to see if another command is using this keyboard shortcut; if so, you can either reassign the keyboard shortcut or press Backspace to delete the contents of the "Press new shortcut key" box, and then press another shortcut. When you've chosen the shortcut, click the Assign button. Then click the Close button to close the Customize Keyboard dialog window.

7. Word now launches the Macro Recorder, which starts recording the macro. Word displays the Stop Recording button, which shows a blue square, on the status bar to give you an easy way to stop the recording.

8. Perform the actions you want to record into the macro. You can

   - Enter text by typing with the keyboard as usual

   - Select text by using the keyboard or ribbon commands (for example, choose Home ➤ Editing ➤ Select ➤ Select All to select the whole document)

   - Give commands from the ribbon or from Backstage by using the mouse

Tip If you need to pause the recording so that you can take an action without recording it, choose View ➤ Macros ➤ Macros ➤ Pause Recording. To start recording again, choose View ➤ Macros ➤ Macros ➤ Resume Recorder.

9. When you've finished performing the actions, stop recording the macro in one of these ways:

    -   Click the Stop Recording button on the status bar.
    -   Choose View ➤ Macros ➤ Macros ➤ Stop Recording.

Running a Macro

After you record a macro, you can run it at any point by clicking the Quick Access Toolbar button or pressing the keyboard shortcut you created for it.

Before you run the macro, make sure you've set up suitable conditions for it. For example, if the macro works on selected text, make that selection first. Or if the macro needs a particular type of document open, be sure to open a document of that type.

If you chose not to create a Quick Access Toolbar button or a keyboard shortcut for the macro, you can run it from the Macros dialog window. To do so, follow these steps:

1. Choose View ➤ Macros ➤ Macros ➤ View Macros to display the Macros dialog window (see Figure 10–39).

Tip You can also display the Macros dialog window by pressing Alt+F8.

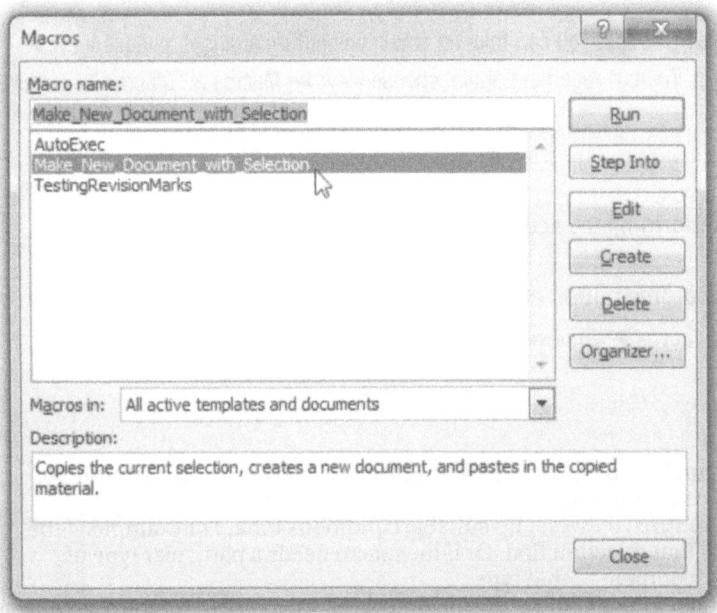

Figure 10–39. You can run a macro by selecting it in the Macros dialog window and then clicking the Run button.

2. In the "Macro name" list box, click the macro you want to run.

3. Click the Run button. Word closes the Macros dialog window and runs the macro.

From the Macros dialog window, you can also take several other actions with a selected macro:

- **Step into a macro**: Click the Step Into button to open the Visual Basic Editor and start running the macro one command at a time. Stepping into a macro is useful for troubleshooting problems with it.

- **Edit a macro**: Click the Edit button to open the Visual Basic Editor and place the insertion point in the macro so that you can edit its VBA code.

- **Start writing a macro**: Type a name for the macro in the "Macro name" text box, and then click the Edit button to open the Visual Basic Editor and start a new macro. Usually, it's easier to open the Visual Basic Editor and then start creating the macro manually.

- **Delete a macro**: Click the Delete button, and then click the Yes button in the confirmation dialog window that Word displays (see Figure 10–40).

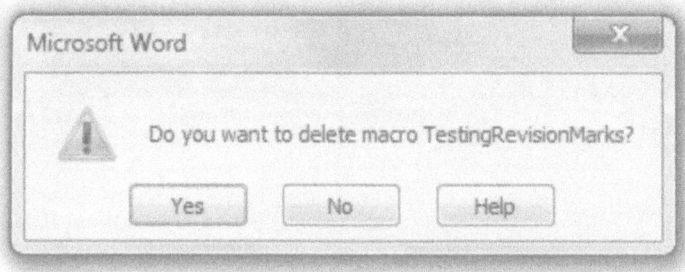

Figure 10–40. Word double-checks that you want to delete a macro.

- **Open the Organizer dialog window**: Click the Organizer button to display the Organizer dialog window, which enables you to move macro project items and styles from one document or template to another. A *macro project item* is either a code module (which contains macros) or a user form, a custom dialog window you create using the Visual Basic Editor. You can't use the Organizer dialog window to move a macro between documents or templates; instead, you must move the code module that contains the macro.

Opening a Macro in the Visual Basic Editor

When you need to change what a macro does, you can open it in the Visual Basic Editor and edit its code. You can also create new macros in the Visual Basic Editor by typing code. This is an advanced subject that goes beyond the scope of this book, but we'll have a quick look to give you an idea of the possibilities. In this case, we'll add a message box to the beginning of a macro that confirms that you want to run it—just in case you've clicked the wrong button or pressed the macro's shortcut by accident.

■ **Note** Programming with VBA is a big topic and has a steep learning curve. If you find this section hard to grasp, don't worry—just leave it for now, and come back if you find you need to write macros in VBA.

To open the macro for editing in the Visual Basic Editor, follow these steps:

1. Choose View ➤ Macros ➤ Macros ➤ View Macros to display the Macros dialog window.

2. In the "Macro name" list box, click the macro you want to edit.

3. Click the Edit button. Word launches the Visual Basic Editor, which opens the module that contains the macro. Figure 10–41 shows the Visual Basic Editor with the sample macro displayed.

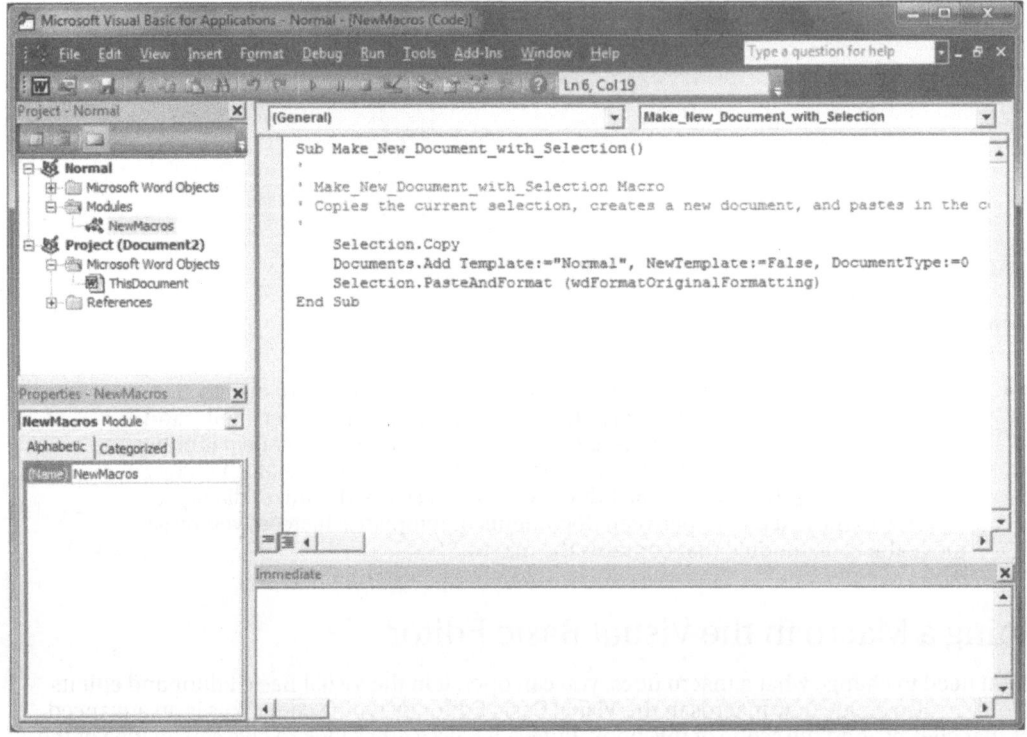

Figure 10–41. You can open a macro in the Visual Basic Editor to examine its code or to edit it.

Let's look at the code quickly, because the macro is short and easy to grasp. The whole of the macro looks like this:

```
Sub Make_New_Document_with_Selection()
'
' Make_New_Document_with_Selection macro
' Copies the current selection, creates a new document, and pastes in the copied material.
'
    Selection.Copy
    Documents.Add Template:="Normal", NewTemplate:=False, DocumentType:=0
    Selection.PasteAndFormat (wdFormatOriginalFormatting)
End Sub
```

Here's what happens in the code:

- **Sub statement and End Sub statement:** The Sub statement begins the macro and gives its name (Make_New_Document_with_Selection). The End Sub statement at the end of the code ends the macro.

- **Comments**: Each line that starts with an apostrophe (') is a *comment*, a line included as information to the human reader rather than a VBA command. The first and fourth comment lines are spacers that Word includes to make the macro easier to read. The second line gives the macro's name, and the third line contains the description you typed in the Description box when creating the macro.

- **Selection.Copy statement**: This command tells Word to copy whatever is selected (the selection) to the Clipboard.

- **Documents.Add statement**: This command tells Word to create a new document. VBA uses the Document object to represent a document, and the Documents collection to represent all the open documents. The VBA command for creating a new document is to add a Document object to the Documents collection. The Template:="Normal" part is a *parameter* (an additional instruction) that tells Word to base the document on the Normal template. The NewTemplate:=False parameter makes the new document a document rather than a template. And the DocumentType:=0 parameter tells Word to create a standard document rather than an e-mail message or a web page.

- **Selection.PasteAndFormat statement**: This command tells Word to paste in the copied material and format it using the original formatting.

So far, so good. Now let's add a message box that makes sure you want to run this macro. Follow these steps:

Place the insertion point at the beginning of the Selection.Copy line.

1. Press the Enter key to create a new line.

2. Press the Up arrow key to move the insertion point up to the new line you created.

3. Type the following code:

```
if msgbox(
```

4. When you type the opening parenthesis, the Visual Basic Editor displays a ScreenTip giving the syntax for the MsgBox function (see Figure 10–42). The Prompt argument appears in boldface, indicating that it's the part of the statement you're currently working on.

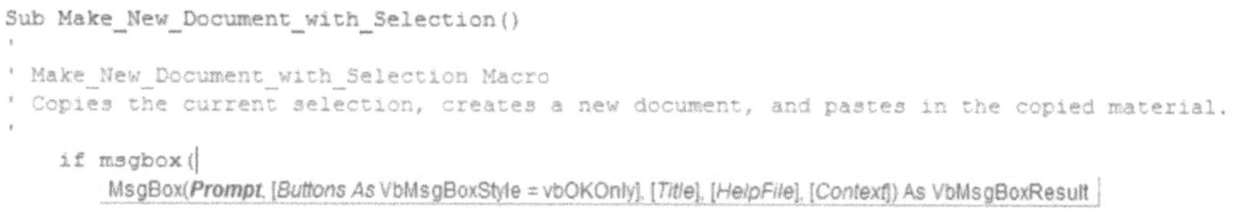

```
Sub Make_New_Document_with_Selection()
'
' Make_New_Document_with_Selection Macro
' Copies the current selection, creates a new document, and pastes in the copied material.
'
    if msgbox(|
        MsgBox(Prompt, [Buttons As VbMsgBoxStyle = vbOKOnly], [Title], [HelpFile], [Context]) As VbMsgBoxResult
```

Figure 10–42. The Visual Basic Editor displays a ScreenTip to remind you of the syntax for the MsgBox function.

5. Type the prompt for the message box—the text that appears in the body of the message box—as shown in boldface here:

```
if msgbox("Create a new document containing the selection?",
```

6. When you type the comma, the Visual Basic Editor moves the boldface on to the Buttons argument in the ScreenTip and displays a menu of options for the argument (see Figure 10–43). This argument controls which command buttons appear in the message box, along with the icon that Word shows in the message box.

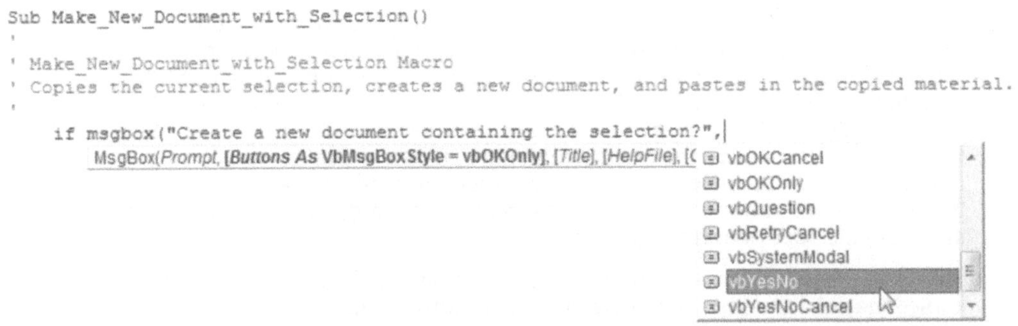

```
Sub Make_New_Document_with_Selection()

' Make_New_Document_with_Selection Macro
' Copies the current selection, creates a new document, and pastes in the copied material.

    if msgbox("Create a new document containing the selection?",|
        MsgBox(Prompt, [Buttons As VbMsgBoxStyle = vbOKOnly], [Title], [HelpFile], [( ⊞ vbOKCancel        ▲
                                                                                      ⊞ vbOKOnly
                                                                                      ⊞ vbQuestion
                                                                                      ⊞ vbRetryCancel
                                                                                      ⊞ vbSystemModal      ≡
                                                                                      ⊞ vbYesNo
                                                                                      ⊞ vbYesNoCancel  ⩙  ▼
```

Figure 10–43. The Visual Basic Editor provides a menu of options for the Buttons argument.

7. Using the mouse, scroll down to the vbYesNo item on the menu, and then click it to insert it in the code.

8. Type a + sign to tell the Visual Basic Editor you want to add to the Buttons argument. The Visual Basic Editor opens the menu of Buttons options again.

9. This time, type vbq to "type down" to the vbQuestion item, and then press the Tab key to enter it in your code. This item tells Word to display a question icon in the message box. Your code now looks like this:

```
if msgbox("Create a new document containing the selection?", vbYesNo +vbQuestion
```

10. Type a comma to move on to the next argument. You'll see that the Visual Basic Editor makes the Title argument boldface in the ScreenTip.

11. Type the title for the message box between double quotation marks, as shown in boldface here:

```
if msgbox("Create a new document containing the selection?", vbYesNo +vbQuestion, "Make New
Document with Selection Macro"
```

12. Type a closing parenthesis to end the MsgBox command, followed by = vbYes to tell VBA the condition is met if the user clicks the Yes button (which returns the constant vbYes). Add Then to complete the If statement:

```
if msgbox("Create a new document containing the selection?", vbYesNo +vbQuestion, "Make New
Document with Selection Macro") = vbYes Then
```

13. Position the insertion point at the end of the Selection.PasteAndFormat line.

Note When you move the insertion point from the line you created, you'll notice that the Visual Basic Editor changes the capitalization of "if msgbox" to "If MsgBox" automatically. This change happens when the Visual Basic Editor checks the code and finds it acceptable.

14. Press the Enter key to create a new line.

15. Type the End If statement, as shown in boldface here:

```
Sub Make_New_Document_with_Selection()
'
' Make_New_Document_with_Selection macro
' Copies the current selection, creates a new document, and pastes in the copied material.
'
    If MsgBox("Create a new document containing the selection?", vbYesNo +vbQuestion, "Make
New Document with Selection Macro") = vbYes Then
        Selection.Copy
        Documents.Add Template:="Normal", NewTemplate:=False, DocumentType:=0
        Selection.PasteAndFormat (wdFormatOriginalFormatting)
        End If
End Sub
```

Click the Save button on the toolbar (or press the standard Ctrl+S keyboard shortcut) to save the changes you've made.

Now, with the insertion point still in the macro, press the F5 key to run the macro. You'll see the Make New Document with Selection Macro message box open (see Figure 10–44).

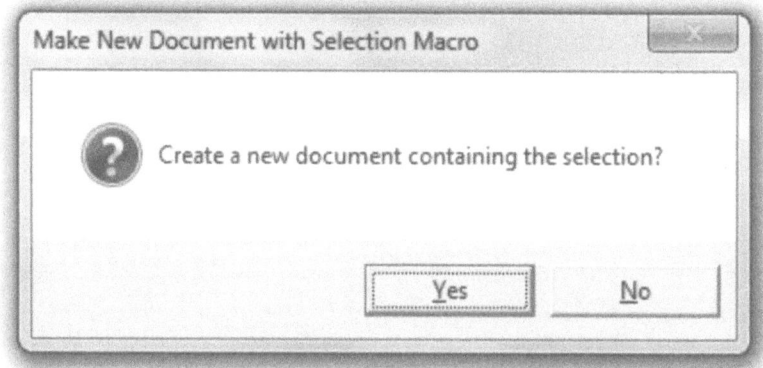

Figure 10–44. Word displays the message box you have created.

Click the No button for now, as you don't want to run the macro.

Choose File ➤ Close and Return to Microsoft Word (or press Alt+Q) to close the Visual Basic Editor and go back to Word.

Now, when you run the macro from Word, you will see the message box you added, and you will be able to choose whether to make the document.

Summary

In this chapter, you've learned how to take your use of Word to a more professional level. You now know how to find the most important options in the Word Options dialog window and choose suitable settings for them. You've gained the skills of collaborating with others on authoring and editing a document using Word's sharing features.

You've learned how to perform a mail merge, and you know how to customize the Word user interface to make Word work your way. You can also record macros with VBA to make Word do parts of your work automatically for you.

Index

■ ■ ■

■ B

■ C

You Need the Companion eBook

Your purchase of this book entitles you to buy the companion PDF-version eBook for only $10. Take the weightless companion with you anywhere.

We believe this Apress title will prove so indispensable that you'll want to carry it with you everywhere, which is why we are offering the companion eBook (in PDF format) for $10 to customers who purchase this book now. Convenient and fully searchable, the PDF version of any content-rich, page-heavy Apress book makes a valuable addition to your programming library. You can easily find and copy code—or perform examples by quickly toggling between instructions and the application. Even simultaneously tackling a donut, diet soda, and complex code becomes simplified with hands-free eBooks!

Once you purchase your book, getting the $10 companion eBook is simple:

❶ Visit **www.apress.com/promo/tendollars/**.

❷ Complete a basic registration form to receive a randomly generated question about this title.

❸ Answer the question correctly in 60 seconds, and you will receive a promotional code to redeem for the $10.00 eBook.

Apress®
THE EXPERT'S VOICE™

233 Spring Street, New York, NY 10013

Offer valid through 2/11.